PLASTIC CAPITALISM

SEAN H. VANATTA

Plastic Capitalism

BANKS, CREDIT CARDS, AND THE
END OF FINANCIAL CONTROL

Yale

UNIVERSITY PRESS

NEW HAVEN AND LONDON

Published with assistance from the foundation established in memory of
James Wesley Cooper of the Class of 1865, Yale College.

Yale University Press books may be purchased in quantity for educational,
business, or promotional use. For information, please e-mail sales.press@
yale.edu (U.S. office) or sales@yaleup.co.uk (U.K. office).

Set in Scala with Scala Sans display type by IDS Infotech Ltd.
Printed in the United States of America.

Library of Congress Control Number: 2023947803
ISBN 978-0-300-24734-3 (hardcover : alk. paper)

A catalogue record for this book is available from the British Library.

This paper meets the requirements of ANSI/NISO Z39.48-1992
(Permanence of Paper).

10 9 8 7 6 5 4 3 2 1

For my father,
Lee Lyon Vanatta

CONTENTS

PREFACE

BUYING TIME

BEFORE I KNEW I WOULD WRITE A BOOK, this project began as an attempt to answer some questions about myself. When I was an undergraduate, I racked up about $3,000 in credit card debt in rather short order. I then struggled for years to bring the balance down. Why, I wanted to know, did I think accumulating the debt was a good idea? How did I convince myself, a college student without a stable income, that I would borrow-to-buy responsibly? I started a graduate program in U.S. history still pondering these questions. In my first attempt to formulate a research topic, I projected them onto the nation's recent past: why had so many Americans taken on so much high-interest debt in the 1980s, the 1990s, and after? What changes in the nation's society and culture convinced them to do so? To frame my thinking, I examined national statistics, where I saw my experience reflected in the parabolic rise of credit card borrowing, indebtedness that peaked in May 2008 at more than $1 trillion. I read books like Robert Manning's *Credit Card Nation*, which offered sociological explanations for the nation's so-called credit addiction. I talked to a marketing professor who had worked on American Express's class-coded branding (green, gold, platinum, black). Yet I couldn't see a viable research design or set of sources that would shine new light on why consumers borrowed so much, so often. Individual borrowing choices were just that, I reasoned—individual, idiosyncratic. Borrowing is also personal and private. Even if people had reflected on their choices, there could hardly be enough evidence to make generalizable claims about American society. My project needed a new direction.

To find one, I transitioned from "why" to "how": how did it become possible for American consumers to take on so much unsecured debt? That question led me to focus not so much on society and culture, but on public policy and business strategy. The story I uncovered begins in the 1930s, with Franklin D. Roosevelt's New Deal. Amid the ravages of the Great Depression, the Roosevelt administration sought to revive the economy by encouraging household borrowing. To do so, the New Dealers created both federal welfare programs that made many American families creditworthy and federal lending programs that made low-cost credit widely available for privileged households. Consumer credit became a tool for American welfare policy, one managed by the federal government and—I discovered—*the states.* Through a mix of federal and state regulation, the New Dealers channeled credit toward social priorities and granted consumers oversight over state-level credit markets. The New Deal created, in effect, a place-based social contract for finance. Throughout the post–World War II decades, state laws restrained finance and financial profits. Bankers, unsurprisingly, chafed under these restrictive rules. They seized credit cards as one way to innovate around them. Cards became the era's fintech—novel financial technology, space-age plastic. In the 1950s and 1960s, bankers used cards to offer high-interest loans outside the bounds of existing regulations. The New Deal financial structure, though, proved resilient. Consumer and labor groups organized for and secured state-level limits on credit card interest rates. State price caps shifted the risk of long-term interest fluctuations onto card issuers, discouraging bankers and other lenders from putting consumers into long-term credit card debt. In the early 1980s, however, opportunistic bankers found another way to undermine state credit rules. They relocated their card businesses to states, like South Dakota and Delaware, with the most favorable regulations, curtailing the ability of all states to regulate the price of credit. Banks then opened the spigots.

Plastic Capitalism thus recovers state regulation as a foundational component of the New Deal's safe and stable financial system and uncovers a missing hinge on which the U.S. turned toward risky, expensive finance in the decades after 1980. I show how, for a time, state-level financial regulation restrained consumer indebtedness. I have tried to do so, however, without being naïve or nostalgic. It's not just that white supremacists defended slavery and later Jim Crow segregation under the tarnished banner of states' rights. State governments were and are centers of political power, where interest groups compete to imprint their goals onto public policy. In this book, I recount how privileged consumers used state interest rate caps to extend a bargain made during the New Deal that guaranteed low-cost credit to white, male-breadwinner-led families. The most sophisticated did so knowing that new rate caps would exclude poor and minority households from credit access, forcing them toward high-cost, fringe finance.

The eventual hamstringing of state regulation changed the terms of financial inequality but not its essential substance. Instead of exclusion, after the 1980s borrowers assigned lower credit scores—often poor and minority consumers—experienced what Keeanga-Yamahtta Taylor has called *predatory inclusion*. They paid higher prices for credit, faced a raft of charges and service fees, and risked debt collection and bankruptcy. Meanwhile, card firms offered middle-income and elite consumers less expensive credit and a buffet of perks and rewards. Freed of regulatory restraints, credit cards became engines of upward redistribution. They also became immensely lucrative for banks and for the networks, Visa and Mastercard, that control the private payment systems in our twenty-first-century economy.

I began this project interested in consumer indebtedness and economic precarity, but through researching and writing, the book also became a story about financial industry growth and banking concentration. The card I received in the mid-2000s was issued by Maryland Bank, N.A. (MBNA). I didn't know it at the time, but Baltimore's Maryland National Bank chartered MBNA as a Delaware subsidiary in 1982, after the bank failed to convince Maryland's legislature to allow annual fees on credit card accounts. Over time, MBNA became one of the nation's largest credit card issuers, in part by partnering with colleges and universities to offer cards to undergraduates. My card came on the letterhead of the University of Georgia Alumni Association. It had a picture of the school's mascot, UGA VI, on the front. In 2006, Bank of America acquired MBNA. With more than 5,700 branches in thirty states, Bank of America was big and growing bigger. The MBNA deal vaulted Bank of America over J. P. Morgan Chase and Citigroup to make it the nation's largest bank card issuer, with 20 percent of the highly concentrated credit card market. These three banks, along with American Express and Capital One, issued three-quarters of the nation's credit cards.

The scale of national financial concentration, while common in other developed democracies, was new in the United States. In the 1930s, Congress
designed the New Deal banking regulations to preserve a political economy
of small finance. Interstate branching rules prohibited banks from building
offices across state lines. Product-line restrictions prevented bankers from
engaging in other financial businesses, like insurance. Together with state
price ceilings, these rules kept most banks small, reinforcing the place-based
social contract. Banking concentration within discrete geographic markets
existed, but never on a national scale.

Several forces converged to erode the New Deal's barriers to concentration. Beginning in 1979, Federal Reserve chairman Paul Volcker waged all-
out war against inflation by unleashing unprecedentedly high interest rates.
The tight money policy, coupled with a bipartisan movement aimed at rolling back New Deal era rules, pressured Congress to initiate moderate price
and product-line deregulation in the early 1980s. Nevertheless, lawmakers
maintained the system's core reliance on state boundaries to restrain national financial consolidation. The financial turbulence caused by the Fed's
policy, though, gave further momentum to deregulatory ideology and ultimately greater banking concentration: as bank failures increased, federal officials encouraged strong banks to rescue weak rivals through interstate
acquisitions. State legislatures, meanwhile, enacted laws that encouraged regional bank mergers ahead of direct competition from colossal New York
and California banks. In 1993, Congress authorized fully interstate branching, unleashing a wave of consolidation. Then in 1999, the New Deal's industry silos fell too, enabling concentration to spread across the financial
services industry. The era of domestic megabanks, forestalled since the
1930s, had arrived.

Credit cards prefigured the larger process of financial consolidation, front-
ing bank strategies to create regional and then national consumer businesses
within the still vibrant New Deal order. This outcome was unintended and
ironic. Bankers developed card plans in the 1950s to help small retailers
compete with expanding department stores. Department stores already offered card-based credit. Bankers merely emulated this service. In doing so,
bankers exerted greater control over local credit markets by shifting credit
relationships, which merchants and consumers maintained outside of
banks, into bank offices. Still, bank card plans remained small and local.

Only with time and experience did bankers settle on transaction volume as a critical component of card plan profitability. As the number of transactions increased, they reasoned, costs per transaction would go down. Geographic expansion would generate more volume and enable banks to compete with travel and entertainment cards, issued by firms like Diners Club and American Express, that already enjoyed nationwide reach. In the late 1960s, bankers connected their local plans into regional and later nationwide networks, enabling consumers to use bank cards from coast to coast.

The geographic expansion of bank card plans advanced in tension with the social ties that held financial markets together. Bankers continued to root their card plans in local relationships. They recruited consumers and merchants within reach of their branch offices. Bank card networks remained fragmented and localized—built and maintained as a collective project by banks that were confined within narrowly constructed geographic markets. Only in the mid-1970s did aggressive banks—led by New York's Citibank—arrogate the networks that the industry had built collectively to solicit cardholders on a national scale. Citi's timing, on the eve of the Volcker shock, proved first ill-chosen, then opportune. When the surging cost of money threatened to wreck their card businesses on the shoals of interest rate risk, large card issuers relocated to job-hungry states without price regulations. No longer burdened by interest rate restrictions, Citi and its peers resumed nationwide solicitations, claiming national market share at the expense of smaller and less sophisticated rivals.

In their quest for scale, bankers initiated what I call *Gresham's law of plastic*, through which high-cost, high-risk credit crowded out lower-cost, less risky alternatives. Here, *Plastic Capitalism*'s themes of concentration and consumer indebtedness merge. Even as market interest rates fell in the mid-1980s, the largest banks maintained heavy card promotions and high prices. Bankers justified high rates in part because they lent to riskier borrowers: high prices compensated bankers for the higher likelihood of credit losses. Predatory inclusion contained a circular, self-reenforcing logic. Expensive credit compensated lenders for extending credit to riskier borrowers; expensive credit made consumer default more likely, justifying high prices. Over time, improved information technology enabled banks to discriminate more effectively among low- and high-risk borrowers. Financial finetuning encouraged still more lending. As credit card debt climbed ever higher, so did consumer bankruptcies, which increased from 288,000 in 1980 to 1.5 million in 2004.

This point merits emphasis: high bankruptcy rates were an expected outcome of lending large, unsecured sums to high-risk borrowers. Yet high bankruptcy rates also undermined the consumer lending markets that fueled the nation's economic engine. Mass consumer credit, emergent in the 1920s, was given robust government support during the New Deal. Even with the scaling back of the New Deal's financial regulations, the new policy regime required an active government role in structuring and policing credit markets. In the same way that policymakers had created rules to protect the pre-1980 system of low-cost consumer finance (for example, by devoting public resources to combatting credit card fraud), so too did policymakers align to protect the new system of expensive and risky lending. In the 1990s and early 2000s, banks and other lenders lobbied for stronger personal bankruptcy rules to enforce credit card contracts. In 2005, Congress enacted the Bankruptcy Abuse and Consumer Protection Act, which made it harder for consumers to discharge debts through bankruptcy. The enhanced provisions of the act, in turn, may have partially motivated Bank of America's takeover of MBNA. Following the acquisition, the *New York Times* reported, "Bank of America elected to follow the MBNA methods it had long admired—from its partnership marketing to its aggressive debt collection techniques and reliance on high fees." With concentration, the most aggressive card issuer practices became the only card issuer practices. Bad plastic money drove out the good.

Together, consumer indebtedness and banking concentration point like a beacon toward the financial crisis of 2008, a drama in which Bank of America, Citigroup, and other protagonists of this book played leading parts. The crisis seemed to affirm economist Hyman Minsky's central insight, that "the tendency to transform doing well into a speculative investment boom is the basic instability in a capitalist economy." In the United States, much of the speculative investment flowed into consumer credit markets—most obviously housing, but credit card lending as well. The nation's longstanding reliance on consumer borrowing to drive economic growth remained but with none of the restraint imposed by the New Deal regulatory order.

As the financial system came crashing down, federal officials rescued the concentrated, systemically important firms. Citigroup, the world's second largest bank (and, by September 2008, world's largest credit card lender), was the quintessence of too big to fail. Citi's role in national and global payment systems was one of the many reasons government officials gave for repeatedly bailing out the bank. "You would go out in a cab, swipe your card, and it wouldn't go through," Citigroup chairman Richard Parsons explained in March 2011, likewise framing the case for rescue around Citi's dominant position in consumer payments. "You wouldn't be able to buy a loaf of bread or clear a check. It would be like Egypt. People would be out in the streets." Presumably, Parsons meant this as hyperbole. Six months later, people *would* be out in the streets, occupying Zuccotti Park in lower Manhattan to protest the government rescue of banks but not of households—and thus the perpetuation of the political economy of big finance and unremitting debt.

Reflecting on the affluent society the New Deal created, Harvard economist John Kenneth Galbraith asked in 1958, "Can the bill collector be the central figure in the good society?" After the 2008 crisis, it seemed like the time had come to renew Galbraith's question, with purpose. Credit card debt peaked at $1 trillion in May 2008, but declined to $832 billion by May 2011. I anticipated a turning point, a recalibration. The Great Depression of the 1930s destroyed much of capitalism and threatened to destroy all of it. In its wake, a new social compromise emerged, which in the United States included an invigorated welfare state and the rigorous control of finance. The 2008 financial crisis threatened similarly epochal destruction. Policymakers, schooled in the lessons of the 1930s, forestalled a similarly catastrophic collapse. We should not lament the rescue. But no new social compromise emerged—no new political economy took command.

Instead, the nation's political leaders sought to preserve the existing system, continuing to rely on household borrowing to spur the economy forward. Piecemeal reforms provided some new consumer protections without fundamentally altering the status quo. The Dodd-Frank Act, which created the Consumer Financial Protection Bureau, is one example. The Credit Card Accountability Responsibility and Disclosure (CARD) Act, enacted in 2009, is another. Momentum for card reform had been building before the crisis. The CARD Act restricted a number of abusive pricing and billing practices, while protecting "young consumers," eighteen- to twenty-one-year-olds (like me), by making it more difficult for them to get credit cards. Yet these reforms came without addressing the underlying reasons young consumers borrowed in the first place, likely pushing cash-strapped undergraduates toward other forms of debt. I finally paid off my card balance with a federal student loan. In recent years, credit card borrowing has resumed its galloping growth, and student loan debt has grown even faster.

This is a book of history, and I will not venture either policies or predictions. It is also a book concerned, at its core, with the fraught relationship between capitalism and democracy. The Great Depression of the 1930s nearly ended both experiments. The New Deal, in different ways, rescued both, in part by making capitalism subject to a greater measure of democratic participation and oversight. In finance, this order was twofold. First, through the institutions of federalism, organized consumers enforced a place-based social contract. That contract proved fundamentally inadequate—it excluded low-income and minority groups from the bargaining table and from mainstream credit markets. Nevertheless, the New Deal regulatory order enabled consumers to shape vigorous credit regulations to match their expectations for economic fairness in America's rapidly changing consumer society. Second, the continued maintenance of the political economy of small finance ensured that most banks remained small. Fear of concentrated finance was elemental to the American democratic tradition. In the postwar era, policymakers worried that large, concentrated financial firms would favor large corporate borrowers over the small proprietors who embodied the ideal of American free enterprise. In league with small bankers, congressional policymakers maintained a fragmented financial system, which limited bank profits and channeled bank lending toward public purposes. This book is about the end of both restraints. Bankers adopted cards to escape the regulatory checks on financial profits. They used cards to escape democratic oversight.

The New Deal emerged from the failure of capitalism to reconcile itself to democracy, and the failure of financial capitalism in particular to provide the stability required by democratic society. The New Deal restrained private finance and bent its powers toward public purposes. Other developed economies followed even more restrictive paths. Yet through its use of private finance, the New Deal opened the door for financiers to grasp the mantle of public legitimacy—to deliver the prosperity promised by the New Deal while disavowing democratic control. Credit cards, as I demonstrate in this book, were central to a long contest between those who sought prosperity through regulation and those who sought prosperity without it. Still, the rise of finance after 1980 was not the result of a grand design. It was incremental, opportunistic, and often clumsy. It operated through a fragmented political system, which offered stakeholders a variety of tools for shaping and reshaping market rules. It rested on a legal system that often struggled to apply inherited legal categories to the strategic deployment of new financial technologies. Although this book ends in the 1980s with bankers' manipulation of the political structure to shield themselves from democratic control, it forcefully demonstrates the long and successful efforts of consumers and other stakeholders to shape card markets through democratic institutions.

Introduction

IN APRIL 2006, CITIGROUP CEO CHARLES "Chuck" Prince III made a special visit to Sioux Falls, South Dakota. Formed by the 1998 union of Travelers Insurance and New York's Citibank, Citigroup was the world's largest financial services company. The merger, which also included Travelers's investment bank subsidiary Salomon Smith Barney, blasted through regulatory silos that had divided commercial and investment banking since the New Deal's 1933 Glass-Steagall Act. Backed into a corner, Congress finally dismantled these barriers the following year. With them went the last vestiges of the New Deal's political economy of small finance, maintained by policymakers through the postwar years of economic growth and financial stability. Citi—giant, complex, sprawling—epitomized the new era of hyperconcentration and turbulence. It was exactly the kind of financial amalgamation the New Deal's rules had been designed to prevent. By the time Prince arrived in Sioux Falls, Citi operated in more than one hundred countries, oversaw more than $1.5 trillion in assets, and offered a one-stop shop for consumer and corporate finance. It was also too big to manage. Citigroup's architect Sandford "Sandy" Weill handpicked Prince, a corporate lawyer, as his successor. Prince began his tenure in 2003 navigating scandals inherited from the Weill era. Conflicts of interest in investment banking, "systematic and widespread deceptive and abusing [consumer] lending practices," and complicity in the Enron and Worldcom frauds had generated massive regulatory fines. By 2006, with these troubles mostly resolved, Prince sought to turn a corner. He was ready to step out of Weill's long shadow. He visited Sioux Falls, a meat packing and agricultural depot, on a mission to chart a new course for Citigroup.[1]

Prince took the stage at Sioux Falls's Washington Pavilion to honor Citi's twenty-fifth anniversary in the Mount Rushmore State. Citibank relocated its credit card division to South Dakota in 1981 as part of a desperate plan to save the card business. In the late 1970s, before it could build branches outside New York State, Citi constructed a nationwide consumer lending business through cards. At the time, New York strictly limited the interest banks could charge on credit card loans. When Paul Volcker, as Federal Reserve chairman, dramatically raised interest rates to beat back inflation in October 1979, Citibank's cost of funds exceeded what it could charge its millions of cardholders. "New York was squeezing us," Prince recalled, "the bank lost nearly a billion dollars." Citi's card business was deep under water, dragging the bank down with it. The move to South Dakota, a state that did not regulate card interest, offered a miraculous solution. "A solution that was good for South Dakota—and that's terrific!—but frankly can be seen to have saved Citibank. Think of that," Prince continued reverently, "saved Citibank." Prince's interest was not historical; he was there to urge Citi employees to grow the bank's card business. "Cards," Prince implored, "is the centerpiece of our North American consumer business. There's no getting around it." Gaining momentum, the CEO of the world's largest financial services company emphasized each of his next seven syllables: "We Need Growth From U S Cards—We need growth in what we sell to people. We need growth in numbers of accounts. We need growth." He continued, his voice a crescendo: "We're going to grow this business. We're going to grow Citigroup." And Prince did; Citi's net-income from U.S. Cards rose 41 percent in 2006, to $3.9 billion. In the financial press, Prince—for a moment—was king.[2]

Citi's achievement marked the outer limit of a credit card bubble, which along with the mortgage bubble, soon erupted with devastating force. The following year, as the global financial crisis began to unfold, Citi's card income fell 26 percent. In 2008, with the collapse fully underway, the bank lost a staggering $523 million on its North American card accounts. The losses underscore the immense growth of consumer indebtedness. Outstanding credit card debt doubled from 1980 to 1985, again by 1990, again by 1995, and again by 2005, topping out in May 2008 at just over $1 trillion. And this figure understates the magnitude. Beginning in the 1990s, consumers often paid down high-interest cards by mortgaging their homes, feeding the motor of American abundance with a steady fuel of debt. The scale of Citi's losses also emphasizes the mammoth size of the top financial firms. By 2005, Citibank claimed 80 million card customers, who collectively spent $229 billion annually, equivalent to 2 percent of the U.S. gross domestic product. Card concentration was but one aspect of a larger phenomenon, encouraged by financial deregulation in the 1980s and 1990s. In 1984, the top four U.S. banks—including Citi—controlled 15 percent of U.S. deposits. By 2008, the top banks controlled more than 35 percent. Citi, gigantic, had been too big to manage. Now, the nation's megabanks were too big to fail. The relocation to Sioux Falls had "saved Citibank," Prince explained in April 2006. During the financial crisis, the federal government saved Citigroup by pumping in more than $500 billion through various bailout programs. It did not save Chuck Prince. When the music stopped in 2007, Prince headed for the exit.[3]

Plastic Capitalism is a history of the bank credit card industry from its origins in the early 1950s until the relocation of card-issuing banks to places like Sioux Falls, South Dakota, and Wilmington, Delaware, in the early 1980s. It is, in the first instance, a business history of the banking industry: bankers developed credit card plans; they signed up merchants and solicited consumers; they incorporated cards into their business models and back office processes; they constructed complex nation-spanning card networks; they lobbied government officials; they filed lawsuits; they made mistakes; they lost money; and they ultimately built private payment systems—Visa and MasterCard—that most of us use today. In doing so, bankers changed not only consumer financial practices but also the social and political structure of consumer financial markets. Their business strategies were fundamentally political strategies aimed at reshaping their industry's regulatory boundaries. Bankers were, in short, innovating around the rules. Although in this book I examine the specific case of credit cards, the point holds for financial change more broadly: in the dense financial regulatory system, innovation always involves the strategic interplay of business practice and political action.[4]

Bankers pursued financial innovation within a regulatory system designed to limit their size, business scope, and political power. During the New Deal in the 1930s, Congress restructured the nation's financial markets, constraining financial firms and channeling their private business activities toward public social goals. In the postwar years, three overlapping regulatory priorities shaped the financial system. The first was *financial federalism*, restrictions on the geographic scope of financial markets, which enabled states to regulate finance within their borders and limited the size of financial institutions by confining firms within states. The second was *industry siloing*, or the compartmentalization of specific financial service fields—like commercial banking, investment banking, and insurance—that limited both financial industry concentration and cross-industry competition. The third priority was *price controls*, which restricted both what banks could pay for deposits, through Federal Reserve Regulation Q, and what they could charge for loans, through interest rate restrictions (called usury limits) imposed by individual states. In all, the New Deal regulatory order relied on a dynamic relationship between federal and state law to create a stable financial structure, which would underwrite liberal social priorities, including mortgage lending, government borrowing, and small business finance. The system preserved private finance and with it the symbolism of free enterprise while making financial rules subject to continuous—often state-level—political negotiation.[5]

Commercial bankers retained status and authority in the post–World War II years, yet they struggled under the regulatory restraints put in place by the New Deal. This may seem counterintuitive. After all, the early postwar years are rightly remembered as an era of unprecedented bank safety. Out of more than thirteen thousand U.S. banks, fewer than ten failed in any given year from 1943 to 1974. Nevertheless, regulatory controls constrained bank growth and curtailed bank profits. New Dealers still dominated congressional policymaking: Illinois senator Paul Douglas and Texas congressman Wright Patman maintained and extended the New Deal's political economy of small finance into the 1960s. Geographic regulations, meanwhile, fixed banks in place as American businesses and households became more mobile. Bankers could not build branches across state lines. In many states, they were restricted to a single office. Locked in downtown skyscrapers, bankers watched as businesses migrated out of central cities, often to the booming Sunbelt. Affluent consumers, meanwhile, flew to the suburbs. Cities became browner and poorer. Hedged in by regulation, bankers endured a decades-long profits squeeze. Inflation raised their costs. Businesses withdrew deposits and sought higher returns than bankers could offer. Commercial banks grew in the postwar years, but the industry withered relative to differently regulated financial firms. Commercial banks controlled 57 percent of U.S. financial assets in 1945 yet only 40 percent in 1958. Savings and loans, credit unions, and other consumer-focused firms gained ground, as did insurance companies and pension plans.[6]

Bankers gradually came to see credit cards as one solution to the regulatory challenges they confronted. Bankers did not invent credit cards, and early on they imitated the strategies refined in other consumer industries. At the turn of the twentieth century, department stores in bustling cities developed card-based payments to identify customers and speed transactions. Gasoline firms like Standard Oil of California and Phillips Petroleum participated in interfirm card networks in the late 1930s, enabling motorists to access credit at service stations across the country. By the early 1950s, when small banks began experimenting with local card plans, Diners Club and similar firms were building global card networks for traveling executives. In every case, firms developed card payments to make credit purchasing convenient for affluent consumers, encouraging them to buy more and pay later. Bank credit cards differed from their predecessors and competitors in that bankers imagined a universal credit service, eventually one that relied on consumer borrowing as the main source of profits. Department store and gasoline cards remained confined to a single retail brand, and they existed to drive retail sales, not to generate profits in their own right. Travel cards targeted an exclusive market of jet-setting executives, generating revenue through merchant and cardholder fees, not interest charges. Bankers sought to combine these markets, transforming cards into a source of universal, credit-driven purchasing power—a new form of plastic money to rival and replace paper cash and checks.

Bankers' credit card plans—and their larger aspirations—took time to develop. As policymakers adopted mass consumerism as a core national goal in the postwar years, cards became synonymous with credit purchasing. Cards also symbolized consumer excess. Bankers, ever cautious, remained cautious. They preferred to lend against solid collateral, like home mortgages and auto loans, where the underlying asset secured the debt. Unsecured consumer lending made them queasy. Bankers entered the card business incrementally, in waves—in 1953, in 1958, and after 1966—at moments when traditional lending proved less lucrative and the industry's future seemed less certain. The inflection point came in 1966, the postwar era's first banking crisis. Bankers seized on cards as the technology that would enable them to compete in the consumer market. Seeing this opportunity, banks mailed tens of millions of unsolicited cards in a desperate bid to capture affluent suburban consumers.[7]

In *Plastic Capitalism*, I examine financial innovation in context; this book is a study of fintech, with all the freight that slogan carries. As such, I reconstruct bankers' evolving business strategies, showing how they crafted new financial services and reimagined the future of their industry through cards. I also emphasize the contingent political processes of market construction, maintenance, and reconstruction that necessarily accompany financial innovation. Within the New Deal regulatory order, the state (*and the states*) created rules and institutions that organized financial markets. Bankers adopted cards to circumvent particular clusters of rules, while nevertheless relying on the state(s) to legitimate and structure the new markets they sought to create. Thus, bankers' pursuit of fintech, in the service of initiating regulatory change, was never about removing government from markets. Rather, bankers used technology to reorganize financial markets and financial rules to favor their interests over those of other stakeholders—a reorganization bankers supported with claims about the necessity and inevitability of the new technologies they promoted.[8]

Put differently, in this book I see cards (qua fintech) as tools for securing power, which motivated bankers deployed in three primary directions. First, bankers used cards to claim power within the banking industry. Confined by New Deal regulations, bankers needed new ideas. They saw information technology—embodied in mainframe computers—as an inevitable, transformative force. Affluent households, meanwhile, offered an expanding market for financial services. Proponents positioned cards as a way to capitalize on these trends. In doing so, card advocates gained resources within their banks and steered the banking industry toward consumer markets. Second, bankers used cards—as private payment networks—to claim power within the economy. Bankers placed themselves at the center of card payment systems. They consolidated local, dispersed credit relationships within their banks and eventually within nationwide payment networks. Bankers controlled who could access cards and set the terms of that access. They made themselves the fundamental financial intermediaries of the consumer economy. Finally, bankers used cards to claim power vis-à-vis the New Deal regulatory order. In the 1950s and 1960s, bankers argued that to best serve consumers, cards should be free from regulatory interference. Regulation came anyway. Then, in the 1970s and 1980s, bankers used the geographic ambiguities of cards, which easily crossed state borders, to undermine the place-based regulatory system and its place-based social contract. Collectively, bankers cooperated to build card networks and to legitimate bank card lending. In industry meetings, through network governance, and in lending markets, they also competed relentlessly to shape the structure and direction of card development. Overall, however, as cards gained traction, bankers' claims to power proved mutually reinforcing, propelling card technology—and banker power—forward with sustained momentum.[9]

Bankers sought to exercise power in a political environment designed to stymie their influence and restrain their ambition. Initially, the New Deal order held firm. New Deal era financial politics—focused on maintaining the political economy of small finance, on ensuring financial stability, and on channeling credit toward social priorities—encouraged continuous congressional and administrative attention on bank card plans. In this context, organized consumer groups drove the regulatory agenda. In line with long-standing pocketbook organizing for fair consumer prices, consumer and labor groups mobilized to control the price of card-based lending. In the post–World War II years, federal mortgage subsidies conditioned privileged households—white, well-compensated, breadwinner-led families—to expect low-cost, widely available credit. Card-based lending, by contrast, tended to be expensive. State by state, consumers brought unsecured card lending under the New Deal price control regime. Banks' mass mailing campaigns, meanwhile, elevated concerns about marketplace safety, which were central to new consumer organizing in the 1960s and 1970s. Consumers and their advocates targeted cards as they sought to make credit marketing, reporting, and billing practices safer, more transparent, and more responsive to consumer complaints. By the early 1970s, middle- and upper-class consumers secured rules that ensured credit markets provided *them* with safe, low cost credit. Yet price controls and consumer safeguards worked against a third strand of consumer politics, one that focused on opening credit access to excluded groups, including women, minorities, and low-income consumers. Bankers and their allies sought to exploit the tensions among consumer

goals, arguing that only markets unencumbered by price and safety regulations would deliver truly egalitarian credit access. Initially, bankers' free-
market arguments went nowhere.[10]

The contests over credit card regulation operated through the complex political structure of U.S. federalism, in which states and the federal government maintained an evolving balance of regulatory authority. Until the 1980s,
the regulatory priorities of the New Deal—financial federalism, industry siloing, and price controls—remained in place. The state rules that implemented
these priorities, however, were never static. As market conditions and business practices changed, as political coalitions changed, or as idiosyncratic
processes (judicial decisions, legal reform movements, moral panics, and so
on) worked through local contexts, financial rules also changed. Federalist
financial regulation created room for flexibility and incremental adjustment.
Confined within individual states, bankers engaged in continuous negotiations with local stakeholders to shape evolving state rules; they participated in
the place-based social contract. Privileged consumer households, represented
by unions and consumer groups, enjoyed significant influence in state policy.
This influence grew as consumerism became a mainstream political force in
the 1960s and 1970s. Democratic and Republican politicians competed for
consumer votes and advanced consumer priorities. Federalist financial regulation thus enabled a measure of democratic control over finance; financial
constituents could change market practices by adjusting state rules. As in
other areas of mid-century American politics, it was a circumscribed democracy. Privileged consumers were well represented; low-income and minority
citizens were not. Through the late-1970s, privileged Americans accepted exclusion as the price for maintaining white credit privileges.[11]

In the New Deal financial order the place of states made sense because financial transactions had fixed, predictable, and knowable locations. Bankers
made loans in bank offices. Those offices—stone and steel—existed in one
state or in another. In the political economy of small finance, banks remained
localized, geographically confined institutions. By the late 1960s, however,
cards and other financial technologies raised difficult questions about where
financial transactions happened and which state's regulations applied. Gradually, bankers used the spatial ambiguities of abstract finance to unravel the
state-based regulatory order.

In part, the regulatory confusion—and conflict—was unintended. When bankers developed card networks in the 1960s, large banks often built card programs over multistate territories, partnering with small banks to sign up merchants and solicit consumers in adjacent states. The large banks issued cards to consumers and expected card transactions to happen, legally, in their bank offices. Consumers, however, struggled to understand how purchases made in Iowa, for instance, became bank loans in Nebraska. Bankers sought uniformity and legal certainty. Consumers and state attorneys wanted transactions that appeared to happen in a state to be governed by that state's consumer protection laws. After a decade-long legal and legislative fight, in 1978 the U.S. Supreme Court settled the question in favor of card-issuing banks. Card transactions, the court decided, would be regulated by the state where the bank was located, not where consumers lived or used their cards. The case, known simply as *Marquette,* became a hinge, a turning point away from the New Deal regulatory order and toward the deterritorialization of U.S. consumer finance.

At the time it was decided, *Marquette* barely registered. Bankers continued to be confined within states; they remained subject to ongoing negotiations with local financial constituents. As long as states maintained regulatory leverage over confined financial firms, the differences among state rules would be meaningful for banks competing across state lines, but they would also be small and subject to renegotiation.[12]

Marquette continued to locate card transactions at a bank in a specific place, and in a larger sense it reflected a shared understanding of bank card markets as geographically circumscribed and tied to local bank offices. Bankers signed up merchants and enrolled consumers in recognizable territories. They expected cards to connect plan participants to their banks and to generate local demand for other banking services. Yet, by the mid-1970s, some enterprising bankers imagined a new future for cards—not as a way to draw customers into physical bank branches but as banks in miniature, plastic branches that could move beyond the spatial confines for the New Deal order. New York's Citibank pushed this idea furthest, fastest. Already Citi straddled the world as a global financial superpower, yet within the United States it could not grow beyond New York State. In its worldwide businesses, Citi executives fostered a culture of regulatory manipulation and aggressive expansion. Turning those ambitions homeward, in the late 1970s, bank executives launched a card solicitation campaign to initiate nationwide consumer banking. Citi gained millions of new cardholders across the country. The bank's competitors, in turn, resumed aggressive card solicitations, now unbound by spatial limitations. At the peak in 1979, banks approved nearly 75,000 credit card applications a day.[13]

By issuing cards across the country, Citi took advantage of a fundamental transformation in the U.S. financial structure. Banks built card networks to connect markets that remained divided by geographic regulations. Until the late 1970s, consumer solicitations and merchant enrollment remained local, even as cardholders used networks to shop on credit when they traveled to other banks' territories. However, once the network infrastructure was in place—with merchants signed up, transactions functioning smoothly, and consumers identifying networks (BankAmericard, later Visa; Master Charge, later MasterCard) with card payments—card networks broke down the spatial divisions altogether. Card networks reordered the nation's payments infrastructure, a fact which contemporaries recognized but struggled to articulate. Bankers, policymakers, and industry observers saw that private bank cards and private bank networks might rival and replace prevailing forms of payment: public cash and quasi-public checks. They promoted the "cashless" and "checkless" society, with bank cards as the inevitable alternative to supposedly outmoded payment media. In effect, bankers created a new universal means of payment, a point BankAmericard made explicitly in the 1970s, urging cardholders to "think of it as money." Through card networks, bankers created private money and gained new gatekeeping power over economic participation.[14]

That power would coalesce over time, but in the late 1970s, bank cards remained highly regulated, their future uncertain. Indeed, as bankers barreled into consumer markets with new vigor, the nation's faith in boundless consumption sagged. The 1970s were racked by high inflation and high unemployment. New competition, from West Germany and Japan, undercut the American industrial machine. The rise of low-paid service work, a constant force throughout the postwar years, became more visible and more concerning. The postwar political economy, built on consumer lending and rising wages, could no longer count on the latter to propel broad-based mass prosperity. Americans used credit more and felt more anxious about mounting debts. Policymakers, who had worried throughout the postwar years

about the economy's dependence on consumer borrowing, increasingly understood indebtedness as a moral and economic problem. President Jimmy
Carter and his administration struggled to contain rising prices. His staff
identified cards as a prime source of inflation and a symbol of national deca-
dence, and in March 1980, Carter initiated a credit control policy to discourage inflationary card purchasing. Controls invited a brief reckoning with the
postwar economy's reliance on consumer debt. Americans reevaluated their
credit habits. They mailed cards to the White House in support of Carter's
policy. Yet by pulling back from credit spending they also contributed to the
sharpest decline in economic activity since the Great Depression. The spring
of an election year was the wrong time to pull the rug out from under the
economy. And Ronald Reagan exploited the moment, rejecting any ambivalence about consumerism. At a pivotal moment, Carter tried to rein in the
credit card economy, yet it had grown past his power to control.[15]

Carter's implementation of direct credit controls demonstrates the extent
to which the New Deal regulatory order remained an active governance
framework, even as financial deregulation—as a solution to the nation's economic ills—gained momentum in the 1970s. In the same month Carter instituted controls, he signed the Depository Institution Deregulation and
Monetary Control Act, legislation that phased out federal control of deposit
interest rates. Together, these actions underscore the long-building tension
between flexibility and control within the New Deal order. Policymakers designed the system to be flexible: Federal Reserve officials could and did adjust deposit ceilings; state lawmakers could and did adjust lending price
caps. Over the postwar era, bankers sought still more flexibility. They made
space at the margins: through new products, in new markets, and—for the
largest banks—offshore. Aggressive bankers saw opportunity and seized it.
Each turn to flexibility created more tension and more risk.

For many card-issuing banks, those risks came to fruition in the months
before Carter's control policy. In October 1979, Federal Reserve chairman
Paul Volcker, determined to quash inflation, orchestrated a dramatic rise in
market interest rates, an event now known as the Volcker Shock. Many banks,
seeking flexibility, had financed card lending by borrowing in variable-rate
money markets rather than relying on price-controlled deposits. The shock
dramatically increased the cost of funding bank card plans, even as state interest rate ceilings prevented banks from passing rising costs onto

consumers through higher credit prices. Citibank had taken the largest risk and faced insolvency. Bank executives frantically negotiated with New York State policymakers to raise the state's price ceilings but to no avail. Schooled in regulatory arbitrage through their international experience, Citi executives found a loophole that allowed the bank to relocate its credit card business to another state, if that state's legislature formally invited them in. It was "a solution that was good for South Dakota," as Chuck Prince later explained, "but frankly can be seen to have saved Citibank." Citi, unable to negotiate regulatory relief in New York, moved its card business to South Dakota.[16]

In the years that followed, other banks moved, or threatened to move, and states rolled back price controls and other regulations to lure financial industry jobs or hold on to the ones they had. Under financial federalism, bankers had a voice in state policy debates. Citi showed them the exit. States and stakeholders lost their regulatory leverage at a critical moment when deindustrialization and economic distress made state policymakers especially eager to compete for financial industry jobs. Bankers, once compelled to negotiate with privileged local stakeholders, now had power to shape state regulatory environments to their whims. "It could have been Missouri," Chuck Prince reminded his audience in Sioux Falls, but "Missouri blinked." His message to South Dakota's political leaders: don't blink. The relocations reshaped the economics of the bank card industry. Cards, marginally profitable before 1980, became extremely profitable, especially for the largest banks. What emerged was Gresham's law of plastic: because they charged higher prices, banks in regulatory havens poured money into marketing and promotion, effectively crowding out low-cost cards. Over the next decade, the bank card industry became increasingly concentrated, rooted in states like South Dakota and Delaware, where there were fewer regulatory controls. State regulation remained—and remains—fundamental to financial governance, yet the states that regulate the largest financial firms are those more amenable to financial industry interests. State political dynamics have thus been an essential—if so far ignored—mechanism for financialization, both by creating new sites for financial extraction and by shielding banks from democratic oversight.[17]

The narrative of this book unfolds in three phases, the first comprises three chapters, the second two contain four each. The first chapter shows how the New

Dealers at once solidified the political economy of small finance and mobilized private credit for economic recovery and later consumer prosperity. In chapters 2 and 3 I uncover the initial development of card plans in alignment with the New Deal's regulatory priorities, and then the adoption and reorientation of cards by large banks in response to the profit pressures created by the regulatory system. In the next group of chapters (chapters 4 to 7) I focus on the banking industry's convergence on credit cards as a technological fix for its regulatory restraints and the resultant surge of bank card solicitations in the late 1960s. Bankers' aggressive marketing, examined in chapter 4, encouraged a variety of countermobilizations at the state and federal level, focused especially on credit prices (chapter 5), consumer safety, and the overall structure of postwar financial markets (chapter 6). Bankers and other card issuers mobilized too, to fight off—unsuccessfully—new price and safety regulations and to fight for—more successfully—active government policing of credit card fraud (chapter 7). Despite bankers' hopes, by the early 1970s, credit cards were securely bound within the New Deal regulatory order.

Yet even as consumer and labor groups used federalist institutions to restrain card plans, bankers were mounting a sustained challenge to the regulatory geography on which those victories relied. In the final four chapters I follow the erosion of the place-based regulatory structure. Chapter 8 uncovers the origins of that process through a series of midwestern legal cases about the regulation of credit cards that crossed state lines, cases that led to the Supreme Court and *Marquette*. In chapter 9 I show how Citibank exploited the resultant case law to develop a nationwide card-based consumer bank, mailing cards to places where the bank could not yet build branches and spurring another round of aggressive bank card marketing. Although consumer groups and the Carter administration sought to maintain the New Deal regulatory order and restrain bank card plans, they failed to re-embed cards (chapter 10). In the final chapter I show how Citibank's relocation to South Dakota in 1981 launched a race to rewrite state-level card rules to retain banks and financial industry jobs—or to steal them. In this sense, place-based regulation and the place-based social contract retained decisive importance for how finance was regulated, but the balance of power to determine the form and content of financial rules fundamentally shifted in bankers' favor.

The New Deal Regulatory Order

Saving Capitalism

When Franklin D. Roosevelt swore his inauguration oath on March 4, 1933, the American financial system had collapsed. Between January 1930 and March 1933, 5,722 distressed banks had merged or permanently closed. To prevent further failures, most states ordered all banks to shut their doors. Whatever Roosevelt's future ambitions, the rescue and reform of the American banking system had to come first. Without safe, stable, and sufficient finance, national recovery could not proceed. Under the leadership of Southern Democrats in Congress, the New Deal's financial reforms hewed conservative. They preserved the existing structure of primarily small, local banks, while imposing new boundaries on price- and business-line competition on all banking firms. In exchange, bankers received government support through federal deposit insurance and recapitalization. New Dealers, however, soon became frustrated by bankers' failure to support recovery. Credit was the lifeblood of the capitalist economy. The government had rescued the banks. It now needed the banks to lend. "Had it not been for the Government support . . . there would be no private banking system in operation today," Treasury official Marriner Eccles wrote to Bank of America chairman A. P. Giannini in October 1934. No one, Eccles continued, "has received more aid from the Government than the bankers and . . . they are the last ones, in their own interests, who should criticize and complain." Eccles, a banker himself, was fast gaining influence over New Deal financial policy.

His message to Giannini, head of the nation's largest bank, was intended for all bankers. The time had come to get in line.[1]

Eccles also recognized that by saving capitalism—as the New Dealers congratulated themselves for doing—the government had left capitalists in power. Their cooperation could not be willed; it had to be bought. With the banks on a sound footing, Eccles and his allies devised policies to encourage bankers to lend in the public interest. In part, Eccles channeled the still-percolating ideas of British economist John Maynard Keynes, who attributed the Depression's severity to a collapse in demand. Famously, Keynes called for government spending to make up the difference. Eccles embraced this idea. He also recognized Roosevelt's antipathy to federal deficits, and he therefore looked to consumer purchasing power, and particularly consumer credit, as an alternate path to recovery. Consumers, borrowing to buy industrial products, would support investment and employment in production industries, generating purchasing power for reemployed workers and yet more consumer demand as workers spent their wages. In June 1934, Eccles helped secure the National Housing Act, which created federal subsidies for consumer installment loans and home mortgages. Federal subsidies convinced bankers to lend. Giannini, for one, strongly supported this program. "Today," Giannini wrote in a widely reproduced October 1936 editorial, the consumer "is a better loan prospect for a bank than ever before." The reason: New Deal policy. "Social security, old age pensions, Federal insurance of bank deposits, and governmental insurance of various types of installment loans, have made bank loans to individuals a preferred investment," Giannini insisted. Few bankers were so publicly effusive. In their offices, though, they followed the federal money and developed new consumer lending divisions, building a foundation for credit-financed consumer prosperity.[2]

The New Deal thus brought commercial bankers into consumer lending markets in service of national recovery, infusing private lending with public purpose. Yet by channeling public policy through private firms, the New Deal's credit programs allowed lenders to maintain pre-Depression beliefs about the superiority of individual economic autonomy and privately ordered markets over governmental planning and control. Building on experience regulating consumer credit during World War II, policymakers like Eccles sought to extend federal credit management into the postwar era to meet the government's new obligations for economic stability and full employment.

Lenders balked. Under the terms set by the New Deal, they, not the federal government, would determine how best to allocate credit in their communities. Some lenders circumvented wartime credit controls, transitioning consumers from fixed-term and regulated installment lending to variable-term and initially unregulated charge accounts. After the war, creditors joined a wide-ranging business effort to roll back federal authority. Private lenders sought and achieved autonomy over local lending decisions. They claimed, through public rhetoric and credit advertising, the mantle of prosperity. By promoting consumer borrowing as a private engine of recovery, the New Deal legitimated it as a private vector of prosperity. In 1936, an estimated 24 percent of households held installment debt. By 1952, 38 percent did, a figure that jumped to 45 percent by 1956. Although bankers remained at the margins of consumer lending, the New Deal's federal credit programs and the wider societal embrace of credit-driven consumer prosperity eventually created pathways for bankers to retake control.[3]

The Roots of the Postwar Financial System

The financial landscape that unfolded before American consumers in the post–World War II years appeared as long-tended farmland, divided by hedges and fences and habits of mind built up over generations. It owed its shape to deep-rooted traditions of local financial control dating to the colonial era, successively reaffirmed by political resistance to big, nationwide banks. Americans—or at least middling American elites spread through townhalls and statehouses across the nation's vast interior—remained committed to local popular sovereignty, expressed variously as states' rights, tax resistance, and antimonopoly politics. They believed, in a general way, that every town should have its own bank managed by its own best citizens. And they succeeded. By the early 1920s, these ideals existed as the stone fronts and columns of almost 30,000 independent banks. An overwhelmingly white, exceedingly male, financial elite controlled these institutions. They justified their financial authority through commitments to community prosperity, commitments which gave moral content to banking's place-based social contract. "Remembering that the banker is a trustee for the community's funds," bank reformer Henry M. Dawes contended in May 1930, "he has no more right to withhold them unreasonably than he has to distribute them

carelessly." As comptroller of the currency in the 1920s, Dawes crafted federal reforms that preserved local financial control. His paean to trusteeship
echoed speeches small-town bankers had made at club meetings and civic
celebrations for half a century. Bankers were custodians. Their community
leadership reflected a symbolic moral economy and paternalistic masculin-
ity, which, while imperfectly practiced, legitimized their financial profits.[4]

America's traditions of local finance provided ideological foundation for
the legal and geographic structure of *financial federalism*, which combined
federal oversight of the financial system with state control of financial institutions within their borders. The dynamic relationship between state and
federal banking law began during the Civil War, when Congress forged a
new national banking system to provide a uniform bank note currency and
to enable the northern states to finance their war effort. The National Banking Acts (1863 and 1864) authorized the federal government to charter and
regulate national banks, while also retaining a competing system of state-
chartered banks regulated by individual states. In what became known as the
dual banking system, national and state banks were confined within state-
defined markets. Most banks remained small. National banks were permitted just one banking office, though state banks could build branches if
permitted by their states. No bank, meanwhile, could build branches across
state lines. Federal banking laws created distinct state and federal banking
regimes, yet they also gave states significant regulatory control over *all* banking institutions within their borders. National banks, for instance, had to
observe interest rate ceilings on loans established by their home state, giving
states significant statutory control over their internal financial markets.[5]

Over time, financial federalism and its political economy of small finance
became deeply ingrained, but countervailing trends toward growth and scale,
always present, gained momentum at the turn of the century. In America's
growing cities, large banks sought to keep pace with consolidating industrial
firms. Big businesses needed big banks. Further, branching restrictions limited the size and scope of banking markets and made individual banks dependent on local economies. Reformers and financial entrepreneurs pursued
branch banking as a safer, more profitable alternative. By the early 1920s, an
exodus of banks from the national system to more permissive state systems
pressured Congress to liberalize rules governing nationally chartered banks.
The McFadden Act (1927), drawn up by Henry Dawes and sponsored by

Louis T. McFadden (R-PA), the House Banking Committee chairman, enabled national banks to operate citywide offices if they were located in a state that permitted branching. California, for example, allowed branch banking, and so a national bank headquartered in San Francisco could branch across the city. A bank headquartered in Chicago, however, could not, since Illinois remained a unit banking state. State rules varied but one constant remained: banks could not branch across state lines. Despite urbanization, industrial consolidation, and the integration of nationwide markets, in banking, financial federalism and state authority over local financial institutions remained paramount.[6]

The Great Depression leveled the political economy of small finance but not the ideology that undergirded it. During the 1920s, a festering agricultural downturn claimed hundreds of banks each year. Successive banking crises in the early 1930s claimed thousands more. In the fires of failure, some bankers lost faith. "Friends whose estates I managed, my family, whose interests I represented, and the community at large, in whose economic life I played a sensitive role, all expected me to find a way out of the pit," Eccles remembered. "All I could find within myself was despair." Despair led Eccles to abandon the free-market principles of his youth, determining instead that the federal government must act to rebalance the economy. Eccles, though, was an exception. While many bankers shared his despair, few willingly abandoned their convictions. Moreover, even after Roosevelt's inauguration in March 1933, federalism remained the structural anchor of the American political order. Members of Congress—elected to represent states and communities—were not prepared to uproot localized finance, despite its profound shortcomings. The most powerful members of Congress, entrenched Southern Democrats, sought to preserve federalism, and with it the racial caste system, at all costs. Even Roosevelt, though his administration shouldered the full burden of national financial safety, remained committed to a financial world ordered, as Eccles recalled, by "small local units of power."[7]

Thus the New Deal financial reforms did not challenge financial federalism; they reinforced it. The Banking Act of 1933—known as Glass-Steagall—embodied complex and sometimes contradictory goals, but at its core the law buttressed local financial control. House Banking chairman and Alabama populist Henry B. Steagall (D-AL) insisted that the law include federal deposit insurance, which shifted risk from community bankers to the federal government. The new Federal Deposit Insurance Corporation (FDIC) protected individual accounts in the case of bank failure. If a bank practiced sound lending but the local economy went bust, the FDIC would preserve the community's financial resources. Small bankers remained in business and in power. Yet the law also contained countercurrents, which encouraged bigger, safer banks. Glass-Steagall further liberalized federal branching rules, allowing nationally chartered banks full parity with state banks. A San Francisco bank could build branches across California. A Chicago bank remained confined to one office, in line with local rules. Overall, banks remained rooted in individual states and subject to those states' geographic and interest rate policies. The New Deal thus centralized financial risk in the federal government while maintaining state authority in financial regulation.[8]

The New Deal financial reforms preserved financial federalism, which distributed authority geographically, and they also introduced or reinforced divisions between different types of financial firms. Congress imposed this fragmentation, or *industry siloing,* to limit what Senator Carter Glass (D-VA) saw as destructive competition among financial service providers. Glass most feared securities speculation. In the 1920s, large commercial banks created affiliate companies, which sold stocks and bonds to the public and ventured on their own account. Glass, the architect of the Federal Reserve System and congressional don of financial regulation, had long opposed "the dangerous use of the resources of bank depositors for the purpose of making speculative profits." To prevent firms from taking excessive risks with depositors' money, businesses were compartmentalized into specific fields, such as investment banking, insurance, consumer finance, and commercial lending. Congress defined these fields by the kinds of liabilities firms could assume (e.g., deposits), the kinds of assets they could hold, and the kinds of services they could provide. Specialization, policymakers believed, meant safety. As New Dealers became more interested in national economic management, siloing created specialized channels for directing the flow of financial resources through the offices of private financial firms.[9]

In addition to confining firms to specific lines of business, the New Deal reforms also limited price competition by establishing *price ceilings,* directly through federal regulation and indirectly through state interest rate laws. First, Glass-Steagall barred commercial banks from paying interest on demand accounts (i.e., checking accounts) and required the Federal Reserve to establish maximum rates for savings accounts, a rule known as Regulation Q. Price controls prevented commercial banks from drawing away deposits from their competitors by taking on dangerously expensive deposit liabilities. Meanwhile, nearly universal state-level interest rate laws, known as usury limits, restrained the prices banks could charge on loans. Federal policymakers understood state interest ceilings as direct compliments to federal deposit rate controls. After observing that Regulation Q fixed low deposit rates for banks, ensuring high profits if banks channeled inexpensive deposits into high-interest lending, a concerned congressman asked Eccles if "there is no attempt to fix the maximum interest" banks "might charge when they loan that money?" Eccles, now Federal Reserve governor, replied, "Most states have usury laws." Through price controls, financial reformers envisioned commercial banks operating safely within closely monitored bands of competition, risk, and profit.[10]

Together, financial federalism, industry siloing, and price controls constituted the New Deal financial reform's three pillars, which would structure the American banking industry until the 1980s. They also reflected tense political compromise. Carter Glass strongly opposed deposit insurance. So, initially, did Roosevelt. Eccles, impatient with the political economy of small finance, wanted to be rid of "mushroom miscalled banks." Nevertheless, although the New Deal reforms grew from different intellectual and ideological ground, by the mid-1930s they interlaced, bound by the institutional gravity of the FDIC and a reformed, centralized, Federal Reserve. Assembled in parts, by the postwar era the financial system resembled a functional whole. Pluralism gave the system strength. By subdividing businesses through policy, the New Deal fragmented the financial services industry politically. Over the next generation, siloed firms spent their political capital protecting their market privileges against less or differently regulated rivals. The system required maintenance, ranging from periodic adjustment to active and vigorous defense. But it was—or at least appeared—solid.[11]

Consumer Credit and New Deal Economic Planning

In the early months of the New Deal, financial reformers worked to reconstitute a financial system that had fallen apart, to provide stability and calm in the face of economic chaos. Once the system stabilized in 1933, their concern turned from rescue to recovery. Here, if possible, debates were larger, more complicated, and more contentious. With the backdrop of massive unemployment and still grinding economic hardship, the New Dealers aspired to save capitalism from itself. They could not agree, however, on the system's primary illness or the appropriate course of treatment. Within the administration, factions prescribing central planning, cartelization, and antimonopoly all vied for influence. Early reform programs, especially the National Recovery Administration, bogged down in these debates. On technical matters, Roosevelt remained ambivalent. He knew that the legitimacy of his reform agenda—whatever form it took—rested on rebuilding the economy, on providing Americans economic security and meaningful work. Those goals, administration officials believed, required the banking industry's cooperation. Roosevelt, along with Henry Morgenthau Jr., his Treasury secretary, and other key advisers remained skeptical of aggressive government spending. Once the financial system was stable, they expected bankers to lend and business activity to resume. Their hopes were disappointed. The 1930s financial crises made lenders cautious. Bankers kept their money on the sidelines. They waited. The New Deal, however, could not wait.[12]

Administration officials, from Roosevelt down, looked for policies that would revive the flow of private credit and in doing so redirect idle capital from bank balance sheets into purchasing power and productive investment. Eccles, who joined the administration in February 1934 as Morgenthau's special assistant, understood the problem clearly. A banker, Eccles thought like a banker. With the economy stagnant and factories empty, private lenders would not risk their funds. "The question is not how bankers . . . can bring about recovery," he told a Utah audience in October 1933, "but why they should do so, so long as there is no incentive offered in any field for profitable investment." In Eccles's view, the root of the nation's prolonged depression was the collapse of consumer spending. Only the resumption of that spending, and with it demand for the products of industry, would generate incentives for new investment. Only then would private capital flow. "The profit incentive," Eccles argued, "will continue to be absent until spending increases, consumption increases, and people get back to work." Eccles initially called for direct government spending to energize the profit incentive. Once in the Treasury, though, he embraced an alternative approach, advocating for federal credit programs that would encourage bankers to lend to consumers, who would then spend, stoke demand, and revive profitable opportunities across the economy.[13]

The New Dealers' embrace of consumer credit in 1934 reflected the transformed place of consumer borrowing in American economic life. Consumer credit changed significantly in the 1910s and 1920s, as consumer durables manufacturers and urban department stores used credit to drive sales and broaden their markets. Industrial firms in consumer goods industries developed *installment credit* to sell expensive products, like sewing machines, radios, and, most importantly, automobiles to salaried and wage workers. For a reasonable down payment and a series of equal weekly or monthly payments thereafter, consumers could participate in the mass consumption economy. New financial institutions—finance companies—emerged at the time to enable small, independent retailers to offer mass installment credit. These firms financed retailer inventories on one side, and then bought, consolidated, and collected on consumer installment contracts on the other. Specialization increased the flow of credit. For proponents, installment selling initiated a virtuous circle. Credit created demand for pricey goods, encouraged economies of scale in manufacturing, drove down unit costs, and made expensive goods less expensive. Opponents saw only vice. Predatory retailers used installment contracts to sell shoddy goods at high markups, especially to poor and minority customers. When borrowers failed to make payments, lenders repossessed the items, leaving borrowers with nothing but debt. Both theories told part of the story. Both reflected reality for some borrowers. During the 1920s boom, installment lending increased significantly, even as debates about its economic consequences and moral efficacy remained unresolved.[14]

While durable goods retailers refined installment credit to sell expansive goods to wage earners, urban department stores experimented with *charge accounts* as a new way to sell soft goods to well-to-do buyers. Charge accounts were a high-status evolution of traditional retail credit, scaled up and systematized through new credit technologies. Like installment lending, department stores developed charge plans to drive sales, in this case by making credit quick and convenient. Charge accounts granted affluent consumers a fixed line of credit that they repaid each month without paying interest. Consumers applied with a store's credit department, and once approved they often received a charge token—a metal badge shaped as a key fob or small plate—that featured identifying information such as the store's name and the customer's account number. To access their line of credit, customers presented charge tokens at checkout, using the metal badges to physically demonstrate their creditworthy status and enabling clerks to recognize valued customers in cities overflowing with strangers.[15]

On the back of these innovations, consumer credit surged in the 1920s, but like the banking system, it crashed when the economy turned south at decade's end. Lenders were not eager to take new risks when the economy was in free fall. Consumers likewise retreated, repaying old debts before assuming new ones. Consumer credit augmented swings in the business cycle. It bolstered consumer purchasing power on the upswing, generating increased consumer demand and drawing in additional investment in manufacturing capacity. On the downswing, consumers stopped spending income *and* credit. Industries dependent on credit-enhanced buying suffered a double loss, leaving factories idle and workers without work. Only by fully replacing pre-crisis purchasing power, officials like Eccles argued, would business investment, and with it industrial employment, return on the supply side.[16]

Forced to action by the slow recovery in 1934, administration officials developed policies that would recreate consumer demand by encouraging lenders to offer low cost, widely available consumer credit. Eccles led this effort. In June 1934, he guided the National Housing Act (NHA) through Congress, legislation that transformed national markets for home mortgage and durable goods credit by introducing government insurance for private lending. Cyclical credit swings had also undercut the housing market. During the Depression, mortgage lending evaporated. Home construction, Roosevelt recognized, was a critical nexus of productive activity, linking industries from lumber to lace curtains. The president was eager to revive home building and recover these jobs. Policymakers developed the NHA to restart private investment in housing. That meant convincing bankers to lend. To draw bankers in, the law created a novel system of federal insurance covering home mortgages and housing-related installment credit, loans made for immovable home improvements like electrification and air conditioning. The insurance protected lenders in the case of consumer default. In exchange, the law required financiers to lend at low, federally mandated rates, prices balanced by the still lower interest banks paid to depositors under the new banking laws. Thus, the NHA enabled lenders to extend credit, risk free, at a modest but guaranteed profit. The approach, Eccles claimed, would generate "a maximum degree of private spending through a minimum of public spending," bolstering purchasing power with borrowed funds.[17]

The National Housing Act laid the groundwork for a U.S. home loan industry that was at once structured by federal policy and managed at the local level by networks of community elites. Private appraisers evaluated residential properties, private real estate agents mediated home purchases, and private banks financed home loans. Federal officials issued standards and provided insurance, but they did so largely out of sight. As a consequence, federally subsidized credit flowed to neighborhoods—white, often suburban—where these publicly empowered private actors expected property values to go up. Mixed race, minority, and urban areas were cut off, redlined into self-fulfilling prophesies of decay and decline.[18]

Credit insurance revolutionized mortgage lending; it also pulled commercial bankers, who traditionally focused on business lending, into consumer markets. Before the New Deal, few commercial banks offered consumer credit. Bankers, as custodians, cloaked themselves in traditionalism and prudence. Bankers lent to businesses. Businesses produced value. Value ensured repayment. Consumption, like the illness, was a wasting disease. In 1934, commercial banks made just 1 percent of all installment loans (though they funded consumer borrowing indirectly through business loans to finance companies). By guaranteeing modest profits, the installment lending provisions of the Federal Housing Administration (FHA), known as Title I, convinced commercial bankers to develop consumer lending departments. By the end of 1934, more than 6,400 banks participated in the Title I program. On the back of this experience, commercial banks steadily increased their lending to consumers. In 1937, banks extended 3 percent of installment loan debt. By 1941, that figure rose to 8 percent. More banks waded into consumer credit markets. By 1946, the American Bankers Association reported that 8,770 of 14,029 commercial banks, or 63 percent, offered some form of consumer credit.[19]

Like the New Deal's financial reforms, federal credit programs created an enduring structure that carried forward into the postwar era. Federal support for credit-driven purchasing power made credit access a defining component of economic citizenship in the United States. Credit citizenship, however, remained circumscribed, reserved for privileged borrowers, who tended to be white and affluent. Under the continued sway of financial federalism, New Dealers vested authority over credit access in financial firms and local financial elites. Doing so, they ensured that credit-driven purchasing power flowed according to local elites' prejudices and in support of their profits. "The watchwords," Eccles intoned in November 1934, were "profits [and] decentralization." Social benefits thus accrued only to the creditworthy, and creditworthiness remained a function of perceived individual traits, including race, class, gender, and sexual orientation. Privileged groups, especially straight white men and their dependents, enjoyed protected access to credit-financed abundance. Others did not.[20]

Moreover, the New Deal's credit programs enabled lenders to maintain fervent belief in individualism and free markets, even as the federal government took responsibility for ensuring those markets provided stability and abundant credit. "No class," Eccles wrote, "received more aid from the government than the bankers." Yet by retaining the political economy of small finance and channeling social policy through it, the New Deal fomented a building tension between lenders, who sought to preserve their economic and social power, and federal policymakers, who, in accepting responsibility for national economic well-being, increasingly favored centralized credit management. The New Deal's financial reforms, built on pillars of financial federalism, industry siloing, and price controls, in conjunction with targeted credit policies like the NHA, gave policymakers a variety of tools for managing the economy through the financial system. By also preserving the position of financial elites, these same programs encouraged ready and sustained opposition to their use.[21]

Credit Control in War and Peace

During the 1930s, the Roosevelt administration and Congress restructured the American financial system, and in so doing created new incentives for private lenders to offer widely distributed, low-cost consumer credit. They did so during the Depression to increase the flow of credit as purchasing power into industries still suffering from excess capacity. They hoped to jumpstart a positive cycle of demand, new employment, and further demand. Soon, however, policymakers needed to twist the knobs the other way. As the United States confronted prospects of international conflict in 1940 and 1941, Eccles, now chairman of the Federal Reserve, feared consumer credit would stoke inflation in an economy geared for war. When the nation's productive capacity turned toward armaments and armor, Eccles believed, the positive cycle of credit-driven demand combined with wartime scarcity of consumer goods would quickly drive up consumer prices. When the storm of war broke, Eccles and Roosevelt acted decisively to curtail credit buying in order, as Roosevelt explained, "to keep the cost of living from spiraling up-ward." But whereas financial firms and business groups had supported poli-cies that expanded credit and guaranteed profits, they resisted policies that pushed in the opposite direction.[22]

For administration officials, wartime credit controls, administered under provisions of the War Powers Act, provided a testing ground for still emer-gent ideas about national economic management and federal regulation of consumer credit markets. In the short term, proponents hoped to channel consumer purchasing power into patriotic saving and redirect the nation's financial flows from consumption to wartime production. "We must dis-courage credit and installment buying, and encourage the paying off of debts, mortgages, and other obligations," Roosevelt demanded, "for this pro-motes savings, retards excessive buying and adds to the amount available to the creditors for the purchase of war bonds." At the same time, some policy-makers saw wartime controls as a means of continuing the New Deal reform agenda. Office of Price Administration (OPA) officials Rolf Nugent and Leon Henderson, who with Eccles designed and implemented the credit control program, wanted to initiate permanent federal regulation of consumer credit. In their pre–New Deal careers, these administrators had worked to protect consumers from predatory lending. States, however, regulated con-sumer credit, and reformers had struggled to achieve consumer protections across forty-eight jurisdictions. Better to have uniform federal regulation, legitimized through wartime experience. Nugent, Henderson, and Eccles all also feared the macro-economic consequences of relying too much on con-sumer borrowing to deliver national abundance. Credit controls, by adjust-ing the price and availability of credit, could temper the swings of the business cycle, first in war and then in peace.[23]

In 1941, Federal Reserve and OPA officials crafted controls to restrain in-stallment lending, but retailers quickly thwarted regulatory efforts by devel-oping new forms of credit which blurred the boundaries between fixed installment credit and more flexible charge accounts. Fed officials sought to curtail consumer purchases of durable goods, such as refrigerators and automobiles. Officials mandated higher down payments and shorter repayment periods on installment loans, increasing the up-front cost of credit purchasing. Although the Fed restricted installment loans, which consumers paid over time, it ignored retail charge accounts, which consumers paid off every month. Charge accounts, regulators believed, made up just a small fraction of overall consumer borrowing and were too complicated to regulate effectively. Retailers capitalized on this omission. First, they lengthened charge account repayment periods, converting short-term credit into long-term financing. Second, retailers began to assess monthly interest charges, so that charge accounts functioned more like installment credit. Retailers thus created a new form of lending, *revolving credit,* which gave consumers a fixed credit limit—like a charge account—but allowed them to pay over time—like installment credit. In short, retailers pursued financial innovation to thwart government regulation.[24]

In response, the Federal Reserve extended controls to cover charge accounts, which prompted further innovation, not to circumvent controls but to comply with them. Under new, complicated rules, Fed officials required retailers to freeze charge accounts of customers who failed to pay off their balances by the tenth day of the second month after each credit purchase. Store personnel, however, often struggled to transmit delinquent account information from the billing department to the sales floor. Charga-Plate technology, a billing system marketed by Boston's Farrington Manufacturing Company, provided an effective solution. Originally developed in the 1920s, Charga-Plate technology employed metal plates embossed with the customer's name and account number. When processing a credit transaction, sales clerks imprinted the account information onto carbon paper sales slips. A clerk could then compare the account number to a list of frozen accounts before finalizing the purchase. By simplifying regulatory compliance, Charga-Plate became the industry standard for large retailers and department stores. The plates—or cards—soon symbolized credit buying.[25]

For many retailers, wartime controls created a tangible link between revolving credit and payment card technologies like Charga-Plate. Charge accounts, which remained more widespread, relied on the same card-based accounting systems. After the war, large retailers transitioned from offering fixed charge accounts to flexible revolving credit, a transformation often re-flected in practice but not terminology. Many retailer "charge account" plans featured revolving credit; others had to be repaid promptly each month. Like-wise, although "credit card" later came to be exclusively associated with re-volving credit, in the 1950s, the term remained ambiguous. What ultimately held these types of credit together was the status attached to them. Charge accounts were for well-to-do people. They were not the installment credit of the working class nor the fringe finance—the pawn shops, loan companies, and loan sharks—of the working poor.[26]

Federal policymakers recognized that formerly distinct credit categories had converged during the war years, but when the United States returned to peace in 1945, they were principally concerned with maintaining controls to restrain inflation. The Truman administration and the Eccles Fed believed that reconversion and the return to mass consumption would cause con-sumer demand to outstrip the supply of goods. Americans had accumulated significant wartime savings. They were eager to buy consumer durables whose production had been limited by the war. To keep credit from bolster-ing already abundant purchasing power, the Fed maintained controls in the months after V-J Day. Anticipating pressure to lift them prematurely, Eccles told a congressional committee in March 1944 that "the danger" of inflation "carries over after peace comes and war-weary people, tired of wartime con-trols and restraints, are eager to throw them off." Truman asked Congress to extend credit control authority in 1947. After Congress assented, the admin-istration maintained controls until the authority expired in June 1949.[27]

Although the administration framed continued controls as essential for war reconversion, Eccles and his colleagues believed permanent federal con-trols could ensure stable economic growth within the context of Keynesian demand management. Federal officials were desperate not to repeat the De-pression experience. In their most ambitious moments, they believed they had the knowledge and authority to tame the business cycle. Under the Em-ployment Act of 1946, they were affirmatively charged with pursuing "maxi-mum employment, production, and purchasing power." Unpredictable credit markets threatened these goals. Drawing on the consensus of postwar economic thought, Eccles told the Senate Banking Committee in June 1947 that installment credit "accentuates the boom and it accentuates the downswing. It tends to make for instability." Instability was exactly what policymakers wanted to avoid. Eccles continued to believe in a virtuous credit cycle that supported employment, production, and purchasing power. Consumers bought industrial products with installment credit, thus supporting well-paid, unionized industrial labor. To keep production stable and unionized workers at work, the credit system required federal management.[28]

Retail and credit industry lobbyists urged Congress to end the administration's control authority, seeking to establish an alternative theory of political economy where prosperity flowed through abundant, privately administered credit, not government management. In the early postwar years, they joined a wider movement of business leaders, who worked to roll back the New Deal's expansion of federal power. The Consumer Bankers Association captured the scope of the credit community's grievances: "Regulation of consumer credit by Federal authority is unnecessary, ineffective, un-American, unsocial, inconsistent, and impractical." The legions of retail and financial trade groups that descended on Congress in the late 1940s hammered these claims: only local lenders, whether department stores, auto dealers, or community banks, had the knowledge and experience to make individual credit decisions. They knew their customers. They knew their communities. Creditors drew on the longstanding values that undergirded financial federalism. They claimed the right to manage, to decide the best course in a free economy. As employers sought to wrest labor negotiations from federal oversight, so too did creditors seek dominion over credit relationships. Following relentless lobbying, they convinced Congress to allow credit control authority to expire.[29]

Although officials lost the fight over direct controls, throughout the 1950s federal policymakers, including Harry S. Truman and Dwight D. Eisenhower, remained concerned that cyclical credit swings threatened postwar prosperity. In their annual *Economic Report of the President,* both Truman and Eisenhower urged Congress to reinstate control authority. For the federal managers of the postwar economy, controlling credit never meant denying credit. Federal welfare ran through the financial system. Suburbanization, a major driver of postwar economic growth, depended on mortgage lending, auto financing, and municipal borrowing. If credit extensions moved abreast of advancements in disposable income, if they did not threaten to exacerbate inflation, and if adequate credit flowed toward social priorities such as home mortgages, agriculture lending, municipal borrowing, and the credit needs of businesses, policymakers were content to let credit follow its course. Such a benign credit environment, however, was never present. Under the tidal force of monetary policy, credit rushed or receded unpredictably. Administration officials wanted to implement, or at least have the authority to implement, credit controls to manage the ebbs and flows of finance, to fine-tune the economy at the micro as well as macro levels. Outside of wartime, policymakers did not get their wish.[30]

Instead, consumer lenders, successful in their campaign against controls, now carried the political burden of the credit-driven economy. They did so eagerly, championing credit as the motive force of broad-based prosperity. In an address to the National Association of Credit Men in June 1951, executive manager Henry H. Heimann praised consumer credit in typically hyperbolic terms: "Next to atomic energy it has the greatest power and influence in the development of industry and commerce, of a high standard of living, and of a happy citizenship." Throughout the 1950s, at trade association meetings and in the banking and retail press, self-identified credit men aligned consumer credit with the broader political compromises between labor and capital which stabilized the New Deal order in the postwar era. Privately administered consumer credit, they argued, not antagonistic labor organizing, would facilitate mass purchasing power and support industrial employment. The legitimacy of consumer credit hinged on its relationship to production; consumer credit was the engine of the Fordist economy because it financed Fords. Within this compromise, lenders maintained coveted power to administer credit—to make day-to-day decisions about who could access credit, for what purpose, at what price—decisions decisively shaped by notions of creditworthiness rooted in race, gender, and social class. Contrary forces remained: the postwar expansion of consumer credit also proceeded under broadly shared understandings, likewise rooted in the legacy of the New Deal, that mass credit should be safe and inexpensive. Meanwhile, credit exploitation continued at the margins and became more visible as credit use became more widespread. Overall, creditors promoted a credit politics closely aligned with mass consumer prosperity and economic growth, channeled through private, locally managed institutions. The watchwords remained profits and decentralization.[31]

Postwar credit advocates' view of consumer credit as a driver of economic growth was (and is still) somewhat circular because it relied on the belief that credit purchasing would raise wages and enable consumers to repay old debts and incur new ones, continuing the growth cycle. With time, key federal institutions accepted that privately administered consumer credit would constitute a driving force in American economic prosperity. In a six-volume 1957 study, the Federal Reserve found that more American families used more credit, year after year. At the end of World War II, consumer debt comprised one-fifth of all private debt. A decade later, it had risen to a third, claiming ground from business and agricultural lending. The report presented such growth as inevitable and beneficial. "Debt," one Fed economist wrote, "flows from and contributes to the achievements of a free economy, and continued growth of debt is to be expected as the economy makes further progress." Yet critics did not retire from the field. In his influential 1958 book, *The Affluent Society*, Harvard economist John Kenneth Galbraith leveled a sustained attack on the ways private consumption crowded out public goods in postwar America. Galbraith had served with Nugent and Henderson at the OPA. He wrote *The Affluent Society* with the Fed's consumer credit report close at hand. "Can the bill collector be the central figure in the good society?" Galbraith asked. Certainly not. Still, whatever audience Galbraith and other critics of debt-fueled affluence found among the public, they did little to turn the tide. Credit, as Galbraith again predicted, intensified swings in the business cycle. For advocates, success came when recovery, fueled by credit, followed each trough with equal conviction.[32]

During the early New Deal, the Roosevelt administration rescued the private financial system and imposed on it a three-part regulatory framework of financial federalism, industry siloing, and price controls. Although the policy motivations undergirding this system emerged from conflicting ideological positions, the regulatory order reinforced the political economy of small finance and restrained the power and profits of financial firms. Within this framework, federal policymakers developed credit programs to channel idle financial resources, through private businesses, into consumer purchasing power. They preserved and bolstered the role of privately administered consumer credit and brought the commercial banking industry into consumer markets. After World War II, officials sought greater regulatory authority to meet their obligations for managed prosperity. But because the New Deal had rescued and built on the ideology of private enterprise and decentralized control, those values retained vigorous force. As Eccles feared, war-weary people, tired of controls and restraints, were eager to throw them off. Credit moved to the center of the business cycle.

In this, the U.S. followed a different path than its peer nations in Western Europe and Japan. In those countries, central governments established, and central banks managed, robust credit control policies, often aimed at restraining consumer lending in favor of supporting business investment, suppressing inflation, and protecting consumers from excessive debt. European countries especially made bureaucratic credit allocation a key feature of postwar economic planning and the backbone of the postwar economic miracle—the trente glorieuses in France, the Wirtschaftswunder in Germany, the miracolo economico in Italy. Considerable national distinctions remained in terms of aims and implementation, yet collectively, developed economies embraced interventionist credit control policies as core to postwar economic management. Public officials, not private elites, determined the course of credit. By contrast, U.S. policy remained decentralized. Without credit control authority, the Federal Reserve managed the business cycle through blunt interest rate adjustments, which refracted through the overlapping institutions of financial federalism, industry siloing, and price controls, and through targeted lending programs like the FHA. In periods of financial disruption, American policymakers would revisit centralized credit controls, looking to wartime experience and foreign examples for inspiration. Overall, however, the U.S. remained an outlier in its commitment to a privately administered, credit-driven prosperity.[33]

That the New Deal laid the groundwork for an unstable, credit-driven consumer economy is ironic. The New Deal's financial reforms and credit policies formed two strands of its broad commitment to economic security, which also embraced the creation of a sustained social safety net along with protections and power for many workers. Taken together, the strands of security had a unified consequence: The New Deal made Americans creditworthy, or at least the white industrial workers and their dependents who primarily benefited from New Deal welfare policies. Giannini argued precisely this point in 1936. Consumer lending became a sound investment because of Social Security *and* government credit insurance. The calculous worked as well for borrowers as for lenders. With security, consumers could hazard more risk. By the postwar era, lenders across the economy shared Giannini's assessment. They clamored for consumer profits, and they did so, conveniently, by forgetting the federal role in securing those profits in the first place.[34]

Charge Account Banking

Charge-Rite

In spring 1955, G. L. Toole, cashier for the Upper Darby National Bank in suburban Philadelphia, published a pair of articles in the *American Banker* newspaper detailing his bank's success developing a charge account credit service, a forerunner of the bank credit card. The program allowed consumers to shop at a variety of local stores using a single, bank-sponsored credit plan, which they repaid at the end of each month. The plan was called Charge-Rite. "Sure, the name can be called corny," Toole conceded, "but it refers to the service it represents, is short, phonetic, and kind of easy to remember." Toole's bank began Charge-Rite in 1953, and by early 1955 the bank had processed more than $750,000 in local credit transactions. After enduring high start-up costs, Charge-Rite was generating modest profits, and the future looked bright. "At my bank," Toole explained, "we believe charge account banking will develop into one of the most successful of our services." Toole was not alone. After detailing the success of charge account banking plans across the country, *American Banker* associate editor Otto C. Lorenz gushed in November, "Where else could the banker invest . . . and get such handsome returns?"[1]

The charge account plans described by Toole and praised by Lorenz were, at first glance, an unlikely innovation for bankers to pursue during the early postwar decades. In the wake of the Great Depression and New Deal banking reforms, the American commercial banking industry was structurally and culturally predisposed toward a custodial obsession with safety, not an entrepreneurial spirit of risk-taking. Commercial bankers, who primarily provided financial services to businesses, tended to be suspicious of direct consumer lending. When bankers did lend to consumers, they did so for purchases with concrete collateral, like automobiles and appliances; for those with firm government guarantees, like Federal Housing Administration Title I loans; or, in the best circumstances, both. They did not finance casual shopping. For a small cohort of bankers, however, the industry's marble-pillared traditionalism was too confining. Consumption was self-evidently the pulsing heart of the postwar economy. Financial institutions that catered to consumers, like credit unions and savings and loans, were growing quickly at commercial banking's expense. If commercial banks wanted a part of this future, self-described "progressive" bankers like Toole believed, they would need to shake the industry's stodginess and find innovative ways to serve consumer markets.

This is not to say that Toole and his peers were bent on destroying the New Deal banking reforms. Just the opposite. Even as bankers pursued financial innovation in the early postwar years, they remained constrained by the era's regulatory barriers and the habits of thought these barriers encouraged. Specifically, although bankers were eager to facilitate consumption, they could not yet imagine marketing their new credit products directly to consumers. Instead, the postwar political and regulatory structure led charge account bankers toward a set of business strategies focused on retailers not consumers, and toward an inherently antimonopoly politics that was pro-small business rather than being pro-consumerism. Charge account banking was a business service designed to help small retailers compete with the credit practices—and overcome the market power—of expanding department stores. Bankers used the plans to deepen business relationships with merchants, who bore the costs of charge account plans, while keeping the primarily female consumers who used the plans at arm's length. The postwar political economy of small banking, which sharply limited individual banks' geographic markets, also allowed charge account bankers to form a collaborative innovation community, since their plans did not directly compete. Through the banking press and new industry groups, charge account proponents organized and legitimized a new field within the banking industry. As they worked together to achieve profitability through the 1950s, charge account bankers adopted many of the features that would later define large-scale bank card systems. In doing so, they pushed the banking industry to embrace unsecured consumer lending.[2]

The Credit Trap

The Federal Reserve's World War II credit controls transformed retail credit in the United States. Controls initially restricted installment loans, which consumers paid in set amounts over fixed intervals, but left charge accounts, which consumers paid in full every month, unregulated. To skirt controls, retailers developed revolving credit, which gave consumers a fixed credit limit—like a charge account—and allowed them to pay over time—like installment credit. Retailers also adopted payment card technologies, which simplified compliance with federal oversight. Wartime controls thus created a tangible link between non-installment retail credit—old charge accounts and new revolving credit plans—and payment card technologies. After the war, large retailers promoted credit plans of all varieties. The National Retail Dry Goods Association, retailers' main trade group, urged members that credit, not accumulated savings, should drive postwar consumption. "Saving should not be relied upon," the association declared. Instead, "the expansion of charge account volume . . . offer[s] a fertile field." Retailers were quick to respond. "In nearly all instances," industry newspaper *Women's Wear Daily* reported in February 1946, "stores are either already aggressive in going after new charge customers or are planning to become so."[3]

In the early postwar years, major urban department stores began building branches beyond city centers, often using the availability of credit to promote new suburban locations. Department stores offered credit at scale: they operated stand-alone credit departments, where specialized employees carefully vetted each credit customer while coaxing efficiency from technically sophisticated credit systems. With their large customer base, department stores enjoyed a diversified lending pool of thousands of individual credit accounts. They could bear the risks of late or missed payments. Importantly, department stores did not operate credit programs at a profit. Credit, as a marketing tool, drove sales. According to the National Retail Credit Association, by 1953 well-managed retailers could offer credit at a cost equivalent to 2 percent of total charge volume. Because credit costs were low, department stores kept financing charges low as well. Charge accounts carried no interest, and revolving accounts carried no interest for the first month, and then usually a modest 1 percent per month (12 percent annually) charge for each monthly billing cycle.[4]

The capacity to offer convenient credit divided large retailers from their smaller rivals, a division that carried sharp political connotations. Small retailers viewed the competitive advantages of larger firms through the lens of antimonopoly. A bright thread of "fair competition" ran through the fabric of the New Deal, woven in through legislation like the Robinson-Patman Act (1936) and the Miller-Tydings Act (1937), which Congress designed to curtail the market power of large retail firms. Even as business leaders rejected federal power after World War II, antimonopoly persisted as a powerful symbol in the retail industry. Wright Patman and Millard Tydings remained in Congress. Retailers, like bankers, continued to negotiate the boundaries of market competition through the political process. Conflicts over market power also played out in the retail and credit trade press. The editors of *Credit World* recognized that not all merchants could afford the mechanical infrastructure necessary to promote mass credit. In the early 1950s, the magazine began publishing a special section, "For the Smaller Businessman," to address the concerns of small merchants. "Occasionally a smaller businessman complains that he is at a terrific disadvantage in competing in credit sales promotion with the bigger stores," the magazine observed in June 1952. Small merchants knew their customers, industry writers argued, and they should use that knowledge to expand their credit operations.[5]

Small retailers, however, recognized that prioritizing credit introduced additional risks as they struggled to compete with larger, more efficient rivals. Small merchants always navigated a precarious existence. Failure was common. Postwar demographic and geographic changes transformed the retail landscape, leaving small firms at a disadvantage. Offering credit necessarily strained merchants' already limited capital, and small retailers often lacked the time or expertise to manage charge accounts. Credit also strained relationships. Denying credit or hounding consumers for repayment were surefire ways to lose customers. In short, small merchants were caught in a credit trap. They needed to offer charge accounts to compete, but offering convenient credit tied up capital and increased costs and risk, potentially making small retailers less competitive or less profitable. Moreover, once most merchants offered credit, individual stores had to bear the higher costs with no gain in competitive advantage. Thus, as consumer credit became an essential feature of postwar consumer capitalism, it created structural advantages for large firms while weighing heavily on smaller competitors. Given the continued rhetorical importance of small business as the lifeblood of American free enterprise and the ongoing—if overdrawn—debates about the survival of small business in the face of competition and government regulation, such competitive disadvantages shaded into political symbolism. Charge accounts would save small merchants or doom them, but there was no question that survival was at stake.[6]

The Origins of Charge Account Banking

Small bankers sympathized with their retailer kin: they too worried about survival in the face of aggressive and expanding rivals—and about the overall survival of small proprietors in a political economy oriented toward big, capital-intensive firms. Small bankers also listened to their merchant customers: some saw opportunity in the new pressures of postwar retailing. "As far back as 1946," G. L. Toole recalled, "our top men were seeking a way to assist the many local merchants who sought help [meeting] the competition of credit buying offered by center city merchants." Yet sympathy did not translate immediately into strategy. New Deal credit programs had nudged bankers into consumer lending fields. They were making home improvement loans and financing automobile and durable goods purchases. These lines of business relied on fixed installment contracts and ran through firms, like auto dealers or appliance sellers, that sold directly to consumers. Most commercial bankers had little retail experience beyond making business loans to retailers. Thus, despite a shared interest in preserving small capitalism against ever-encroaching big business, prevailing experience did not offer bankers like Toole an obvious path to follow.[7]

Experimentation started small and at the margins. In the mid-1940s, John C. Biggins, an executive at Flatbush National Bank, a small bank nestled in a growing Brooklyn neighborhood, noticed that his merchant customers were facing increased competition from New York City's downtown department stores. After the war, Manhattan department stores had branched out across the East River and enticed Brooklyn consumers with charge accounts. Biggins's merchant customers needed to offer convenient credit too, but doing so was expensive and risky. "The number of merchants who have been knocked out of business by supplying their own credit is enormous," Biggins explained in August 1946. "Charg-It," a plan for "providing the small storekeeper with a credit arrangement that wasn't a losing proposition for everyone concerned," was Biggins's answer. Under this plan, Biggins's bank provided consumers with a revolving credit account they could use to shop at a variety of local retailers. The bank would pay merchants for the goods consumers purchased and assume the bookkeeping costs and credit risk.[8]

Biggins conceived of Charg-It as at once a credit service and a means of maintaining community integrity in the face of external competition. Charg-It, however, got its first trial not in Brooklyn but in Bay Shore, an outlying community linked to New York City by the Long Island Rail Road. While Biggins was developing Charg-It, Manufacturers Trust Company, a large Manhattan bank that was also expanding into Brooklyn, acquired Flatbush National. Manufacturers Trust executives considered implementing Biggins's plan across New York City but chose not to, perhaps because Charg-It would have competed with the charge account plans of their department store customers. Instead, Biggins tested his plan in partnership with the First National Bank and Trust of Bay Shore. The program was small: a 1946 ad listed eleven participating merchants clustered on Bay Shore's Main Street. "Charg-It will give you the advantages of a department store charge account in your favorite local stores," one ad promised, offering suburban residents an incentive to do their shopping in town instead of downtown. Biggins continued to hone this community-shopping strategy at Paterson Savings and Trust Company in suburban New Jersey, where he introduced Charg-It on a larger scale in 1950. Paterson merchants also competed with New York department stores, and Charg-It offered these retailers a "vital community service" by keeping business local. "You can shop in your own neighborhood," a Paterson Savings ad promised. "*Charg-It* [at] stores and receive the same credit courtesy available [at] the biggest stores in the city."[9]

Biggins designed Charg-It to help small retailers compete with department stores, but the plan had a critical weakness: it did not replicate the social prestige embodied in department store charge accounts. By the late 1940s, most department stores had adopted charge plates—embossed metal cards—which, as part of an otherwise invisible accounting and billing infrastructure, enabled stores to monitor and control credit purchases. For consumers, the card appeared only as a means of identification and a medium of credit. As such, it marked class status, not credit control. Such class symbolism, bankers and retailers believed, was especially important for female customers. "There is . . . a certain prestige for particularly the woman shopper," G. L. Toole observed, "who could present her credit card and merely say, 'Charge it—please.'" On the contrary, Charg-It operated through credit scrip. The bank gave customers paper certificates equal to their preestablished credit limit, which they could spend like money at participating stores. Scrip put bankers firmly in command. Consumers could never use more scrip than the bank provided and they received new scrip only when they paid their outstanding Charg-It balances. Scrip, however, was inconvenient. Issued only in denominations of $1 or more in whole dollars, it annoyed consumers, since purchases inevitably did not come out in round figures. Scrip was also oversight manifest; it physically argued that consumers could not control themselves. "There is a certain stigma attached to the carrying of scrip," Toole observed. Because of that stigma, his bank chose not to adopt a scrip-based plan.[10]

Biggins initiated bankers' shift into revolving retail credit, but the industry largely rejected credit scrip. Instead, to bring charge account banking into alignment with female shoppers' status expectations, innovative bankers emulated department store credit practices. The Franklin National Bank, also of suburban Long Island, led this effort, introducing the similarly named "Charge-It" plan in 1951. The bank developed Charge-It, executive Edward Donohue explained, following a conference it hosted to consider how the bank's merchant customers could better promote their businesses. Charge account services, the assembled retailers argued, were "perhaps the greatest need." As they considered how to help these firms, Franklin executives decided that if department stores were the threat, they should also be the standard. "In order to make this program completely acceptable to the ultimate consumer," Donohue observed, "we could not change habits; we would have to emulate exactly the technique and methods of department stores." Franklin National made the card both the form of identification and credit medium. Charge-It customers would experience charge account purchasing at their local merchant exactly as they did at a department store.[11]

With merchant buy-in seemingly assured, Franklin National executives looked to recruit creditworthy consumers. In a model that later charge account programs would widely adopt, Franklin executives made retailers the frontline of consumer enrollment. Under the bank's plan, "Mrs. House-wife," applied for a bank charge account through a participating merchant. "We stressed," Donohue explained, "that a merchant should attempt to so-licit and originate charge accounts in his store." The bank performed its own credit check later, but by relying on its merchant partners to sign up custom-ers, the bank embedded Charge-It within existing relationships between merchants and consumers, relying on established social bonds to anchor the new credit program. Using retailers in this way both expanded and con-strained consumer access to bank credit programs. The bank's merchant network reached more customers than the bank could and engaged consum-ers at the moment when credit purchasing would be foremost in their minds. Retailers also policed card programs, soliciting customers who matched ra-cial and class expectations about creditworthiness (which bankers would in turn monitor by enrolling merchants who served desirable clientele).[12]

Once she passed the credit check, Mrs. Housewife was issued a charge card by Franklin National, imprinted with her husband's name and their ac-count number. When making a purchase, she handed the retailer her card, and—if the advertisements are any indication—proudly exclaimed, "Please charge it!" The retailer, duly impressed, completed a carbon paper sales slip with the purchase details and imprinted the embossed card on the slip, which Mrs. Housewife signed. If the purchase was above $10, or some simi-lar predetermined "floor limit," the merchant called the bank to confirm Mrs. Housewife's account was in good standing. As far as Mrs. Housewife was concerned, the transaction ended there. She took her goods and left. Every month the bank consolidated Mrs. Housewife's account and mailed her a bill containing carbon copies of her sales slips. She paid her bill in full each month, without paying interest.[13]

Behind Mrs. Housewife's transaction lay a second series of transfers be-tween the merchant and the bank, which hid the mechanics and—more im-portantly—the costs of her charge account. At the end of the business day, Franklin National's merchant-customers consolidated their charge sales slips and transferred them to the bank. The bank then credited each mer-chant's checking account for the full value of these purchases, less a fixed percentage called the *merchant discount*. Merchants also paid fees to join the charge account plan, to rent the imprinter that recorded the customer's information on the sales slip, and to participate in advertising tie-ins with the bank.[14]

As Donohue's invocation of "Mrs. Housewife" suggests, bankers designed their charge account plans to facilitate female-led, family consumption. Charge account bankers imagined their market as white, female, married, and affluent, a vison prominently portrayed in charge account advertising. Toole's customer was "Mrs. John Shopper"; other bankers preferred plain "Mrs. Shopper." Charge account banking, advertisements promised, made wifely tasks like provisioning and budgeting more convenient, consolidating small purchases into one monthly bill. Bank charge accounts thus operated in contrast to predominantly male modes of credit, like automobile loans and durable goods purchases. Large purchases like these tended to require a husband's presence and approval. Likewise, the husband's approval was a necessary step in obtaining a Charge-It account since the family's credit was in his name. Charge account bankers thus promoted wholesome abundance and familial safety, central middle-class family values in the Cold War era.[15]

When Charg-It and Charge-It emerged in the early 1950s, the business press hailed the plans as important new banking services for aiding small retailers. Clearly reflecting the narratives employed by Biggins and Dono-hue, *Business Week, Banking,* and other publications portrayed bank charge accounts as products imbued with small business, antimonopoly politics. Franklin National's "Charge-It" plan could "support private enterprise at the small retailer level" and even "stem the disappearance of the small store which finds it difficult to compete with the large units opening branches in suburban areas." Charge account bankers needed allies; to recruit them, they leaned into these narratives. At industry conferences and in the banking press, charge account bankers reiterated their politically coded origin story: banks initiated charge accounts to help their small merchant customers compete with department store credit plans. They did so in part to convince other bankers to adopt, develop, and sustain the new financial technology. The message was also aimed at merchants, whom bankers understood as necessary partners in any charge account plan—and indeed as necessary al-lies in their pursuit of financial innovation.[16]

Press enthusiasm was one of several currents that drove a wave of banks to launch charge account plans in the early 1950s. First, the end of the Korean War and with it another round of wartime credit controls cleared the way for the growth of consumer borrowing. In this market, charge account plans promised significant revenues—as high as 20 percent, *American Banker* estimated in October 1952. Firms that manufactured credit-processing equipment, such as Addressograph and Diebold, also encouraged bankers to imagine profits flowing from retail credit plans. So did charge account bankers, like Biggins and Donohue, whose banks marketed franchise arrangements to their industry colleagues. Whether they signed with an established plan or developed their own, at least 91 banks launched charge plans by the end of 1953. "'Charge accounts for banks,'" Donohue declared confidently in March 1953, "is here to stay."[17]

Donohue's optimism hid the impending difficulties bankers faced as they brought their new charge account plans to market. High equipment and supplies costs, difficulty enrolling merchants and consumers, inexperience managing retail credit accounts, and regulatory scrutiny would all challenge firms as they tailored charge account banking to their local markets. Their banking peers, meanwhile, remained skeptical that charge accounts were a legitimate banking service. Rather than confront these challenges alone, bankers quickly formed formal and informal networks to promote charge account banking. They worked together to determine best practices and to develop new profit-making strategies. In doing so, they also refined their social and political arguments that charge accounts were a rightful banking service, constructing a vision of commercial banking's future with consumer borrowing at the center. Such cooperation was possible because, under the New Deal order's geographic regulations, charge account bankers did not directly compete.[18]

American Banker editor Otto Lorenz led the promotional campaign within the banking industry. Lorenz, a veteran of the industry's expansion into installment lending in the 1930s, seized on charge accounts, turning commercial banking's leading newspaper into a claxon for consumer lending. In June 1953, Lorenz began publishing multipage quarterly reports in *American Banker*, which detailed statistics on charge account sales volume, expenses, and profits and also featured extensive commentary from Lorenz and practicing charge account bankers on plan management. Through his reports, Lorenz forged a community of practitioners—whom he fondly called "pioneers"—giving them a virtual space to test new ideas. Together, Lorenz and his contributors identified the methods that made charge account banking profitable and even formulated the statistical categories that defined profitability in the first place. Was the size of a bank's "trading area" a factor in charge account success? What was the best way to report delinquency data (while not scaring off potential adopters)? How much overhead should the charge account program be accountable for? By reporting and analyzing the strategies employed by exemplary performers, and by using such information to critique underperforming firms, Lorenz and his contributors crafted a proscriptive guide to charge account banking. They sought to demonstrate that charge accounts were a legitimate banking function and to entice more bankers to adopt the plans. Budget targets, accounting principles, explanations of plan management procedures, and Lorenz's enthusiastic boosterism opened charge account banking to more firms and guided bankers over the early shoals their plans inevitably encountered.[19]

As charge account bankers built a community through Lorenz's *American Banker* reports, they developed institutions to solidify innovation within their banks and spread them to the wider industry. At first, practitioners cooperated informally. As one banker recalled, "Many of us . . . had been exchanging ideas and discussing problems, both through correspondence and during personal visits to each other's offices." In March 1954, at the American Bankers Association's National Installment Credit Conference, 24 banks from 13 states formed the Charge Account Bankers Association (CABA) to "promote generally the interest of charge account banking." CABA became a clearinghouse of information about bank card plans. Through annual conferences and frequent late night phone calls between overworked bankers, CABA members gradually settled on a common set of charge account practices, more closely resembling Franklin National's department store-style card than Biggins's scrip plan (Biggins did not join CABA). Once bank charge accounts found a stable footing, CABA transitioned into a self-regulatory institution. The group developed and disseminated standards for charge account banking programs to reassure bank management, regulators, and other stakeholders that the seemingly risky credit plans were in fact safe and sound.[20]

At the same time that Lorenz and CABA members tried to convince skeptical bankers that charge account plans merely extended established banking practices, they sought to convince government officials that the plans should not be held to the same standards as traditional banking. As a new financial technology, charge accounts existed in ambiguous regulatory space, and bankers worked to shape regulatory interpretations to their advantage. Government officials, bankers argued, should evaluate their novel credit service on the same basis as the retail firms that banks emulated—firms that were not subject to banking's strict accounting and oversight standards. Charge account bankers focused special attention on charge-offs, the mandated delinquency period after which banks had to write off non-performing loans, and on state interest rate limits, which restricted rates on bank loans but usually did not extend to retail credit. "We have been examined four times— once by F.D.I.C., twice by State, and once by Clearing House," one banker complained. Frustrated with the rapid charge-offs mandated by officials, he continued, "We believe 90 day charge off is impractical on retail charge accounts. I know of no retailer who acts so soon." Lorenz urged CABA to educate oversight officials by creating uniform standards for charge account write-offs that officials could then apply. Some bank examiners agreed to follow the account delinquency rules that CABA published in 1959, but others maintained stringent lending standards. "Some banks," Lorenz reported, "had unhappy management" as a result.[21]

Variations in state law also complicated charge account bankers' efforts to offer revolving credit. Through the 1950s, retailers gradually shifted from charge accounts that consumers paid off monthly to revolving credit that allowed consumers to carry balances by paying interest. Retailers' revolving credit plans fell under a legal exemption to usury laws called the time-price doctrine and were largely unregulated. Even when states specifically regulated retail credit sales, rates were higher than for money loans. After 1960, New York retailers could charge 1.5 percent a month (18 percent annualized) on unpaid revolving credit balances, whereas banks could charge only 6 percent per year for personal loans.[22] Over the long term, state interest rate restrictions became the most visible and politically contested regulatory barrier constraining bank card plans. In the 1950s, however, official oversight of charge account banking largely proceeded out of sight, without public pronouncements or obvious political conflict.[23]

In the mid-1950s, the future of charge account banking remained uncertain. Bankers struggled to win industry, merchant, and regulatory allies. Most plans tended to lose money for several years before turning modest profits, and about half of the firms that jumped into the field in 1953 did not wait long enough to turn the corner. Bankers lacked experience developing, staffing, and promoting retail-related services. Some—sold on the merits of charge account banking by aggressive equipment salesmen—bought more processing equipment, carbon forms, and card imprinters than they needed. For several years, the charge account banking "fraternity" endured a slow attrition. Few new banks started plans. The economy boomed from 1954 to 1957, and the banking industry enjoyed many safe, profitable outlets for bank funds. Despite Lorenz's best efforts, commercial bankers largely remained suspicious of direct consumer lending.[24]

The Merchant Approach

The charge account banking plans that survived grew significantly in the 1950s, making gains in consumer accounts, credit volume, and overall profits. Early practitioners solidified their merchant-centered approach to unsecured consumer credit, recruiting retailers into charge account plans and then encouraging them to sign up creditworthy consumers. The merchant approach derived from commercial bankers' business lending experience and their ongoing rhetorical commitment to antimonopoly retail politics. It enabled bankers, Lorenz and CABA emphasized, to make profitable consumer loans and to deepen their business relationships with merchant members. Charge account bankers engaged constantly with their retail partners. Through their charge plans, they promoted additional services, including commercial and mortgage loans. And because retailers maintained a checking account at their charge account bank—where the bank deposited funds against their charge sales receipts—the plans also provided inexpensive funding. "The charge account banking business," Lorenz argued, "finances itself."[25]

Despite claims that smaller merchants desperately needed charge accounts to compete with large department stores, bankers still had to sell charge accounts to retailers. Bankers breathlessly advertised the many benefits offered by their plans. The first should have been obvious. As the Pan American Bank of Miami, Florida, explained in a brochure, "Mr. Merchant: Here's a New Avenue of Revenue!" The bank's Charge Plan "enables the local merchant to offer his customers a charge-account service comparable to that of a large department store." Merchants, the bank explained, would receive immediate cash for all their charge account sales and did not risk any credit losses. The Pan Am Bank Charge Plan guaranteed "INCREASED SALES," "INCREASED NET PROFITS," and "INCREASED NUMBERS OF POTENTIAL CUSTOMERS." Other plans promised to reduce bookkeeping, personnel, postage, and supply costs, allowing merchants to focus on what they did best—merchandising. Summing up these advantages, the Florida National Bank of Orlando explained that its "F.N.B. Charge Plan Acts as the Credit, Accounting, Bookkeeping, and Collection Departments, *And Actually costs participating merchants and professional men, and their customers less.*"[26]

Merchants would have to pay for these services, of course, and they did so through the merchant discount, which operated at once as a service charge and set of legal relationships between the merchant, the consumer, and the bank. Discounts, a longstanding banking practice, are effectively interest in reverse, paid upfront instead of over time. The merchant discount—calculated as a percentage of the final sales price—compensated the bank for the time it took to collect the balance, the cost of administering the account, and the risk associated with the transaction. In the case of a 5 percent discount, when a merchant sold a $10 pair of shoes, the bank paid the merchant $9.50. The remaining 50 cents accrued to the bank, covering the cost and risk of lending. Discounting also created legal safeguards for both merchants and bankers. When a consumer signed her charge account receipt, she actually signed a debt contract with the merchant. The merchant then sold—or "discounted"—this debt to the bank. Bankers purchased charge account contracts on a *non-recourse basis,* meaning if the customer failed to pay, the bank could not pass the losses back to the retailer. Bankers became *holder in due course,* meaning that if the merchandise was faulty or the merchant had committed fraud, the consumer still had to pay the bank.[27]

Through the merchant discount, merchants, not consumers, paid for charge account banking. While John Biggins claimed that his Charg-It plan "doesn't cost" consumers "a penny more" than purchasing with cash, merchants handed over 8 percent of their Charg-It sales. Franklin National's plan was less expensive, charging merchants 5 percent on 30-day charge purchases and 6 percent on 60-day charges. When later plans allowed consumers to spread their charge account payments over 30, 60, or 90 days, many banks raised the merchant discount on longer repayment periods. Eventually, some banks reduced their merchant discounts by rebating merchants if they met certain sales volume targets. Still, during the 1950s, discounts remained high. From 1954 to 1959, *American Banker* calculated that profitable bank plans charged an average discount of 5.21 percent. In charge account banking, consumers borrowed, and retailers paid the interest.[28]

Although bankers promoted charge plans as a mutually beneficial service, many retailers remained doubtful about the merits of charge account banking. "Strange as it may seem," Franklin National's Donohue remarked, "the merchant requires a good deal of education in this program." Merchants were getting a good deal of education from the retail trade press, often of a character unfavorable to banks. "Granting credit on credit cards issued by others," *Credit World* bluntly warned readers in September 1953, "is a mistake." Many merchants, faced with high discounts, doubtlessly agreed. Banks' fees, a writer in the trade magazine *Stores* argued, cost more that managing an in-house credit department. For efficient department stores, credit costs averaged about 2 percent of charge volume versus the 5 percent commanded by banks. Bankers disputed these figures. They argued that the increased sales generated through charge accounts more than compensated for these costs. For merchants without existing credit departments, the *Stores* writer conceded, a bank's charge plan might be an appealing alternative to investing in equipment and personnel, but the merchant would need to promote credit purchases, turning potential cash sales into 5 percent markups.[29]

High merchant discounts strongly influenced which types of retailers would join bank card plans, limiting participation to those that charged high markups on their merchandise. Clothing and shoe stores, which competed directly against department stores, were obvious targets. Drug stores and hardware stores also joined charge account plans, as did gas and service stations. Florists and photographers often participated, and so did optometrists and dentists. In small towns, local department stores occasionally joined bank charge account plans, though they tended to negotiate lower discounts, giving the sponsoring bank high sales volume but little added profit. More often, department stores with established credit plans declined to join, as did discount retailers that offered low prices and no credit. Grocers, especially supermarkets that likewise sold on low margins, seldom adopted bank card plans in the 1950s. In a 1960 report, the U.S. Department of Agriculture suggested that the first grocery store to join a bank plan might increase its profit by pulling customers away from its competitors. But if a city's other grocers also adopted charge accounts, the opportunity to gain new customers would disappear. All the grocers would then be stuck paying high merchant discounts, costs that would either subtract from profits or lead to higher consumer prices. This was exactly the kind of credit trap retailers sought to avoid.[30]

High costs were just one reason retailers resisted charge account programs: they also worried about banks intervening in their relationships with customers. Instead of returning to the store each month to settle up—and perhaps make additional purchases—customers paid off their charge accounts at the bank or by mail, costing smaller stores valuable foot traffic. Merchants also feared that by sending their accounts to the bank, they would lose their customers to competitors who adopted the bank's charge plan. Some banks, like Marine Midland, a banking group in upstate New York, tried to counter this fear by enrolling only one type of retailer in a particular location, like a new shopping plaza. Some merchants took matters into their own hands, sending more troublesome credit accounts to the bank while keeping their prompt-paying customers for themselves. Throughout the 1950s, the retail trade press remained suspicious of bankers' retail credit plans. The same spirit of independent proprietorship that fueled retailers' impulse toward antimonopoly also led them to resist what one writer in *Women's Wear Daily* called banks' "long-range . . . campaign to establish themselves as the principal source for all types of credit."[31]

Despite these ongoing tensions, bankers convinced many merchants to join their plans. Between June 1953 and November 1958, the number of merchants accepting bank charge plans rose from 5,000 to 12,000, or from about 170 to about 360 merchants for each reporting bank. Merchants wanted to offer credit. Although charge account banking had drawbacks, bank plans allowed merchants to participate in the expansion of the private credit economy without investing heavily in the infrastructure necessary to do so on their own.

In their pitch to retailers, bankers often promised to unite merchants into local shopping communities, a process that manifested in the spatial strategies banks adopted to serve their local markets. In smaller towns, charge account banks worked to preserve and revitalize downtown shopping. Of the 74 merchants listed in the directory of the Industrial Savings and Trust of Muncie, Indiana, 54 were clustered within four blocks of the main downtown intersection, where the bank had its offices. Expanding automobile ownership placed many small-town merchants into direct competition with large stores in nearby cities. Bank charge accounts kept retail business local. After describing how the new four-lane highway created "the tendency . . . for the ladies to go to Indianapolis to shop," Columbus, Indiana, banker J. Irwin Miller explained to Congress how, thanks to the bank's charge account plan, "by and large, business . . . stays in Columbus."[32]

Banks on the outskirts of major cities, meanwhile, adopted suburban strategies for their charge account plans. When merchants moved into the nation's shiny new shopping centers, they were often short on capital and lacked established ties with local customers. Financing consumer credit was a risky burden. Bank charge plans banded merchants together into shopping center-wide credit services. Charge account plans that emphasized suburban shopping, however, threatened downtown merchants. As one worried *Credit World* author observed, "Banks all over the country are sponsoring new consolidated 'charge account' services, the single purpose of which is to *get people to buy in the neighborhood* instead of going 'downtown.'" The geographic diversity of charge account plans suggests that the programs were flexible and could be adapted to different retail environments, even as, like the banking industry more broadly, the service remained confined by geographic regulation.[33]

Geographic restrictions were not always insurmountable barriers. In a preview of networking strategies banks developed in the 1960s, some charge account bankers experimented with *interchange,* where banks separated by geographic regulations participated in the same card plan. The first interchange system began in 1955, when five small banks in rural Michigan approached the larger Citizens Commercial and Savings Bank of Flint, which operated a plan called "Charge-O-Matic." As a Citizens executive explained in *American Banker,* the smaller banks wanted to offer charge accounts in their towns but feared they would not generate adequate volume to make the plans profitable. Citizens Commercial had long-standing relationships with the banks; its executives, sensing an opportunity to profitably deepen these ties, devised a cooperative interchange system that enabled the smaller banks to offer charge accounts in their communities. The small banks recruited merchants in their towns, and the merchants recommended consumers to participate in the plan. The small correspondent banks—later called agent banks—managed the merchant side of the business, collecting charge slips, taking floor limit calls, and crediting merchant accounts for consumer purchases. Merchants, in turn, opened checking accounts with their local agent bank, and the agent bank earned a portion of the merchant discount on each local transaction. Citizens Commercial handled the consumer side, collecting merchant slips from the small banks, billing consumers, and retaining any interest consumers paid on their accounts. "Will it work?" the Citizens Commercial executive asked. When he explained the plan in May 1956, "it [was] a little too soon to know."[34]

The banks that experimented with "correspondent charge account plans" in the 1950s did so to capitalize on investments in managerial expertise and credit-processing equipment and to expand the geographic reach of their plans. Citizens Commercial and the First National Bank and Trust of Kalamazoo, which began the second such plan in 1957, were both located in Michigan, a state that limited branch banking to a 25-mile radius from a bank's primary office. Correspondent plans incorporated merchants and consumers from outside the card-issuing banks' restricted market, increasing transaction volume and lowering individual transaction costs. Still, bankers remained careful to root their correspondent plans in their agent banks' communities, relying on cross-branding to ensure that the agent bank was the prominent face of the plan in their markets. While Citizens Commercial claimed its plan covered a 100-mile radius, in the small towns serviced by Charge-O-Matic, the program's emblem carried the agent bank's name in bold letters. Cardholders also received their Charge-O-Matic cards in a letter from the agent bank. The small community banks thus maintained local relationships with merchants and consumers, and added income as well.[35]

The Consumer Question

Bankers anticipated how charge accounts would benefit local merchants and deepen their relationships with small business customers, but they struggled to conceptualize how they would interact with consumer cardholders. We now think of card-issuing banks as intermediaries connecting cardholders to merchants and merchants to cardholders. Through the card, consumers' relationships are now firmly with the bank. In the 1950s, charge account plans ran through merchants. Banks relied on their retail partners to promote charge accounts to their customers and to encourage credit spending at each transaction. Enrolling consumers was the first step. From

Fig. 1: Brochure promoting the charge account service of the First National Bank and Trust of Kalamazoo. Mrs. Smith, who feels a charge account would be "more convenient" than cash, approaches a shopkeeper, who then helps her apply for the bank's charge account in his store.

Source: "First National Charge Account Service Shoppers Guide," First National Bank and Trust of Kalamazoo Clipping File, Kalamazoo Public Library (ca. mid-1950s). Reprinted with permission of PNC Bank, N.A.

that point forward, as Lorenz and other *American Banker* contributors emphasized, when the consumer chose between cash, check, or credit, bankers needed merchants to promote their credit plans.[36]

Charge account bankers worried constantly that merchants were not encouraging credit sales enthusiastically enough. At Marine Midland Bank,

executive Douglas A. Freeth confronted the issue directly in a memo titled
"What's Wrong with Midland Charge Plan?" Five of Midland's subsidiary
banks had adopted charge accounts in the 1950s and all were losing money.
For Freeth, *the heart of the whole problem* was "the host of merchants, of all
sizes, who do not realize the value of credit selling or know how to accomplish it." Without sufficient merchant cooperation, the Midland banks could
not generate sufficient sales volume to cover their plans' fixed costs. Bank
personnel had to sell merchants on the virtues of the Midland Charge Plan,
and they had to convince merchants to sign up consumers and push credit
sales. "We need to stimulate, through merchants, more card holders and
increased card usage," Freeth concluded. "Such a result will not just happen.
It must be *made* to happen—by selling—hard!" In the banking press, charge
account bankers reinforced this sentiment, uniformly arguing that bankers
had to convince merchants to sell on credit, not convince consumers to buy.[37]

Although bankers praised charge accounts as a way to gain and deepen
business lending relationships, they seldom discussed how charge accounts
could generate new consumer deposits or consumer loans. Commercial
bankers specialized in business lending. In other lines of consumer credit,
they usually worked through consumer-facing firms, such as car dealers
when making auto loans. Bankers structured charge accounts in the same
way, creating a debt between the consumer and the merchant, which the
merchant then sold to the bank. Most bankers simply did not feel that they
could make an all-out pitch to consumers. As Freeth concluded, "An individual's attitude toward debt and his paying habits are not easily predeter-
mined or readily changed." Other bank card promoters agreed. Recall
Edward Donohue's exhortation that "we could not change habits." Instead,
bankers built their charge plans on relationships that already existed, first
between consumers and merchants, and then between merchants and the
bank.[38]

Bankers' image of their ideal charge account customer—Mrs. Housewife—also inhibited aggressive customer solicitation. Bank offices were
overwhelmingly male spaces and charge account bankers self-consciously
styled themselves a "fraternity." Bankers worked within a hierarchy of social
and gender divisions: merchants and bank tellers served female customers,
while bankers dealt with other men. For such bankers, female-led shopping
carried transparent sexual undertones. Warning bankers against soliciting

consumers directly, Lorenz cautioned, "Nobody uses a charge card unless a buying impulse has been aroused. That buying impulse must be stirred up by the merchant and his wares." Bankers would facilitate credit sales. The charge account fraternity, however, had no business between the sheets with Mrs. Housewife and the draper.[39]

Still, just because bankers did not feel they could solicit consumer participation directly did not mean that consumers were not active agents in the growth of charge account banking. After all, banks developed charge account plans so that small merchants could meet customers' credit demands. So long as consumers borrowed while retailers paid the interest—so long as the costs of the system remained hidden from consumers by prices that weighed heavily on merchants—consumers continued to pressure retailers to take their new bank cards. For Pan American Bank in Miami, "Each customer [was] an ambassador of good will and usually demand[ed] new merchants . . . inquire and join this service." Retailers, however, seldom appreciated being arm-twisted by their customers. As Marine Midland executive Raymond Alm discovered after surveying his bank's merchant partners, "Most of these merchants did not need (or desire) this bank service, but joined the plan in order to retain present customers who might wish to use the bank charge card in their stores." As more consumers carried bank cards, retailers faced a stark choice: accept bank cards and pay the merchant discount or refuse bank cards and lose sales entirely.[40]

Although merchant discounts remained consistent throughout the 1950s, charge account bankers slowly adopted revolving credit, which allowed consumers to carry purchases over time by paying interest on their outstanding balances. In October 1953, Lorenz reported that only a fifth of charge account bank plans incorporated revolving credit, "surely an omission of major magnitude." As charge account bankers gained more experience, Lorenz urged them to adopt revolving credit "both as a means of increasing volume and as another source of valuable income." By August 1958, nearly 60 percent of charge account banking plans incorporated revolving credit, and consumer interest payments accounted for about a quarter of the income for profitable bank plans.[41]

Bankers, though, were unsure how to promote revolving credit, because, as Alm found, consumers remained apprehensive about credit purchasing. In addition to surveying Marine Midland's merchant customers, Alm also surveyed the bank's inactive cardholders "to determine their reaction to the charge plan and their reasons for not using this service more often." Here, Alm discovered a paradox. He found that 31.2 percent of inactive cardholders claimed they preferred not to use credit, yet only 9.8 percent reported they did not use charge accounts. Alm considered this "an obvious inconsistency." Was it? Perhaps consumers, in the throes of postwar abundance, remained uncomfortable with the insecurity and indebtedness that came with credit use. For Alm and Marine Midland Bank, the solution to consumer reluctance was simple: do not talk about credit. "The economy and convenience of only one bill a month should be emphasized," Alm wrote, "thus creating the image that the bank is performing a billing service, not a credit service." To convey this image, Marine Midland renamed their Midland Shopper Credit Service the Midland Charge Plan. The bankers who oversaw Charge-It, Charge-Rite, and Charge-O-Matic had long taken the same approach.[42]

The Travel Cards: Credit Unbound

At the same time that bankers were developing charge accounts to serve merchants and families in local communities, entrepreneurs in New York City developed a different kind of credit card, one for jet-set executives. Origin stories of the credit card industry often begin here, with Frank X. McNamara. The tale has evolved over time, but the basic version is that in 1949, McNamara was transacting business over an expensive yet "wholesome"— as in, hold the martinis—lunch in New York City. As the waiter was about to bring the check, McNamara realized he had left his wallet at home in one of his other suits. Ignobly waiting for his wife to drive in from suburban Long Island so he could settle the bill, McNamara got to thinking. "Why," he wondered, "should people be limited to spending what they are carrying in cash, instead of being able to spend what they can afford?" That thought launched the Diners Club. Initiated in February 1950, Diners was the first travel and entertainment card and, in most journalistic and scholarly accounts, the first "universal" credit card.[43]

As origin stories go, McNamara's wayward wallet worked well. It made the Club's cards instantly elite and masculine, perfect for the man who couldn't keep track of his wallet among his many suits. It also encoded the card as safely straight and white, wedded—through McNamara's wife—to the clean family living of the all-white Long Island suburbs. And it made the card functionally distinct, different than the charge accounts and department store cards used by households and housewives. Also, like many origin stories, it was a fabrication. As the tale filtered through marketing materials and news accounts, few have asked how a businessman who forgot his wallet would have remembered his Diners Card.[44]

The story was no less powerful for being implausible—it stuck and so did the Diners Club. Begun as a way for New York executives to dine on credit at restaurants and nightclubs, Diners expanded to provide a variety of services for its elite clientele, enabling them to charge hotel rooms, car rentals, and even freshly cut flowers. In the Club's estimation, such services made the card the "Indispensable New CONVENIENCE for the Executive—the Salesman—the man who gets around!" By its one-year anniversary Diners claimed more than 40,000 members and 300 participating restaurants and nightclubs, and it had offices in Boston, Hollywood, and Chicago. The company began international operations in 1953 in Italy and France, by which time it claimed more than 100,000 members and 3,000 merchant partners. Growth continued: Diners went public in 1955. Membership reached 260,000 in April 1956 and 560,000 in February 1958. By then, the firm was billing $92 million a year.[45]

For executives in the 1950s, wining and dining clients was at once an expected social practice and a valuable tax write-off. Like charge account banking, Diners sold cardholders convenience, not credit. The phrase "charge it" featured prominently in company advertising; "credit" never did. Convenience, moreover, reflected status. "You don't have to be a top executive to enjoy the many benefits of this man-about-town charge account privilege," the Club claimed. For all the implied prestige, Diners offered a practical product. The "biggest advantage to business members," Time magazine reported, is that "it gives them ready-made accounting of their expenses for income-tax purposes." Early on, the firm found its top users were "advertising men; closely followed by public relations men, [and] men in various selling businesses." These men needed to drink with clients and track the receipts; Diners helped them do both.[46]

As with the early bank charge plans, restaurants and other participating merchants bore the costs of the system, while cardholders used credit for free. The Club demanded a high discount. It kept 7 percent of what its card-holders charged, arguing that cardholders entertaining clients on credit would spend more. Meanwhile, Diners built its membership by giving cards to anyone who passed an initial credit check. Managing the plan, however, required significant capital. Diners had to pay merchants immediately, while waiting for cardholders to settle their accounts. Unlike banks, which accessed low-cost funding through consumer and business deposits, Diners had to borrow the money it lent to cardholders in financial markets. Even with its high merchant discount and short repayment period, the firm could not generate a profit until it added a $3 annual membership fee. Cardholders who did not regularly use the card dropped out, but demand for new memberships continued to grow. The fee added prestige. Although the Club lost more than $300,000 in its first year, the annual fee enabled the firm to turn a profit by 1955.[47]

Diners Club spawned numerous rivals and imitators, especially as it expanded from offering just meals to a full suite of travel and entertainment services. Alfred Bloomingdale, department store heir and early backer of Diners, built his own card plan in Los Angeles called Dine-n-Sign. Eventually, Bloomingdale bought out McNamara and merged the two plans. Now-forgotten cards like Trip-Charge, the Esquire Club, the Gourmet Guest Club, the Golden Key, and the Playboy Club all pursued a similar elite male clientele. The most lasting were Hilton Hotel's Carte Blanche, which grew out of the hotel chain's in-house charge card, and American Express, a firm specializing in business and travel services which began issuing cards in 1958. The remaining firms either folded or were absorbed by Diners, Hilton, or American Express.[48]

Bank charge accounts and travel and entertainment cards thus served distinct markets, distinguished by function—family shopping versus business entertaining—and by location—neighborhoods and suburban communities versus major cities. Nevertheless, these parallel products were tightly connected. Both bank charge accounts and the Diners Club developed between New York City and its Long Island suburbs in the early postwar years. Donohue and McNamara may have occasionally shared a train. Both products were part of the continued redefinition of male, homosocial workspaces, on the one hand, and idealized white, affluent, female-led suburban life, on the other. They operated in separate and distinct spheres, earmarking specific kinds of consumption while overlapping in the wallets and pocketbooks of middle-class families. The plans grew together. In the first quarter of 1958, Diners had 560,000 members, while the charge account banks that reported to *American Banker* accounted for 754,000 cardholders between them. Travel cards, which served male elites in major cities, gained wide press attention; bank cards, which served housewives in the suburbs, continued steady, if inconspicuous, growth.[49]

In 1958, California's Bank of America and New York's Chase Manhattan, the two largest banks in the United States, entered the charge account business. Bankers deluged Lorenz with questions. Should they, too, begin offering charge accounts? And why, after all, had so many banks dropped out of the business over the past few years? Lorenz had little patience for these inquiries. Through relentless promotion of charge account banking over the past half decade, Lorenz believed he had demonstrated the viability of charge account programs. Through such demonstrations, moreover, he revealed that bankers needed to escape the confines of their marble-clad imaginations and embrace progressive methods of granting credit. "Charge account banking stands on its own feet," Lorenz retorted. "It is profitable."[50]

The very visible rise of travel and entertainment plans like Diners Club and the later entry of major banks like Bank of America and Chase have eclipsed the history of charge account banking, and with it our understanding of early postwar financial innovation. In one sense, charge account banking reveals a process through which bankers innovated within the rules rather than around them. The structure of charge account banking followed from the New Deal regulatory order and the politics of small-business antimonopoly that undergirded it. Bankers developed their novel card plans within the confines of a political economy designed to constrain their firms' geographic reach, which ultimately enabled bankers to cooperate and innovate together. Through the banking trade press and newly formed national trade associations, bankers shaped a shared social vision for the charge account field and a common set of business practices. On the ground, they built plans through existing relationships with retailers and, through the retailers, with consumer cardholders. Their pricing strategy, which placed the cost of card plans fully on retailers, reflected these relationships. By the late 1950s, charge account banking was a viable, if still evolving, financial service. As later chapters will reveal, many of the pioneering banks, including Marine Midland and the First National Bank of Omaha, would go on to play critical roles in the card industry's future.[51]

Still, although charge accounts emerged from within the political economy of small finance, they nevertheless represented tentative steps to reshape the regulatory environment by opening new consumer markets. CABA bankers worked to convince financial regulators that charge account plans were different from traditional banking—that the old rules did not apply to innovative financial products. Moreover, just because bank card plans were local did not mean that bankers' ambitions were small. Banks, W. Albert Hess, vice president of the Bank of Virginia, explained in October 1953, "should be the reservoirs for every type of credit in their communities." Hess predicted that soon "banks may be handling the bulk, maybe all, charge account financing." Expressing similar sentiment, *Bankers Monthly* editor J. H. Peters reflected, "When you really get to thinking about 'charge account' banking, in all of its ramifications, it doesn't shrug off very easily." These ramifications would take time to develop. Charge account banks created the foundation for private credit networks, which would gradually draw merchants and consumers into a permanent credit—and payments—trap.[52]

3

Profits Squeeze

Creative Management in Banking

David Rockefeller, president of Chase Manhattan, regretted his bank's brief experiment with charge account banking. Encouraged by reports from Otto Lorenz and the *American Banker,* Chase initiated the Chase Manhattan Charge Plan (CMCP) in 1958 as a part of a broader effort to expand its retail banking presence across New York City. Chase bankers determined that "there was a ready market for this type of credit-card service," Rockefeller recalled, and they "liked the prospects." However, by 1964, when Rockefeller reflected on the experiment in a lecture at Columbia University, published as *Creative Management in Banking,* the program had gone bust. In 1960 alone, CMCP lost $1,790,000, almost 20 times the start-up costs Chase executives had projected. The creative banker needed the courage to risk failure, Rockefeller explained, and the wisdom to move past mistakes. For Chase Manhattan, charge account banking had been a mistake.[1]

Creative Management in Banking was not primarily a reflection on CMCP; it was instead Rockefeller's attempt to answer a larger question: was the New Deal regulatory order capable of meeting the evolving demands of the postwar economy? Rockefeller—whose grandfather John D. had built the family fortune on Standard Oil and whose older brother Nelson began his fifteen-year reign as governor of New York in 1959—had tried to answer that question as a member of the Commission on Money and Credit (CMC). The commission convened in 1958, at the request of President Eisenhower, to evaluate the postwar financial structure in light of the nation's evolving economic circumstances. Within its wide-ranging analysis, the commission revealed the extent to which the New Deal regulatory priorities of financial federalism, industry siloing, and price controls had constrained commercial banks. Banks, like Rockefeller's Chase Manhattan, which traditionally served the financial needs of businesses, had lost significant ground to consumer-oriented financial firms. They suffered, bankers complained, from an acute "profits squeeze." The commission urged immediate reform. Yet restrictive policies continued to enjoy robust political support, especially in Congress. Well-placed lawmakers, notably Representative Wright Patman (D-TX) and Senator Paul Douglas (D-IL), stridently defended the system's limits on concentrated financial power. While Rockefeller and other members of the commission sought space for financial firms to grow and change, Douglas, Patman, and their allies maintained the New Deal order's regulatory constraints.[2]

Through his service on the Commission of Money and Credit, Rockefeller worked with bankers and other elites to reform the New Deal financial rules through the political process; his bank's simultaneous experiment with charge account banking reflected an effort to innovate around regulatory restraints. But, as Rockefeller learned, the financial regulatory order, for all its contradictions, was not easily reformed or circumvented. After Congress barred the door on direct growth through merger, larger banks turned to new services, including charge accounts, that might open windows onto new markets. Chase and Bank of America, its West Coast rival, both launched card plans in 1958. As with the first wave of charge account banking, they did so as consumer spending lifted the economy out of recession, presaging commercial banks' full-scale pivot toward consumer markets. Within the banking industry, the entry of these giant firms signaled a new phase for card-based credit. Still, most bankers watched and waited. Chase and Bank of America experienced significant operational challenges, and both banks suffered major public losses. By the early 1960s, Bank of America's resilience—and Chase's capitulation—solidified a new business model focused on consumers rather than merchants. As the banking industry pursued consumer markets in the next decade, the industry adopted Bank of America's consumer-focused strategies. Charge account banking faded from view.

The New Deal Regulatory Order in Transition

The Commission on Money and Credit was the product of President Dwight D. Eisenhower's persistent concern with achieving sustained growth within a context of economic stability, low inflation, and fiscal responsibility. Ike, a Republican, had made his peace with the New Deal welfare state. Unlike his Democratic predecessors, successors, and critics, he resisted making federal spending a perpetual engine of economic expansion. Instead, he and his advisers believed monetary rather than fiscal policy was a more appropriate tool for managing the U.S. economy. Monetary policy, however, worked through the fragmented financial system, generating unexpected— and often politically contentious—outcomes. When the Federal Reserve tightened the money supply to tamp down on inflation in 1956, mortgage rates and municipal borrowing costs surged. Congressional investigations followed in short order. The financial infrastructure seemed incapable of effectively transmitting the will of policymakers. Considering new policy directions as he began his second term in 1957, Eisenhower sought to determine whether the financial structures inherited from the New Deal could deliver stable, long-term growth. During his State of the Union Address that January, Eisenhower called on Congress to create a commission "to conduct a broad national inquiry into the nature, performance and adequacy of our financial system." Eisenhower wanted the commission to be nonpartisan— to keep matters of expert economic analysis beyond the reach of partisan politics.[3]

In banking, though, politics always intervened. In this case, Eisenhower's proposal landed amid a long-running conflict between congressional Democrats and national business groups over how to evaluate—and possibly reform—the financial structure. Since the late 1940s, the Committee for Economic Development (CED), a business-led policy institute, had pressed for the kind of independent investigatory commission Eisenhower now proposed. Congressional leaders, however, would not cede policy authority. They stonewalled CED's efforts even after Eisenhower's endorsement. Patman and Douglas, guardians of the New Deal financial order, instead sought a congressional commission, one that would be sympathetic to their antimonopolistic vision of the postwar credit economy. Yet they too failed to win congressional approval. Finally, with support from the Rockefeller and Ford

Foundations, the CED undertook Ike's project on its own initiative, establishing the Commission on Money and Credit in 1958.[4]

Despite its contested origins, the commission assembled a prominent membership and proceeded to examine the financial system in light of the economic, social, and political demands placed on it. In addition to Rockefeller, CMC members included former Federal Reserve chairman Marriner Eccles, future Treasury secretary Henry Fowler, labor leaders, New Deal veterans, and other leading financial executives. Paul Volcker, future chairman of the Fed, served as Rockefeller's assistant, and economist Hyman Minsky wrote one of its supplemental reports. The commissioners framed their study around the widely accepted goals of price stability, low unemployment, and persistent economic growth. Growth, they believed, required credit. Consumers needed credit to buy homes, cars, and household goods; businesses needed credit to make these products and bring them to market; government units needed credit to build infrastructure, maintain the armed forces, buttress the welfare state, and otherwise secure the blessings of liberty for Americans and their posterity. In contrast to Western European nations, which channeled credit largely toward business investment, American politicians wanted to direct scarce credit to consumption, to production, and toward an eclectic mix of more specific goals like housing, agriculture, and small business. Given the disparate public objectives, commission members struggled to identify a tangible agenda beyond that of a general loosening of regulatory restraints. As the report's lengthy argumentative footnotes indicate, they struggled to agree on anything at all.[5]

At the level of policy, commission members labored to find a viable direction, but their work also placed a spotlight on the postwar growth of the U.S. financial system and the diminished place of commercial banks within it. In broad strokes, the news was encouraging. American households turned their rising incomes into savings. Corporations turned their profits into capital. "We have witnessed a very rapid growth in financial institutions," the commission reported, adding, "The assets of all private financial institutions have increased at a growth rate well above the rate of growth of population, real output, or national wealth." The financial business boomed. Total assets of private financial firms grew from $280 billion in 1945 to $614 billion in 1958. Commercial banks were growing too, but slowly. Over the same period, commercial bank assets increased from $159 billion to $238 billion, but they declined relative to the financial sector, from 56.5 percent to 39.5 percent. The regulatory structure, the commission argued, clearly benefited some firms more than others. Thrifts, like savings and loans and credit unions, could not offer checking accounts as did commercial banks, but they paid higher interest on consumer savings. As mortgage specialists, thrifts also led the postwar housing boom. Meanwhile, less or differently regulated firms, particularly investment companies, pension funds, and insurance firms, competed with commercial banks for business loans without the geographical impediments of interstate branching boundaries.[6]

Commercial bankers were slow to recognize the ways that regulatory differences and their own conservative strategies undermined their competitive position. In the early postwar years, commercial banks easily met the credit needs of their primary customers, business firms. They did so primarily by selling U.S. bonds accumulated during the Depression and war years instead of seeking new deposits from businesses and consumers. At the peak in 1946, Treasury securities represented more than half of total commercial bank assets. Banks sold these securities and used the proceeds to invest in business loans, transitioning from one asset to another rather than seeking new deposits to expand their balance sheets. From 1946 to 1956, commercial bank deposits increased only 38 percent, compared to GDP growth of 100 percent and non-bank deposit growth of 172 percent. Bankers blamed their meager gains on regulatory disadvantages. In material written under the CMC's auspices, bankers warned policymakers that weak deposit growth threatened the entire economy. The ability of commercial banks to provide adequate credit, the American Bankers Association warned, "depends to a large extent upon the way in which banks serve—*or are permitted to serve*—as deposit institutions." If they could not grow their deposit base, bankers belatedly realized, they would not keep pace with the growing needs of their business customers.[7]

Commercial bankers felt particularly hard pressed when it came to expanding consumer markets. At the end of World War II, commercial banks held 53 percent of household savings, but by 1960 they retained only 41 percent. As the commission's study highlighted, American consumers enjoyed a diverse market for financial services. With their deposit rates fixed by the Federal Reserve, commercial banks often competed for consumer accounts through non-financial incentives. Some were quaint, including toaster and

Table 1. Distribution of Assets of Private Financial Institutions,
1945 and 1958 (by percent)

	1945	1958
Commercial banks	56.5	39.5
Mutual savings banks	6.0	6.2
Savings and loan associations; credit unions; and finance, mortgage, and loan companies	3.9	13.2
Life and other insurance companies	19.1	22.8
Pension funds and investment companies	2.1	7.4
Trust departments and securities brokers and dealers	12.3	10.9
Total	99.9	100

Source: Commission on Money and Credit, Money and Credit: Their Influence on Jobs, Prices, and Growth (Prentice-Hall, 1961), 155.

steak-knife giveaways. Yet entrepreneurial bankers also experimented with new products and services, like charge accounts, to draw consumers into their banks. Even so, geographic regulations prevented many banks from following white, affluent customers as they migrated out of central cities, where banks had their offices, and into the suburbs. Americans were on the move, the commission recognized, as their banks stayed in place. "While the migration of people and industry had not been restricted by city, county, or state boundaries," the commission observed, "the migration of banks by branching often has been restricted." Consumers were, in more ways than one, leaving commercial banks behind.[8]

Not only had bankers been slow to compete for deposits, but in the early postwar years the deposits they did possess become increasingly expensive, squeezing bank margins between expensive deposits and loan rates subject to price controls and public pressure. Persistent inflation made depositors price conscious. Over time, consumers and businesses shifted their money from accounts that did not pay interest to those that did. In 1945, 81 percent of commercial bank deposits were checking accounts that paid no interest. By 1958, they were down to 73 percent. Conversely, savings and time deposits, which paid rates set by the Federal Reserve, rose from 19 percent to 27 percent over the same period. They continued to rise to 33 percent in 1961 and 49 percent in 1972. "A principal factor" in Chase Manhattan's "persis-tent rise in expenses," Rockefeller's bank noted in 1961, was "the growing importance of time and savings deposits for which interest must be paid." Banks, however, could not easily pass on rising costs through higher prices. State usury laws restricted rates on consumer loans and mortgages. Mean-while, competition and political pressure held down business lending rates. Any increase in the prime rate—the rate banks charged their most credit-worthy business customers—ensured vocal criticism from politicians and negative headlines in the nation's mainstream press. Trapped between ex-pensive deposits and low loan rates, commercial banks confronted what Rockefeller and his contemporaries termed the "profits squeeze."[9]

Commission members saw clearly—and, in Rockefeller's case, experienced personally—the ways the regulatory structure constrained commercial bank-ers' role in the American financial order. The commission also recognized that some banks sought to retain profitability through aggressive growth, es-pecially via merger. Rockefeller's bank provided the salient example. In 1955, Chase National Bank, a wholesale bank that served large business clients through offices in Manhattan, merged with the Manhattan Company, a retail bank with branches spread through the Bronx, Brooklyn, and Queens. The new Chase Manhattan became the second largest bank in the country—be-hind only California's Bank of America. The combination also ignited a merger boom among Chase's competitors. The *New York Times* hailed a "New Banking Era." Congress was not so enthusiastic. Patman and Douglas, along with allies like Emanuel Celler (D-NY) and Estes Kefauver (D-TN), rose to defend the New Deal's political economy of small finance. "The businessman and merchant," Celler warned as he prepared a congressional inquiry, "will be at the mercy of a financial colossus." Throughout the 1950s and 1960s, Con-gress extended the New Deal's political economy of small finance through a raft of antimonopoly legislation, including the Bank Holding Company Act (1956) and the Bank Merger Acts (1960, 1966). Even as the CMC debated regulatory liberalization, Congress remained committed to fragmentation and restraint.[10]

Congressional antagonism to bank mergers did not bode well for the commis-sion's recommendations. In its June 1961 report, the Commission on Money and Credit offered 91 proposals aimed at increasing financial competition and improving the federal government's economic management and credit programs. For commercial banks, the report recommended loosening branching restrictions to enhance competition with non-bank financial firms, liberalizing bank investment powers, and equalizing limits on savings account rates. President John F. Kennedy praised the report and called on Congress's Joint Economic Committee (JEC) to propose appropriate legislation. Patman and Douglas, however, jointly chaired the JEC. With their allies, they remained hostile to concentrated economic power, defensive of state regulatory prerogatives, and protective of the New Deal banking reforms. "I think we should have local banks run and owned by local people," Patman explained. David Rockefeller, scion of a monopolist and president of a monopolist bank, embodied the antithesis of their vision. When Rockefeller appeared before the JEC's hearings in August 1961, Patman grilled the Chase president on the dominance of New York banks and attacked the commission's branching recommendations (never mind that Rockefeller was there to discuss federal lending programs). With Patman and Douglas in charge of the agenda, the JEC buried the commission's proposals.[11]

Congressional leaders remained committed to the political economy of small finance, rejecting both the practical efforts of bankers to grow through merger and the theoretical claims of the CMC that financial liberalization would encourage the policy trifecta of low inflation, high employment, and steady growth. Patman and Douglas found an eager constituency among the thousands of small financial firms, which collectively sought to preserve their competitive positions against the forces of consolidation and monopoly. Small, local finance also reflected the commonplace understanding that financial relationships were social relationships, embedded in communities (and in community power structures, including race, gender, and social class). Although banks would chip away at the edges through innovation, Congress remained committed to the New Deal regulatory order into the 1960s.[12]

Within the nation's larger banks, the regulatory system's unyielding restrictions on commercial banks vis-à-vis other financial firms bred an increasingly vigorous regulatory resentment paired with an anti-regulatory, free-market ideology. This was especially true for a cohort of young, midlevel bankers who built their careers in the 1950s and 1960s. In succeeding decades, men—and they were all men—like Citibank's Walter Wriston, First National Bank of Omaha's John R. Lauritzen, and Seattle National Bank of Commerce's Dee Hock would press against the political economy of small finance. In doing so, they turned antimonopolists' language of fair competition against the regulatory state, arguing that the solution to the unfair regulatory standards was free competition in the market. Like the profits squeeze, this ideology would develop over time, and as it did, many of its proponents reached for credit cards as a strategic embodiment of its ideals: as a way to pursue regulatory reform through market means.[13]

The Divergent Paths of Chase
Manhattan and Bank of America

The financial order, built on financial federalism, industry siloing, and price controls, created wide channels for growth for some firms but restrained commercial banks. Congressional leaders, eager to maintain the political economy of small finance, watchfully guarded the system. As bankers reexamined their competitive positions at the end of the 1950s, they looked for new ways to generate profits within the system or, barring that, to plot a course beyond its confines. In boardrooms, the inviting call of the charge account bankers sounded louder and clearer. Charge account bankers reported 750,000 cardholders, $40 million in transaction volume, and $12.5 million in credit outstanding in 1957. The charge account fraternity aimed for one million cardholders and $45 million in volume in 1958 and expected to achieve it. "This hard-working, resourceful and successful little corps of pioneers have come through with better results year after year," Otto Lorenz gloated. Charge account banking had direction and momentum.[14]

The course of that momentum shifted dramatically in 1958 when Rockefeller's Chase Manhattan and California's Bank of America launched charge account plans. The two firms were orders of magnitude larger than their commercial bank competitors. The average (mean) U.S. bank in 1958 had $38.5 million in total assets, whereas the average (mean) card-issuing bank had—as a rough estimate—about $250 million. By comparison, Chase and Bank of America were huge: at the end of 1958, Bank of America had $11.2 billion in assets, Chase had $8.3 billion. Although they shared size in common, they operated fundamentally different business models shaped by their distinct state regulatory contexts. These elemental differences determined how their executives understood the challenges their new card plans would face—and what strategies they would adopt to overcome them.[15]

Chase entered the charge account business at a moment when its executives were uncertain about the bank's identity and future direction. The original Chase National Bank had been a wholesale bank, serving large corporate
clients in New York State and across the country. Chase executives recognized that postwar inflation was encouraging these clients to shift their deposits from interest-free demand deposits to interest-bearing time accounts
at the bank or to new financial instruments outside of it. Chase bankers determined that the bank needed to diversify its deposit base and asset portfolio. They did so, in 1955, by merging with the Manhattan Company, a firm
that focused on the consumer market. The merger created double vision
within the bank. Former Chase National executives like Rockefeller saw a
nationwide—even global—corporate market. Their ambition stretched as far
as planes could fly from New York City. Former Manhattan Company executives, meanwhile, saw their customers from their office window, in the
neighborhoods where the new Chase Manhattan Bank maintained its branch
offices. Under state law, the consolidated bank could not build branches outside New York's five boroughs; only in 1960 could they extend to neighboring Nassau and Westchester Counties. The merger agreement called for
joint leadership by the Manhattan Company's consumer-focused executives
and Chase's traditionally wholesale bankers. The two visions might coexist,
but they could not co-lead.[16]

In 1958, as the internal power struggle remained unresolved, the bank
introduced the Chase Manhattan Charge Plan (CMCP). Bank executives
modeled the plan on the charge account programs promoted in *American
Banker,* adopting the methods and goals developed there. Through CMCP,
executives argued, Chase would forge new relationships with small retailers,
while helping those merchants compete with credit-granting department
stores. As Rockefeller recalled, "Our studies strongly indicated that there was
a ready market for this type of credit-card service, designed to give customers
of smaller retail establishments credit facilities comparable to those of major
department stores." Advertising to retailers, Chase emphasized that "the
merchant is able to improve his competitive position" by offering "a modern
charge account service." Chase also followed the charge account bankers'
model when courting consumers, promoting the CMCP as a boon to middle-
class, female-led, family shopping. In a typical ad from April 1959, "One
woman tells another . . . the Chase Manhattan Bank Charge Plan is the

smartest way to shop!" Spring shopping, back-to-school shopping, Christmas shopping, the CMCP was the "convenient, modern way to shop" for all seasons. In an arrangement familiar to charge account bankers, while women did the shopping, husbands got the credit. CMCP made "back-to-school shopping a pleasure!" for a mother of four; the card she used belonged to "Jonathan Q. Public," not Jane.[17]

The Chase executives soon learned that the strategies medium-sized banks pioneered in towns and suburban communities proved less successful for a massive bank in a major city. Chase struggled to develop successful merchant or consumer recruitment strategies, and with them sufficient volume to generate reliable profits. Merchants were lukewarm to the plan. Large retailers with existing credit programs refused to join CMCP, and small merchants complained about the 6 percent merchant discount. CMCP also alienated Chase's existing business customers, like department stores, which viewed CMCP as a competitive threat. By mid-1961, an internal report found that CMCP had produced only $2.5 million in new deposit accounts, or $379 per merchant. The bank struggled to recruit creditworthy cardholders. Because Chase executives used CMCP to establish relationships with merchants, they could not immediately tap into merchants' relationships with their customers. Instead, Chase ran newspaper ads and mailed applications to existing checking account customers. The bank required potential cardholders to submit a credit application. Executives tried to be diligent: they rejected half the consumers who applied. Nevertheless, Chase's mail-order credit screenings lacked the intimate formality of department store and smaller bank card plans. Instead of securing the personal recommendation of a participating merchant or sitting for a credit interview at the bank—methods that added social weight to consumers' credit responsibility—consumers applied through the mail. Fraud became a significant and mounting problem. The bank's blacklist of cards reached seventeen pages.[18]

As Chase executives struggled to identify promotion strategies that would yield adequate transaction volume, they also refused to charge prices that would produce adequate revenue. Chase initially charged CMCP cardholders 1 percent per month on their outstanding balances (12 percent annually). Even with CMCP's high merchant discount, these rates proved too low. Under New York law, the bank could have charged up to 1.5 percent (18 percent annually) on most balances, but executives ruled out raising rates. "When we

evaluated this service in the context of our over-all banking activity," Rockefeller recalled, "we simply could not see ourselves charging customers 18 per
cent—even though the servicing costs fully justified the charge." Chase specialized in safe business lending, where 18 percent interest was unthinkable.
In 1960 Chase earned just 4.5 percent interest on its entire loan portfolio, up
from 4.05 percent in 1959. Further, politicians like Paul Douglas were mobilizing against high consumer credit prices, and Chase executives worried
that charging consumers 18 percent would draw unwanted political attention. Finally, Chase's internal accounting rules allocated more expenses to
the CMCP than was common at other banks, while executives balked at re-
tooling their billing machinery to tabulate higher rates. In November 1961,
the bank's federal examiners found that CMCP had lost between $4 and $5
million in three years of operation. Executives were not encouraged.[19]

Unlike Chase, Bank of America was fundamentally a consumer bank,
built to sustain founder A. P. Giannini's famed commitment to help "the
little fellow." That help came through a far-reaching branch network
and through the bank's savvy embrace of postwar federal lending programs.
California did not restrict branch banking, and when it launched its
BankAmericard program in November 1958, Bank of America had 638
offices across the rapidly growing state. These offices generated 7 million
individual deposit accounts, or 486 accounts for every 1,000 residents of
California. Bank executives channeled household savings back into consumer lending. In contrast to Chase, Bank of America made just under 40
percent of its loans to businesses. Instead, more than 20 percent of the
bank's lending supported consumer installment purchasing. The bank invested another 40 percent in real estate, primarily home mortgages, compared with just 4.5 percent at Chase. Fully a quarter of Bank of America's
loans were "guaranteed or insured by the United States Government or its
agencies" through programs like FHA and VA mortgage guarantees and
FHA home improvement loans.[20]

Government lending programs provided guaranteed profits for Bank of
America, and they also required executives to manage millions of consumer
loan accounts across a large and diverse state. The principal challenge of
lending to "the little fellow" remained the high costs of administering small
loans. In the 1950s, Bank of America executives blended their past focus on
consumer services with a future-oriented commitment to new technologies

that would make small transactions more efficient and less expensive. The bank invested heavily in large mainframe computers. In 1955, it unveiled Electronic Recording Machine, Accounting (ERMA), an electronic check-processing system. Engineers also developed installment and real estate loan software that ran on IBM machines. Experience with these new systems convinced top management that the right mix of technology could make credit cards a profitable service. Bank executives had considered starting a charge account banking plan in 1953, when the first boom was at its peak, but held off fearing they did not yet know how to make a card plan work. By 1956, executives were ready to move forward with serious planning.[21]

Bank of America's consumer-focused, technologically-driven culture led executives to reorient their charge account plan from merchants—where Chase and the charge account banking pioneers were focused—to consumers. By shifting their perspective, executives fundamentally changed how they understood the business problems associated with card plans, reshaping in turn the subsequent strategies they adopted to overcome them. Heading this effort was Joseph P. Williams, who led the bank's Consumer Research Service Department. Williams ardently embraced Bank of America's consumerist philosophy. In the 1940s, he drove across the country to seek a job at the bank (no small feat before the construction of the interstate highway system). Williams propelled the development of what would become the BankAmericard as a consumer-focused product—not primarily a means of offering charge account services to merchants, but a way to sell revolving credit to consumers.[22]

From the outset, bank executives imagined the BankAmericard as a vehicle for consumer lending, and they established an 18 percent interest rate on revolving credit balances. At the time, just over half of charge account banks offered revolving credit, and few—if any—charged 18 percent.[23] California, unlike New York, did not regulate interest on revolving accounts. Bank of America executives, unlike their counterparts at Chase, had no qualms about charging a price that would make the BankAmericard profitable. And consumers were paying these rates already. Williams simply copied the prices that retail firms, specifically Sears and Mobil Oil, were charging. On the other side of the card transaction, Bank of America followed Chase and the other charge account banks by charging merchants 6 percent on each card purchase but found merchants resistant to this high fee. To meet merchant concerns, Bank of America lowered its discount and introduced graduated rate reductions based on a merchant's monthly charge volume. And unlike other banks, which often negotiated discounts privately with individual merchants, Bank of America provided clear tables and pricing transparency. The bank thus streamlined merchant enrollment and likely made merchant discounts easier for their computer systems to process.[24]

Bank of America executives also revolutionized consumer and merchant recruitment. Instead of relying on merchants to recommend creditworthy cardholders, Bank of America launched its program by mailing out millions of unsolicited cards directly to bank customers. Such direct consumer marketing was anathema to charge account bankers. In their view, banks designed card plans to serve merchants; merchants, in turn, promoted bank card plans. "Once you have your merchant signed your work is only beginning," Charge Account Bankers Association president Charles Landrain observed at a banking conference in November 1958. "From that time on . . . you have to roll up your sleeves to keep your merchant under control and producing." Charge account bankers understood that they needed to recruit enough consumers and merchants to make participation worthwhile for each group. They had resolved to make merchants the vector of the process and to accept a slow buildup of creditworthy cardholders. Bank of America executives inverted the prevailing logic: instead of using merchants to recruit consumers, the bank used consumers to draw in merchants. Executives made unsolicited cards the center of this bold and risky strategy. "It would be impossible to start a major program with a small amount of cards," a BankAmericard spokesman explained to *Women's Wear Daily*, "'because it would be impossible to interest merchants.'" Card-carrying consumers would pull merchants in.[25]

The unsolicited mailing of cards went against the experience and inclination of the commercial banking industry. It was, *American Banker* editor Otto Lorenz declared, "Mistake No. 1." Williams, however, believed the bank could build adequate volume and sustain the new credit program only by putting cards into consumer hands. Lorenz, reflecting the experience of small and mid-sized banks, understood consumer credit as rooted in communities, embedded in social relations. Williams and his team did not abandon social embeddedness entirely. Although Bank of America dispensed with merchant recommendations and in-person credit checks, in its early campaigns the bank sent cards only to established customers. Bank of America built its program on a vast infrastructure of bank branches, which connected the BankAmericard to local communities. Williams, who had no direct lending experience himself, believed that the bank's community presence would en-sure that customers used their cards properly and paid their debts promptly. There was no need to plumb the depths of cardholders' souls before giving them cards, no need to subject them to the steely-eyed stare of a bank credit manager. Odds were, if they were already Bank of America customers, they would use their cards properly.[26]

Because the bank had branches across California, Williams and his team had the luxury of testing the waters before fully committing to the plan. Ex-ecutives chose to unveil the BankAmericard in Fresno, then a city of 130,000 midway between Los Angeles and San Francisco, where Bank of America controlled 45 percent of the banking market. If the plan flopped, bankers hoped, no one in San Francisco or Los Angeles would notice. In late 1958, the bank enlisted over 300 community retailers before mailing credit cards to every bank customer in the area, nearly 60,000 in all. Williams dubbed the experiment "the drop." To inform consumers where they could use their new BankAmericards—and to demonstrate to merchants that their compet-itors had already enrolled in the plan—the bank ran full-page ads, listing all participating merchants, in the *Fresno Bee*. Initially, the mass-mailing ap-proach had the desired effect. Facing competitive pressure and the knowl-edge that half their customers now had BankAmericards, merchant enrollments tripled over the next five months.[27]

The BankAmericards mailed in September 1958 presented Fresno con-sumers with another innovation: the cards were made of plastic. Before then, payment cards were either metal, integrating with mechanical information systems popular with service stations and department stores, or paper, requir-ing clerks to record account information by hand. Bank of America, working with the small technology firm Dashew Business Machines (DBM), pioneered plastic credit cards. Founded by entrepreneur Stanley A. Dashew in 1951, DBM primarily contracted with the U.S. Navy and was one of California's many technology firms weaned on the military industrial complex. DBM spe-cialized in card-embossing equipment, which the Navy used to keep track of spare parts. By his own recollection, Dashew saw the expanding card industry as a potential application of his firm's technology. The Databosser, DBM's flagship product, could read and transcribe information directly from IBM punch cards used by both the Navy and big banks, at a speed unmatched by its competitors. That DBM's Databosser could churn out 1,000 cards in an hour would have meant little to BankAmericard recipients. But the new plastic cards fit seamlessly into the era's prevailing feeling of boundless technological progress. "The citizens of Fresno gather[ed] around the checkout counter to watch someone pay with a BankAmericard," business writer Joseph Nocera observed. "This was the 1950s . . . a time of wonder at the miraculous march of progress. The BankAmericard was part of that march."[28]

Based on the promising results in Fresno and rumors that competitors were planning to launch plans in other key California markets, Bank of America's managing committee moved to rapidly implement the program on a statewide basis. The bank rolled out the BankAmericard in Sacramento, San Francisco, and Los Angeles in early 1959. By the end of the year, the bank announced, "Nearly two million California families hold our BANKAMERICARD, which is honored by more than 25,000 merchants and professional members."[29] This bold pronouncement proved premature. Bank of America soon revised down its tally of cardholders—counting not simply households to which the bank had mailed cards but those actually using them.

Indeed, Bank of America's computerized credit future did not materialize quite as planned. While Williams's mass-distribution strategy succeeded in recruiting cardholders and merchants, it also invited criticism from consumers who were less eager to accept the bank's new plastic liabilities. In early 1960, *Consumer Reports* magazine joined a growing chorus critical of the BankAmericard, "which appears to lead in the sales-persuasion chants in praise of debt." Bankers also critiqued unsolicited card mailing. Charge Account Bankers Association president Charles Landrain mocked Bank of America: "It is agreed by most operators that broadcasting credit cards to the public is a waste of money." In Bank of America's offices, executives saw that Landrain had a point. Aggressive marketing came at the price of delinquency and fraud. Williams expected an initial delinquency rate of 4 percent; the actual rate was close to 20 percent. "The degree of credit checking we did was somewhat limited by the urgency to get the card out on the wide basis," a BankAmericard spokesman later explained. "We had to move fast." Moreover, like Chase, the bank failed to sign up large retailers who already had credit departments, who disdained the bank's high discount, and who feared the loss of their customer base—objections which denied Bank of America access to key sites of high dollar consumption. The bank reported nearly $9 million in BankAmericard losses for 1960 alone.[30]

Nevertheless, Bank of America's top management remained committed to the card and with it a future defined by convenient credit. At the end of 1959, Williams left the bank. The card plan's losses, he realized, would be an indelible mark on his career. After Williams's departure, top management transferred the BankAmericard to the bank's installment lending division. For a time, Bank of America stopped mailing unsolicited credit cards and focused on weeding out unprofitable accounts. Meanwhile, the bank's very public losses scared away competitors. Bank of America maintained a virtual monopoly over the bank card business in California into the mid-1960s, enabling bank executives to identify and overcome organizational and technological challenges and to achieve steady profitability.[31]

Chase suffered similarly but lacked Bank of America's commitment. The New York bank was initially unable to recruit large retailers and experienced greater than anticipated expenses from equipment, personnel, account delinquencies, and the cost of funds. Consistent with its retailer focus, Chase lowered merchant discount rates to bring in more retailers and generate more volume, which further eroded income, especially because the bank's executives refused to consider raising consumer interest rates. Importantly, John J. McCloy, the chairman who had pushed Chase National into retail banking through the Manhattan Company merger and who had been a strong supporter of the CMCP, retired in 1960. He was replaced by George Champion, a Chase National veteran and lifelong commercial banker. Champion, according to David Rockefeller, had "worked hard to make Chase the country's foremost wholesale domestic bank, catering primarily to large U.S. corporations." After an internal audit of the program, Champion decided that CMCP was a poor bet to produce significant future earnings. Chase ultimately sold CMCP to Uni-Serv, a company Joseph Williams founded after leaving Bank of America in order to have another crack at the card business.[32]

The early charge account programs found success and profits by developing through established community relationships and operating at a scale that was manageable for small bank executives. Following Otto Lorenz's advice,

they were frugal with equipment and personnel. They used their card programs to expand their merchant customer base, slowly warming to profiting
from consumer lending. Charge account banking, nestled in the political
economy of small finance and nurtured by a community of like-minded pioneers, had—and retained—forward momentum. Yet for Chase and Bank of
America, the stakes and the scale of the challenges were dramatically larger.
By the early 1960s, Chase remained committed to a future that looked much
like its past, lending wholesale to large corporate clients. Its executives were
not patient enough to allow their plan to develop slowly and not adventurous
enough to take an aggressive risk on consumer banking. Bank of America
executives also followed a path defined by the bank's corporate culture, but it
had a longstanding commitment to consumer lending, bolstered by the New
Deal's federal loan guarantees. The bank's commitment to consumer lending, in conjunction with its statewide reach, led executives to make sustained
investments in information technology. Despite experiencing higher initial
losses than Chase, Bank of America executives stuck with their card, reaching profitability by 1962 and maintaining it through the decade.

The very visible struggles of both firms caused other banks to steer clear
of charge account banking for nearly a decade. For their part, charge account
bankers continued to pursue steady, incremental growth, overshadowed by
their giant competitors and the flashy travel cards developed by Diners Club
and American Express. Charge account bankers lost their most vocal advocate in January 1960, when Lorenz died following a long "wasting illness."
Without his leadership and enthusiasm, *American Banker* discontinued its
charge account coverage. Although many of the charge account pioneers remained active in the card market, the eventual profitability of Bank of America's consumer model, in line with a wider eclipse of antimonopoly politics
by consumer politics in the 1960s, propelled bankers to follow its lead.[33]

Bankers developed early credit card programs within the social and political
framework of the New Deal regulatory order before turning cards into a technological weapon against that system. Put another way, bankers' use of financial
technology to innovate around the rules was an incremental process, one that
required them to fit the technology within the existing social and political structure. Charge account bankers understood cards as an organic outgrowth of
their relationships with retail firms, which shaped both the business strategies
they developed and the antimonopoly narrative they promoted. Charge

accounts, as a business service for merchants, slotted in commercial banking's regulated silo. The programs, geographically circumscribed and inexpensive for consumers, matched the spirit of financial federalism and price controls. Regulatory negotiations—over charge-offs and revolving credit—unfolded at the margins. For Bank of America, charge accounts followed from the bank's entwined commitments to information technology and consumer lending. By developing the BankAmericard on a statewide basis and charging consumers 18 percent interest, executives pressed against the spirit of geographic restrictions and price ceilings. In this, California's distinct rules shaped Bank of America's strategy. The bank's experience, in turn, prefigured later approaches used to affirmatively challenge both financial federalism's geographic restrictions and price controls in more restrictive states. Chase, for its part, lacked the internal resources or compelling future vision to sustain card-based innovation.

Ultimately, the 1950s were a seedbed for dynamic changes that reshaped the industry in later years. Some of this dynamism, like the accelerating investment in information technology, aligned with immediate regulatory goals while encouraging financial concentration in the long run. Information technology made banks more efficient and helped bankers reduce the mounting costs of processing financial transactions. Big banks could invest in mainframe computers and other back-office technology. Small banks could not. Economies of scale and scope worked against the political economy of small finance. In other areas, bankers pressed more directly against the regulatory boundaries or sought to escape the New Deal system altogether. Large banks expanded abroad into less or differently regulated foreign markets, achieving growth overseas that Congress would not allow at home. They also developed ways of circumventing federal price controls on deposit rates by borrowing in financial markets. The regulatory order structured all these strategies, which, like charge account banking, reflected efforts to grow at the margin of the rules. Moreover, a rising cohort of bankers, not chastened by the Depression years, were increasingly not satisfied to innovate at the margins. They wanted to be entrepreneurs, not mere custodians. They wanted to tear down the rules altogether. Political stasis fed a rising tension, building competitive pressures that soon would pop.

4

Deluge

Self-Fulfilling Prophecy

Following the strategy pioneered by Bank of America, from 1966 to 1970 bankers flooded American mailboxes with tens of millions of unsolicited credit cards. They did so, they argued, because they had no other choice. "In the competitive climate that exists, if we had depended upon applications alone our plan could not have been launched successfully," David M. Kennedy, chairman of Continental Illinois Bank in Chicago, explained to shareholders in January 1967. "There never was any possibility that we could have proceeded at a more leisurely pace." For the next four years—until Congress banned unsolicited card mailing in October 1970—bankers repeated versions of Kennedy's argument. Mass mailing was simply the only way to launch a successful bank card program. In one sense, bankers spun their self-fulfilling prophesy out of hopeful visions of the future. Most states did not yet regulate the price of credit card lending. Bankers increasingly saw consumer markets as the key to growth and profits, an emphasis steadily ingrained by the profits squeeze of the 1950s and increasing financial turbulence in the 1960s. At this pivotal moment, card technology captured the industry's imagination. If managed properly, bankers believed, cards would not only produce profits on their own but would also create lucrative and long-lasting consumer banking relationships. Further, bankers saw cards as a logical step toward the industry's technological future, where computers and data processing would expand the range of bank services and drive down operations costs. With these hopes came intense anxiety. The number of creditworthy customers was limited, bankers reasoned. No one could afford to wait while rivals scooped them up.[1]

As they sprinted into the credit card market, bankers developed regional and national payment networks, which enabled their banks to integrate local plans into far-reaching credit systems. Bankers, confined by geographic regulations, had long used interfirm relationships to conduct business in distant markets. Card networks built on these traditions. They were necessary, bankers believed, to compete with travel card firms, like the Diners Club and American Express. Whereas travel cards catered to male business elites, bankers envisioned universal cards, equally useful for shopping trips and business trips. Drawing on a common pool of technology and industry know-how, rival network-building firms developed card systems with distinct organizational styles that reflected financial federalism's diverse, state-based regulatory environments. Bank of America began franchising its BankAmericard plan to select licensee banks in early 1966, modeling the network on its centralized control of its California branches. Many bankers viewed BankAmericard's expansion as a threat. To counter, rivals developed regional card associations and, eventually, a competing national network, the Interbank Card Association. Taken together, the flurry of network building rested on established modes of interfirm cooperation, along lines of long-standing interbank rivalry and within geographic strategies dictated by financial federalism. Put another way: the regulatory structure shaped bankers' networking strategies.[2]

Even as bankers developed card networks to merge the gendered retail and travel markets, they retained implicit class and racial boundaries on consumer participation. As one Continental Illinois banker explained, the "demographics of the 'best' credit card customers point to married couples between the ages of 24 and 34, with family incomes of from $7,000 to $15,000, probably living in high-growth areas." Bankers coded creditworthiness—their governing criteria for credit access—as young, white, middle- to high-income, straight, and suburban. Young suburban families, bankers believed, would consume now on the promise of higher future incomes. They would use their cards *and* pay their bills on time. While the best customers lived in high-growth, all-white suburbs, geographic regulations often cloistered large urban banks, like Continental, in racially diverse downtowns. Bank network-building thus also aimed at reaching suburban consumers, propelling credit from city centers into leafy enclaves of white privilege. In Chicago, where downtown banks began issuing cards in October 1966, network expansion occurred alongside demonstrations led by Dr. Martin Luther King Jr. against segregated suburban housing. Although Continental's David Kennedy spoke solemnly about finding "the solution of our urban problems," card network building conformed with the broader pattern of "Jim Crow credit," the disinvestment from browning cities and reinvestment in white suburbs that defined postwar American finance. In their haste to get cards in the hands of suburban families, bankers narrowed their potential market and increased the competitive pressure. They pursued mass mailing to achieve volume and scale, ultimately stoking a suburban backlash.[3]

In the mid-1960s, cards offered bankers a path out of the postwar regulatory confines, particularly the price controls and geographic restrictions that anchored the New Deal financial order. States did not yet regulate credit card interest rates. With card networks, bankers could begin recruiting consumers across state lines. In their eagerness, bankers swamped the nation in cards just as consumer politics and protection were emerging as a bipartisan political force. Bankers embraced cards as a means of innovating around the New Deal rules; by decade's end, political backlash against relentless credit expansion firmly ensconced cards within them.

Competing with Diners Club

In the mid-1960s, the bank credit card industry was poised for renewed expansion. The sustained economic boom of the 1950s burned even hotter early in the next decade. From January 1960 to January 1967, the economy grew at 6.6 percent a year. Incomes and expectations for material comfort grew apace, especially among the white, increasingly suburban middle class. A series of federal tax cuts, proposed by President John F. Kennedy in 1963 and enacted after his death, further spurred growth. The cuts, Lyndon Johnson explained, put "$25 million a day in the hands of the American consumer." Johnson urged Americans to spend the money. They did, often augmented with credit. Feeling more affluent, consumers borrowed more freely. Recognizing widespread prosperity, lenders extended more credit. Consumer borrowing, growing at 9 percent a year, significantly outpaced economic growth.

The virtuous cycle of consumer purchasing power, juiced by credit, continued to spin, at least for Americans fortunate to be considered creditworthy.[4]

In this environment, universal card plans gained momentum. "Credit Card Companies Are Enjoying a Fresh Surge of Healthy Growth," the business magazine *Barron's* announced in a March 1964 headline. Incumbent firms, which the magazine divided along established lines of travel and entertainment cards for male executives and retail cards for city and suburban shoppers, had seen steady increases in cardholder spending. Card issuers had also expanded merchant and cardholder membership, while curtailing bad-debt losses. Newspapers and the business press touted BankAmericard's success as evidence that bank card plans had found solid ground. In 1965, several large regional banks debuted new card ventures, including Valley National Bank in Phoenix and Mellon National Bank in Pittsburgh. "Alert banks," Mellon president John A. Mayer observed, "realize that there have been major social changes in the United States. People who weren't candidates to do business with banks now are." The New Deal political economy, bolstered by relentless postwar growth, continued to make more Americans creditworthy. Bankers were bullish. The cover of the December 1966 issue of *Burroughs Clearing House,* the magazine "for Bank and Financial Officers," greeted readers with a picture of a red-cheeked Santa with bank and travel cards tumbling from his billfold. The industry, once skeptical of charge account banking and unsecured consumer lending, seemed ready to embrace cards.[5]

Nevertheless, Mayer's invocation of "alert banks" hinted at the industry's continued apprehension about falling behind their differently regulated financial competitors. Commercial bankers chafed at restraints. Affluent consumers continued migrating to the suburbs, where, in states with branching restrictions, downtown banks could not follow. Thrifts, like credit unions and savings and loans, offered consumers better rates on savings and lower prices on home mortgages. Beginning in 1966, regulatory differences contributed to a series of acute crises. When the Federal Reserve raised interest rates to fight surging inflation, investors moved money out of price-controlled bank deposits and into higher yielding financial assets. To meet existing loan commitments to large corporate borrowers, bankers raised cash by selling municipal bonds, promptly crashing that market. In this unstable environment, bankers remained torn between their custodial duty to make safe loans and an entrepreneurial itch to develop new services. They sought a greater share of consumer lending markets and, through those relationships, more stable consumer deposits. By the 1960s, a new generation of bank executives, men who had not weathered the Depression and bowed to its regulatory compromises, moved into bank leadership. With the well-publicized success of the BankAmericard, credit cards looked like a service ambitious bankers could call their own.[6]

Bankers' hopeful vision for cards centered in large measure on automation, especially new computer technologies that promised to streamline labor-intensive credit account processing. As noted in Mayer's Mellon Bank 1965 annual report, "A prime factor in making this service possible is the degree to which the Bank has developed the use of computer equipment, which is economically essential to the operation of a program of this magnitude." California's Crocker National likewise hailed the credit card as a "development made possible by the use of electronic data-processing equipment." And cards were just the start. The banking press anticipated the imminent arrival of the "cashless" and "checkless" society, imagined futures of computerized payment systems that would lift the mountainous weight of processing paper cash and checks. Across the financial system, the steady growth of transactions, from stock purchases to check usage, placed enormous pressure on firms' accounting and processing capacities. Computers would, bankers believed, solve these back-office problems. They could also generate new lines of business. "The trick is going to be to combine money and computers to create a whole new range of services," one observer wrote. Bank of America had pioneered commercial bank applications of computer technology with its ERMA check-processing system in the late 1950s. It developed the BankAmericard to utilize these systems as well. Major banks, seeking advantages in electronic scale, followed Bank of America's lead.[7]

The potential reach of computer technology remained limited, however, so long as bank cards operated in circumscribed geographic and product markets. As Barron's highlighted, travel cards enjoyed a global reach, while retail cards were confined by financial federalism: "The largest [retail credit plan] is that of the Bank of America, which operates exclusively in California." A few dozen other bank cards served smaller markets, limited to smaller states and individual cities. Geographic divisions mirrored the continued gender division among travel and retail plans. For travel cards, the *New York Times* reported, "The average card holder is: male, married, earns between $10,000 and $20,000 a year, travels frequently, and is a college graduate." Such assertions combined reality as it was with what travel card marketers wished to project: creditworthiness coded as high-income, male, and straight (whiteness was assumed, if unstated; a vanishingly small number of Black workers received high salaries). To maintain their masculine exclusivity, travel firms policed the division between their cards and feminized retail markets. "We believe women account for 95% of the spending on the BankAmericard," Diners chairman Alfred Bloomingdale wrote in a letter published in *Forbes* in October 1966, "while men account for 95% of the spending on the Diners Club card. We do not believe that the Bank of America is a competitor of the Diners Club." Bloomingdale wanted the gender divide to remain stark and explicit.[8]

Bloomingdale may have accurately described card markets as they were when he wrote, but only because banks had just begun to merge gendered credit markets. Bank of America led the transformation. Initially, bank executives promoted regional card use within the rubric of female-led consumption. BankAmericard ads highlighted "*statewide* shopping convenience," emphasizing that the card was "the sound, modern plan for making the most of your family dollars." BankAmericard's early advertising seldom featured men; when it did, the focus remained family shopping. It was, after all, "The Family Credit Card." As executives sought to increase transaction volume to maximize investments in electronic equipment and personnel, the bank turned to travel services. In 1964, Bank of America signed ten airlines into the BankAmericard plan. By then, more than three thousand hotels, restaurants, and travel agencies across California accepted the card. Incorporating travel features expanded BankAmericard's market from affluent female shoppers to their upwardly mobile husbands. Unlike travel cards, the bank offered these services without charging an annual fee. Combining retail and travel created economies of scale, making the BankAmericard cheaper for merchants and consumers. It also created network effects: More consumers would carry the BankAmericard, more businesses would accept it, and participation would be more valuable for both groups. Still, Bank-

Americard operated exclusively in California. Bloomingdale was right; it was not yet a competitor of the Diners Club.[9]

At the end of 1965, the two largest New York banks, First National City—today's Citibank—and Chase Manhattan, sought to enter the travel card business with an eye toward geographic expansion. In September, First National City partnered with third-ranked travel firm Carte Blanche. The companies initially planned to extend Carte Blanche's services internationally by linking the then-nationwide card plan to Citibank's global branch network. Federal law prohibited U.S. banks from expanding across state lines, but after World War II federal officials encouraged large banks to develop overseas branch networks. With their foreign branches American banks supported multinational U.S. firms and projected U.S. economic power. Citibank, Chase, and Bank of America all operated significant overseas businesses, with Citi boasting more than one hundred international branches. As Citi's negotiations with Carte Blanche developed, bank executives decided to purchase the travel business outright. Not to be outdone, Chase, Citibank's chief New York rival, moved immediately to purchase Diners Club. The acquisitions offered clear strategic advantages. The banks could finance card lending more cheaply than the stand-alone travel firms, making the businesses more competitive and profitable. Moreover, travel cardholders—elite, male business executives—were the banks' ideal customers, opening pathways for new business lending.[10]

Commentators readily observed that travel cards remained "a totally different business" than retail credit, yet rival firms anticipated that Citi and Chase held larger ambitions: to use travel cards as the basis for nationwide, universal card plans. If Bank of America was moving from retail to travel, Citi and Chase could go in the other direction. "We're in the money business," a Citi spokesman quipped. Such a move aligned with the New York banks' broader strategies. Citi and Chase pressed against the New Deal order's regulatory boundaries, waging constant battle against state and federal officials who restrained their geographic growth through branching and merger restrictions. With nationwide—and international—reach and experience managing far-flung plans, Carte Blanche and Diners could serve as platforms for breaking down the geographic and gender divisions in card markets. American Express executives saw these possibilities clearly. In

December 1965, Amex made its own bid to combine the travel and retail markets by acquiring Uni-Serv, a retail card company that had taken over Chase's ill-fated Charge Plan. The Department of Justice saw the same thing. The Antitrust Division sued to block Citi's acquisition of Carte Blanche and threatened suit if Chase closed its deal with Diners. Allowing the largest banks to take over established travel plans would reduce competition in the card market, federal antitrust attorneys reasoned (a risk apparently not immanent in Amex's purchase of Uni-Serv, which the department allowed). Citibank, the department wrote, "is especially qualified to enter the credit card business on its own . . . and such entry is likely if the proposed merger is enjoined." The Antitrust Division's actions effectively foreclosed acquisition as a strategy that banks could use to enter the card market and expand geographically.[11]

The Department of Justice's intervention constrained the territorial growth of individual bank card plans at a time when bankers increasingly saw the geographic scope of their card programs as important for recruiting middle-class consumers, for building transaction volume, and for maximizing the value of credit processing technology—for, in short, competing with Diners Club. Instead of large banks operating stand-alone nationwide card plans, as Citi and Chase had intended, the decision encouraged bankers to construct networks that would combine their local retail credit programs into regional and national card systems. This path was perhaps the likeliest outcome anyway. Although some aggressive bankers sought to push past regulatory restraints, most of the nation's nearly 14,000 banks continued to embrace localism and community embeddedness as fundamental values. Alert bankers saw wide vistas for expansion into consumer markets. They also wanted to maintain bulwarks against the market power of Citi, Chase, Bank of America, and their ilk. From the 1960s onward, bankers continued to develop card plans as local services, built to sell convenient credit and to deepen relationships with consumer and merchant customers in geographically restricted markets. They did so recognizing that even to compete locally they needed to offer credit that could move across states and around the country. Doing so required cooperation: bankers could not build where they could not reach. And they needed to build quickly. Citibank's and Chase's aborted acquisitions sent a clear signal: competition was coming.[12]

Top-Down Network Building: BankAmericard

Given the constraints of financial federalism, both legal—in that banks could not build branches across state lines—and ideological—in that bankers could not easily think beyond state borders, it was not obvious that banks would develop nationwide credit plans in the 1960s. In 1958, Otto Lorenz writing in *American Banker* had suggested that a "liaison" connecting distant bank card plans would enable them to compete with nascent travel cards. Lorenz, though, remained an outlier. Market participants and observers understood retail bank credit as bound in space. In this environment, the path to BankAmericard's nationwide expansion appeared essentially by accident. As bankers around the country realized that the BankAmericard had found a stable, profitable market in California, they sought to understand and replicate its success. Bank of America executives capitalized on this interest. In 1965, the bank began to market its proprietary credit card accounting software, repackaging a financial information system developed in its local market for sale to a global cohort of large, computerized banks. Executives focused on U.S. banks with existing card programs—like Marine Midland in upstate New York—and on foreign banks—specifically Barclays in England, which planned to initiate its own card plan. Building on this experience, executives concluded that a nationally (and, in the case of Barclays, globally) compatible accounting system run on efficient computers could provide a technological foundation for expanding the BankAmericard beyond California. Bank of America could sell more than its accounting software; it could sell its entire card plan, recruiting consumers and merchants at scale.[13]

To do so, Bank of America executives developed a national cooperative network in the style of its California operation. The bank adopted a franchise model, selling licenses to participant banks, setting their geographic territories, and ultimately controlling entry and competition within the network. Bank of America executives designed the system so they could manage it from the top down, replicating their experience managing a statewide card network across California's diverse markets. To join the network, banks paid a $25,000 franchise fee and 0.5 percent of their card plan's gross credit sales. In return, participant banks gained, according to executive Ken Larkin, "a nationally-known product . . . a card which is not limited to one regional area." Initially Bank of America restricted participation to large regional

banks and assigned territories to licensees. The bank encouraged licensees
to market cards aggressively, teaching participants how to use the unsolicited
mailing strategy it developed in California. In theory, participant bankers
would not compete to enroll the same merchants and consumers, or if they
did, competition in any market would be confined to a few "reputable banks."
The franchise model also meant that licensee banks were fundamentally
subordinate. The BankAmericard system had a clear hierarchy, with the nation's largest bank firmly at the top.[14]

Bank of America adopted the franchise model to replicate the local ties created by its branch network, using licensees' community relationships to root
the BankAmericard in markets across the country. Bank of America's executives first recruited banks in large cities not yet served by bank card programs.
The bank also sought large banks, which could afford the technological systems and costs associated with launching the plan on a massive scale through
unsolicited mailing. Licensee banks, in turn, recruited merchants and consumers in their immediate market area. They also expanded across their assigned regions by signing agent agreements with smaller banks—partnerships
similar to those used by charge account bankers who built small-scale card
networks in the mid-1950s. Agent banks recruited local merchants and suggested potential cardholders to licensee banks, which managed all consumer
accounts. Although card networks hinted at a future where bankers could
decouple their services from the physical constraints of their branch systems,
in the 1960s bankers saw cards as a tool for connecting consumers and merchants to their branches. Bankers worked to embed card plans within community relationships, efforts that extended to plan branding. "We give other
banks the benefit of our experience in helping them set up their own cards,"
Larkin explained in October 1966, indicating that although banks were joining Bank of America's network, they would retain control of their card plan
locally. Like the correspondent charge plans, BankAmericard cards and advertising carried the local licensee's name to tie the BankAmericard program
into the local community. Unlike the earlier plans, "BankAmericard" appeared centrally in bold text, signaling which bank was paramount.[15]

Bank of America developed its network to facilitate nationwide "interchange," the process of registering card transactions, discounting sales slips,
debiting merchant accounts, and billing cardholders. In California, Bank of
America handled these steps internally, managing interchange among its

branches through a subsidiary, BankAmericard Service Corporation (BASC). To expand its network nationally, Bank of America organized franchising through BASC, which then coordinated interchange procedures and established operational rules among participating banks. When a cardholder, signed up by Seattle's National Bank of Commerce, purchased goods from a California merchant enrolled by Bank of America, the merchant first discounted their sales slip at their local Bank of America branch. Bank of America then credited the merchant's account for the cost of the merchandise, less the merchant discount, and forwarded the slip to the National Bank of Commerce. The National Bank of Commerce reimbursed (rediscounted) Bank of America for the purchase and added the charge to the cardholder's bill. As interchange networks developed, the "issuing bank" (National Bank of Commerce) would also deduct an interchange fee from the funds it reimbursed to the "acquiring bank" (Bank of America). Although card networks were new, bankers understood interchange. Since the nineteenth century, they had developed a variety of private institutions, from correspondent networks to clearinghouses, to facilitate transactions across financial federalism's geographic barriers. The credit card system, "is one of exchanging valuable pieces of paper," one commentator argued. "Bankers are no strangers to this process, which is fundamentally the same as the existing check clearing system."[16]

Bank of America announced its plans to license the BankAmericard in May 1966, and over the next two years the program grew rapidly. By the end of 1966, Bank of America counted 8 licensees, growing to 17 the following year. By the end of 1968, 41 licensee banks issued BankAmericards, and 1,823 agent banks signed up merchants and recommended consumers in their territories. With this growth came building tension. Although Bank of America relied on its partners to build the network, executives also intended the BankAmericard as the steppingstone for Bank of America's eventual nationwide expansion. "The ultimate objective of this program," Larkin wrote in a March 1966 memo, "is to make the name BankAmericard a household word throughout the nation." These ambitions, well known within the banking industry, undermined trust in BASC among participant banks, especially when Bank of America seemed to place its own interests ahead of the franchisees and the success of the system. Cooperation without competition was at best a strained compromise, which placed Bank of America as at once competitor and referee. At the same time, the BankAmericard's expansion

How the systems work

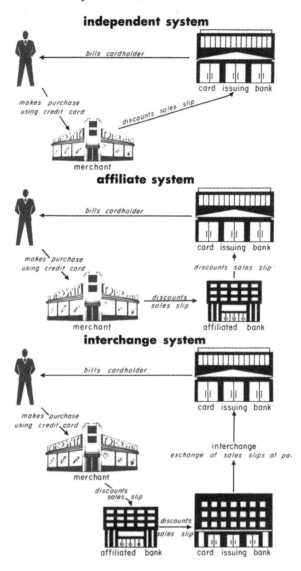

Fig. 2: A schematic illustration of consumer-merchant-bank connections fashioned by different bank credit card networks. The figure also reflects the increasing scale and complexity of these networks, from stand-alone charge account banking plans (independent system), to regional plans that connected card-issuing and agent banks (affiliate system), to regional and then nationwide card networks that linked smaller systems together (interchange system).

Source: Karl A. Scheld, "Bank Credit Cards: Saturation in the Midwest?," *Business Conditions* (June 1968): 14. Reprinted with permission of the Federal Reserve Bank of Chicago.

inspired a competitive fervor among rival firms, especially large regional banks that topped the local financial hierarchies in the nation's geographically segmented banking markets. They recognized Bank of America's ambitions, and they sought to use its mass promotional strategy to secure their card plans before the California colossus came crashing in.[17]

Cooperation *with* Competition: Regional Bankcard Associations

For bankers able to buy a franchise, the BankAmericard offered a clear path to the credit card future. Most banks, however, could not or would not join. Bank of America restricted franchises to a handful of large banks. Others refused to participate as junior partners to the California giant. For bankers outside the BankAmericard system, its nationwide expansion posed an acute, monopolistic threat. Bank of America, the nation's largest bank, sought to dominate convenient retail credit. The card industry "could not be something . . . jealously guarded by an individual bank," Marine Midland executive Karl Hinke recalled. To counter, rival bankers began to build their own regional and then national card networks. Just as California's regulatory geography influenced BankAmericard's structure, the geographic regulations governing these bankers' markets shaped the networks they built. All were constructed with one eye on the local market and one on the national competitive picture.[18]

Bankers in Chicago developed the first alternative to Bank of America's top-down network, under the leadership of the city's largest bank, Continental Illinois, and its chairman, David Kennedy. Continental and Kennedy were unlikely credit card pioneers. Kennedy, a devout Mormon raised in rural Utah, began his banking career in 1930 as a clerk at the Federal Reserve in Washington, D.C., where he eventually served as assistant to Fed chairman Marriner Eccles. After World War II, Kennedy moved to Continental and rose quickly. Through the 1950s, the bank remained deeply conservative, taking deposits from large businesses and investing in business loans and government securities. Continental scorned consumer banking. Its 1924 neo-classical headquarters, situated in the heart of the Loop, embodied stodginess. The building's most distinctive feature, its Grand Banking Hall, was a three-story financial temple of thick Ionic columns and entablatures decorated with gentlemanly quotes. "All of the progress of men and nation is based on the sacredness of contracts," a typical one reads. When Kennedy became chairman in 1959, Continental was, his biographer emphasized, "'an old man's bank.'"[19]

Kennedy set out to remake Continental, a campaign he advanced in evolving relationship with the racial and economic transformations of urban Chicago. Stodginess aside, Continental's main limitation remained Illinois's unit banking laws, which confined the bank to its single downtown office. Within these constraints, Kennedy established Continental's consumer banking business, rebranding Continental as "the big bank with the little bank inside" and creating a "family banking center" to lure customers downtown. Chicago, though, was changing. White residents steadily migrated to the suburban periphery. Black residents, following the triumphs of the Civil Rights (1964) and Voting Rights Acts (1965), escalated claims for racial and economic justice. In summer 1966, Martin Luther King Jr. began his Chicago campaign, leading marches through the city and its all-white suburbs. Like other urban business leaders, Kennedy worried that with rising racial tensions, consumers would avoid downtown altogether. Continental, though, could not move. Kennedy sought to foster urban economic opportunity. He allied with Chicago mayor Richard J. Daley to promote redevelopment. Continental actively hired Black employees. Such actions, while well-intentioned, failed to address the deep structures of segregation and credit redlining that continued to undermine Black opportunity. Kennedy also looked beyond the city. Continental expanded its international operations in the 1960s and lobbied state lawmakers for branching liberalization. Credit cards, which bank executives hoped could serve the Chicago region and wider Midwest, sat uneasily between urban engagement and abandonment. Cards also reflected a third front of Kennedy's strategy: technological modernization. In a widely reproduced speech to Continental's shareholders, Kennedy explained that "advancing technology not only makes charge cards more feasible and economical for general use but singles them out as an important milestone on the road to the future."[20]

As Continental executives plotted their move into the card business, they considered the scope of their markets—which merchants and consumers to target—and the design of their network—how to achieve scale given the bank's geographic confinement. To address the first question, Continental commissioned a market research study in the summer of 1966. Focusing initially on retail rather than travel services, the researchers interviewed merchants enrolled in the First Wisconsin National Bank's charge plan, which had recently begun operations in Milwaukee. Even more than their peers in the 1950s, these retailers felt compelled to offer credit. "Many said their customers expect to charge purchases," the report observed, emphasizing the ever-present competition of firms, like Marshall Field and Sears, with in-house card plans. Consumer expectations opened a door for the bank, especially in affluent suburban communities. "Retailers in or near wealthy or high-status suburbs . . . seem to offer an excellent potential for the bank card plan," the report argued, "since people in these areas appear to be extremely charge conscious." Retailers still harbored significant reservations, especially about the costs of accepting bank cards. They fumed, as well, "that they are unfairly being forced to pay for the customers' credit." Consumer demand left them little choice.[21]

Although Continental executives focused narrowly on retail credit, they appear to have contemplated a racially inclusive card plan, one that could serve urban and suburban markets. Continental's researchers convened seven focus groups. Five represented suburban communities—three from Evanston, north of the city, two from Hinsdale, to the west. Two more represented "Negro consumers." Perhaps bankers sought to extend the card market's racial boundaries to include Black customers. Yet the groups' responses, which were not disaggregated by race, suggest a wide gulf in credit experiences and expectations. Most interviewees valued "convenience," especially the convenience to shop at a variety of stores without securing charge privileges at each one. These consumers expected credit access. Others shunned convenience. They wanted cards as a backup in emergencies or to establish credit with the bank. Consumers also held different views on price. Some argued that Continental charged too much, too quickly; they expected longer repayment periods without interest common in informal credit plans. "Who pays for this?" others asked, skeptical that the card and initial thirty days of credit could come free of charge. The report did not identify which consumers fell into which categories. It seems likely, however, that charge conscious consumers, from white, high-status suburbs, expected convenient, inexpensive credit. Likewise, Black consumers, who were often denied access to mainstream financial services and channeled into expensive credit relationships with

inner-city merchants, likely sought economic security and access to traditional banking relationships. Based on their experience, Black consumers expected to pay.[22]

Researchers presented interviewees' divergent perspectives while nudging Continental executives away from non-white borrowers with coded language of creditworthiness. The bank should avoid marketing that "might
associate the charge card too closely with poor credit risks," the researchers
advised. These "could be a strong negative association for many people."
Instead, the researchers urged Continental to take a conventional approach,
marketing the card "as a convenience," to support high-status, family shopping. To expand the market, bankers needed to maintain the symbolic power
of aspirational consumerism. Extending cards to non-white people would
threaten their exclusivity and prestige. To be blunt, it would *blacken* the cards.
To expand the networks into white suburbia, bankers believed they needed to
maintain racial exclusion. Bankers might blend the gendered travel and retail markets without sacrificing status; crossing racial boundaries risked
shrinking the market rather than widening it. Yet by prioritizing a narrow
vision of white, suburban, affluent creditworthiness, banks also increased
the pressure to reach those consumers, and quickly.[23]

As Continental executives debated marketing strategy in summer 1966,
they also partnered with other Loop bankers to develop a new kind of card
network that would enable Illinois's unit banks to expand throughout the
city, into the suburbs, and beyond. In June, a consortium of Chicago's four
largest banks revealed plans to study a statewide, "compatible bank credit
card system." Unlike BankAmericard, the *Wall Street Journal* reported, "the
group stressed that the plan won't be a franchise agreement." Under what
became known as the Midwest Bank Card System, participants both cooperated and competed; cooperating to manage interchange among the separate
plans while competing to enroll consumers and merchants. Without
branches, Chicago's bankers reasoned, their individual card plans would
struggle to enroll enough merchants or consumers. Moreover, if several
large banks entered the market at once, their competing plans would sow
confusion and deny any bank adequate charge volume. Under the Midwest
system, each bank created its own card brands, setting individual policies on
interest charges and merchant discounts (though given the banks' close cooperation, these tended to converge). All cards and store decals, meanwhile,

carried the Midwest logo, an abstract blue, green, and white dollar sign, marking the network clearly for merchants and consumers. Unlike Bank-Americard, the participant banks managed the Midwest Bank Card System as partners. The association standardized processes for the interchange of sales slips between banks, enabling participants to work together in the collective interest of the system while pursuing their own profits.[24]

Midwest Bank Card organizers designed the network to extend far beyond Chicago. This choice reflects their stated ambitions to generate charge volume as well as an unstated desire to expand their consumer businesses outside the city's urban core. Each Midwest bank adopted the agent bank structure, relying on established "correspondent" relationships to develop proxy branch networks through smaller banks across the region. Given Illinois's unit banking laws and banks' expressed intention to mail unsolicited cards, Midwest Bank Card members needed agent banks to embed the individual card plans in the neighborhoods, suburbs, and towns where they operated. "We . . . stand a reasonable chance of having our newly introduced card widely accepted and used through the ties [correspondent banks] provide with their own communities," Kennedy explained to Continental's shareholders. By that time, Continental had recruited 380 agent banks in Illinois, Indiana, and Michigan to offer its Town & Country Charge card. The other Midwest banks pursued a similar path. Collectively, Chicago's bankers expressed hope that Midwest would "dovetail into a national system of similar regional bank credit card plans" and eventually challenge the BankAmericard. Their expansion efforts also demonstrated the extent to which Loop bankers saw their future outside Chicago. At Continental, the name tells the story. Executives named the plan "Town & Country Charge," evoking suburbs and golf clubs, not urban shopping.[25]

To overcome geographic regulatory constraints and to confront competition from BankAmericard as it enrolled large banks across the country, bankers quickly developed cooperative bankcard associations in other regions. In October 1966, four major California banks announced a similar cooperative-competitive network that would compete against the BankAmericard in its home state. Likewise contrasting themselves with Bank of America's top-down approach, the participants stressed that "they won't sell participation to banks outside the state" and instead "encourage[d] banks in other areas to establish similar ventures and affiliate themselves with the group." By 1968, fourteen regional associations, including the New England Bankcard

Association, the Southern Bankcard Association, and the Eastern States Bankcard Association, formed to coordinate local interchange in their regions. With banks across the country rapidly entering the credit card market, the pulse of competition beat ever faster.[26]

Growth and Consolidation: The Interbank Card Association

As banks new to the card field used regional associations to build bulwarks against BankAmericard's expansion, several banks with established card plans began to plot a rival nationwide network. Marine Midland Bank Group, a large New York bank holding, led the effort. Several of the corporation's banks operated a unified card program, the Midland Charge Plan, which its Binghamton bank initiated in 1953. When Bank of America announced it would license the BankAmericard in 1966, Midland Charge was the second largest bank card program in the country, with more than 400,000 cardholders and 6,500 participating merchants.[27]

Seeing an opportunity, the largest bank in the group, Buffalo's Midland Trust, applied for a BankAmericard license. The previous year, Midland Trust had purchased Bank of America's credit card accounting software, encouraging Bank of America executives to imagine a nationwide card market. Although Bank of America advertised that "the plan is available to any bank," Midland Trust's application was turned down. "Buffalo wasn't that important a community," Midland executive Karl Hinke recalled, "and [Bank of America executives] were looking for larger game." Hinke suspected that BankAmericard planned to grant an exclusive license for New York State to a large New York City bank. If that happened, Midland executives feared, the New York City bank would then enlist merchants and customers in Midland's upstate territory, bringing the BankAmericard into direct competition with the Midland Charge Plan. Midland executives resented this possibility. Upstate banks had long defended New York State's branching restrictions, which kept powerful New York City banks geographically confined to the city's boroughs and out of upstate markets.[28]

Now, instead of becoming a BankAmericard licensee, Midland executives feared Midland Charge could soon face the competitive weight of the nationwide BankAmericard and a New York City rival. If the Midland Charge Plan was going to compete, it needed to go national as well. In the summer of 1966, Hinke and vice president for consumer credit Douglas "Doug" Freeth listed banks that had existing card plans and might be viable partners in a cooperative national venture. They also hedged their bets. Because Midland had longstanding relationships with Bank of America, Hinke and Freeth decided to try again with the California bankers in person. The meeting went badly. Hinke and Freeth arrived at Bank of America's San Francisco headquarters for a 10:30 a.m. meeting with Vernon Richards, the executive in charge of BASC. It is unclear if they again raised the issue of securing a BankAmericard franchise, or instead proposed joining Midland Charge and BankAmericard into a cooperative-competitive system. In either case, Richards wanted no part in their proposal. "There is nothing we want to or can do," he said. He didn't even invite them to lunch. In the clubby world of banking, this was a stinging rebuff.[29]

When Hinke and Freeth emerged from Bank of America's offices, Hinke recalled, they looked across the intersection and saw, like a beacon, the Wells Fargo sign. They knew Wells Fargo, then a midsized California bank, had recently co-founded the California Bankcard Association to challenge Bank-Americard across the state, and they knew the Wells executive, Jack Elmer, who headed the association. That day Elmer proved receptive to a nationwide cooperative network (though, because he had a prior appointment, he didn't take them to lunch either). Encouraged, Hinke and Freeth flew to Phoenix to negotiate with the Valley National Bank, which operated a statewide Suncard across Arizona. They eventually recruited the Bank of Virginia in Richmond, Citizens and Southern National Bank of Atlanta, and the Mellon and Pittsburgh National Banks in Pittsburgh, all leading card issuers eager to stymie the BankAmericard's progress.[30]

Representatives for these banks met in Buffalo in August 1966, determined to pursue a different organizational model than the top-down Bank-Americard. By November, the banks had agreed to form a nonprofit cooperative, the Interbank Card Association, which would manage a national interchange network. Hinke became Interbank's first president. Like the regional bankcard associations, Interbank's members rejected the franchise model. Through licensing, Bank of America set network policies and skimmed revenue from every transaction, even as licensee banks worked to expand the BankAmericard network. "Interbank was and would always be an operating association rather than governing entity that might someday grow into dictatorship," an Interbank executive explained in *Bankers Monthly* in July 1968. Although Interbank began as a network connecting individual bank card plans, many regional associations joined as well. The California Bankcard Association joined in early 1967, as its members prepared to mail out cards under the "Master Charge" brand. In January 1969, Midwest joined. As a foil to BankAmericard's top-down policies, Interbank became the antimonopoly network.[31]

Like the regional associations, Interbank balanced unified system branding with the desires of individual banks to maintain local identity. Within the BankAmericard system, all cards and merchant decals carried the program's blue, white, and gold emblem (retained by its successor, Visa). The issuing bank's name appeared in small type in the top blue bar, with "BankAmericard" in bold in the central white stripe. On the contrary, Interbank did not offer a unified national brand; instead, its members placed an *i* enclosed in a circle on their cards and decals. Midland and its peers had invested heavily in their local brands. They were not ready to give them up. "The association approach allows each bank—large or small—to keep its own identity," Wells Fargo president Richard Cooley explained, adding, "It allows the small bank to compete with the largest . . . [with] a card that would be honored anywhere in the country." Interbank made this pitch directly to bankers: "Give your customers the *national* charge *they* want. Keep the *local* identity *you* want."[32]

More was at stake than brands, of course. The competing networks embodied different responses to tensions embedded in financial federalism, between local and national markets, and between local and national control. The organizers of both Interbank and BankAmericard sought to overcome geographic regulatory barriers, within states and between states, to create nationwide credit and payment networks. Doing so enabled them to compete with travel firms not subject to these boundaries and, as Hinke reckoned, with one another. Both networks, to greater and lesser degrees, foregrounded local bank identity. All believed that bank card plans needed to build on the existing relationships of local bankers, merchants, and consumers to gain traction and grow. For Interbank, local bank identity was paramount; for BankAmericard, the network was. The starkest difference reflected the most enduring conflict: Bank of America centralized power and authority; Interbank diffused it. These orientations were not permanent;

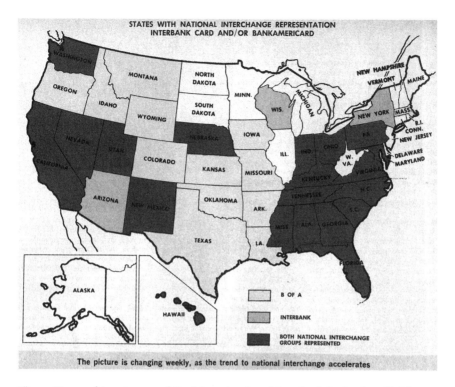

Fig. 3: Geographic coverage of BankAmericard and Interbank in April 1968. The extent of each card network is depicted as conforming strictly to state boundaries, suggesting the importance of state borders in defining financial space under regulatory federalism. At this time, only Arizona, Wisconsin, and New York were exclusively Interbank territory.

Source: Thomas C. Franklin, "The Significance of Interchange for Bank Card Plans," Burroughs Clearing House (August 1968), 28.

they could—and would—change. To better achieve nationwide recognition, the Interbank plans would adopt Master Charge as a unifying brand. Bank-Americard licensees, meanwhile, soon demanded more autonomy and control. These developments were in the future. In the mid-1960s, the battle lines were sharp and clear.

The Deluge

In retrospect, bank network-building strategies appear calm, orderly, and rational. Bank of America and its licensees developed a cooperative system with minimal internal competition to extend consumer credit across the country. Competing banks responded by spontaneously organizing regional and national cooperative-competitive platforms, coalescing into the rival Interbank network. Network expansion enabled bankers to offer travel services, generating system volume by combining a market previously divided by gender, even as cards remained privileged products for creditworthy, white Americans—Town & Country rather than inner city. Network building, however, facilitated a competitive process that was anything but well-ordered. The multiplication of bank card plans begins to suggest the scale. At the end of 1965, 68 banks operated credit card plans, and few competed against other banks. Four years later, 1,207 banks operated card plans, all competing for shares of local and regional markets. These figures include only card-issuing banks, not the agent banks that signed up merchants and solicited consumers. By April 1970, more than half of all commercial banks, 7,810 out of slightly less than 14,200, had affiliated with either the BankAmericard or Interbank. The networks claimed 450,000 merchant participants each and almost 60 million cardholders altogether.[33]

Facing breakneck expansion, commercial bankers were seized by excitement and fear, expectation and doubt. Bankers saw cards as their road to a profitable, technologically modern, consumer-focused future. They believed transaction volume was the key to card profitability. They aggressively built network infrastructure and recruited consumers to secure it. Mapped from above, the drama looked like a sweeping military campaign. BankAmericard licensees fought to command new markets. Regional cooperatives sprang up to resist them. As *Bankers Monthly* explained, "When BankAmericard started its franchising program, banks that did not sign up for this plan hurried to get their own cards as a competitive counter weapon." The martial metaphor is apt. Bankers viewed card competition as zero-sum: neither consumers nor merchants were likely to maintain relationships with two banks. A gain for one bank was a loss for another. Bankers were especially concerned about consumers. Guided by their racially- and class-inflected assumptions, bankers reasoned that the number of creditworthy households was limited. Consumers would, they expected, accept the first card that came their way. If that card was issued by a competitor, bankers feared, the customer might be lost forever.[34]

The consequences of such zero-sum thinking played out most vividly in David Kennedy's Chicago. There the downtown Midwest banks all sought to enroll medium- to high-income suburban consumers. Bank cards, though, were novel, unproven. Suburbanites, Loop bankers believed, would not commute in to apply for cards in person. The civil rights marches of 1966 and violent white reaction likely reinforced this view. Meanwhile, the city's banking industry swirled with rumors that "one of the big, national credit-card companies was about to mount a special campaign to get Chicago cardholders." Chicago's bankers could not wait for the merchant-initiated signups used by charge account banks. They never considered it. Instead, they embraced Bank of America's unsolicited mailing strategy. Competition, David Kennedy explained, "necessitates a new—and to some surprising—approach to the concept of credit: Banks did not ask for applications for charge cards but instead mailed the cards directly to creditworthy people." It was a fateful decision.[35]

In their initial deliberations, Midwest banks had planned to wait until 1967 to begin their solicitation campaigns, so that they could calmly study operating procedures, screen card recipient lists, and implement appropriate security measures. In August, however, the Pullman Bank Group, a small, South Side bank holding company, announced that its banks would introduce a statewide card plan, Illinois Bankcharge, in November 1966. The Loop banks accelerated their timelines. Unwilling to cede the valuable suburbs and believing their preparations were more advanced than their competitors', Continental executives moved their launch date forward to October. The remaining banks followed, swamping the holiday mail with millions of unsolicited cards. The numbers were staggering. Continental mailed 3.25 million Town & Country cards, two to a family. The First National Bank of Chicago issued cards to one million families, as did Harris Trust. The remaining Midwest banks issued cards merely in the hundreds of thousands.[36]

In his January 1967 speech to shareholders, Kennedy described what Continental hoped to gain by entering the card market, but his ultimate goal was to rationalize the unfolding chaos. By launching their programs in October and November, Chicago's banks dropped millions of cards into a postal system oversaturated with holiday mail and staffed by sticky-fingered seasonal employees. The banks publicly announced their plans, lighting a beacon for Chicago's well-organized underworld. As credit cards mingled with Christmas cards, criminals scooped them up by the thousands at the post office and from mailboxes; some apparently targeted multifamily homes and apartments, where they collected dozens of cards at once. Unlike modern cards, which require activation using private personal information, these cards were live and ready to use. They required nothing but a signature—any signature—to facilitate fraudulent holiday shopping. Some merchants colluded with criminals, billing the banks for merchandise purchased with stolen cards and splitting the proceeds with card thieves. Eventually thirty business owners were indicted, and many others were charged with stealing cards from the mail.[37]

Criminals may have been thrilled, but many consumers were not. "I object," one angry card recipient wrote Continental, "to the manner in which these charge cards are promoted and to the inflationary pressures they cause by encouraging people to extend their indebtedness." Kennedy sympathized with consumer concerns. He quoted the letter in his speech. Bankers, Kennedy explained, were not trying to "lure people into debt over their heads by offering the enticement of easy spending" or by "asking for repayment at excessive rates of interest." They were instead upholding their age-old obligation to make credit available to their communities. Kennedy felt these accusations keenly. His religious upbringing and continued leadership in the Mormon church instilled a strong aversion to the bondage of debt. "Many of us," he told Continental's shareholders, "were brought up under more conservative financial and banking circumstances and feel a natural reluctance to accept some of the seemingly radical innovations that are upon us." Yet this reluctance, Kennedy urged, "must give way in the face of increasingly strong competition." Kennedy, chairman of one of the nation's largest banks, could not follow his conscience. He had to follow the market.[38]

Or so he claimed. Kennedy's pretensions to responsibility clashed with widespread evidence of recklessness. Chicago's bankers had purchased rosters of likely cardholders from third parties. In their rush to get cards out, they did not vet them. Continental had only issued cards, Kennedy explained, to "bank customers and shareholders and *a few others in whom there was reason to place confidence.*" His vagueness was suggestive. The press sharpened the picture, highlighting a litany of bank blunders. People with strong credit histories or relationships with multiple banks received as many as a dozen cards. Graver mistakes occurred. One woman received cards from two separate banks, which was unfortunate, since she had been dead five months. Small children received credit in the mail. As Federal Reserve governor Andrew F. Brimmer later explained to congress, "Babies with sizable savings accounts—frequently opened by grandparents—could not be distinguished from adults."[39]

The trouble all came back to competition. "If we were to enter the field at all," Kennedy explained, "the necessity to be among the first was compelling." Before Continental launched its plan, one of Kennedy's subordinates argued that if it took the bank fifteen years to recover its start-up costs, the expense would be worth it, so long as Continental beat the other Chicago banks to market. Zero-sum thinking prevailed. Yet in the plan's first months, even fifteen years might have seemed optimistic. For the six months ending June 30, 1967, Continental reported an increase in "other" operating expenses of $7 million from the same period in 1966, a loss equal to 30 percent of the bank's annual profits. Kennedy attributed the increase to start-up costs, especially "a relatively high proportion of fraud losses." The other Midwest banks gushed money too. Three eventually withdrew their cards from circulation, reissuing new ones after completing more thorough credit checks. "For other banks around the country," the *Wall Street Journal* explained, "the Chicago credit card program could have been a how-not-to-do-it demonstration staged for their benefit."[40]

Despite the enormous losses and widespread embarrassment of these banks, the difference between their experiences and what the rest of the banking industry soon endured was one of degree rather than kind. Bankers convinced themselves that unsolicited mailing and intense mass promotion were indispensable. "A basic formula for success in credit card banking consists largely of two basic ingredients," the American Bankers Association (ABA) reported after surveying card-issuing members in 1967: "1) a bank must be consumer oriented; and 2) it must be willing to implement its program with vigorous merchandising efforts." The Federal Reserve offered a similar assessment. "All of the banks that we have contacted . . . found it desirable in launching their credit card plans to send out cards unsolicited," a Fed official reported. By design, the strategy was seductive and coercive. Unsolicited mailing enticed "charge conscious" consumers, feeding their expectations of widely available credit. To satisfy these expectations, merchants had to join card plans. Success required speed and scale.[41]

Competition created an inescapable cycle, reinforced from above by trade groups and card networks and on the ground by local rivals. The ABA found that almost half (49 percent) of banks admitted to entering the credit card field solely because of competition from other banks. "It is becoming abundantly clear," wrote a Dallas banker, "that many banks have gone into the credit card program as a defensive measure and without first doing their homework." Fear brought on recklessness. The same ABA survey found that only 54 percent of banks checked consumers' credit before mailing unsolicited cards. Congress later heard that closer to 80 percent of banks failed to perform adequate credit checks. As the number of card-issuing banks expanded, so did the competition. Gasoline companies and department stores mounted aggressive campaigns as well. By 1970, one journalist estimated, firms had mailed over 100 million unsolicited cards. With so many cards in the mail, bankers discovered, "there's no good solution to the fraud problem." The incidents that made Chicago's banks the laughingstock of the financial press multiplied, year after year, undermining the credibility of the industry as a whole.[42]

Some bankers urged caution, but most ultimately argued that only free, unbridled competition would give the public the full benefits of the new card plans. Speaking at the ABA conference in March 1967, Bank of America president Rudolph A. Peterson called for restraint: "The public is becoming confused and more than a little concerned about the unseemly spectacle of banks competing frantically to be the first in their region with their own particular cards." He warned of the "credit card hysteria now sweeping our industry." Bank of America, of course, had initiated that hysteria. Peterson could hardly hope to restrain the bedlam that followed. Instead, a year later, Marine Midland banker Thomas L. Bailey argued before Congress that "banks should be encouraged to develop new methods of serving the credit needs of their communities." Unimpeded mass distribution was essential, Bailey claimed, because "to deny banks without credit card plans the privilege of issuing cards unless requested would completely limit this business—which is a most natural one for banks." Driven by competition to undertake unsolicited mailing, bankers appealed to competition to defend it. Bankers had long faced disadvantages in consumer markets, an area that represented their best hope for future expansion. As the proper conduits of credit in their communities, bankers believed, they should be encouraged in these endeavors. To remain custodians, they needed freedom to also be entrepreneurs.[43]

Arguments for market freedom were met with a rising tide of consumer and political anger. *Life* magazine columnist Paul O'Neil perhaps best captured the mood in his March 1970 article, "A Little Gift from Your Friendly

Fig. 4: Banks' adoption of new financial technologies and the public's experience of mass credit card mailing were given visual form in the illustration that accompanied a *Life* magazine article aptly titled "A Little Gift from Your Friendly Banker."

Source: Paul O'Neil, "A Little Gift from Your Friendly Banker," *Life* (March 27, 1970). Illustration by John Huehnergarth.

Banker." Banks undertook card distribution, O'Neil wrote, "in many cases, with a kind of eager innocence which none of them would have countenanced for a moment in firms with which they did business." O'Neil went further. "A few of them, caught up in the excitement of the unfamiliar chase, seem to have become as blithely careless of consequences as a drunken sailor shooting craps in a Mexican whorehouse on New Year's Eve." The article explored the litany of problems caused by unsolicited mailing: fraud, fears of impersonal technology, inflation, unsteady gender dynamics, and threats to the safety and soundness of irresponsible card-issuing banks, all of which spurred new regulatory efforts. O'Neil's characterization highlighted the moral concern many felt about traditionally austere banks pushing credit on consumers and called into question whether the credit card business really was "a most natural one for banks."[44]

In the mid-1960s, the banking industry converged on cards as the road to the future, with new computer technologies facilitating low-cost, geographically expansive consumer financial services. Certainly some bankers traveled more warily than others, but once the competitive cycle started the destination was never in question. The cascading momentum built on several fronts. The banking industry, squeezed by the New Deal regulatory order, turned to consumer markets with energy—and desperation. As it did so, a new generation of bankers, committed to less restrained competition and freer markets, assumed leadership. Competition with Diners and American Express led bank executives to combine masculine travel and feminine retail credit, covering regional and nationwide markets. State and federal geographic regulations and federal antitrust policy pushed bankers toward network building and shaped the strategies adopted in differently regulated markets. Below the surface, network-building bankers harbored even greater ambitions. Kennedy argued that cards would "replace on a direct retail basis" credit that flowed through merchants or other consumer financial firms. With cards, banks could become the center of consumer finance. With universal credit cards, bankers envisioned universal payment systems under their control.

Nevertheless, although bankers presented values like convenience as universal, their network building evidenced a racial and class politics that favored high-income, "credit conscious" suburbanites over less affluent, often minority inner-city residents. For banks, the road *to* the future implied a road *from* the past, one inscribed in the geographic legacy of nineteenth-century commercial districts and twentieth-century urban industrialization. Banks, especially big urban banks, stood immobile in transforming downtowns: Continental in Chicago, Midland in Buffalo, Mellon in Pittsburgh, Citibank and Chase in New York. White Americans continued their flight to the suburbs. Cities became browner and poorer. Large banks faced a dilemma: engage urban consumers or plot an escape. In different cities, bankers pursued different strategies. In the aggregate, large, urban, card-issuing banks built networks as conduits to the suburbs. When a Continental banker described the "demographics of the 'best' credit card customers" as "married . . . with family incomes of from $7,000 to $15,000, probably living in high-growth areas," he drew a de facto racial boundary. Fewer than 20 percent of Black families earned such high incomes. By prioritizing white suburbanites, bankers increased the pressure to enroll these consumers ahead of their competitors. In their fear, they carpet-bombed the crabgrass frontier. They also did so at an inopportune time. For while the politics of American cities were changing, so were the suburbs. Bankers expected to set the terms by which well-off Americans accessed convenient credit, but a rising consumer movement soon challenged bank practices. As urban citizens rose to demand economic and racial justice, suburban consumers sought to maintain the New Deal's promise of low-cost, widely available credit.[45]

In the final analysis, the bank card networks embodied a paradox. Bankers designed their networks to embed nationwide card plans within the local ties between merchants, consumers, and card-issuing or agent banks. Place still mattered. BankAmericard and Master Charge linked circumscribed markets, they did not overlay them. A Marine Midland Charge Plan, bankers believed, was different than a Wells Fargo Master Charge. Credit cards were not commodities. Instead, they were grounded in each bank's market area, inextricably linked to the physical edifice of the bank and its branches, where consumers and merchants would come to make deposits and engage other banking services. But unsolicited mailing set in motion several disembedding forces. It divorced the process of receiving credit from the experience of consumption; to access credit, consumers no longer had to endure an interview with a credit manager, "something," characterized in *Bankers Monthly* as "akin to a prisoner-of-war interrogation." Credit came in the mail. But while bankers hoped cards would still be coupled with their branch offices, and through them with the social relationships that undergirded their role as responsible guardians of credit, consumers experienced cards differently. Like Kennedy's mysterious "few others," many consumers were unknown to the banks who issued them cards. When bankers bought lists of likely credit risks to reach beyond their existing customer base, they eliminated social connection in the process. For some consumers, this meant they were less careful with their spending and more likely to default. Other consumers were outraged that credit invaded domestic space. Over the long term, it meant that most consumers associated their credit with the network, BankAmericard and Master Charge, rather than the issuing bank. Credit cards became commodities, divorced from local markets, and as such tools to break down financial localism.[46]

5

Regulating Revolving Credit

Pocketbook Politics

In January 1968, a new credit disclosure law went into effect in Washington State and quickly unsettled the local politics of retail credit. The law required lenders to publish consumer interest rates in simple, annual terms. For retail and bank card issuers, the change was sharp. Instead of telling consumers they were paying *only* 1.5 percent a month on their revolving credit accounts, these firms now had to advertise rates of 18 percent a year. Although technically identical, interest calculated on an annual basis looked much more expensive. Consumer groups responded immediately. The Washington State Labor Council, the umbrella organization for the state's labor unions, collected over 100,000 signatures for a ballot measure to restrict credit card and installment interest rates to 12 percent a year. In November 1968, the initiative succeeded by a wide margin. As the president of the Labor Council explained afterward, "The campaign brought home to the consumer for the first time the fact he was actually paying 18 percent." Once consumers understood the full cost of convenient credit, they organized and used state-level regulation to curtail credit prices.[1]

Washington State was at the head of a national wave of political mobilization aimed at expensive consumer credit. Large retailers, for example, Sears and J. C. Penney, had heavily promoted card-based revolving credit during the postwar years. Bankers joined this effort slowly in the 1950s, then suddenly in the 1960s, cementing expectations of convenient retail credit as foundational to middle-class purchasing power. Revolving credit, however, remained more expensive than other forms of consumer lending. It also remained unregulated, situated outside state-level price controls that restrained other borrowing costs within the New Deal's place-based social contract. For consumer and labor groups, especially the National Consumers League and the AFL-CIO, expensive credit contradicted the postwar promise of low-cost, widely available borrowing. They resolved to fight. They did so at an important moment for the consumer-labor coalition, which had pursued a purchasing power agenda of high wages and fair prices since the New Deal. Persistent postwar inflation strained this alliance, especially as union wage demands seemed to drive up the cost of consumer goods. Consumer groups, meanwhile, became more concerned with securing protection from harm—caused by unsafe products or environmental degradation—than fixing prices. Nevertheless, these groups continued to find common cause in the struggle over expensive credit. Together, and in concert with state officials, they worked to secure state regulation of credit card interest rates, joining the continuous negotiations between government officials and industry groups over the state rules that comprised the New Deal regulatory order.[2]

Consumer and labor groups pursued rate regulation in opposition to stakeholders who argued that competitive markets, not restrictive state laws, should set the price of credit. Senator Paul H. Douglas, a liberal Democrat, stood firmly against state rate ceilings. Douglas authored the federal Truth-in-Lending Act (1968), which—like the Washington State law—mandated uniform credit price disclosure. Douglas shared consumers' and labor's desire for low-cost credit. With price disclosure, he believed competitive markets would provide it more effectively than price controls. As a regulatory strategy, disclosure offered more flexibility than the New Deal's blunt product and price restrictions, relying on informed, free-contracting consumers to make credit markets work more efficiently. Douglas's federal Truth-in-Lending Act, in turn, created a pathway for state-level regulatory reform. The law allowed states with equivalent disclosure rules to seek exemption from federal regulations in order to maintain state control of local financial rules. Federalist-minded legal reformers took the state exemption clause as an invitation to rationalize what one called the "crazy-quilt pattern" of state-level credit regulations. In 1968, the National Conference of Commissioners on Uniform State Laws (NCC) published the Uniform Consumer Credit Code

(UCCC), a model state law designed to match Truth-in-Lending's disclosure provisions, to simplify and standardize state credit regulations and to promote competition in consumer credit markets. NCC members then campaigned to secure the UCCC's adoption, with the aim of replacing restrictive state price controls with competitive markets. "If the market is competitive," they argued, "rates will find their own level without regard to the ceiling"—a level in the best interests of consumers.[3]

Douglas and the NCC staff developed their reform arguments to address new political demands on the postwar financial system. In the mid-1960s, Lyndon Johnson's Great Society and War on Poverty initiatives drew attention to the continued exclusion of poor and minority Americans from postwar abundance. Civil rights advocates shifted their attention from political rights to economic inequality. During major urban uprisings, Black protesters targeted retailers who employed exploitative credit practices—what legal scholar Mehrsa Baradaran calls "Jim Crow credit." Poor Americans, Black and white, demanded access to the low-cost, convenient credit enjoyed by privileged white households. Lenders, however, expected to charge higher prices to borrowers they perceived as riskier. Including low-income households meant raising or eliminating state rate limits, the UCCC drafters argued, "to permit most credit-worthy consumers to have access to the legitimate consumer credit market." Consumer and labor groups rejected this argument. They expressed sympathy with poor and Black borrowers. Yet in the debates over Truth-in-Lending and the UCCC, consumers fought to maintain the privileged credit economy, protecting themselves from high credit costs and dangerous levels of debt. Consumer and labor groups recognized that imposing low price ceilings would shrink consumer credit markets, ensuring credit access for only the most creditworthy. They accepted that tradeoff.[4]

Political conflict over credit prices began before bankers surged into the credit card market and continued as banks rained millions of cards down on suburban households. Bankers had entered the card market because revolving credit was not yet regulated. They joined retailers in the fight against price caps; when regulation became inevitable, bankers lobbied for higher statutory rates. Truth-in-Lending, and the state rate regulations that followed, decisively structured the bank card industry, creating distinct markets, state by state, subject to continuous negotiation and renegotiation among competing interest groups. In the short run, new rules hemmed in the profitability of bank card plans. In the long run, distinct state rules created advantages for some banks over others, opening space to undermine the system altogether.

Truth-in-Lending

The Truth-in-Lending Act grew from long-building momentum for consumer credit reform. Since the 1940s, prominent policymakers, among them Marriner Eccles, chairman of the Federal Reserve, had worried that fluctuations in consumer lending could upset stable economic management of the postwar economy. The rapid growth of consumer credit through the 1950s, interrupted by the recession of 1957 and 1958—which some economists attributed to declines in credit purchasing—provided further evidence of the disruptive consequences of unchecked consumer borrowing. For the public, newspaper and mass-market magazine articles expounded credit's virtues and its vices, which the readers encountered alongside advertisements that displayed the glowing wonders of credit purchasing. All the while, consumer advocates, legal reformers, and social critics amassed evidence that the credit economy was not meeting the needs of many consumers, that it instead perpetuated social, economic, and racial inequalities which mass prosperity supposedly erased. Calls for reform sounded from many corners of postwar society and grew louder over time.[5]

Nationwide momentum for consumer credit reform coalesced around Douglas's Truth-in-Lending Act. In January 1960, Douglas introduced legislation requiring creditors to publish credit prices as simple, annual interest rates. Douglas, a former University of Chicago economist, had been mulling mandatory rate disclosure since serving in the New Deal's National Recovery Administration. Through his high-profile leadership of Congress's Joint Economic Committee in the postwar years, Douglas became a prominent liberal voice on federal economic policy. For Douglas, Truth-in-Lending combined two interrelated goals. First, market competition would lower consumer prices and increase employment. Truth-in-Lending, by "facilitating more informed bargaining between customer and creditor," aligned with his pro-competitive, purchasing power agenda. Second, Douglas also argued that rate disclosure would improve federal economic management and support Democratic social priorities. If price-conscious consumers knew the true cost of credit, they would slow credit purchasing when the Fed, in response to an overheating economy, raised market interest rates and made credit more expensive. Likewise, consumers would increase credit purchases when the Fed, in response to a cooling economy, lowered rates and made credit cheaper. Privately, Douglas recognized that by requiring lenders to publish credit prices as annual, and thus higher-seeming, rates, Truth-in-Lending would dampen overall consumer credit demand. Lenders would then reallocate credit toward Democratic priorities like small business, housing, and municipal borrowing.[6]

Faced with powerful and nearly unanimous creditor opposition, Douglas knew he could not sell credit disclosure as competition policy and macroeconomic management. Refining his pitch in 1961 and 1962, Douglas prioritized combatting deceptive credit practices, a subtle pivot with transformative implications. In Douglas's hands, Truth-in-Lending became a vehicle for reorienting Democratic consumer politics from provision to protection—merging the New Deal's pocketbook politics of fair prices with an emerging consumer politics of protection in the marketplace. Through legislative hearings and grassroots organizing, Douglas used Truth-in-Lending to develop a new consumer constituency, adopting the mantle of consumer protection that would, over the next decade, transform American economic policymaking.[7]

The movement scholars now call third-wave consumerism was not Douglas's creation alone: by the mid-1960s an emerging cohort of activists, lawyers, and lawmakers swelled to the consumer cause. Privileged white Americans enjoyed unprecedented abundance in the postwar years. With that abundance came high expectations about product quality and safety. When markets failed to meet these expectations, consumers organized and turned to government. Douglas recognized the budding consumer movement earlier than most Democrats. As he pursued Truth-in-Lending, he foregrounded consumer protection to appeal to affluent, suburban voters. "Passage is extremely important not only for itself," Douglas explained as he lobbied President Kennedy to continue supporting the legislation in December 1962, "but because of the real problem we Democrats face in the suburbs which are growing and which tend to be Republican." Although Truth-in-Lending debates eventually encompassed the kinds of deceptive practices that plagued poor and minority borrowers, Douglas initially aimed at mainstream credit markets. In doing so, he lit an organizing beacon for a new branch of liberal politics. Kennedy, who had endorsed Truth-in-Lending in his "Message to

Consumers" in March 1962, appeared to share this vision. So did Lyndon Johnson, who continued the commitment after Kennedy's death, both publicly and through plodding, behind-the-scenes policy work as the legislation stalled, shuddered, and then, in 1968, almost suddenly succeed.[8]

Truth-in-Lending induced a grinding, gouging legislative fight, one in which the new consumer politics—although decisive for final passage—initially proved a sideline to the main issue. By promising to bring consumer credit under permanent federal oversight, Truth-in-Lending threatened the prevailing division of federal and state authority. Traditions of localized finance undergirded a broad consensus that states should regulate the terms and price of credit. Within this framework, segregationist Southern Democrats, amid their scorched-earth battle against 1964 Civil Rights and 1965 Voting Rights Acts, vigorously resisted any federal intrusion on state prerogatives. Preserving state authority was not only about preserving Jim Crow, however. For a wider audience, including legal reformers, state-level officials, and even consumer and labor groups, federalism remained foundational to American democratic governance and the place-based social contract, ensuring that credit rules reflected local conditions and responded to local interests.[9]

Federalism's supporters nevertheless recognized that state-level consumer credit regulation needed simplification and revision. When lawmakers and legal reformers surveyed the state regulatory landscape, they found local credit rules that were, as one legal scholar observed, "poorly-organized, subject to redundancies, and unnecessarily complex." Methods for calculating, disclosing, and restricting interest varied substantially within and among states. To be specific, in 1965 almost every state maintained a *general usury limit,* a restriction on the maximum rate lenders could charge on loans of money, usually between 6 and 12 percent annually. General limits originated in the nineteenth century, and state legislatures often updated them to reflect evolving conditions. States also managed a host of exemptions to the general limit. Beginning in the 1910s, states enacted small loan laws, enabling lenders to charge higher rates to risky urban borrowers. Credit unions, industrial loan companies, commercial banks, and even pawnbrokers gradually sought exemptions to legitimately enter consumer markets. States obliged, often codifying the innovative practices such lenders had used to circumvent existing rules. Legislatures also enacted laws governing installment sales—first auto loans and then retail installment credit. Installment loans had traditionally been exempted from usury limits under the "time-price doctrine," a legal distinction between lending money and selling goods over time—one which revolving credit issuers still clung to. In all, by the mid-1960s each state's consumer credit laws reflected specific, layered responses to changing market practices, constituted through legislation and legal interpretation and constantly negotiated to balance creditor and debtor interests.[10]

For legal observers who sought consistency, uniformity, and predictability, the multiplicity of regulations made it difficult to address "the consumer-credit problem as a total process." More directly, caked-on local law impeded consumers' ability to make informed credit decisions, costing them money. States' subdivision of usury exemptions by industry, and the further division between loans of money and retail credit, meant that states regulated substantially similar forms of lending in different ways. Lenders calculated some rates, like those for small loans and revolving credit, monthly instead of annually. In other transactions, lenders charged add-on rates and discounts that made credit prices seem lower than they were in fact. A charge of $6 in interest on a $100 installment loan looked like a 6 percent annual rate but was actually 12 percent.[11] Consumers also paid extra for credit investigation or life insurance, non-interest costs that increased the overall price of credit. In many transactions, no rates were quoted at all. Rates did not have to be intentionally deceptive to be unintelligible. During the exhaustive Truth-in-Lending hearings, supporters and opponents used complexity to justify their cause: supporters to show the need for simple annual rates, opponents to show that such rates were impossible to compute. Ultimately, although state usury laws should have established clear lines between legal and illegal lending, the Truth-in-Lending debates demonstrated that lenders often benefited from the profusion of local rules.[12]

Uniform credit disclosure would cast bright light into the dark corners of this system without, Douglas continuously insisted, interfering with state authority to regulate credit terms and prices. "The purpose," Douglas claimed, "is to require that the American consumer be given the truth, the whole truth, and nothing but the truth, about the interest rates and finance charges." Douglas did not, he assured his colleagues, intend "to control credit" or "to preempt State authority over the level of rates and charges." Instead, he wished to "invigorate competition in the consumer credit market by requiring a return to price competition." Through the nearly decade-long fight over

Truth-in-Lending, Douglas remained stubbornly consistent. He refused to modify his demand for uniform annual disclosure of all consumer credit prices. He also resisted more transformative proposals, like direct federal credit controls and national usury ceilings. By enabling consumers to police firm behavior in the market using standardized, comparable information, disclosure—in credit markets and across the broader arena of consumer protection policy—promised less intrusive government control of ostensibly private economic activity. After Douglas lost his reelection bid in 1966, the bill's new shepherd, William Proxmire (D-WI), continued to reassure lawmakers and lenders that, "the bill does not regulate credit. The bill does not tell lenders how much they can charge. The bill contains no assumptions that credit is bad."[13]

Despite their posturing, Douglas and Proxmire certainly recognized that Truth-in-Lending's nationally uniform disclosure standards would impose nationally uniform methods of calculating interest rates and finance charges. Over time, these standards would compel states to address their byzantine usury laws once the disparities they created were spelled out in simple interest. Douglas, the economist, hoped Truth-in-Lending would eliminate rate regulation in favor of pure market competition. State interest rate regimes, however, remained deeply entrenched, both as legal mechanisms for managing competition among different lending firms and as embodiments of social ideals about fair credit prices. Gradual change was more likely than dramatic reform.

As Douglas cultivated support for Truth-in-Lending, he faced intractable opposition from within the Senate Banking and Currency Committee, whose members squelched the bill through four successive Congresses. In committee hearings, Wallace Bennett (R-UT), whose family owned the largest department store in Salt Lake City, peppered witnesses with complicated credit scenarios to demonstrate the difficulties ordinary clerks would have computing uniform rates. Bennett's tactics frustrated Douglas, but the more strident opposition came from the committee's chairman, A. Willis Robertson (D-VA). Robertson, a fierce civil rights opponent, fought any expansion of federal authority. Writing Douglas in March 1964, after Douglas finally advanced his bill to the full Banking Committee and just as the Senate prepared to debate the 1964 Civil Rights Act, Robertson laid out his objections in clear terms: "You are aware, of course, of my strong opposition to the bill.

I consider it unnecessary, because the States can regulate the disclosure of credit terms as well as they can regulate other matters relating to credit. . . . I consider it undesirable because I think this is a field which should be left to the States under the Constitution." Still, Robertson agreed to allow the bill to come before the full committee, "with the expectation that . . . the bill will be rejected." It was, by a single vote.[14]

Douglas and Robertson both failed to win reelection in November 1966, clearing the way for action on Truth-in-Lending. Favorable appointments to the Banking Committee in January 1967, followed by President Johnson's strong endorsement in February, convinced observers that the bill was likely to succeed in the Ninetieth Congress. As the legislation advanced, however, new forces pressed in on the debate. In urban uprisings, Black Americans targeted exploitative lenders, vividly demonstrating the differences between the privileged credit of the suburbs and the exploitative credit of the inner city. Black demands for fair credit access flowed through legislative debates as the bill neared passage, as did the concerns of poor borrowers who likewise faced expensive and exploitative credit markets. Nevertheless, the adminis-tration remained focused on protecting middle-class borrowers. Reflecting on Truth-in-Lending, an aide wrote Johnson in June 1966, "I think . . . you can pass about any bill you want [that] does not carry racial or religious impli-cations." As Johnson put his full support behind the law, he instructed staff he wanted "a bill and not an issue." Ultimately, revolving credit prices, not racist lending practices, made the bill an issue.[15]

For credit-granting firms, Truth-in-Lending's fresh start dictated a change in legislative strategy, from outright opposition to whittling down its most onerous provisions. The law posed a special threat to national retailers. Firms like J. C. Penney, Sears, and Montgomery Ward operated nationally uniform credit plans across diverse state regulatory environments. They relied on re-volving credit to drive sales and generate profits. J. C. Penney provides a case in point. Before World War II, the firm grew by selling everyday necessities to working-class Americans for cash. The middle name of the founder, James C. Penney, was, improbably, "Cash." As the postwar era progressed, however, the firm's core customers became more prosperous and moved to the suburbs. J. C. Penney followed, and found that competitors there offered a broader array of goods, which they sold on credit. Credit increased sales, and retailers gradually transitioned from closed-end charge accounts that consumers repaid every month to open-end revolving credit to keep consumers buying. Retailers also raised credit prices, from 1 percent per month to 1.5 percent to make their credit departments self-sufficient. J. C. Penney adopted revolving credit in the late 1950s, though James Cash Penney voted against it. By 1968, the firm sold $1.2 billion of goods on credit, 36.1 percent of its total sales on 6.5 million accounts. At Sears, J. C. Penney's larger rival, 9 million revolving credit users accounted for 31.3 percent of $8.2 billion in net sales. Although bank card mailing and travel card marketing made universal card plans increasingly visible, in the 1960s retailers still dominated revolving credit.[16]

Before Truth-in-Lending, most states regulated installment credit but not revolving credit. Instead, retailers relied on a nineteenth-century legal distinction, the time-price doctrine, to shield their card plans from states' general usury laws. Federal courts defined usury as dealing only with money: "a loan and a taking of usurious interest, or the taking of more than legal interest for the forbearance of a debt or sum of money due." Such a transaction was distinct from a time-price sale, where a seller established different prices for an immediate cash sale and a sale made over time. In 1861, the Supreme Court formalized the rule as follows: "If A propose to sell to B a tract of land for $10,000 in cash, or for $20,000 payable in ten annual instalments, and if B prefers to pay the larger sum to gain time, the contract cannot be called usurious." Here, the difference in price represented the time preferences of both parties, not a loan of money and not usury. Retailers, and later banks, extended this logic to their card plans. They argued revolving credit sales were likewise sales on time, not loans of money.[17]

The time-price doctrine proved a durable legal fiction, but it provided an unsteady foundation for billion-dollar credit plans. Large retailers, which operated across heterogeneous state law environments, needed to maintain this distinction rooted in federal precedent. With uniform price disclosure, however, retailers recognized that their revolving credit plans would appear to consumers—and courts—as what they were: loans of money. Then, under the bill's provisions, J. C. Penney would report its 1.5 percent monthly revolving credit rate as 18 percent annually. In states without a specific revolving credit exemption, such charges would look like egregious violations of local usury laws. As Truth-in-Lending gained momentum, large retailers lobbied vigorously to exclude revolving credit from the law's disclosure provisions.

Consumer and labor representatives, along with allied policymakers, fought to include revolving credit in Truth-in-Lending, predicting that what started as a small loophole would grow as retailers pushed consumers into unregulated revolving accounts. Organizing against the exclusion of revolving credit, National Consumers League representative Sarah Newman argued that "to give the fastest growing segment of consumer credit preferential treatment . . . would strike a blow at the very heart of the protection this legislation should be extending." Yet, to finally move the bill out of the Senate Banking Committee, Proxmire cut revolving credit regulation from the Senate version in 1967. Consumers objected and rallied in the House, where they found allies in financial industry groups opposed to giving retailers a regulatory advantage. Johnson administration staff convinced installment lenders and banks to support the bill with revolving credit included. With the administration's support, House consumer advocates eliminated the revolving credit loophole, and the House passed the bill in February 1968. Johnson signed it into law on May 29, with the disclosure provisions set to take effect on July 1, 1969. "Had the financial community not fought the bill so bitterly, it would have been a milder one," Douglas later boasted. "This thought may not yet have dawned upon them."[18]

That the inclusion of revolving credit marked the finale of Truth-in-Lending's legislative saga indicates the extent to which the law remained captive to its original suburban consumer politics. As the legislation moved through the House, liberal members, led by Missouri Congresswoman Leonor Sullivan, also tried to address abusive credit practices, such as wage garnishment, that disproportionately harmed poor and minority borrowers. Yet the Johnson administration, focused on securing popular, middle-class legislation, opposed the House provisions. If Johnson supported garnishment limits, aides predicted, he would be criticized for "only sending up legislation that benefits the Negroes and the poor." Opponents "may call it a 'civil rights bill' in disguise, one that rewards rioters," aides observed. Middle-class voters, meanwhile, "would conclude that you are trying to bail out people who do not pay their debts." Only after Truth-in-Lending proved secure did Proxmire convene hearings on "the problem of obtaining adequate consumer credit in the ghettos." The law also remained captive to financial federalism. The House version had contained an 18 percent national usury limit, which the conference committee firmly rejected. Although interest rates needed reform, consumer credit remained a matter for local regulation among state-level stakeholders. With dis-closure, Douglas argued, usury limits were unnecessary and potentially harmful. Proxmire continued to support state rate caps to protect consumers and manage competition among financial firms. Ultimately, Truth-in-Lending generated state-level reform momentum not to eliminate usury limits but to strengthen them.[19]

Uniform Consumer Credit Code

When Paul Douglas drafted the Truth-in-Lending Act in the early 1960s, he intended the federal law to transform the nation's consumer credit mar-kets, but he also created a legal pathway for maintaining federalism's role within the financial regulatory system. Douglas favored extending federal power directly to solve social and economic problems, especially in his advo-cacy for civil rights legislation. He also recognized the value of state admin-istrative power, particularly in finance, and he needed the support of conservative Democrats, who urged him not to extend federal regulation to states with adequate disclosure laws. Douglas's draft bill, in addition to not intruding on state authority to regulate credit prices, exempted states with "substantially similar" disclosure laws from the Truth-in-Lending Act. Such states could continue to regulate financial activity within their borders and try consumer credit cases in state courts. Enforcement of consumer laws would then rely on state, not federal, precedents, preserving and strengthen-ing local control over consumer credit markets.[20]

Douglas's concession to local financial authority encouraged legal reform-ers to address the tangle of state consumer credit law, moving beyond price disclosure to consider the full sweep of local credit regulation. The National Conference of Commissioners on Uniform State Laws undertook this proj-ect. Founded in 1891, the NCC was (and is) composed of lawyers, judges, and law professors appointed by state governors to draft model legislation. By publishing model statutes and encouraging state legislatures to adopt them, the NCC promotes legal uniformity at the state level in place of—and in op-position to—expanded federal regulation. By the 1960s, the organization had promulgated dozens of model laws, including the near-universally ad-opted Uniform Commercial Code, which modernized and harmonized the law of commercial transactions. The Truth-in-Lending debate and Douglas's proposed state disclosure exemption convinced the NCC to take up state consumer credit reform. In 1964, when Truth-in-Lending remained stalled in the Senate, the NCC formed a special committee ("credit committee") to develop a Uniform Consumer Credit Code (UCCC). New York attorney Alfred Buerger headed the group, which was staffed by financial industry lawyers and law professors with expertise in consumer credit regulation. The committee intended the UCCC to replace accreted state law with one statute, which balanced creditor and debtor interests to regulate the rates and terms of credit. The code went through several draft and comment stages before the NCC published the final version in early 1968. The drafters wanted the UCCC to be available for state legislatures to adopt before Truth-in-Lending went into effect on July 1, 1969.[21]

Like Douglas, the drafters of the UCCC hoped to encourage more robust competition in consumer credit markets. "The successful American way of permitting competition to determine prices . . . should also be allowed to apply to the pricing of money and credit," declared the commissioners when they introduced the final version of the code. Toward this end, the UCCC offered a system of credit regulation based on defined loan types—mortgage lending, auto loans, revolving credit, and time sales—rather than by type of lender, as state law usually did. The code then applied uniform interest rate limits to each lending category, rates that were substantially higher than those allowed in most states. The commissioners believed market rates would develop below the legal maximums as lenders competed and borrowers shopped for low prices. High rate ceilings would protect marginal consumers from "unconscionable" credit abuses. High rates also compensated lenders for consumer-friendly provisions of the code, like limitations on wage garnishment, that made offering credit riskier and more expensive. Finally, the UCCC invited competition by removing state-level barriers to entry that restricted participation in consumer lending markets.[22]

Although competition remained a potent symbol, industry representatives and consumers objected to the regulatory changes required to achieve it. During drafting, Buerger's committee struggled to unite the politically divided credit industry. Lenders strongly favored competition in the abstract, but they jealously guarded the legal exemptions, loopholes, and niches created by their siloed credit markets. Retailers, for instance, objected to plans to eliminate the time-price doctrine. They advocated instead for a separate "retail credit code." Commercial bankers adamantly opposed the "free entry" of less regulated competitors, which drafters included to promote rigorous price competition. Small loan companies, credit unions, and even encyclopedia sales firms all lodged industry-specific objections.[23]

The credit committee's quest for competition shaped their strategy on what would become the fundamental battle surrounding the UCCC: the price of credit. At the beginning of its project, the committee recognized that "the rate structure in each state is more the result of a fought-out compromise between competing political forces than the rational selection between alternative theories of rate regulation." Commissioners described state interest rate laws as "neurotic" and "highly haphazard." As long as segments of the consumer credit industry were regulated separately within each state, they argued, rate limits would ensure profits for politically connected businesses rather than protect the public. The UCCC offered a radical simplification: it proposed bringing all consumer credit transactions under the ambit of a single, unified, rational state law. Committee members recognized their plan would be controversial. "I am every bit as aware as anyone that so-called usury legislation involves political and emotional implications of great magnitude," committee member Walter Malcolm explained to his colleagues in 1965, "but . . . we must first seek sound solutions and only secondarily consider political feasibility." Commissioners understood the fraught politics of rate regulation. In their high-minded ambition—and naiveté—they determined to eschew politics altogether.[24]

To establish uniform ceilings under which credit providers would compete, the Buerger's committee set the UCCC's rates high. For revolving credit, the code allowed 24 percent interest on the first $500 and 18 percent on balances in excess of $500. These rates significantly exceeded what most retailers and banks charged on their credit card plans. Still, retailers and banks objected. With the time-price doctrine in place, most states did not regulate revolving credit at all. Citing recent state-level litigation, the committee argued that retailers' sacred time-price doctrine would inevitably wilt under the bright lights of price disclosure. When it did, it would also undercut mushrooming bank card plans, which relied on the same legal fiction. "Banks are now rushing headlong into the credit card business," Malcolm observed in August 1968. "If bank credit card operations are . . . loans, a charge of 18% per annum on credit card accounts will violate the law . . . in

40 states." Anticipating consumer pushback, committee members insisted that market rates would develop below the code's high ceilings as creditors competed on price. Many observers were not so sure. In a statement to the committee, New York City's consumer affairs office expressed the widely held view that "the trend is for the legal maximum rate to become the final resting place for competition between creditors." If state law established high rates, then consumers would pay high prices.[25]

The UCCC drafters were undeterred, for they had invested their project with deep moral purpose. With the War on Poverty as a backdrop, welfare rights advocates pressing for credit access, and urban rioters targeting exploitative merchants, committee members argued that raising rate ceilings would expand the size of consumer credit markets and extend credit citizenship to more Americans. "Are the poor to be denied the opportunity to participate in the American economic life though the use of credit?" asked William Pierce, president of NCC, of members of Congress who criticized the UCCC's rate ceilings. Robert W. Johnson, an economist for the committee, went further. "The net result of a ceiling," Johnson argued, "is to throw out of the legal market the poor consumer, the ghetto consumer, and to give only the image of protecting the consumer who deserves rates well below the ceiling." By contrasting poor and ghetto consumers with consumers who deserved low rates, Johnson made a revealing shift between structural and moral categories. Rate ceilings, market efficiency advocates emphasized, excluded poor and Black consumers because of their structural positions in America's class and racial hierarchy. Poverty and racism made them uncreditworthy and locked them out of regulated markets. To overcome structural inequality, the committee proposed to charge for access. High credit prices were the price of inclusion "in the American economic life." Then the shift: once inside legal credit markets, credit prices reflected moral responsibility *not* structural hierarchy. Deserving consumers, Johnson emphasized, were "entitled, because of [their] credit worthiness, [their] bill-paying ability and record, and [their] affluence," to low credit prices. In UCCC's framework, markets, not policymakers, would divide the entitled from the unentitled, the deserving from the undeserving. Instead of addressing the inequalities that shaped assessments of creditworthiness, the credit committee offered to transfer the burden of inclusion to the market.[26]

Ultimately, members of the credit committee shared with liberal members of Congress the goal of expanding consumer protections and credit access, but they argued that achieving such goals would impose costs on lenders best managed through less regulated price competition. Consumer and labor groups, fresh from their Truth-in-Lending victory, rejected this trade-off. For them, securing inexpensive credit was more important than ensuring wide credit access. Although the UCCC's drafters sought to unify the concerns of privileged and nonprivileged borrowers through competitive markets—arguing that privileged, deserving borrowers might enjoy even lower rates in the absence of legal ceilings—consumers sought to preserve their privilege outright. Consumer and labor groups fought to maintain rate ceilings, not because they disputed Johnson's moral judgments but because they shared them. The New Deal had created the expectation among middle- and high-income white borrowers that credit would be inexpensive and widely available *for them*. This guarantee, moreover, operated through the morally inflected credit decisions of private lenders. White consumers believed they deserved low-cost credit. They were entitled to it. And the credit markets they used provided it. In this framework, rate ceilings ensured fair prices and also aligned with the new consumer protection politics. Rate ceilings discouraged lenders from lending too much. They shielded consumers from over-indebtedness and bankruptcy. "If some customers, high- or low-income, are denied credit occasionally because of the new law, then it will be to their advantage," a Wisconsin official argued after securing tight rate regulations. Indeed, if such ceilings limited access for poor and minority borrowers, then they rightly protected the undeserving from overextending themselves.[27]

When credit committee members unveiled the UCCC in 1968, they were sure they had made a significant contribution. "In a social and economic problem extending back for at least 4,000 years," Walter Malcolm declared, "the Code offers, for perhaps the first time in history, a reasoned solution of the problem of the cost of money and credit." Members had reason to be confident (though not *that* confident). In September, the committee received major funding from retailers to support state-by-state promotion. The Johnson administration, which had participated in the final comment stage, also endorsed the UCCC. The code, Betty Furness, special assistant for consumer affairs, argued, was "a significant and realistic step forward which will be of benefit to the consumer." In January 1969, Paul Douglas appeared before the Massachusetts legislature to encourage consideration of the UCCC:

"I strongly indorse the Code's attempt to foster meaningful price competition on credit charges." The code met quick success. Utah adopted it in March 1969; Oklahoma in May. According to internal committee data, by June 1969 the UCCC had been introduced or placed under official study by most state legislatures.[28]

Resistance, though, developed quickly. Consumer and labor groups sharply criticized the code, arguing that it was drafted to serve creditors, not consumers. Organized labor groups headed the movement to restrain credit prices, focusing, as they had during the Truth-in-Lending debate, on revolving retail credit. Labor leaders, like their consumer allies, sought low credit prices that would enhance consumer purchasing power. They also believed, in an environment of credit scarcity, that revolving credit necessarily grew at the expense of other forms of lending, like mortgages and auto loans, that indirectly employed unionized workers. The AFL-CIO had strongly supported the national 18 percent usury limit in the House. When it failed, the union turned to the states. In November 1968, consumer advocate Sidney Margolius highlighted the victory of Washington State's Labor Council in securing a 12 percent limit on revolving interest rates. This, he argued in *AFL-CIO News,* "is a lesson for credit-exploited working families and their organizations everywhere." At its annual convention in October 1969, the union initiated a nationwide campaign, directing its state chapters to lobby for revolving credit limits of not more than 12 percent a year. Contrasting its effort with the "outrageously high finance charges" contained in the UCCC, the convention resolved that "the current exorbitant interest rates on charge accounts border on usury and eat away at the hard-won economic gains achieved at bargaining table." Union leaders expected low-cost credit access, but as an adjunct to wage-driven economic citizenship not as a replacement for it.[29]

Mounting opposition revealed the credit committee's error in "only secondarily consider[ing] political feasibility" of interest rate levels. The UCCCs' drafters were unprepared for the adverse national response. Over the two-year drafting process, the committee had promoted consumer interests against continuous industry pressure. Although the *price* of credit was more favorable to lenders under the code, the *terms* of credit were far more favorable to consumers than under the Truth-in-Lending Act or the existing laws in most states. Within an intellectual framework that prioritized market efficiency, committee members had made a good faith effort to balance borrower and lender interests. The committee, however, suffered from bad optics. Through September 1968, more than 90 percent of the project's funding had come from the credit industry. Its chairman, Alfred Buerger, was a prominent lawyer and lobbyist for Marine Midland Bank. Still, committee members were shocked by claims that the UCCC aimed to subvert the Truth-in-Lending Act. Defending the code against such criticism, Harvard law professor Robert Braucher contended (fairly) that the Truth-in-Lending Act was equally influenced by business lobbyists, and that it was "weaker than the [UCCC] on every point on which they differ." By then, the code had become a target for consumer organizing and a springboard for state-level price regulation.[30]

As its members crisscrossed the country, lobbying state legislatures to adopt the UCCC, the committee's confidence faded. In state after state, local opposition impeded the committee's efforts. Consumer and labor groups led the public fight against high prices. Meanwhile, state banking associations undermined the law, which threatened to introduce new, less regulated competitors into commercial banking markets. Writing in September 1969, NCC educational director Nathaniel Butler confided that "the rate has been the focus of consumer attack in the states," yet "although the most vocal opposition has come from consumers, we all know the more important and effective opposition has come from banks." With public consumer and labor opposition and banks working behind the scenes, Malcolm worried that the UCCC "can be another major accomplishment of the Conference or it can be a complete flop." The latter outcome looked increasingly likely.[31]

The Fate of the UCCC

For the UCCC committee the national picture looked grim, in part because its proposed code had landed amid perpetual state-level negotiations over the price and terms of credit. These negotiations involved not only state legislatures, the focus of committee lobbying, but also a fluid mix of administrative officials and courts—a combination of market structuring institutions that made local credit policies highly contingent. Still, across states, broad trends are visible. Savvy state officials, Republicans and Democrats alike, recognized the rising salience of consumer protection. They understood, as Douglas had explained to the Kennedy administration, that working on behalf of consumers made for good politics. They attended the

political winds. And they used their positions within state bureaucratic institutions and interstate policy networks to advance pro-consumer policies. The
committee's effort to promote uniformity also ran into an abiding state-level
tension between local norms and national trends. State legislatures, regulators, and courts looked to their peer states for guidance and authority—but
never the final word.[32]

In Wisconsin, state officials had long sought to regulate the price of revolving credit. When Wisconsin retailers began charging consumers 1.5 percent
per month on their charge accounts in 1956, their policies drew scrutiny
from the state's supervisor of consumer credit, John Doyle. Writing in *Personal Finance Law Quarterly* in 1958, Doyle disputed retailer claims that revolving credit fell under the time-price doctrine—that it constituted a
difference in price, not a loan of money. "Revolving credit plans are not time
sales and cannot be considered as such," Doyle argued. Doyle, though, lacked
authority to act. Instead, he sought an opinion from the state's attorney general on the legality of such transactions under Wisconsin law. He waited—
for seven years. In December 1965, attorney general Bronson La Follette also
concluded that retail credit plans were not time sales and that they violated
the state's usury laws. Yet La Follette further determined that a test case was
necessary to settle the matter. His office, however, was reluctant to single out
one retailer for judicial action.[33]

With their revolving credit plans on shaky legal ground, the Wisconsin
Retail Merchants Association lobbied for an explicit exemption to Wisconsin's 12 percent general usury limit. Association members met with Republican governor Warren Knowles in 1967. He instructed them to work with
the state's banking commissioner to craft "a bill which would be agreeable to
both parties." Instead, retailers introduced their own bill, which the Banking
Commission blocked because it lacked balancing consumer protections. A
meeting of the two sides in April 1968 ended in acrimony. Retail representatives predicted "chaos" if they "were to reduce the revolving charge to 12
percent per annum." Citing the industry's earlier subterfuge, the assistant
attorney general suggested a test case might be necessary to gain "leverage"
over the industry. "Leverage or blackmail?" the retailers replied.[34]

La Follette had hesitated to target one firm, but in 1968 his office sued
J. C. Penney, arguing that the national retailer's revolving credit plan was
usurious, constituted a public nuisance, and should be enjoined. The trial

court initially found that Penney's revolving plan did violate Wisconsin's usury law, but that the state had no legal right or interest in credit contracts between individual consumers and J. C. Penney. Penney may have violated the state's usury law, but it did not constitute a public nuisance that the state had the power to stop. On appeal, the Wisconsin Supreme Court upheld the trial court's determination that the plan was usurious and further held that the issue was worthy of injunctive relief. "There is no reason defendant should be permitted openly, notoriously, and flagrantly to violate our laws enacted for benefit of our people," the court concluded. "The state would be weak indeed if it were powerless to prevent it." The state was not weak, and now it had leverage.[35]

J. C. Penney drew new battle lines in the national fight over the price of credit. Doyle recognized that the trial court's initial finding—that Penney's revolving credit plan was not a time sale—provided an opening for his administrative counterparts in other states. In April 1969, he wrote several state officials, boasting, "It can be finally said that . . . revolving charge account plans cannot be considered time sales[, and] must be . . . subject to the provisions of the Usury Statutes." Doyle activated networks of state administrative enforcement, which, when combined with national media coverage of the case, enabled peer states to press for advantage. Attorneys general of Minnesota and Iowa, both of whose state legislatures were considering the UCCC, used the Wisconsin precedent as the basis for successful suits against major retailers in their states. Several state AFL-CIO chapters also initiated private class actions against retailers and banks on the same grounds. Nationally, the usury cases yielded mixed results. Some state courts followed *J. C. Penney*. Others viewed it as an aberration. Nevertheless, by pursuing Wisconsin's strategy, state administrators and private actors used the courts to exert significant pressure on ongoing legislative negotiations over the price of credit.[36]

In Wisconsin, *J. C. Penney* polarized the local debate over retail credit prices as the legislature considered the UCCC in 1970 and 1971. Consumer interest rates remained the most contentious issue. The "credit community," led by the Wisconsin Bankers Association, advocated for the code's high rates, claiming that the code's consumer-friendly credit terms necessitated higher credit prices. The AFL-CIO and Wisconsin Consumers League refused to budge from the 12 percent rate established by *J. C. Penney*. They were encouraged by peer organizations in other states. The Washington State Labor

Council reported positively on that state's 12 percent rate referendum. "When Wisconsin consumers see this occurring in other states," a Wisconsin Consumers League representative explained to the legislature's UCCC advisory committee, "consumer advocates have a hard time selling them the fact that Wisconsin must raise its rates." With legislators desperate for a compromise, the committee stalemated. Although participants found considerable common ground, they recognized that "the whole committee effort would die if the rate question is not answered." Neither side would budge. The legislature made what hash it could, incorporating consumer-friendly credit terms while also compromising on revolving credit prices. The Wisconsin Consumer Act—not, tellingly, the Wisconsin Consumer Credit Code—cleared the legislature in 1971, allowing 18 percent on the first $500 and 12 percent on all exceeding balances.[37]

The terms of the compromise are less important than the process through which it was achieved. At the state level, credit regulation developed through iterative, multilayered, contingent, and imperfectly democratic negotiations. What the process lacked in system and method, it made up for in pluralism— though certainly a circumscribed pluralism that excluded poor and minority stakeholders. Sometimes creditor interests succeeded (though siloed industries as often checked each other as advanced a common interest). Sometimes consumers or other interest groups won out. Most often, as in Wisconsin, idiosyncratic compromise prevailed. Nevertheless, Wisconsin Democrats claimed the Wisconsin Consumer Act as a major victory. "The consumer revolution has begun," legislative leaders rejoiced. The law constituted "a big gun in that revolution." The state's banking industry also remained upbeat. The act was "a victory" and "a testament to those who represented the industry in negotiations." Bankers achieved some concessions and maintained the political good will necessary to negotiate again in the future. "The agreement," Wisconsin's bankers concluded, "demonstrates the viability of our political system." Financial federalism worked.[38]

As credit committee members crisscrossed the country to sell their uniform law, they invariably found similarly complex state credit negotiations— and labor and consumer groups determined to undermine their efforts to raise credit prices. The travels of Harvard law professor and credit committee member Robert Braucher provide a glimpse of this quixotic process. As the committee finished its work, Braucher was on a visiting appointment at the University of Minnesota Law School. There, state lawmakers believed "it imperative that the legislature enact statutes . . . which would retain for the State of Minnesota administration of the federal Truth-in-Lending Act." They supported local control. Prospects for the UCCC looked good. Braucher testified at legislative hearings in October and November 1968. Many legislators felt the code's rates did not compare favorably with the state's recently reaffirmed 8 percent general usury rate. One state senator asked Braucher pointedly, "Are [we] in effect voting to cost the borrower more money?" Bankers also remained staunch opponents of the code's free entry provisions. They sidelined the bill. Minnesota bankers *did* want the code's high revolving credit rates, but consumer opposition defeated a separate bill setting revolving credit prices at 18 percent. In a later session, the legislature explicitly capped them at 12 percent.[39]

In February 1969, Braucher went to Montana. There, he convinced the House Business and Industry Committee to recommend the legislation. The full bill, however, proved too large and expensive to print. The Montana House debated it and defeated it without ever reading it. "The misinformation that was circulated by consumer groups," the credit committee's local correspondent explained, "and the failure to receive affirmative recommendations from Labor groups was disastrous when we requested the Legislature to accept the Code on faith." Montana's labor groups may have been undecided when Braucher visited the state in February; by September, when he visited Arizona, labor organizations there had made up their minds. Arizona retailers supported the code, Braucher found, but the state's AFL-CIO chapter martialed decisive opposition. The UCCC "is no more a *consumer* code than a corporate charter is a statement of employee rights," the union argued. Arizona instead passed less ambitious regulations for retail charge accounts, setting interest rates at 18 percent for the first $1,500 and 12 percent thereafter.[40]

The credit committee could not develop a viable strategy to achieve widespread enactment of the UCCC. Bankers continued to undermine their efforts, seeking to preserve their protected position by attacking the code's free entry provisions. At the same time, consumer and labor groups, bolstered by *J. C. Penney* and the continued salience of low credit prices, fought for lower rates. Of the first six states to adopt UCCC, five lowered the revolving credit limits from 24 percent a year to 18 percent. The credit committee's argument that competition would generate prices below the code's high ceilings repeatedly failed to gain traction. State legislators and policymakers applied their own experiences, which taught them that usury limits always began as a rate ceiling and ended as a price floor. Moreover, instead of accepting the idea that nationally consistent rates would make for a uniform credit market, local lawmakers evaluated the code's rates against local conditions. "Are the rates proposed in [the] Uniform Act appropriate in Michigan?" a legislative aide asked lawmakers considering the UCCC, suggesting that "rates appropriate in California might not be appropriate in Michigan." Michigan's lawmakers agreed. The legislature did not seriously consider the UCCC.[41]

By 1975, the UCCC had flopped. By then, nine states had adopted the code. The final total would reach only eleven. Instead, most retained their fragmented credit laws. "The dry pages of a law review article are completely inadequate to portray the depths of distrust and bad feelings between consumer and creditor groups," concluded credit committee member William Warren. "Their standoff on rate regulation reform leaves undisturbed the present segmented, totally illogical patchwork of rate-ceiling laws in most states." The New Deal regulatory order, though, was designed to be democratic, not logical. State-level credit regulation encouraged constant local adjustment as firms found new ways to offer credit or as market conditions changed. Within this system, state officials developed local solutions through multifaceted negotiations with consumer groups and financial firms. In state after state, local officials regulated credit card interest rates, clustering around 18 percent annual interest as an acceptable price for convenient credit.[42]

In the late 1960s, consumer and labor groups began an extended campaign to control the price of revolving credit. In concert with enterprising state officials, they extended price controls over credit card accounts, defeating federal politicians, legal reformers, and industry participants who all favored disclosure and price competition over price controls. Federal Truth-in-Lending, in this sense, reflected the growing federal enthusiasm for disclosure as a consumer protection strategy that aligned with percolating ideas about the efficiency of less regulated markets. Disclosure, as an alternative to more interventionist regulatory policies, promised to increase overall consumer welfare by making more consumers market participants and, as such, well-informed market regulators. Informed consumers, free to choose, would vote with their dollars. The veil of market freedom cloaked preexisting economic and social advantages, representing them instead as categories of moral worth—creditworthiness, repayment record, affluence—expressed in prices. As federal policymakers, in the wake of the civil and women's rights movements, sought to expand access to markets formerly reserved for privileged consumers, disclosure gained momentum as a way to simultaneously promote market safety and market access.

The story of state-level credit regulation, by contrast, demonstrates the continued salience of proscriptive government controls over market behavior, pursued by organized citizens and bureaucratic officials through democratic political institutions. Organized consumers, free to choose, pursued their self-interest through the political process. Enterprising bureaucrats, channeling consumer objectives, developed pro-consumer strategies and disseminated them through their policy networks. Consumer and labor groups, meanwhile, fought at once for pocketbook politics, marketplace protection, and privileged status. Reflecting their self-perception of innate creditworthiness, they expected low credit prices. They also sought protection from dangerous levels of household debt. Price ceilings offered both. As one Wisconsin official explained, "If the new law increases the quality of credit-granting, and reduces the need for people to resort to bankruptcy, all of us should be better off." Indeed, although industry opponents and free-market advocates portrayed rate ceilings as irrational, credit price controls operated through a clear logic. Low legal rates ensured that creditors lent only to the most creditworthy borrowers and did not extend additional credit to those already burdened with debt. By organizing to maintain their privileged status in credit markets, consumers declined an alternative that offered more inclusion—and more risk. Deregulated interest rates would enable lenders to expand the scope of credit markets by charging poor and minority borrowers higher prices. Consumers rejected predatory inclusion—out of paternalism, certainly, and out of fear that they would be subject to it. Within the postwar political economy, prosperity flowed through credit markets while price ceilings shifted risk onto creditors and encouraged them to manage prosperity safely: this was the foundational moral economy of the New Deal financial order.[43]

Banks launched their card mailing campaigns just as consumer and labor groups mobilized against high credit prices. They could not have chosen a worse moment. Bankers hoped cards would create new, unregulated channels of consumer lending, and they joined retailers in lobbying to maintain the dubious time-price doctrine. Federal Truth-in-Lending debates focused attention on high credit prices and generated momentum for state regulation. They also encouraged congressional scrutiny of bank card mailing and other business practices that put consumer households at risk. In the face of mounting criticism, bankers continued to assert that self-regulating markets would best serve consumer interests; the countermovement to embed card plans in state-level price regimes, however, proved robust and successful, at least in the short term. In the long term, bank cards that increasingly crossed state lines would provide the key to unraveling state price controls altogether.

6

Confronting Cards in Congress

"If There Was Ever an Unsound Banking Practice"

Elected in 1928 to represent the piney hills of northeast Texas, Wright Patman tirelessly championed the political economy of small finance. As chairman of the House Banking Committee beginning in 1963, the populist crusader did so with institutional force and authority. For bankers and many of his colleagues, "Rep. Don Quixote" was a relic, a gadfly, a crank—an arthritic opponent of financial progress. Patman, though, was no fool. He remembered well the bank failures that caused the Great Depression; he had made his career fighting for fair consumer prices. He grasped the 1960s consumerist revival. When Patman came to the House floor to denounce the onslaught of unsolicited card mailing in August 1967, he launched a major fight over bank card regulation. Recalling "those catastrophic days of the 1930's," Patman anticipated a new source of calamity: "If there was ever an unsound banking practice, it has to be the sending out . . . of millions of unsolicited credit cards to an unsuspecting public." Indiscriminate card mailing jeopardized bank stability. It diverted credit flows from national social priorities. And it endangered consumer households. Patman called for a "statutory moratorium on credit cards." He would fight the "credit card racket" for the remainder of his career.[1]

Patman had reason to worry. From 1966 to 1970, more than one thousand banks rushed into the credit card market, mailing tens of millions of unsolicited cards in a mad scramble for market share. The card explosion coincided with unprecedented turbulence in the postwar financial system. The

fragmented, siloed, and price-controlled financial markets strained under the
1960s economic boom. Escalation of war in Vietnam added yet more pressure.
Inflation increased in the red-hot economy. Interest rates followed as the Federal Reserve tried to cool things down. As it had during the 1950s, tight money
disrupted the regulatory channels that guided credit toward national priorities.
During the "credit crunches," which squeezed tightest in 1966 and 1969,
money moved in unpredictable ways. The groundswell of Lyndon Johnson's
Great Society, meanwhile, generated new demands for scarce credit from poor
and minority borrowers, who sought access to federal credit programs that had
subsidized white suburbia. With interest rates up, however, bankers had little
incentive to participate in government-guaranteed, low-cost lending. Instead,
where they could, investors and bankers pulled money from low-yielding sectors, like housing, small business, and municipal lending. They pursued the
highest returns available, snubbing social priorities in pursuit of profit.[2]

As Congress struggled to rebalance the regulatory structure—to coax and
compel private lenders to fund public priorities—credit cards piled up. High-
interest bank cards, already the target of state-level price control efforts, became integral to larger debates about preserving the financial structure. Many
politicians imagined a zero-sum contest for finite resources: credit delivered
through cards did not build houses or schools. Others viewed consumer
credit as procyclical, inflationary, and in need of direct federal control. Financial turmoil also invited regulatory skeptics: They argued that freer competition, rather than continued regulation, would ease flows of scarce credit.
Such ideas, however, remained inchoate and marginal. Most lawmakers remained committed to the New Deal's regulatory priorities—financial federalism, industry silos, and price controls—even as they struggled to make them
work. Confronted by unpredictable financial flows, Congress shored up the
regulatory structure with sandbags and particleboard. Lawmakers even
granted the president new authority to enact peacetime credit controls, enlist-
ing the administration in increasingly difficult credit allocation decisions.[3]

The 1960s credit crunches made the debates over bank cards more ur-
gent. The sudden and massive shift into cards continued commercial banks'
transition from primarily serving businesses to aggressively targeting consumers. Lawmakers, too, saw the road to the future. Few, other than Patman,
yanked toward the off ramp. Congress's financial policy community was
transforming, from a cohort dominated by Southern New Deal veterans like

Patman to a new generation of postwar politicians, most prominently Senator William Proxmire. Unlike their senior colleagues, Proxmire and allies like Senator Thomas J. McIntyre (D-NH) had not navigated depression and war from seats in Congress. They were open to new regulatory ideas. As they grappled with the onslaught of unsolicited cards in the context of turbulent financial markets, they sought some middle ground that would at once encourage competition and financial innovation, preserve the regulatory structure, and protect consumers.[4]

The balance, however, was difficult to strike. On one side, bankers, the Federal Reserve, and some Republican politicians argued that bank credit cards would benefit consumers. To achieve these benefits, banks had no choice but to mail cards to build adequate transaction volume. With time and experience, bankers would adjust their practices to match consumer preferences. Markets would self-correct. Legislative interference would only stifle natural market evolution. Consumers, however, along with congressional and administration allies, sought safety in the marketplace. Unsolicited cards stoked consumer fears about financial insecurity, credit-fueled inflation, and impersonal technology. Bankers pressed cards unbidden into consumer homes, and into the hands of wives, children, and not a few irresponsible husbands. One congressman labeled unsolicited cards "financial pornography." Criminals also stole cards, exposing consumers to liability for cards they had never requested and never seen. None of these problems could be solved by more efficient markets; rather, they were the kinds of externalities, like environmental degradation and product safety, that the larger 1960s consumer rights movement sought to sharply limit through regulation. As Congress debated different ways to maintain card mailing in the name of competition, consumers, federal agencies, state legislatures, and outside experts pushed the process toward limited consumer liability and an outright ban on unsolicited mailing. Bankers could proceed down the road to the future, but they would do so with guardrails firmly in place.[5]

The New Deal Regulatory Order in the 1960s

The explosive credit card growth came at a moment of intense concern in Congress about the American financial system. Such concerns were not new, of course. Since the New Deal, policymakers had struggled to balance targeted policies, which channeled credit toward sectors including small business, agriculture, housing, and public borrowing, against the Federal Reserve's blunt monetary tools, which allocated credit by raising or lowering overall prices. When the Fed tightened the money supply, critics like Paul Douglas and Wright Patman had argued in the 1950s, large firms cornered scarce financial resources. In a June 1957 letter to Douglas, Senator Joseph S. Clark Jr. (D-PA) explained his party's position succinctly. "I have no desire to leave our social priorities to the market place." Yet, by relying on private lenders to allocate credit-based social provision, liberal policymakers had already left social priorities in the hands of market actors. At best, well-designed policies would align private interest with the public good. The Commission on Money and Credit, established by Eisenhower in 1958, arrived at different conclusions. It favored liberalizing financial rules in order to free up credit and stimulate economic growth. Although President John F. Kennedy praised the commission's report upon its release in 1961, Congress ignored its recommendations. By the mid-1960s, the CMC was largely forgotten.[6]

The problems, however, remained. The credit crunch of 1966, the first major financial crisis of the postwar era, validated many of the predictions of the CMC report. For example, declining commercial bank profitability led these firms, especially those that were large and publicly held, to expand their balance sheets. As corporate, household, and municipal borrowing increased during the 1960s boom, interest rates and inflation climbed steadily higher. The Fed sought to temper credit growth by increasing the legal reserves banks held against their loan portfolios. Raising reserve requirements, however, only compounded banks' scramble for funds to meet existing loan commitments. Demand for money rose. So did its price. By June 1966, market interest rates exceeded what banks could legally pay on large-denomination certificates of deposit (CDs) and consumer savings accounts. Investors sought higher returns elsewhere. Funds fled the banking system. Bankers responded in two ways. First, they offered smaller, negotiable CDs, diverting consumer savings from thrift institutions. Thrifts, which specialized in low-interest home mortgages, could not readily offer high-interest deposits. Money moved from thrifts to banks; mortgage lending froze. Second, banks stopped investing in low-yield municipal bonds, freezing that market as well.[7]

At once, the credit crunch affirmed the convictions of regulatory advocates and critics. In commercial bankers' aggressive pursuit of funds, congressional Democrats saw proof that big banks would always favor big business over small borrowers. By leaving financial markets to sort the winners and losers of tight credit policy, the Fed likewise appeared to favor large corporations over national social priorities. Democrats renewed calls for controls that placed credit allocation in the hands of policymakers, not markets. For bankers and their allies, the crunch held the opposite lesson. The system's regulatory priorities were the problem; more controls were not the solution. In the wake of the crisis, Congress sought to satisfy both sides. It adjusted federal limits on deposit interest rates (Regulation Q), giving thrifts a slight deposit-rate advantage over commercial banks. Congress also authorized federal bank supervisors to adjust deposit ceilings, enabling them to forestall rapid movement of deposits—a process called disintermediation—between financial sectors. The law, though, had to be renewed biannually, forcing congress to constantly revisit debates about financial regulation. As inflation and interest rates reached new postwar highs year after year, frustration mounted on all sides. Bank cards, which appeared to channel credit away from social priorities and toward high-interest consumer borrowing, added fuel to this volatile mix. Liberal lawmakers did not trust banks to begin with. Unsolicited card mailing cemented these views.[8]

Unsolicited Mailing Comes to Congress

Bank card plans drew congressional attention during the Truth-in-Lending debates. In House hearings in August 1967, Betty Furness, the Johnson administration's special assistant for consumer affairs, recounted her experience receiving two unsolicited cards from the First National City Bank of New York (Citibank). To launch its "Everything Card" that summer, Citibank mailed more than a million cards in and around New York City. "I bitterly resent having the card," Furness explained. "I did not ask for it, I do not want the card, and when you think of the unwise hands those cards fall into, it is a shocking thing." William Windall (R-NJ), the subcommittee's ranking Republican, agreed. He urged his colleagues to investigate "mailing out [cards] without anybody looking into the background of the person." By then, national media had trained its spotlight on the madcap mailings in Chicago the previous winter, while banks continued to inundate their local markets. Eager to halt further mass mailing, Patman introduced legislation prohibiting FDIC-insured banks from issuing unsolicited cards. Mass mailing, Patman argued, endangered bank safety and through federal deposit insurance it risked taxpayer dollars. With public criticism mounting, Patman's gambit earned wide approval. Even the *Wall Street Journal* endorsed his goals: "Mr. Patman's idea would make bankers seem more like responsible businessmen. That impression surely has not been enhanced by the seeming carelessness of the scattergun mailings."[9]

Patman convened hearings in November 1967 as a show trial for unsolicited mailing. Ostensibly, participants debated the risks of financial innovation and considered which groups—consumers, bankers, or taxpayers—should bear them. Patman, however, as an aide later wrote, was determined "to strike at the heart of the bank credit card system." The New Dealers had designed the political economy of small finance to limit the market power of financial firms. With cards, Patman argued, big banks sought to "totally dominate consumer credit." Card issuers stood between consumers and merchants, collecting charges from both. As Patman put it, "I think the banks, ever since the moneychangers were driven out of the temple of God, have been trying to perfect some plan whereby they can collect from both sides." Inflation was the likely outcome. Consumer prices would necessarily rise to pay the new financial middlemen.[10]

Bank cards, other critics feared, threatened the tenuous balance between ensuring widely available credit and protecting consumers from unsustainable debt. Leonor Sullivan (D-MO), architect of the House's ambitious Truth-in-Lending bill, observed that "these cards are a tremendous temptation when they get into the wrong hands." By the "wrong hands" she meant what Furness termed the "compulsive buyer." "It is usually those least able to handle and understand credit—the poor, the uneducated—who become the most hopeless addicts," Furness had explained. Patman endorsed this critique. Cards were "anti-thrift." Impersonal technology compounded the danger. Banks' use of "automatic data processing equipment," Patman warned, meant "numbers will displace persons' names." Depersonalized credit encouraged households to sink into debt. Outraged consumers demanded action. "I protest violently your act of endangering my financial security, credit rating, and peace of mind," a North Carolina consumer wrote his local bank, forwarding a copy to Furness. "If this is not illegal on your part, it should be." Members of Patman's committee received "many letters from constituents . . . protesting the credit card issued to them unsolicited from various banks." Credit card mailing, the Banking Committee feared, was completely out of control.[11]

To committee members, mass card mailing appeared random and indiscriminate, upsetting their notions of creditworthiness as elementally individual, rooted in the work and responsibility of the male head of household. For the middle-class, white, married men that served as the ideal type of creditworthiness, borrowing carried the cultural freight of personal honor and self-worth—what Patman called "honest and honorable" credit. Creditworthiness reflected prudence, diligence, and care, not something mailed to every family on the cul-de-sac. Credit and individual identity were inseparable. Bank solicitation flattened distinctions between households. By targeting female dependents, banks also undermined male household authority. "My wife and my two teenage daughters have these cards and it tends to make me nervous," Tom Gettys (D-SC) observed. Furness, a former actress and Westinghouse spokeswoman, fretted about her own capacity to use cards responsibly. "I am only a girl and I have more than nine credit cards. I use a great many of my credit cards, and I use them with joy and I hope with wisdom." As bank cards cascaded into consumer mailboxes, committee members determined, they undermined the solvency and social foundations of American households.[12]

The growing threat of credit card crime compounded consumer anxiety. By mailing tens of millions of cards, banks provided easy targets for crooks and con artists. When thieves lifted cards from the mail, they appropriated consumers' identities. When thieves used stolen cards, they exposed consumers to liability for credit charges, often on cards consumers had not requested—or even anticipated. Banning unsolicited mailing, Patman argued, would solve the fraud problem. Yet widespread card use meant that card fraud already exceeded the scope of unsolicited mailing; thieves stole cards from wallets as well as from envelopes. Consumers feared financial liability for charges made with lost or stolen cards. Card issuers and merchants squabbled over fraud losses. Some lawmakers believed only strong criminal sanctions would deter card criminals. Building on a campaign led by American Express, two committee members introduced bills to "prohibit transportation, use, sale, or receipt, for unlawful purposes, of credit cards in interstate or foreign commerce." Fraud provisions, however, were outside Patman's legislative jurisdiction. They belonged to the House Judiciary Committee, where similar legislation had stalled since the early 1960s.[13]

Faced with mounting consumer concerns, federal bank officials urged calm, caution, and patience. Congress, they argued, should permit banks to innovate. "We need to be careful," Federal Reserve governor Andrew Brimmer cautioned, "not to discourage banks from experimenting in developing improved ways to serve the public." Brimmer, the Federal Reserve's first Black governor, headed the system's Task Group on Bank Credit-Card and Check-Credit Plans. Some early initiatives, he acknowledged, had been flawed. With Fed guidance, Brimmer assured, bankers would learn from their colleagues' mistakes. Officials were paying close attention, collecting data, and documenting best practices. "Given the fact that plans are just developing, the practices are just unfolding, and we are still in the process of innovation, should we not permit some time for the practices to settle down so that the best of the practices become the general practices?" Brimmer asked. Through constant engagement with banks, federal oversight officials were better positioned than Congress to guide that process. Brimmer appealed to the ideal of fair competition. Many banks had already launched card plans using unsolicited mailing. Prohibiting the practice would advantage those incumbents over new entrants. Bankers, their federal supervisors argued, could weigh the risks.[14]

Oversight officials urged congressional inaction until the Fed completed its bank card study. "Time is available—and we think it should be used," Brimmer argued. After two days of hearings, Patman's committee accepted the wait-and-see approach. (Patman later blamed Fed officials for preventing him from nipping card mailing in the bud.) Over the next several months, numerous lawmakers introduced or cosponsored legislation to mitigate the worst features of unsolicited mailing without eliminating the practice and, with it, competition. As Senator Walter Mondale (D-MN) argued, introducing legislation in December 1967, "Some form of Federal regulation is required that will not hamper the generation of new business." While Congress waited on the Federal Reserve, banks flooded the mail with plastic.[15]

In July 1968, the Fed Task Group on Bank Credit-Card and Check-Credit Plans released its report, drawing congressional attention back to unsolicited mailing. The Fed offered a wide survey of bank card plans. It explored their impact on bank operations and market structure, along with their implications for consumers. The task group endorsed bank cards as a valuable service and argued that banks should be allowed to advance credit innovation. The report raised and dismissed the concerns of Patman and other card critics: cards did not raise consumer prices, lead consumers to make larger purchases, draw consumers easily into debt, or contribute significantly to inflation. Such fears reflected inexperience. They would pass with practice and time. "In the final analysis, of course, it is the consumer who stands to benefit most from the heightened competition arising out of bank cards," the task group reported. Ensuring competition meant preserving unsolicited mailing. In this, the Fed fully adopted bankers' claims that mailing was the only reliable way to launch a card plan. "Admittedly," the report concluded, "unsolicited cards are a nuisance to some recipients, but the problem is not large over-all." For bankers, the Fed's report constituted a full-throated endorsement of unsolicited mailing.[16]

William Proxmire did not accept the Fed's judgment, and in October 1968 he convened hearings to consider the report's findings and to build support for a regulatory agenda that would allow competition while rebalancing risk among consumers and card issuers. Proxmire was sensitive to bankers' arguments that banning card mailing would advantage incumbent firms. As lead Senate sponsor of the recently enacted Truth-in-Lending Act, Proxmire shared Paul Douglas's faith that informed consumers, acting in transparent, competitive markets, were their own best advocates. To maintain competition among card issuers, Proxmire opposed a ban on unsolicited mailing. Instead, he favored a two-pronged approach: first, requiring card issuers to screen potential recipients against a uniform set of credit standards; and second, shifting most financial risk from lost or stolen cards from cardholders to card issuers.[17]

As with Patman's hearings, Proxmire's considered an avalanche of consumer concerns; they also focused attention on difficult questions surrounding credit access, creditworthiness, and credit risk that had been central to the Truth-in-Lending debates. At that time, consumer and labor groups accepted that low prices would limit credit access for borrowers deemed less creditworthy. Similar concerns emerged in the Banking Committee's investigations of Black urban unrest, which revealed the sharp credit practices of many "ghetto" retailers. In both contexts, arguments that competition would make credit more widely available at lower prices ran headlong into deeply entrenched assumptions about which groups were inherently creditworthy. Proxmire probed these issues further. Although bankers primarily targeted middle- and upper-income consumers, unsolicited cards reached borrowers further down the income scale. The national reliance on consumer borrowing—through home mortgages, auto loans, and retail credit—created risks for moderate-income households. Many teetered on the edge of insolvency. At the margins of the affluent society, bankruptcies increased year after year, from just over 10,000 in 1947 (that is, 11 filings for every 100,000 Americans aged twenty and over) to more than 190,000 in 1967 (161 per 100,000). For struggling households, a federal bankruptcy official explained, an unsolicited card "comes like a gift from heaven." In their courtrooms, bankruptcy judges saw how the unrequested lifeline, carrying unrequested financial risk, often pulled struggling families into bankruptcy.[18]

Consumer advocates pressed these arguments, portraying unsolicited cards as an acute danger to consumer households. Betty Furness accused banks of turning consumers into "hopeless addicts." Unsolicited cards were like a drug—one that could ruin the lives of families as well as individuals. Bank cards were uniquely addictive, others argued, because banks were motivated to keep consumers in debt. "There is a reverse incentive for the bank to try to get people who are not going to pay promptly to take the credit card," Proxmire observed. Law professor Eric E. Bergsten developed this point. Retailers used card plans to facilitate goods purchases, on which the retailer profited. Travel cards, like American Express, profited from high merchant discounts and annual fees paid by cardholders. They did not allow customers to run balances. "It may be that it is only with the bank cards that we are talking about the credit aspect of credit cards being a significant feature," Bergsten explained. Banks, Proxmire and Bergsten surmised, benefited from putting consumers into high-interest debt and keeping them there. Proxmire advocated for "some minimum standard of credit worthiness," to protect the "low-income," "slow payer . . . who will be lured in." More than half of banks, the committee learned, mailed cards without performing adequate credit checks. Only responsible consumers should receive addictive cards, and bankers could not be trusted to sort the risks themselves.[19]

The framework of creditworthiness and responsibility, which would remain consistent throughout the unsolicited mailing debate, obscured the deeper mechanisms that at once made consumer debt necessary and dangerous for

American households. Credit, channeled by the public-private welfare state, provided essential rungs up the social ladder, but only for households fortunate to enjoy stable employment and rising incomes. Creditworthiness was structural. Access to high incomes and government support fell unevenly. So did the risks of credit-financed abundance. The language of responsibility hid these fundamental inequalities, rooting them in the agency of individuals rather than in the underlying economic and social structure. Rising bankruptcies cracked the picture window. Instead of reevaluating credit-fueled abundance, liberals like Proxmire, who favored more active market competition, doubled down on personal responsibility. It had to be deadbeats not paying their bills. The alternative—that credit-based social provision was flawed—remained unthinkable. Bank cards entered at the boundary of this system, and Proxmire and his colleagues were genuinely conflicted about how they fit. Were cards, by facilitating consumer spending, consistent with national social goals? Did cards, by introducing new risks of indebtedness and bankruptcy, undermine them? Proxmire's proposal placed cards on a spectrum of credit citizenship, where creditworthiness (i.e., social class) determined access to affluence. Protecting the low-income, slow payer from bankruptcy protected the integrity of the system. It did so by placing the government, rather than private lenders, in the business of drawing visible lines between borrowers.[20]

Proxmire's credit standards proposal proved controversial, and he was on steadier ground with cardholder liability. In this, Proxmire looked to recently enacted laws in Massachusetts and Illinois, which limited cardholder liability for lost or stolen cards. As "laboratories of democracy," in Justice Louis Brandeis's famous phrase, states often developed novel regulatory policies ahead of federal lawmakers. Here, state legislatures responded to state-level court decisions, which tended to hold cardholders liable for charges made on lost or stolen cards. These decisions reflected a major shift from rules governing checking accounts, explained Massachusetts Consumers' Council representative (and co-drafter of the UCCC), William Willier. Liability for check forgery rested squarely with banks. To distribute fraud risk more appropriately between consumers and lenders and to encourage both to protect card systems, Massachusetts limited cardholder liability to $100. In theory, consumers, facing $100 liability, had a significant incentive to report missing cards to issuers, after which they were not liable for further charges. The law also deterred reckless card solicitation, since it shifted the risk of mail theft squarely onto banks.[21]

Proxmire also heard from federal bank officials, who created and enforced regulatory standards, and from bankers, who had to abide by them. Brimmer echoed the findings of the Fed's report. Focusing on banks' mailing of cards without prior credit checks, Proxmire asked: did the Fed want authority to create minimum standards of creditworthiness for unsolicited card recipients? Brimmer demurred. Such authority was unnecessary. Thomas L. Bailey, vice president of Marine Midland Bank, responded more forcefully. Bailey's bank had provided the Fed with its most systematic evidence for unsolicited mailing's effectiveness (the fact that Midland had built the nation's second largest card plan before 1966, without unsolicited mailing, went unremarked).[22] "Problems associated with the mailing of credit cards are being solved by the banks themselves," Bailey assured the subcommittee. Like banning unsolicited mailing, fixing credit standards would only create a "competitive disadvantage" for banks not already in the market. Although they agreed about the efficacy of competition, Brimmer and Bailey disagreed about consumer liability for lost or stolen cards. Brimmer endorsed legislation to limit consumer card liability: "The liability on the customer should be small, inasmuch as the issuers are better able to bear the losses and control them." Banks' policies on fraud losses were designed in consumers' interests, Bailey countered, and state laws could provide adequate protection. Consumers could also look to the market: "Low-cost credit card insurance is available to holders of all types of credit cards," Bailey observed.[23]

Following the hearings, Proxmire drafted legislation designed to protect consumers from the most harmful aspects of unsolicited card mailing without erecting insurmountable barriers to bank card competition. The bill, which Proxmire introduced with ten cosponsors in January 1969, required the Fed to set guidelines for unsolicited card mailing, including credit checking procedures. It also included a limited cardholder liability provision, as pioneered in Massachusetts. Proxmire incorporated his unsolicited mailing bill into a comprehensive strategy, which he explained in *Banking* in April 1969. Card mailing, as testimony before both Patman's and Proxmire's committees revealed, threatened consumers' credit ratings. Impugned credit, in turn, denied consumers access to basic credit citizenship. Proxmire introduced a separate bill, the Fair Credit Reporting Act, to authorize consumers to access their credit reports and "protect themselves against arbitrary, erroneous, and malicious credit information." As with Truth-in-Lending, Proxmire believed that informed consumers could make competitive markets work better, without questioning the fundamental premise of credit-financed social policy. He also recognized the growing popularity of pro-consumer politics. Proxmire introduced a "whole series of consumer protection bills," complained Wallace Bennett, Proxmire's perpetual opponent on the Banking Committee, "whose real purpose is not consumer protection but Proxmire election."[24]

The Credit Control Act

As card regulation gained momentum in congress, national credit markets remained unsettled. The card debate dovetailed into wider concern about how to ensure that the financial system supported national policy goals without causing inflation. By the late 1960s, the U.S. economy had never been stronger. Businesses continued to invest, especially in new, high-tech industries. Government spending, through Lyndon Johnson's Great Society programs and the escalating war in Vietnam, remained high. On the back of this stimulus, the unemployment rate fell below 4 percent in February 1966. It remained there until the end of the decade. Robust economic activity, however, fueled inflation and continued financial disruption—what economist Hyman Minsky termed the "transition to turbulence and fragility." Inflation, held to just below 3 percent in 1966 and 1967, jumped to 4.2 percent in 1968, and to 5.4 percent in 1969. Rising prices and tight monetary policy stoked rising interest rates. Markets for home mortgages, municipal bonds, and other priorities remained, in Minsky's polite phrase, "disorganized." Republican Richard M. Nixon, elected president in November 1968, shared his predecessors' commitment to low-cost finance, especially for the Silent Majority's suburban mortgages. Yet Nixon offered little new policy substance. He filled his administration's core economic posts with bankers, including Continental's president David Kennedy as Treasury secretary. Administration officials, in turn, sought vague regulatory "flexibility" to better nudge capital to and fro. Like Dwight Eisenhower, Nixon also organized a presidential commission to study the financial system. In the meantime, he left the difficult credit allocation decisions to Congress and the Federal Reserve, which continued to pull markets in competing directions.[25]

After the 1968 election, Democrats maintained control of Congress and the legislative agenda. Without administration guidance, lawmakers struggled to cope with rising credit prices. The New Dealers designed their financial reforms in the 1930s to bring idle credit into circulation. In the early postwar years, national expectations solidified in an environment of inexpensive and abundant credit. Now, the nation's social priorities and credit-dependent interest groups remained. Indeed, they expanded as Congress made new promises of mortgage access to Black Americans in the 1968 Housing Act. Credit, however, had become expensive and scarce. The political task of balancing competing interests grew more onerous. In early 1969, lawmakers sought to shift some responsibility onto the administration, offering Nixon unprecedented financial power. The Credit Control Act (CCA), advanced by Proxmire in the Senate and Patman in the House, authorized peacetime credit controls similar to those actively employed in other developed economies. Whenever the president determined controls were necessary for "preventing or controlling inflation," he could authorize the Federal Reserve "to regulate and control any or all extensions of credit." Republicans, led by Nixon, objected to new power that "the administration did not request and does not desire." Democrats, however, viewed controls as necessary for mediating inflation, rising interest rates, and social priorities. A House report stated the matter clearly. "The unrestricted extension of particular forms of credit in excessive volume, based only on the highest interest rate creditors can obtain not only raises the level of interest rates" but also distorts "the whole credit picture. Short of direct lending by government itself, there is no mechanism available for channeling credit into those activities which national policy requires." Lawmakers could not contemplate direct government lending. Under the still dominant New Deal framework, private lenders, whether enticed or coerced, were responsible for directing credit toward the public good.[26]

In their fight against rising prices and expensive credit, congressional Democrats believed credit controls and a mass-mailing ban would work in tandem. By putting millions of cards into consumer hands, unsolicited mailing pressured small businesses to accept bank credit, raising their costs. At the same time, small business owners had to pay higher rates on business loans, meaning they paid bankers more to stock their shelves *and* to sell their goods. Higher credit prices, plus high credit card service costs, meant higher consumer prices. Some Democratic lawmakers hoped the administration would use the Credit Control Act to restrain inflationary consumer borrowing. "I am sure," Leonor Sullivan contended, "most Americans would be willing to forego or postpone some unnecessary purchases." Days before Congress enacted the CCA, Proxmire likewise expressed outrage at the inflationary behavior of card-issuing banks. "It is ironic," the senator inveighed, "that in these inflationary times commercial banks continue to send out still more credit cards urging the consumer to buy more at a time of 18 percent-a-year interest." Proxmire urged fellow lawmakers to "bring unsolicited credit cards under control." Despite his reservations, Nixon considered invoking credit control authority but ultimately declined. The authority, though, remained available. In time, one of Nixon's successors would use it to bring cards to heel.[27]

Proxmire Takes Charge

Congressional inaction on unsolicited mailing opened the door for consumer advocates elsewhere in the federal government. In May 1969, the Federal Trade Commission (FTC) entered the fray, announcing a proposed rule barring unsolicited card mailing. Paul Rand Dixon, a former counsel for the Senate Antitrust and Monopoly Subcommittee, headed the FTC. Appointed by John F. Kennedy in 1961, Dixon transformed the commission from a lethargic patronage repository into an alert consumer watchdog. Although consumer advocates like Ralph Nader criticized the agency for inaction, in the 1960s Dixon expanded its autonomy and ambitions. The agency issued important consumer rules, including on cigarette labeling, and it had sought authority to craft Truth-in-Lending guidelines. Action on unsolicited mailing reflected the agency's new assertiveness. It also revealed the growing scope of consumer anger: the FTC received more than one thousand consumer complaints about the deluge of credit cards arriving in their mail. Yet the agency's proposed rule also threatened to create a major disparity. The FTC could not regulate banks, and its rule, ironically, would advantage bankers over retail and other card issuers.[28]

Despite these potential problems, the Nixon administration supported FTC action. Like Kennedy and Johnson, Nixon embraced emergent consumer politics, recognizing, as his Democratic rivals had, consumerism's strong pull in the affluent suburbs. To this end, Nixon appointed Robert Meade director of legislative affairs for the President's Committee on Consumer Interests, replacing Betty Furness as the White House's consumer liaison to Congress. Before his appointment, Meade had headed the Massachusetts attorney general's Consumer Protection Division, where he had enforced the state's Truth-in-Lending law and other consumer financial protections. Meade was exceptionally qualified to address unsolicited mailing. At FTC hearings in September 1969, Meade argued that consumers were justifiably concerned about card mailing on two counts: first, "the [moral] principle involved," and, second, "the direct problem of jeopardy to his credit rating." Meade made the administration's position clear: "unsolicited credit card mailings should be prohibited." Although the FTC could not regulate banks, Meade was not deterred. "Strong Federal Trade Commission regulation," he argued, would "prompt hearings on the practice as carried out by establishments not under FTC jurisdiction." Strong FTC regulation would force Congress to act.[29]

Retailers and other card issuers decried the FTC rule, especially since bankers' recklessness had sparked the public outcry. After describing Montgomery Ward's rigorous credit screening and fraud prevention procedures, the department store's representative argued, "The banks . . . have drawn the most attention and been subjected to the greatest criticism." Yet, "under the proposed rule, banks . . . are, with impunity, free to engage in mass mailings of unsolicited credit cards." Bankers, "as a matter of principle," also opposed the FTC's rule. In letters and testimony, they uniformly invoked the Federal Reserve's conclusion that generating a viable customer base required mass card mailing. Bankers downplayed consumer concerns and took little responsibility for problems, like card fraud, caused by unsolicited mailing. Instead, they blamed the Post Office, arguing that postal officials were not doing enough to protect the mail. Fed officials continued to support the bankers. Speaking before a banking group two week after the FTC hearings, Brimmer insisted again that federal bank examiners, informed by the task force study, were guiding bank managers to adopt appropriate practices. The invisible work of bank oversight, though, offered small defense against the growing consumer outcry.[30]

Members of Congress recognized the implications of FTC action and, concurrent with the agency's hearings, moved to address card mailing. The

House Postal Subcommittee, which led the regulatory effort in that chamber, focused not on banning unsolicited mailing outright but on requiring firms to send cards by registered mail. The subcommittee pursued this approach in light of its ongoing efforts to regulate another form of unwanted mail: pornographic solicitations. Throughout the late 1960s, the subcommittee held constant hearings on the "Offensive Intrusion of Sexually Oriented Mail." Pornographers, the committee learned, bought consumer lists from companies that specialized in mass-mail marketing and widely distributed explicit advertisements, hoping for a small but profitable uptake. These practices were not exclusive to porn: consumer information, compiled, categorized, and sold by mass mailing firms, facilitated an onslaught of direct mail advertising. American consumers were drowning in junk mail; pornography was merely the most contemptable case. Banks, buying lists and mailing cards, operated a similar model. Although the subcommittee heard many of the concerns raised during the Patman, Proxmire, and FTC hearings—card mailing encouraged "families to go too deeply into debt" and facilitated "criminal activities"—members invariably read unsolicited cards through the lens of porn. One subcommittee member criticized the "promiscuous use of credit cards." Another warned that "the mailing of unsolicited credit cards is much more serious and sometimes more unsettling than pornography." This rhetoric paralleled fears of credit temptation, but more specifically it reflected concerns about consumers' rights to privacy. Firms surveilled and commodified consumer households. They sold private information to other businesses, which invaded private space with unwelcome solicitations.[31]

Because Postal Subcommittee members conceptualized pornographic and card mailings as parallel problems, they applied the subcommittee's same regulatory approach to both. In 1967, Congress authorized consumers to insulate their households from "erotically arousing or sexually provocative" mail by prohibiting senders from mailing to them. Mass-mailing firms, however, challenged the law on free speech and other constitutional grounds. With the outcome uncertain, lawmakers pivoted and sought to make pornographic mailing "economically unfeasible," requiring advertisers to use more expensive registered mail. The subcommittee applied this approach to cards, while also requiring card-bearing envelopes to read "unsolicited credit card—addressee may refuse," enabling recipients to reject cards outright. Competition shaped this approach as well. Informed consumers could shield their households from unwanted intrusion without shutting down card marketing entirely.[32]

When the subcommittee met in November 1969, administration witnesses urged an outright prohibition of unsolicited card mailing. Robert Meade repeated his concerns about morality and consumer risks. Registered mail failed to address these problems. Speaking for the administration, Meade explained, "We believe that the most effective solution . . . would be . . . restrict[ing] the mailing of unsolicited credit cards without exception." Seymour Rotker, a Bronx district attorney, along with the Post Office general counsel and chief postal inspector, shared Meade's concerns. Rotker and the postal officials had been policing card fraud since mass mailing began in 1966. They had cooperated with card issuers, identified best mailing practices, and built lines of communication with bankers. Nevertheless, banks appeared willing to accept fraud losses to the extent that the costs required to prevent fraud were greater than the losses themselves. Banks, though, did not bear costs alone. Private actions necessarily placed demands on public resources, especially on the Postal Inspection Service, which investigated and prosecuted credit card crime. Bankers continued to reject calls for regulation, now with vehemence. Representing the Midwest Bank Card System—the network of Chicago banks responsible for the 1966 fiasco—Earl Pollock challenged every critique leveled against banks' mailing campaigns as he sought to shift blame from banks to the government. The imposition of an unsolicited mailing ban, Pollock insisted, "would represent simply a tacit admission that the Post Office Department is incapable of safely transporting such mail." Subcommittee members objected to Pollock's charge. The hearings dissolved in acrimony.[33]

Before the House Postal Subcommittee finished its work—it held additional hearings in early 1970—Proxmire convened hearings to consider his unsolicited mailing bill. The FTC ban worried Proxmire. He continued to believe that transparent, competitive markets best served consumers. A ban would protect banks that had used unsolicited mailing to build large customer bases; it would reward bad behavior with monopoly power. Proxmire and ally Thomas McIntyre struggled to balance protection and competition. The senators tested different ideas on a parade of consumer, agency, and industry witnesses. They suggested mandating a "positive pre-mailer," a solicitation that would require a consumer to mail back an acceptance before an offered card was issued. They considered requiring issuers who had already used unsolicited mailing to renew these cards at consumer request. There was no middle ground. Consumer advocates demanded an outright ban. Banks and retailers pushed the subcommittee to avoid regulations altogether.[34]

Proxmire scheduled additional hearings for Friday, December 5, but Senate Republicans employed an archaic procedural rule that prohibited committees from meeting while the full Senate was in session. As they had with Truth-in-Lending, Senate Republicans resisted Proxmire's efforts. They knew the issue was too popular to vote against and hoped that, through delay, they would never have to vote at all. Proxmire outflanked them, taking the unusual step of convening hearings on Sunday, when the Senate was out of session. Wallace Bennett, the subcommittee's ranking Republican, "almost fell out of his chair." As Ken McLean, the committee's professional staff member, recalled: "A hearing on Sunday! . . . He thought this was sacrilegious." Proxmire opened proceedings with a moment of silent prayer to appease those with religious sentiments. He then got down to business. The FTC and postal hearings had generated significant media attention. Congress, the administration, and federal agencies appeared ready to converge on significant card regulation. Proxmire had the spotlight. As McLean recalled, "It was a Sunday, so it was the only game in town . . . there were dozens of reporters . . . and TV cameras." Proxmire and McLean would not waste the opportunity. They had a surprise in store. But before they could spring it, the Nixon administration delivered a surprise of its own.[35]

Meade appeared first and initially offered unremarkable testimony. He began as he had with the FTC and the House Postal Subcommittee, recounting the importance of consumer credit in the economy and the sudden recent rise of the bank card industry. He repeated his objections to unsolicited card mailing. He assured that "the problem is one which is most appropriate for Federal Regulation." Previously, however, Meade had called for restricting unsolicited card mailing "without exception." Now he urged a "limited prohibition on the mailing of unsolicited cards." Previously he had known what regulatory actions to take. Now he asked for time to study which method would be most appropriate. Proxmire was incensed. "You apparently have changed your position," he snapped after Meade delivered his statement. "This seems," Proxmire continued, "to be a program of delay."[36]

Meade was in a tough spot, and not one of his making. In the weeks prior to the hearings, Meade had requested clearance from the Nixon administration to send Congress a strong consumer bill restricting unsolicited mailing, requiring accepted cards be sent by registered mail, and limiting consumer liability for unauthorized card use. As Meade explained when he presented his plan, "Point is: Administration has taken position favoring restrictive feature of" the House Postal Subcommittee bill, and "will be required to take position on liability feature in [Proxmire's bill] S. 721. Since the Administration will be thus committed anyway, and since this is a persistently high consumer frustration, we believe Administration should go ahead and introduce its own bill." Instead of cementing Nixon's pro-consumer stance, Meade's memo focused critics and turned the administration against the legislation. In the internal debates, the Council of Economic Advisers attacked both the unsolicited mailing restriction and the limitations on consumer liability. The Commerce Department also objected and suggested rolling study of card mailing into the National Commission on Consumer Finance, a body authorized by the Truth-in-Lending Act. Doing so would let the administration capture the issue and control its outcome. Although administration officials initially decided they "could afford to support the consumerists on this one," more important interests intervened. Meade, to that point a forceful advocate for consumer protection, would have to take a different tack.[37]

Sitting across the committee room from Meade, Proxmire did not know that an earlier failure of communication within the White House had led Meade to slow walk the legislative process. Meade's flip, though, was emblematic of the very challenges Congress faced: Nixon administration officials had no idea what to do about credit cards. They wanted time to strike the right balance between regulation and competition, and they wanted to capture the political credit for protecting consumers.

Proxmire would give them neither. Before the hearing, McLean had handed Proxmire an unsolicited card the senator had received from the North Carolina National Bank, along with a large pair of scissors. As he admonished Meade for flip-flopping, Proxmire pulled out the card and began cutting it into pieces. "This is a difficult process," the senator observed, "I imagine some consumers of the fair sex might have difficulty cutting up this credit card." Proxmire, scissors drawn, appeared on the front page of the *New York Times*. News accounts reported the administration's change in policy, though they were more concerned with the testimony that organized criminal groups were paying top dollar for lost or stolen cards. Ultimately, by December 1969 a reinforcing momentum had developed. Consumer activists fought for financial safety, members of Congress sought to capture a popular issue, new banks joined the card market and mailed out more cards, criminals developed ingenious strategies to profit from ill-gotten cards, and the media breathlessly sensationalized the consumer risks and household dangers. Banker arguments that cards were a welcome innovation collapsed.[38]

Proxmire moved quickly. In early February 1970, he convened his subcommittee to advance his bill. The legislation charged the Federal Reserve with creating unsolicited mailing standards, with guidelines to "determine the creditworthiness of the prospective recipient." The bill also incorporated a $50 cardholder liability limit modeled on Massachusetts law, which shifted most fraud risk from consumers to card issuers. Bennett, the indefatigable opponent of Truth-in-Lending, objected that strict regulation would hamper the long-term development of credit card technology. "Looking down the line . . . the combination of the credit card and the computer is going to represent the basis of our accounting between companies and individuals and banks," he predicted. With encouragement, a private infrastructure of cards and computers would propel American enterprise. He pled for his colleagues to embrace innovation instead of being "overconcerned about making it difficult for people to get credit cards." Bennett spoke to Proxmire's bill, but he was anticipating an amendment from McIntyre, who sought to align the legislation with the FTC's mailing ban. Before they could take action, a floor vote interrupted the meeting, pushing the decision to the full committee.[39]

When the Senate Banking Committee met on February 26, 1970, Bennett and his Republican colleagues were unprepared. Coaxed by the administration, Republicans had drafted a counterproposal that sought to legislate simple mailing rules rather than empowering the Fed to write regulations. They planned to authorize "negative pre-mailers," to notify consumers that an unsolicited card would come, unless they responded declining the offer. The minority staff had secured administration approval, but when they consulted with industry representatives, the lobbyists objected. The proposal "would kill them," they warned. A staff lawyer pulled an all-nighter redrafting. "There are all kinds of cards out there," Bennett discovered. Republicans—and indeed most committee members—had ignored the issue. Now they had no constructive proposals to offer. Only in the final negotiations did

some senators bother to pull cards out of their wallets, read the relevant liability provisions, and ask basic questions about how the card systems worked.
Proxmire and McIntyre, lawmakers who built expertise and cultivated support, controlled the process.[40]

Still, the committee understood that either McIntyre's or Bennett's proposal would replace Proxmire's. The Fed's reluctance to accept rulemaking
responsibility, combined with a preference for statute over agency regulation, convinced the senators to support statutory restrictions. By moving
away from Proxmire's proposal, the committee foreclosed a novel regulatory
path. Proxmire intended for the Fed to set minimum credit standards for
card recipients. "We had good testimony . . . that these credit cards have
come into the hands of people who have either erratic or low income and
poor credit records who have gone into bankruptcy because they have run up
enormous bills," Proxmire reminded the committee. Under Proxmire's proposal, the federal government, rather than private lenders, would establish
the lower boundary for card access. The law would protect "the Georgia jani-
tor who ran up $3,000 in bills in less than a week" by closing him—and with
him a large class of low-income and minority borrowers—out of card markets. State interest rate and consumer liability limits had similar effects. Yet
under these rules, private firms still struck the balance between risk, price,
and creditworthiness. Lenders decided who would access credit, even as the
legal system invisibly structured who could meet private credit standards.
Alarmed at the rising toll of consumer bankruptcy that followed from channeling prosperity through credit markets, Proxmire proposed shifting this
decision from private lenders to a public agency. Perhaps Proxmire's policy
would have made the government's role more visible and contestable, but
his committee favored shifting risk within ostensibly private markets rather
than asserting public power. They adopted McIntyre's unsolicited mailing
ban along party lines.[41]

The Senate began the carefully choreographed movement of Proxmire's
bill in April 1970. In the sweep toward passage, lawmakers advanced two
major changes. First, Harrison "Pete" Williams (D-NJ), supported by Republican Banking Committee members, sought to fix the committee's awkward
effort to preserve competition. McIntyre's amendments required all cards
issued through unsolicited mailings to be reissued in line with the new
rules. Concerned that the renewal provision would cause "confusion and

inconvenience," Williams and his cosponsors urged that cards already accepted by consumers be eligible for automatic renewal. Although automatic renewal would advantage firms that had already used unsolicited mailing, Williams insisted that this outcome was preferable to the "undue burdens" businesses and consumers would experience if every credit card had to be replaced. Second, Russell Long (D-LA), advanced an amendment making credit card fraud a federal crime. Fraud sat outside the Banking Committee's jurisdiction, and members expressed concern about adding a criminal statute that they had not considered in hearings. They were satisfied, however, that the issue could be worked out in conference with the House. The Senate unanimously adopted the amendments and the measure passed 79 to 1. The House, meanwhile, continued working on its own legislation requiring card issuers to use registered mail. When the bill came to the floor in September, some House members contrasted their registered mail approach with the Senate's mailing ban, arguing that registered mail was a better solution to the problem of competition. Others argued that, in light of the FTC ban, "permitting continued mailing of unsolicited cards if they are sent registered mail no longer makes sense." How many of the 380 other House members who voted for the bill felt the same way is unclear, but none voted against it.[42]

The conference committee, composed of members of both chambers' Banking Committees, met in October and largely adopted the Senate bill. The only change was an amendment that limited criminal penalties for use of illegally obtained cards to cases involving amounts of $5,000 or more. The high threshold was necessary, Proxmire explained, because "the Justice Department felt such a provision would be extremely costly to administer." The Senate adopted the bill by voice vote on October 9, 1970. Leonor Sullivan introduced the conference report to the House. Although she noted the House conference committee members' discomfort with adopting the Senate's liability provisions, since they had not been considered by the full House, she insisted that the issue had been thoroughly examined by the House Banking Committee. Action was necessary, she argued. House members could take it in good conscience. The House adopted the conference bill by voice vote on October 13, 1970. President Nixon signed the bill on October 26. Members of Congress took the bill home to their districts just in time for the midterm elections. Proxmire bragged in his constituent newsletter that

"Prox Makes Triple Play for Consumers." The purpose of his bills was both consumer protection *and* Proxmire election.[43]

Bankers predicted Armageddon, but Congress's unsolicited mailing ban proved a godsend to the industry. Bankers had eagerly embraced credit cards as a road to the future, one that led out of the New Deal's price controls and geographic confines. But that road also led into a tempest of competition and spiraling costs, one that, with their experience within tightly regulated local markets, bankers were ill-prepared for. By 1970, they were ready to call a truce. By then the burst of unsolicited mailing had done its work, establishing card plans for individual banks and the nationwide bank card market. "There is much more of an awareness of the public about credit cards," Marine Midland's Thomas Bailey testified in December 1969. Consumers could now be solicited without "automatically sending out cards." When bank cards were new, bankers believed they needed unsolicited mailing to convince consumers to take up an unfamiliar financial product, but once the industry was established, card mailings were unnecessary. Bankers settled into maintaining and gradually expanding their card programs, while weeding out delinquent borrowers. Credit card debt grew by 20 percent a year from 1970 to 1976, by which time BankAmericard and Master Charge together claimed 100 million active cardholders. In the mid-1970s, when cards next became an object of congressional attention, lawmakers sought to extend these numbers to include women and minority groups, who were still excluded from full credit citizenship. By that time credit access, rather than credit prices, was the dominant policy paradigm, in large measure because credit prices were rigorously controlled by states.[44]

Congress adopted the unsolicited mailing ban and associated consumer protections at a moment of wider turmoil for the postwar financial system. "We are closer to a crisis than at any time since 1933," Treasury secretary and former Continental Illinois banker David Kennedy wrote President Nixon in December 1969. The credit crunches of 1966 and 1969 revealed that the system of geographic restrictions, industry silos, and price controls were under tremendous pressure as financial firms struggled to find profit in a system racked by inflation. Congress was racked by its own divisions. New Deal liberals favored reinforcing the system of government controls. Postwar Liberals were willing to consider market-based solutions. Republicans, ever the minority, favored greater liberalization, but like their Democratic peers, they faced powerful industry constituencies seeking to retain their advantages within the thicket of financial rules. In this environment, Congress was only capable of patchwork, ad hoc policies. The Credit Control Act was one of those. David Kennedy called it "a very bad piece of legislation." Nixon reluctantly signed it and declined to use its authority. A decade later, President Jimmy Carter, operating in similarly troubled financial circumstances, dusted it off. One legacy of this moment was a policy tool that Carter, driven by impulses similar to those that led lawmakers to label credit cards financial pornography in the 1960s, would use to orchestrate his own countermovement against the credit card economy in 1980. By then, though, it would be too late.[45]

Indeed, because the credit card debates largely occurred within the framework of consumerism, lawmakers—Wright Patman and Wallace Bennett perhaps excluded—did not consider how card technology and newly expansive credit networks were reshaping the banking industry. Cards, like banks, seemed bound in regulatory space. Lawmakers—and indeed most bankers—believed that cards complemented local banking relationships, drawing cardholders into bank offices, where they might deposit money or take out a mortgage. The unsolicited mailing ban reinforced this connection—and with it, the place-based social contract. The mailing ban made it harder for banks to reach beyond their existing markets. In concert with the Truth-in-Lending Act and state interest rate ceilings, the legislation legitimized the bank card industry by regulating it, in effect binding credit cards within postwar liberalism's regime of (relatively) low-cost, safe consumer credit. Cards, like other areas of closely governed bank lending, were unlikely to generate significant profits. Bankers, however, had gotten into the card business to break free of the New Deal order's onerous restrictions; some would continue to seek and seize opportunities to innovate around the rules.

7

Risk Shifting

Fraud Means Movement

In June 1970, the radical magazine *Scanlan's Monthly* ran a feature article, "How to Counterfeit Credit Cards and Get Away with It." The timing was opportune. Over the previous half decade, the card market had grown feverishly. Gasoline, airline, and travel firms had expanded their programs, and hundreds of banks entered the market frantic to reach consumer-borrowers. To the dismay of card issuers, loosely organized networks just as rapidly developed parallel, illicit markets in stolen and counterfeit cards, building on established fraudulent practices and crafting new, card-specific schemes. *Scanlan's* offered readers a piece of that action. The article's protagonist, "Todd," detailed various cons a "passer" could use to turn stolen credit into ready cash. Fraudulent practices required sophisticated knowledge. "I know how the cards work," Todd bragged. Todd's schemes all hinged on a simple strategy: making moderate purchases with cards issued by out-of-state firms. This way, Todd confided, even if he was caught red-handed, the cost of prosecution was not worth the time or expense for the card issuer or local law enforcement. Todd knew how policing worked too. With that knowledge, the street-smart fraudster would seldom lose.[1]

Card issuers had always been concerned about fraud, but in the late 1960s swindlers like Todd threatened to overwhelm the nation's expanding credit networks. Card firms quickly turned to government for help. Like credit regulation, criminal policing remained primarily a state responsibility within the federalist system. Most states had enacted basic card fraud laws in the 1950s. These statutes reached only a limited range of fraudulent actions, however, and state policing did not easily extend beyond state borders. As card networks expanded nationally, and as criminal knowledge spread with them, card firms faced a fraud problem that exceeded the capacities of individual states. Seeking a greater quotient of government power, card issuers turned to Congress. They lobbied for a federal "law with teeth." Federal officials, however, were not keen to serve as nationwide card police. Card firms, officials argued, placed marketing and convenience above system safety. As cards increased exponentially, so did card fraud, a prosecutorial burden that threatened to overwhelm federal resources. The Department of Justice was eager to pass.[2]

Lawmakers and law enforcement officials necessarily weighed governments' responsibilities for protecting credit markets against preserving limited public resources when private firms ought to protect themselves. As card firms sought to privatize the payment system, transitioning consumers from public cash and semi-public checks to private plastic, card networks needed to be secure to be legitimate. Card firms, consumers, and government officials all negotiated the boundaries of card crime and the responsibilities for system security, with each group seeking to imprint their interests in the structure of nationwide card markets. Consumers and their advocates bundled fraud protection within their larger demands for market safety, which included restrictions on interest rates and aggressive marketing practices. Card firms had placed liability for fraudulent card use on consumers to encourage consumers to protect their cards. Consumers resisted this responsibility and sought to renegotiate their card contracts through the political process. Card issuers could generate profits only through secure networks, yet security was expensive. If pursued too vigorously, it could make credit inconvenient. Card issuers needed to socialize the cost of policing by harnessing governments' policing power; they needed to disassociate card purchasing from fraud punishment by outsourcing security to government actors; and they needed fraudsters thrown in prison. Thus, even as card firms sought to limit government oversight of their relationships with consumers, they sought active government partnerships to punish illegitimate card users. They wanted the feds to do their dirty work.[3]

Ultimately, at both the state and federal levels, legislatures responded by undertaking a two-part risk shift: lawmakers shifted fraud risk from

consumers to card issuers by limiting cardholder liability, and they shifted
fraud policing from issuers to the state through more comprehensive card
fraud statutes. Travel card firms, like American Express, had hoped for more.
Led by Amex, card issuers promoted state-level card fraud legislation by at-
taching their project to the politically salient War on Crime. Yet reckless bank
card mailings undercut the industry's claims of vigilance, increasing momentum for consumer protection. By 1970, when Congress enacted legislation
containing both limited liability and a new federal card fraud law, risk shifting
offered a workable compromise. This compromise proved short-lived: fraudsters and their attorneys undercut the expansion of federal policing by asserting their rights through the courts. They rendered the hastily drawn federal
law practically unenforceable while also hamstringing existing federal tools
for combating organized card fraud rings. In the 1974 case, *U.S. v. Maze*, the
Supreme Court sharply curtailed the federal policing role, cementing fraud
prosecution in the states even as card networks continued to expand beyond
state borders. Despite card issuers' best efforts, through the 1970s the safety
of their card plans rested on the uncertain protection of state law.[4]

Beginning in the mid-1960s, bankers had grasped credit cards as a means
of innovating around the New Deal's restrictive financial rules, especially
state-level limits on the scope of banking markets and the prices banks could
charge consumers. Even as bankers used financial technology to circumvent
existing regulations, they also sought active government intervention to
structure the new markets they were creating. Bankers and other card issuers wanted a strong state to protect their card plans. They got less than they
wanted. Nevertheless, together with the emerging consumer protection regime, federal and state card fraud legislation legitimized the national credit
card industry, backing private payment networks with state authority. Card
networks became embedded in the fragmented institutions—state and federal; legislative, administrative, and judicial—that structured national and
local financial markets.

From Status Stealers to Professional Criminals

During the 1960s, enterprising swindlers transformed credit card fraud
from a niche specialty into a booming business. In the previous decade, the
first generation of card crooks had primarily crafted false identities to obtain

cards from issuers and then use them to finance indulgent spending sprees. Such fraud, which harmed companies and not consumers, aligned with travel firms' marketing narrative of risqué credit practices. When the media ran breathless accounts of novel—and legal—travel card adventure, reporters often included sensational stories of fraudsters creatively bilking the card companies. In 1959, *Life* magazine profiled Joseph Miraglia, a nineteen-year-old New Yorker who financed an international spree using a clutch of ill-gotten cards. "I had collected a truckload of loot and charged almost $10,000 worth of fun," Miraglia boasted. As cards became more widespread, seasoned fraudsters learned how card systems worked. They incorporated card fraud into existing networks of criminal labor that relied on stealing consumer identities rather than fabricating them. At first, the press incorporated organized card fraud into the still jaunty narrative of fraudulent adventure. Yet mounting illicit activity soon threatened to destabilize and delegitimize the industry. New practices not only harmed card companies, as earlier crooks had by fashioning false identities, they also endangered consumers, who faced potential liability when their cards were misappropriated and misused. In response, the media narrative gradually transformed from moral ambiguity into moral panic.[5]

Entrepreneurial fraudsters developed methods of harvesting value from card systems while minimizing risk of punishment. Mirroring legitimate practices, they engaged in intricate divisions of illicit labor. First, thieves developed strategies for obtaining cards from cardholders. In an era when business and heavy drinking were close companions, traveling businessmen proved easy marks. Before the 1960s, the highwaymen and -women who targeted unwary travelers usually discarded cards they found in stolen billfolds. As card networks expanded and cards became more valuable, market signals increasingly attracted the attention of low-level criminals. Stolen cards became a commodity with a price. They could be sold up the illicit supply chain. In addition to burglars, pickpockets, and prostitutes, low-paid workers with access to cards—busboys, car attendants, hotel clerks, and waiters—might lift cards from unwary victims. "With a little help from one of the clerks," Todd explained, tourists "often forget their cards." Once banks began mailing millions of unsolicited cards, mail theft became easier still.[6]

Thieves passed cards into the illicit supply chain by selling to a "fence," a dealer in stolen goods, who commodified, bundled, and distributed them.

Pimps or dishonest barkeeps took this role; Todd "bought three wallets from a pimp named Joey," paying "a hundred a piece." Fences made markets, mediating a price hierarchy that reflected cards' value in the legitimate economy. Affluent travel cards and airline cards, with the highest credit limits and inherent mobility, commanded the highest prices. Bank cards, with lower credit limits, were less valuable. Department store and gasoline cards might be bartered or tossed in for free. In all cases, the physical plastic remained necessary. Fraudsters could not yet make cards themselves—their industry was distribution, not manufacturing. Timing also mattered. Cards needed to be "fresh," recently stolen. "Hot" cards, long on the lam, were more likely to appear on a company's stolen card list, increasing the risk of detection.[7]

When a passer like Todd obtained the cards, many profitable opportunities opened. Todd described using bank cards to obtain cash advances, small swindles that netted several thousand dollars. "Jesse James," he bragged, "without a gun." Most fraudsters bought goods, which they either kept or sold back into the underground economy. Here again, criminals incorporated cards into established practices of acquisitive crime, like passing bad checks, which all became more common as inflation cut into consumer purchasing power. From 1960 to 1965, consumer prices increased 1.3 percent a year on average, before accelerating at 4.3 percent a year for the remainder of the decade. Rates of acquisitive crime more than doubled from 1960 to 1970, compounding with the rise in inflation. As the cost of goods went up, many Americans were willing to sustain their faltering purchasing power off the back of a truck.[8]

Fraudsters also got creative; they innovated. By the late 1960s, card firms frequently complained about sophisticated airline ticket fraud: a swindler in Los Angeles would buy or steal several airline or travel cards and make for the airport. "There are five United Airlines clerks in a row," Todd reported. "I hit each end, buying tickets and working toward the middle." After buying fistfuls of tickets, some fraudsters hopped a plane to New York. Upon arrival, they repeated the process, buying more tickets before the issuer could freeze the account. Airline tickets were fully transferable. Crooks offloaded them through established distribution channels in the city, turning pilfered plastic into clean, untraceable cash. As syndicates became better organized, customers could order "discount" tickets in advance.[9]

Card firms expected merchants to serve as the front line of fraud defense, but some merchants colluded with fraudsters, an arrangement an American

Express security officer dubbed the "Unholy Alliance." A thief might feign to buy goods with stolen cards. The merchant would bill the card company, but no merchandise would change hands. Once the card issuer repaid the merchant for the goods they had supposedly sold, the merchant split the proceeds with the thief. In another version, which two Texas swindlers called the "split ticket," the card thief ordered a $3 cocktail from a friendly bartender, then tipped $97, which the two split. Merchant collusion wasn't always voluntary. Some merchants repaid Mafia debts by knowingly accepting stolen cards. In one scenario, known as the "bust out," mob operatives would take over a company that owed them money and use its travel and bank cards to purchase valuable merchandise and airline tickets. The firm would eventually go bankrupt, leaving its legitimate creditors with irredeemable debts.[10]

Card thieves were, in a manner of speaking, disruptive innovators who actively reordered card markets in search of illicit profits. They, too, innovated around the rules. Still, not all card crime was directed at feeding black markets or maximizing the gains from illicit trade—though industry and government sources both focused on "professional criminals . . . attracted to the credit card as a new way of making a dishonest dollar." Thieves took joy rides and racked up charges for the pleasure of consumption and status. Card fraud, in this sense, was plastic capitalism's dark mirror. Rising wages and widespread credit made affluence widely available, especially for white male breadwinners and their families. Yet the postwar political economy promised universal affluence that it did not and could not deliver. Not everyone was paid well enough to enjoy mass prosperity. Not everyone qualified for credit. Life circumstances, individual "nonconformity," and deep-rooted discrimination all barred access to consumer abundance. As the postwar commitment to consumerism made status seeking a defining feature of American life, fraudsters, to paraphrase sociologist Robert Merton, ignored socially acceptable means to attain socially approved goals. They participated in the affluent society while avoiding the debt collector. They just had to stay ahead of the law.[11]

To combat status stealers, card issuers needed to get fraud laws on the books. As with credit regulation, states oversaw most criminal lawmaking within U.S. federalism. In the 1950s, state lawmakers had discovered that card fraud did not map well onto traditional common law crimes, like fraud and embezzlement. These crimes linked deception and harm, yet card fraudsters often deceived merchants (posing as legitimate card users) but harmed card issuers (who bore the loss). Modern credit relationships did not fit squarely within inherited legal categories. With urging from local card issuers, state lawmakers developed an eclectic mix of card fraud laws. Enforcement, however, remained geographically circumscribed. Card swindlers learned, as Todd explained, that "mobility [was] crucial." State laws, an attorney for gasoline retailer Standard Oil of Ohio (SOHIO) complained in 1964, "are inadequate for use in apprehending credit card criminals, who . . . sometimes make charges in several states in a single day." To supplement state-level enforcement, card issuers turned increasingly to existing federal law and, when that failed, to Congress.[12]

In the late 1950s and early 1960s, when card fraud remained the business of individual grifters rather than organized networks, card issuers focused on the Stolen Property Act (1934), which outlawed transporting stolen "securities" across state lines. Coordinating with local U.S. attorneys, issuers argued that credit cards and the charge slips generated through card transactions both constituted "evidence of indebtedness," one category of security defined in the law. Judges, however, were not persuaded. "A credit card is nothing more," a federal court in California ruled, "than a means of identification which tells the merchant that the holder is entitled to charge merchandise. . . . It is not a 'security.'" After similar decisions eroded the theory in 1960 and 1961, a U.S. attorney confided that "the general position of the Department of Justice has been that credit cards are not covered by" the act. The Ninth Circuit, an appeals court covering much of the western United States, fully foreclosed the stolen securities argument in *Barack v. U.S.* (1963), ruling that sales slips also did not constitute securities. The decision, a Carte Blanche representative complained to House Judiciary chairman Emanuel Celler, "effectively strips our company, as well as any company issuing credit cards usable in more than one state, of all protection under Federal law."[13]

As the judicial path faded and vanished, card issuers turned to Congress, seeking to incorporate cards into the Stolen Property Act. In summer 1962, SOHIO attorney Douglas Wick contacted Frances P. Bolton (R-OH), the congresswoman who represented Cleveland's suburbs. Card fraud, Wick explained, was on the rise. Wick compiled data from gasoline and travel firms showing that fraud losses increased from $266,850 in 1958 to $1,915,556 in

1962. Wick pled for Bolton to act. Bolton took up the issue, becoming a leading crusader against interstate card fraud. Working closely with Wick, she
introduced legislation in 1962 amending the Stolen Property Act to include
cards. Despite support from card issuers and House colleagues, Bolton's
bill repeatedly stalled in Celler's Judiciary Committee, which through the
mid-1960s remained focused on civil rights legislation. In his frequent letters, Wick practically stamped the floor with impatience.[14]

Finally, in February 1966 Celler prepared to advance Bolton's bill, but a
scathing evaluation from Lyndon Johnson's Justice Department derailed the
legislation. The department, deputy attorney general Ramsey Clark explained, had adequate authority to pursue card fraud cases under the federal
mail fraud statute. Merchants, Clark argued, always mailed charge slips to
card issuers. The time delay created by mailing the slips, Clark continued,
was an essential element of any fraud scheme, since it enabled the swindler
to escape detection. Mail fraud better fit the facts. Card issuers, however,
maintained that mail fraud did not provide adequate protection. The law was
reactive, not proactive. The government could only pursue fraudsters after a
transaction had occurred and sales slips were in the mail. Federal authorities
could not track down cards that had been stolen but not yet used. Clark emphatically supported such limits. "The Department of Justice," Clark insisted, "would assume a staggering burden if it undertook to investigate all
cases of credit card misuse."[15]

Ultimately, Clark opposed card issuer efforts to shift security costs onto
the federal government because card firms engaged in reckless marketing
and credit granting. Writing before the eruption of unsolicited bank card
mailing, Clark worried that Bolton's bill would protect "credit arrangements
which are intrinsically loose and susceptible to fraud," requiring the federal
government to investigate and prosecute "the users of a credit card which is
part of a system having no effective internal safeguards." The legislation
could even be read, Clark argued, to apply to legitimate borrowers who did
not repay their debts. Card industry lobbyists disputed Clark's interpretation. "It is not the intention of credit card issuers to use the Department of
Justice as a collection agent," a Shell Oil representative responded. Nevertheless, Clark's objections killed the bill and, with it, card firms' immediate
hopes of securing federal legislation. The Justice Department believed "the
improper use of credit cards should be left for state prosecution," a resigned

Bolton explained in July 1966, "in other words, the department does not want to take on the responsibility."[16]

To be clear, the Johnson administration and Congress did not oppose expanding federal policing resources or prosecutorial authority. Rather, they focused their attention on politically salient issues, primarily organized crime and Black urban unrest, which Johnson brought together in 1965 under his War on Crime. A series of high-profile investigations by Democrats Estes Kefauver, John McClellan, and Robert Kennedy had trained national attention on organized criminal activity since the early 1950s. The waves of urban violence that accompanied the Civil Rights Movement, meanwhile, gave momentum to racialized "law and order" politics, which the Johnson administration sought to capture and redirect. Beginning in 1965, Congress significantly increased federal spending on policing, investments which would ratchet up over subsequent decades. When Clark objected to Bolton's bill in 1966, card fraud did not yet align with federal policymakers' understanding of the nation's crime problems. Individual swindlers, not organized gangs, remained the primary culprits. Likewise, credit cards remained a middle- and upper-class product. Black Americans, less likely to be legitimate card users, were less likely to be illegitimate users as well. Thus, to harness federal and state policing resources, card firms needed to make card fraud a salient political issue. As organized rings became more active in card fraud, card firms drew attention to these nascent operations, emphasizing the dangers they posed to consumers and to social order more broadly.[17]

American Express and the Return to the States

With the federal path foreclosed and card fraud mounting, American Express led the effort to secure new state-level criminal legislation. Amex cultivated a reputation for rigorous fraud policing: "From its entry into the credit card field in 1958," vice president Milton Lipson explained in the *FBI Enforcement Bulletin,* "American Express has maintained the philosophy that each and every known criminal misuser of a credit card should be arrested and prosecuted." By the mid-1960s, the firm employed more than three hundred investigators, staff recruited after an average of twenty years of law enforcement experience. Lipson, who headed corporate security, had served as a Secret Service agent in Franklin D. Roosevelt's administration and an instructor in the army and navy intelligence schools. Lipson's overriding concern was the professional criminal. "The major factor in credit card fraud losses is the professional thief," he told a meeting of police chiefs in 1969. "The amateur does not constitute a threat." By emphasizing the professional criminal, Lipson sought to shift attention to evolving card fraud practices and encourage a media narrative that tied card fraud to organized crime.[18]

Although it is difficult to disentangle panicked rhetoric from facts, organized swindlers seem to have cornered a larger share of illicit markets as the decade moved on. In cities like Los Angeles and New York, hubs of both business travel and criminal activity, legitimate and illegitimate markets converged. In Los Angeles, law enforcement observed a rapid increase of card fraud in the first half of 1966. Cards lost in the area, city police found, often turned up on the East Coast, and cards from around the country likewise ended up in Los Angeles. "A loosely-organized import-export operation is responsible," one officer reported, leading city police to establish a dedicated card fraud unit. In New York, the story was much the same. In February 1966, the Nassau County paper *Newsday* ran a three-part series, "The Hot Card Racket," documenting the movement of New York City's crime families into the card fraud business. The card industry estimated that 300,000 cards were stolen and fraudulently used each year, the paper reported, amounting to over $20 million in card issuer losses. Firms could not sustain such losses, while the growing association of cards with fraud undermined the legitimacy of the business.[19]

American Express took action in 1967. Working to provide local officials new tools to combat professional fraudsters, it assembled a staff to draft a model law. The company hired Columbia University law professors Jack B. Weinstein and Tom J. Farer, along with a research staff of twenty-five investigators, to compile and analyze all relevant federal and state-level card fraud statutes and case law.[20] The final law and accompanying report combined intellectual and—at nearly 450 pages—physical heft, reflecting the diversity of state fraud rules. Consistent with Lipson's concern with the "professional criminal," the model law, which Amex dubbed the State Credit Card Crime Act, targeted the entire fraudulent supply chain, from initial theft to ultimate card use. Weinstein and Farer gave prominent attention to such schemes as airline ticket fraud and merchant collusion. Overall, they tried to define and criminalize every card offence imaginable. Their model law incorporated a host of weighty presumptions to increase the power of state prosecutors working to protect card companies. "A person," the section on credit card theft read, "who has in his possession . . . credit cards issued in the names of two or more other persons is presumed to have violated" the law. In an era where criminals' rights received increased political and judicial attention— including, in later years, from Weinstein himself—such presumptions pushed against the tide of legal reform.[21]

With the model law drafted, American Express worked to sell state law-makers on the professional criminal narrative. The company created the National Credit Card Fraud Legislation Project (NCCFLP), headed by company attorney Guy Capel and incorporating other card issuers like Diners Club and Bank of America. The NCCFLP coordinated with state legislators and industry representatives to develop state-level policy networks that linked local lawmakers across the country. The NCCFLP initially focused on four states—California, North Carolina, Florida, and New York—but the group's goal was to enact the model bill nationwide. Given the rising prominence of professionalized card crime and the spread of law-and-order politics, Amex and its allies were right to feel optimistic.[22]

In New York, the NCCFLP partnered with Republican state senator John R. Dunne, who would play a prominent role in efforts to protect card issuers—and later consumers—from card fraud. Dunne, an attorney, won election to the New York State Senate in 1965, representing suburban Nassau County. As a first-year lawmaker looking for signature issues, card fraud drew his attention, especially after he read *Newsday*'s "Hot Credit Card Racket" series. Governor Nelson Rockefeller appointed Dunne to the state's Temporary Commission on the Revision of the Penal Law and Criminal Code (Penal Law Commission) in July 1966. Dunne, in turn, used his appointment to call for a crackdown on credit card fraud. Dunne pursued this agenda over the next several years, while *Newsday* provided continuous favorable coverage, generating a partnership between card firms, politicians, and friendly media—one which developed similarly in other states. Dunne and Capel formed a close partnership. In February 1967, Dunne introduced Amex's model bill, and in March, American Express's public relations firm organized a press conference to promote the legislation, which quickly passed the New York Senate. The Penal Law Commission, however, halted its progress. Inspired by a long-running penal reform project organized by the American Law Institute, New York undertook penal law revision to clear the detritus of old and outdated criminal law. By introducing a host of new fraud categories, the commission's chairman Richard J. Bartlett argued, Dunne's bill was counterproductive. As Bartlett told the press, "If it passes both houses and goes to the governor, we might have to take a stand." Instead, the bill died in the assembly's Rules Committee.[23]

New York was an outlier. The three other states American Express targeted (California, North Carolina, and Florida) adopted the State Credit Card Crime Act in short order. In California, John F. McCarthy, a Bay Area Republican, sponsored the law, which the legislature enacted with near unanimity. In a letter to Governor Ronald W. Reagan, McCarthy explained that the legislation was necessary because California's 1961 card fraud law had been narrowly interpreted by state courts. State prosecutors had pursued card fraud cases using both common law crimes, such as forgery, and the 1961 card fraud statute. Presaging a flaw that would later plague federal law, state courts determined that the legislature intended the card fraud law to serve as the sole vehicle for pursuing card crime, invalidating other approaches. This "grave defect," McCarthy argued, "hampered efforts of law enforcement officers and credit card issuers seeking to protect themselves against criminal activities." Reagan, a law-and-order champion, needed little convincing. He signed the California Credit Card Crime Act into law in September 1967. The legislation, the *Los Angeles Times* emphasized, was part of a national project "to obtain more or less uniform legislation throughout the country . . . aimed at curbing the activities of nationwide rings." The professional criminal had to be stopped.[24]

Dunne and his business allies prepared to push the legislation again, but they faced the persistent counterweight of criminal law reformers who opposed industry-specific crime statutes. In 1968, Dunne's bill cleared both legislative chambers, yet he failed to convince his colleagues on the Penal Law Commission. "The bill is obviously a special interest one," wrote Richard Denzer, counsel to the commission, which "seeks to attach criminal sanctions to every conceivable type of conduct relating to credit cards which its sponsors feel might be injurious to their business." Denzer was uncompromising. He eviscerated the bill, provision by provision. In his veto message, Rockefeller quoted Denzler's memo extensively. Dunne again returned to the drawing board, and in 1969 submitted a revised bill that amended existing law rather than concocting a host of new credit card crimes. He also

scheduled hearings, set to meet in February 1969, to elicit public support at
the beginning of the next legislative session. In the meantime, Massachusetts and New Jersey adopted American Express's model law, although it
failed in New Hampshire. "Possibly the basis of the bill is very good," a state
lawmaker noted, "but it had some horrible aspects to it." As ever, state lawmaking resisted uniformity.[25]

Unsolicited Mailing and On-the-Ground Enforcement

As Dunne and his allies prepared to try again, the card fraud narrative
shifted. American Express had driven the debate about card fraud in 1966
and 1967, but bankers' massive unsolicited mailing campaigns—and the
waves of fraud and consumer anxiety that accompanied them—changed the
current of conversation. Although American Express, with its three-hundred-
strong inspection force, could credibly claim to uphold security standards
even as it lobbied for more state policing, banks carelessly put consumers at
risk—and they did so while demanding government protection, calls that
taxed law enforcement resources and ultimately alienated would-be allies.
Federal officials who worked with banks to prosecute card fraud rings quickly
became vocal critics of banks' reckless marketing practices.[26]

In New York, Citibank initiated the state's first major unsolicited mailing
campaign, one that was, from the outset, plagued by theft and fraud. Citi
launched its "Everything" credit card in 1967 by mailing one million cards to
New York consumers. As executive John Reynolds later explained, thieves
quickly discovered that stealing cards from the mail was easier than stealing
them from cardholder wallets. The bank had enrolled hundreds of merchants to accept the cards, many of whom proved less than trustworthy. By
February 1968, fraudsters had used eighteen "Everything" cards to make
$80,000 in illicit charges in Bronx County alone, numbers that rose to sixty
cards and $125,000 two months later. When Citi executives discovered the
scale of their fraud problems, they enlisted the Bronx district attorney. The
DA had experience with card fraud and had been investigating Unholy Alliance collusion between gas stations and card crooks since 1966, pursuing
cases under the federal mail fraud statute. In Citibank's case, assistant district attorney Seymor Rotker later explained, officials arrested and charged
eighteen individuals and five store owners with illegal card use, all of whom,

investigators believed, had ties to organized crime. Although Rotker acknowledged Citibank's assistance, he attributed the scale of the fraud to the
bank's recklessness, especially cards "which were mailed unsolicited." Protecting card companies from their own strategies, Rotker explained, required
"many man hours," detracting from scarce law enforcement resources that
could be better employed elsewhere.[27]

Even with the Bronx DA's help, Citibank endured almost $3 million in
fraud losses in 1968, figures bank executives attributed to Mafia infiltration of
the postal service in New York City. Anticipating similar losses in 1969, Citi
executives approached Emanuel Celler, whose congressional district covered
parts of Brooklyn and Queens. The bank sought not legislation but influence.
Local postal authorities were not taking card fraud seriously, Citi executives
complained. They hoped the powerful Judiciary chairman would intercede.[28]

When Celler made inquiries on Citibank's behalf, he encountered concerns like those expressed earlier by Ramsey Clark: federal officials were
frustrated that card issuers demanded protection even as their credit systems
lacked effective safeguards. Celler called on chief postal inspector William
Cotter. Initially, Cotter determined that the Brooklyn Post Office lacked sufficient inspector manpower, and he assigned a special task force to address
New York's security problems. Postal inspectors made quick progress, ar-
resting and charging two mail carriers accused of stealing Citibank cards.
Still, Citibank vice chairman Thomas Wilcox told Celler, "We continue to
face monthly fraud losses at an unacceptable level." Cotter now objected. Citi
and other banks had brought the fraud problems on themselves. When they
saturated the mail with what Cotter described as "'attractive' letters," the
postal service struggled to protect the public and the banks. Writing to Celler,
Cotter explained that "the continuing mass mailings . . . together with the
increasing general crime rate . . . are imposing heavy and increasing demands on Postal Inspector manpower." While Citi's security personnel were
eager to work alongside state and federal authorities, law enforcement officials struggled under the added workload. The story repeated itself across the
country. In 1964, before mass mailings began, the Postal Inspection Service
investigated only 15 cases of mail theft and fraud involving credit cards. By
the end of 1970, the service had completed 754 mail fraud investigations and
had 1,048 more underway. The attractive letters had unattractive consequences for thinly stretched federal investigators.[29]

Risk Shifting

In Albany, when Dunne convened hearings in February 1969 on his card fraud bill, unsolicited bank cards topped the agenda. First, Dunne focused on the challenges fraud posed for card issuers. In this vein, Citibank vice president John Reynolds invoked the specter of the Mafia, concerns echoed by representatives from the travel card, airline, and gasoline industries. Dunne's views, though, were evolving. "During the course of our study," Dunne later explained to a congressional committee, "an avalanche of new credit cards— the bank credit card, in particular—appeared throughout the state, bringing new problems for the consumer as well as an intensification of prior problems faced by law-enforcement officials." Banks' headlong rush into the card market reshaped the political landscape. Consumers feared liability for charges accrued on unsolicited cards. Law enforcement officials continued to criticize bank card marketing. And banks and other card issuers howled about fraud losses. To make card markets functional and legitimate, lawmakers had to balance these competing claims. At the state and federal level, they followed a similar pattern: protecting consumers from fraud liability by shifting fraud risk onto card-issuing firms, and adopting stronger criminal laws to shift the policing burden from card issuers to the state.[30]

Dunne's newfound concerns for consumer protection did not weaken his resolve to combat card fraud, and the hearings and redrafting drove the fraud bill forward. Once the bill cleared the assembly in March, the Penal Law Commission dropped its opposition. "Such legislation," Richard Denzler acknowledged, "must, of course, be viewed in the current setting of an exploding credit card world beleaguered by fast growing criminal activity already of gigantic proportions." When Nelson Rockefeller signed Dunne's bill later the same month, lawmakers and industry representatives emphasized that the law would "combat organized crime's stolen credit card racket." At the signing ceremony, Milton Lipson asserted that, "without question" the law "will be an effective weapon against professional criminals." In its article documenting the signing, *Newsday* emphasized its own leadership on the card fraud issue, while continuing to stoke the fires of moral panic, even naming the mobsters involved in ripping off the industry.[31]

Although initially championing the interests of his business allies, Dunne turned to addressing consumers' concerns about fraud liability and their widespread resistance to banks' unsolicited mailing campaigns. Dunne pressed industry representatives to admit that they had compounded the problem by mailing unsolicited cards. They had not, Dunne indicated, taken adequate security measures to protect consumers from fraud. He also called for follow-up hearings "to determine who should be responsible for losses." Soon after his fraud law was enacted, Dunne introduced bills to limit cardholder liability for lost or stolen cards and to ban the unsolicited mailing of credit cards. Dunne eventually accepted card industry claims that an outright mailing ban would be too restrictive and prevent competition. But Dunne was also losing control of the now popular issue. New York's attorney general, Republican Louis Lefkowitz, endorsed much stronger measures. Reflecting the gender politics attached to the issue of card distribution, Lefkowitz framed his effort as a salve to worried husbands. "I have had numerous letters from husbands," Lefkowitz told a meeting of the National Association of District Attorneys in November 1969, "who have said that the forwarding of these cards is nothing more than a temptation to their wives to make purchases that are beyond their capacity to pay." New York adopted consumer liability protection in May 1970.[32]

In doing so, New York lawmakers completed the increasingly commonplace risk shift, transferring fraud risk from consumers to card issuers and at the same time shifting the policing burden from card issuers to the state. Massachusetts, California, and Illinois took different paths to the same point. The Massachusetts legislature first protected cardholders through limited liability before later adopting Amex's model fraud law. California adopted the Amex law in 1967. After Congress enacted limited liability in 1970, California lawmakers adopted a sweeping consumer protection law that matched federal liability provisions and also included new protections for credit billing and credit discrimination. Illinois had enacted a card fraud law in the wake of the Chicago banks' mass-mailing debacle of 1966 and followed thereafter with limited liability. Into the early 1970s, Illinois lawmakers debated Amex's model bill, but they remained concerned about taking on additional law enforcement responsibilities when card firms continued to recklessly market convenient credit. "We have concluded that legal restrictions on the fraudulent use of credit cards in Illinois are pitifully out of touch with reality," a commission studying card fraud reported in 1972, yet "mere legislation without a complementary increase in security by the credit card companies will not deter the mounting incidence of credit card frauds." Card firms could not expect state protection until they protected themselves.[33]

The same concerns vexed Congress members as they finalized a federal consumer protection package that banned unsolicited card mailing and imposed limited liability on a national basis in 1969 and 1970. Throughout the legislative process, Congress considered protecting consumers through enhanced federal fraud policing (even if card firms were the ultimate beneficiaries). But law enforcement officials repeatedly argued against greater federal responsibility. Card issuers, they charged, willingly sacrificed consumer safety to make credit convenient. When the House Postal Subcommittee considered an unsolicited mailing ban, for instance, Seymour Rotker and William Cotter recounted their experience investigating Citibank's fraud losses. Although bank security personnel wished to reduce fraud losses, Rotker testified, bank marketing staff wanted the widest possible card distribution. "It appears that from a business standpoint," he observed, "the firms may be willing to sustain losses to some extent through illegal use which may be less than the necessary expense to cut these losses." If so, Rotker implied, card firms could hardly expect the government to pick up the tab; if they wanted a policing partner in the state, card issuers needed to put system security above credit marketing.[34]

In the march to passage, Russell Long amended the Senate bill, adding a provision making card fraud a federal crime under the Stolen Property Act. Although the text had not been debated in either chamber, William Proxmire, head of the conference committee, integrated the provision into the final bill, possibly as a concession to card issuers to soften the impact of the unsolicited mailing ban and liability provisions. Proxmire initially supported an expansive federal fraud statute, but, he explained to Senate colleagues, "The Justice Department felt such a provision would be extremely costly to administer." Instead, the committee amended the federal Stolen Property Act, placing unauthorized card use under federal jurisdiction only when fraudulent purchases aggregated to $5,000. The high threshold limited the statute's reach, but it accomplished the double move adopted by states. At the federal level, the risks and costs of card fraud shifted from consumers to issuers through limited liability, and from card issuers to the federal government through the criminal law.[35]

By instituting this double move, state and federal policymakers buttressed the expanding scale and scope of private, nationwide card networks. In the

1940s and 1950s, local card systems, whether department store or charge account banking plans, relied on interpersonal embeddedness—trust created through webs of relationships among consumers, store personnel, local bankers, and credit managers. With national card systems and mobile consumers (and crooks), such linkages were no longer sufficient. Policymakers thus created new legal, institutional embeddedness more suitable to the era of impersonal credit. In doing so, policymakers recognized and protected the methods of card use prescribed by card firms, and they criminalized the methods of card use employed by innovative fraudsters. Given lawmakers' willingness to adopt card issuer arguments before banks launched their unsolicited mailing campaigns, firms like American Express might have secured a greater measure of state protection, with fewer legal commitments to consumer welfare, had banks not careened into the market. Nevertheless, the consumer and criminal protections that emerged from the swell of credit activism in the late 1960s provided the entire card industry with a foundation of state-sanctioned legitimacy. The consumer protections, from expanded state usury laws, to limited liability, to unsolicited mailing bans, all, in the sense that the social theorist Karl Polanyi intended, embedded and legitimized plastic capitalism. State policing commitments, in turn, represented a foundational government investment in private card markets, which, despite policymakers' embrace of credit-driven purchasing power, was not obligatory or guaranteed. All of this redounded to the benefit of bankers, who would in turn use this foundation to launch sustained offensives against the complex web of federalist financial regulation in the decades to come.[36]

The Location of Credit Card Crime

When Proxmire set a $5,000 threshold for card fraud to mollify Justice Department concerns, he hardly captured the department's hostility to any new card policing mandate. An October 1970 letter from Richard Kleindienst, deputy attorney general, to Proxmire, as the conference committee weighed fraud legislation, made clear the department's position: a federal card fraud law would overwhelm federal resources. "It has been estimated that there may be as many as five million unauthorized use of credit card violations in the United States annually," Kleindienst objected. "The Federal

Bureau of Investigation would not have the personnel to investigate this large a number of cases." Even if it could, he continued, "there are not enough Federal prosecutors or judges to even begin to make a dent in the volume of cases that would arise." The problem had grown too big for the federal government to handle.[37]

Kleindienst sought to preserve limited resources, but he was equally concerned that new fraud legislation would interfere with ongoing and successful efforts to prosecute organized card criminals: a joint task force of Justice Department and Postal Inspection officers had been pursuing organized card thieves using the mail fraud statute since 1964. The federal government had long used the far-reaching mail fraud statute to combat novel commercial crimes. When courts curtailed the reach of the Stolen Property Act in 1963, U.S. attorneys turned to mail fraud, increasing card fraud prosecutions from 5 in 1964 to 246 by 1970. "We believe," Kleindienst explained, "that the proposed amendments . . . are unnecessary and possibly could adversely affect the enforcement program directed at the prosecution of large scale, organized unlawful use of credit cards." Prosecutors often used mail fraud in areas where Congress had not yet legislated, but once Congress defined card crime as distinct from mail fraud, the elastic mail fraud statute might no longer apply.[38]

Curiously, the federal government's success prosecuting card swindlers had remained outside the policy debates surrounding card fraud in the 1960s. There were several reasons for this absence. First, the federal court that developed the most robust mail fraud jurisprudence, the Fifth Circuit, covered Texas, Louisiana, and Mississippi. The cases involved gasoline cards, issued by firms like Shell and Standard Oil, not the bank and travel cards embroiled in the national debate. Until other federal jurisdictions adopted the Fifth Circuit's precedents, a process which began only around 1970, the court's rulings remained a local curiosity, not settled law. Further, mail fraud cases were the province of the Postal Inspection Service, an effective investigatory agency housed in a much-maligned institution. The mutual antagonism unsolicited mailing created between banks and the Post Office meant neither party welcomed sustained working partnerships. Card issuers wanted to call on the FBI. Finally, card firms and their attorneys still believed that mail fraud was inherently limited: the mail became an element of a fraudulent action only once a transaction was completed; it offered no method for breaking up the criminal supply networks. Or at least that's how matters seemed in the mid-1960s.

As card firms lobbied to expand the Stolen Property Act and enact Amex's model card crime act, prosecutors and judges in the Fifth Circuit crafted a wide-ranging interpretation of the mail fraud statute. They reimagined card fraud, from a singular event that happened at a checkout counter at a fixed moment, to a process that necessarily unfolded over space and time. In doing so, they engaged in policy entrepreneurship through the federal courts, in much the same way that state attorneys general, seeking to hold card issuers accountable to usury statutes, had done at the state level. That reimagining began with Felix Adams. When Adams deceived a gas station clerk by offering his stolen Gulf Oil Company credit card, Adams's attorney argued in 1962, the fraud began and ended. At that moment, at one of the many checkout counters where Adams racked up $2,953.55 in charges over several months, nothing was being mailed. Adams's actions were deceptive, but they did not constitute mail fraud. On the contrary, the court reasoned, "The practice of extending credit was inseparably connected with the use of the mails to forward the sales slips to Gulf Oil Company." Adams's fraud scheme depended on the use of the mails, because it "occasioned a delay in . . . detection . . ., and that delay permitted [Adams] to expand the scope of his operations." Thus, the court concluded, "When the scheme is viewed in its entirety, it is obvious that the use of the mails constituted a part of it." Adams never licked a stamp or sealed an envelope, but he caused these actions to happen.[39]

Still, to establish criminal intent, judges inferred that fraudsters understood the back-office processes that afforded the time delay. In their appeals, convicts adamantly contested this claim. Their purchases were immediate, they argued. Although possibly crooked in intent, that intent did not contemplate the mail. The Fifth Circuit rejected these arguments. In a 1965 case, the court ruled that "the use of the mails . . . inheres in the credit card system." The mailing of sales slips could not be separated from the credit-granting process. By 1970, the court brushed aside a defendant's claim that his scheme was complete at the time of purchase as not worthy of oral argument. In the Fifth Circuit, card fraud was, *per se*, mail fraud.[40]

The full scope of this theory became apparent in *U.S. v. Kellerman*, a 1970 case from the Second Circuit (Connecticut, New York, and Vermont) that built on the doctrine developed in the Fifth. In 1967, a mechanic working for Dashew

Business Machines, which produced plastic cards for Diners Club, Bank of America, and other card issuers, tried to sell embossing equipment and card blanks to his neighbor, John Kellerman. Kellerman and a group of coconspirators planned to establish a counterfeit Diners Club ring, producing and selling cards into the black market. But the would-be manufacturers could not get the embossing equipment to work. In the meantime, one of the coconspirators used a stolen card for his own amusement, got pinched, and offered details of the larger scheme to save his skin. Kellerman and three others were subsequently convicted of conspiracy to commit mail fraud. Appealing, Kellerman argued that all he tried to do was buy the embossing machine and card blanks. He never contemplated the use of the mails. The court was not convinced. "The card has no value qua card," the court argued, but only as a credit device the conspirators would sell, and which they then knew would be used to commit fraud. "Since the fraudulent use of a credit card constitutes mail fraud, so also does a conspiracy to put spurious cards into circulation." The government did not need to wait for a transaction to take place—the possibility of a future transaction involving the mail was enough. The reach of mail fraud was wide indeed.[41]

Although Kleindienst had worried in October 1970 that the new card fraud law would complicate federal prosecutions under the mail fraud statute, initially such complications did not materialize. The Postal Inspection Service extended the reach of its investigatory authority and its monthly *Enforcement Report* teemed with descriptions of successfully foiled fraud cases. Once Congress enacted the card fraud law, the Justice Department placed investigative jurisdiction with the experienced Postal Service, not the Federal Bureau of Investigation. Meanwhile, the Fifth Circuit's jurisprudence continued to spread to other courts. "Every court of appeals case involving credit card schemes," the Third Circuit (Delaware, New Jersey, and Pennsylvania) observed in 1972, "has held that such schemes fall within the mail fraud statute." Disputes, however, soon crept in. The first Kleindienst had anticipated. If Congress created a specific category of credit card fraud, could activities within that category also be defined as mail fraud? The second centered on knowledge and intent. Could courts reasonably assume that fraudsters understood card systems well enough to contemplate the entire credit-granting process when they made fraudulent purchases? Did fraud happen in the store or, by contractual translocation and the convenience of the modern mail, in some far-off credit office?[42]

These questions converged in the case of Thomas Maze. In early 1971, Maze took up residence with Charles Meredith in Louisville, Kentucky. "In the spring of that year," Supreme Court Justice William H. Rehnquist later wrote, Maze's "fancy lightly turned to thoughts of the sunny Southland, and he thereupon took Meredith's BankAmericard and his 1968 automobile and headed for Southern California." Embodying the happy-go-lucky fraudster, Maze made out for the California coast, lodging at hotels in Huntington Beach and San Diego. Then he headed east for New Orleans, and on to Fort Lauderdale, all financed by Meredith's BankAmericard. Finally, Maze returned to Kentucky, where Meredith's '68 Pontiac ran into some trouble. Maze took it to a garage and borrowed a 1964 Chevy on Meredith's credit. Two days later, Maze, drunk, wrecked the Chevy. He was subsequently arrested.[43]

Federal prosecutors indicted Maze for one count of auto theft and four counts of mail fraud, one for each hotel bill charged to Meredith's BankAmericard. A jury convicted Maze of all five counts, but in October 1972, the Sixth Circuit Court (Kentucky, Michigan, Ohio, and Tennessee) reversed the mail fraud convictions, arguing that Maze did not contemplate the use of the mails as part of his fraud plan. In doing so, the court rejected the expansive view of the card transaction—and of criminal knowledge—implied by the other federal circuits. "It was immaterial to [Maze] how (or whether)" the hotel owners "collected their money or who eventually paid for the purchases," the court argued. "As far as appellant was concerned," it continued, "his transaction was complete when he checked out of each motel." The court went further, asserting that Congress, in enacting the 1970 card fraud statute, shared this view. Card fraud was not, as the Fifth Circuit would have it, *per se* mail fraud. Federal prosecution should be limited to cases over $5,000, as the law stated. "Casual or incidental misuses," among them Maze's, should be left "to local prosecution."[44]

The Sixth Circuit's ruling, along with a similar one delivered by the Tenth Circuit (Colorado and surrounding states) the same year, created significant disagreement among the federal courts, encouraging the Supreme Court to clarify the relationship between the card fraud and the mail fraud statutes. The court heard Maze's case in November 1973. William T. Warner, a court-appointed Louisville attorney, represented Maze, who was serving out his auto theft sentence in federal prison. Warner's argument was simple: courts could not assume that persons committing credit card fraud knew their actions would involve the mail. The cases that gave rise to the *per se* doctrine of the Fifth and other circuits involved knowledgeable defendants and complex, long-term schemes, Warner explained. Yet Congress's and the card firms' moral outrage over organized crime should not shape the law for all defendants. Maze hadn't thought twice. The court should curtail the federal government's reach, Warner argued. If it did so, he assured, card systems would not go unprotected. "Kentucky statutes are more than adequate to cover every aspect of the so-called scheme." State law could do the job just as well.[45]

A bare majority of justices accepted Warner's argument, and only then with some reservation. On the dissenting side, it was patently obvious to Justice Harry A. Blackmun that card fraud contemplated the use of the mails, as it was to Justice Byron White, who wrote the primary dissent. Hoping to add meat to White's dissent, Chief Justice Warren E. Burger wrote a short treatise on the history of the mail fraud statute, arguing that the court should maintain it as a robust tool for combating commercial fraud. Enough justices, though, were persuaded. Justices Thurgood Marshall and William J. Brennan Jr. believed that Proxmire's amendments demonstrated Congress's intent to limit card fraud jurisdiction. In conference, Justice Lewis Powell confessed that he "could toss a coin," but he concluded that "credit cards ought to be at the state level." William Rehnquist, a former president of the National Conference of Commissioners for Uniform State Laws and strong advocate of state prerogatives, likely agreed. But in his majority opinion, Rehnquist focused only on criminal knowledge and intent. Maze's "scheme reached fruition when he checked out of the motel," Rehnquist wrote. "There is no indication that the success of his scheme depended in any way on which of his victims ultimately bore the loss. Indeed, from his point of view, he probably would have preferred to have the invoices misplaced by the various motel personnel and never mailed at all."[46]

In concluding his oral argument, Warner tried to clarify the stakes of the case. "The Government," Warner observed, "has lit off a kind of a smoky bonfire," that "unless the Court overturns the Sixth Circuit decision that the entire credit card system is going to breakdown. I don't think that's true." From Warner's perspective, states like Kentucky, which had adopted the State Credit Card Crime Act proposed by American Express in April 1970, were more than capable of defending national card systems using local law.

In Maze's case, the Louisville Bank that issued Meredith's BankAmericard could provide all the evidence a local prosecutor would need. Because Maze ultimately defrauded the Louisville bank, Kentucky had the necessary jurisdiction, no matter how far Maze roamed. Justice White also saw the continued primacy of state criminal enforcement as the ultimate outcome in *Maze*, but with dramatically different consequences. Maze, in White's view, "must now be charged and tried in California, Louisiana, and Florida. This result, never intended by Congress, may precipitate a widespread inability to apprehend and/or prosecute those who would hijack the credit card system."[47]

Maze left federal card fraud law in a messy heap. In his dissent, Chief Justice Burger emphasized that the majority ruling did not preclude the use of the mail fraud statute to prosecute card crime. Prosecutors, though, had to demonstrate that the use of the mail was an essential element of the fraud scheme. And in areas like Unholy Alliance frauds, where colluding merchants undoubtedly knew the mail was in play, the federal government retained authority. At the same time, Proxmire's fraud law proved difficult to enforce. The $5,000 threshold Kleindienst requested applied to "a transaction" involving an improperly obtained "credit card." As written, "transaction" and "card" were singular. If Congress imagined an aggregation of multiple fraudulent purchases on a single card, or on many cards, it had not said so. Only the Fifth Circuit took an expansive view of the text, allowing that Congress meant an aggregation of multiple transactions on multiple cards. On the contrary, "the interpretation of the majority of courts of the aggregation requirement," one commentator wrote, "renders the statute too narrow to effectively combat credit card fraud." Thus, while Justice White had been incensed that card fraud prosecutions would have to rely on the hodgepodge of state law, even within the federal courts, the location of specific fraudulent acts led to varied legal outcomes. The place of prosecution still determined whether certain actions were federal crimes or not.[48]

The issue of location permeated *Maze* in another way. The majority concluded that prosecutors had to demonstrate that defendants knew how card systems worked well enough to have incorporated the geographic distances, which divided fraudulent purchases from the institutions ultimately responsible for them, into their schemes. To commit mail fraud, card fraudsters had to be sophisticated users of financial technology. Criminals who understood their transactions as occurring, in Maze's case, in hotels in Florida and California, not in a bank office in Kentucky, were literally pardoned for that lack of sophisticated understanding. As consumers began to use cards from out-of-state banks, some confronted situations where their lack of knowledge about the geographic scope of card systems was, instead, distinctly punishing. The laws of the state where they lived and used their card were not necessarily the laws that applied to their credit card transactions. But unlike criminals, for whom knowledge and intent had to be proven to be enforced, courts were more comfortable assuming consumers knew what they were doing. The entire federal consumer protection regime rested on just this notion of informed, autonomous, discerning consumers.

Finally, for card issuers, who craved uniformity and predictability, the saga demolished their faith that state policing could protect their card systems. Instead, card firms turned their attention to new technologies, which they hoped would enable stricter system security while still making credit convenient. Magnetic strips, point-of-sale terminals, and electronic funds transfer systems held out the promise of augmenting card issuers' newly crafted institutional embeddedness with complex technological systems that could defeat the most enterprising criminals. If constructed properly, these new systems of surveillance and control would enable bankers to cut out untrustworthy merchants and extend bank control even deeper into consumers' lives. That, however, was a big if.[49]

8

The *Marquette* Decision

Where Is Fisher?

In the days preceding oral arguments in *Marquette National Bank of Minneapolis v. First of Omaha Service Corporation*, Justice Harry Blackmun pondered a teasing question: "Who is Fisher?" The issue in *Marquette*, argued before the Supreme Court in October 1978, was whether the First National Bank of Omaha, Nebraska, could charge its credit card customers living in Minnesota the 18 percent interest rate allowed under Nebraska law, or if the bank instead had to conform to Minnesota's 12 percent usury limit. The case hinged on the question of *where* First of Omaha's card plan was legally located, which in turn would dictate which state's interest rate applied. Nearly a decade of legal struggle culminated in the case, as states sought to protect their citizens from high interest rates delivered through border-crossing credit cards. The state of Minnesota stood beside the Marquette bank as a plaintiff-respondent, with conservative legal scholar Robert H. Bork delivering the oral argument for the Nebraska bank. In a similar case, the Iowa Supreme Court had recently decided against First of Omaha. *Marquette* would reshape the credit card market. It began, indirectly, with a man named Fred Fisher. Blackmun wanted to know who he was.[1]

In the decade before *Marquette*, state consumer leagues and labor union chapters waged a pitched political battle against the financial community over the price of credit, specifically the interest rates and fees tied to credit card accounts. In some states, these groups secured new laws that limited the rates lenders could charge. In others, state attorneys general challenged the time-price doctrine and brought revolving credit under existing state usury regulations. Across the country, consumers, politicians, credit reformers, and bankers all understood consumer credit as bound within space and properly regulated by states. This patchwork of local regulation stood in the way of a unified, national credit card market. Growth-oriented national banks, situated in states with less restrictive interest rate rules, quickly put pressure on state-based consumer protections. Under federal law, nationally chartered banks could charge interest according to the laws of the state in which they were located. Although a bank's location was fixed, its cards could readily cross state lines. Bankers located in states that allowed high interest used financial technology to offer profitable, expensive credit in neighboring states. By mailing differently regulated cards across state borders, they used financial technology to undermine local democratic efforts to control credit prices.[2]

Consumers and state officials saw what was happening and tried to stop it, developing legal strategies to hold out-of-state card-issuing banks accountable to local interest rate rules. Examples in two states—Iowa and Minnesota—involving two sets of cases—*Fisher* and *Marquette*—illustrate the difficulties in doing so. The cases unfolded as consumer and labor groups in both states successfully challenged the high rates promulgated by the Uniform Consumer Credit Code, and as both states' policymakers used Wisconsin's *J. C. Penney* decision to rein in retail credit prices. In both states, the primary antagonist was the First National Bank of Omaha, a large regional bank that used cards as a tool to break out of the New Deal's geographic and regulatory confines. From the late 1960s forward, states, banks, and individual citizens worked to shape the institutional and legal structures of the bank card market within the complex matrix of financial federalism. For all parties, federalism offered legal instruments that might advance their interests, though ultimately, in *Marquette,* the banks would turn the system to their advantage. In the years after the decision, bankers would relocate their card plans to states without any price restrictions and use *Marquette* to export the rules from those states to cardholders across the country.

Geographic Structure of Bank Credit Card Networks

The questions at the heart of Fisher's case—and later in *Marquette*—grew out of bankers' efforts to build nationwide card networks that linked their geographically constrained credit card plans. Banks could not branch across state lines when they began building networks in the mid-1960s, and in many states, local law constrained their markets even further. Within these confines, bankers envisioned cards as tools for recruiting local customers— whether merchants or consumers: new customers would visit local bank branches and use their other services. Over time, Bank of America and Interbank built national card systems by combining participating banks into nationwide branch networks, making cards at once local in character and national in scope. Consumers held BankAmericard and Master Charge cards that featured the name of their local bank and often the insignia of a local card plan. Merchants joined card systems at the urging of their community banker. Bankers built their card networks to reinforce financial localism and to retain the interpersonal embeddedness that undergirded older credit relationships. All participants expected these local relationships to be regulated by local—that is, state—law.

Bank card plans remained fundamentally local in the 1960s, but bank networking strategies ensured that cards crossed state lines, even when the banks issuing them could not. Network builders had to deliver efficient nationwide—and eventually global—infrastructure, while maintaining close on-the-ground relationships. Bank of America executives approached this challenge by adopting a hierarchical structure. Bank of America partnered with large, regional banks, often assigning them multistate territories. Regional, licensee banks then drew on "correspondent" relationships to recruit smaller "agent banks" in their service area. The local agent banks signed up merchants in their communities to accept BankAmericards and recruited consumers, either by recommending them for direct solicitation by the licensee bank or by accepting and forwarding applications to the licensee bank. The licensee bank issued BankAmericards and extended credit to consumers within its geographic territory. Bank of America's hierarchical network enabled agent banks to offer local card services. The licensee bank and the network, in turn, gained the agent bank's local knowledge and community relationships. Interbank coalesced after the bank card associations, like Chicago's Midwest, had organized, and its architecture was more decentralized. Nevertheless, large banks likewise recruited agent banks to expand the network and embed the card system locally.[3]

Licensee banks distributed cards across multistate territories, yet because state interest rate rules varied, licensee banks had to determine which rates applied. This problem had two layers. First, when bank card networks expanded in the late 1960s, it was often unclear *within individual states* whether state interest rate rules applied to bank cards at all—because of the time-price doctrine—and if so which of a state's interest rate laws applied. Rate rules within states could also work differently for state and nationally chartered banks. Under the "most favored lender" doctrine, national banks could charge the same rates as any competing state chartered or licensed financial institution, including small loan companies that could charge 30 percent a year or more. James Saxon, comptroller of the currency (1961–66), who oversaw the national banking system, encouraged banks to interpret this rule liberally to make their card plans profitable. State policymakers challenged this approach. When two Oregon national banks used the comptroller's ruling to justify charging 18 percent interest on their BankAmericard plans under the state's small loan law, rather than the 10 percent allowed for commercial bank loans, Oregon's attorney general ruled that the card plans violated state usury laws. The banks backed down, accepting that it was better to negotiate with state policymakers than to defy them on the basis of federal authority—a stance which would only make future negotiations more difficult. *Within* states, then, national banks tended to defer to local authority and to work with local policymakers to set statutory rates. Banks operating plans *between* states, however, had no influence over rate policies in other states. When their cards crossed state lines, bankers adopted the rate rules of their home states, but it brought them into conflict with consumers and officials of other states, who fought to enforce local rules.[4]

The *Fisher* and *Marquette* cases centered on one such bank, the First National Bank of Omaha, Nebraska (First of Omaha). First of Omaha pioneered charge account banking, introducing the "First Charge" service in January 1953. First Charge experienced growing pains similar to those of other charge account banks—resistance from large retailers, high consumer defaults, cultural opposition from conservative bank executives. Still, the program grew steadily in Omaha where the bank had its office (Nebraska was effectively a unit banking state). When the card market took off in the mid-1960s, First of Omaha joined the fray. In 1966, it launched a major campaign in Omaha, increasing active accounts from 12,000 to approximately 30,000. Executives soon looked to expand across Nebraska, then regionally, relying on the new national card networks to facilitate growth. First of Omaha considered joining

To Find Out What's in the Cards (First Charge/BankAmericard) For You, Call Bill Henry.

Bill Henry is a card expert. He's marketing officer in charge of marketing and promotion for First National's First Charge/BankAmericard credit card.

First National Bank of Omaha has become affiliated with BankAmericard, the all-purpose, worldwide credit card. If you want to make BankAmericard available to your customers, call Bill Henry. He can show you how it can increase deposits and profits for your bank.

FIRST NATIONAL BANK OF OMAHA

MEMBER F.D.I.C.
Always the FIRST to Serve You.

Northwestern Banker, July, 1968

Fig. 5: First of Omaha ran ads, such as this one in the July 1968 *Northwestern Banker*, to recruit agent banks to its BankAmericard program. Bill Henry (pictured), who was employed and paid by First of Omaha, traveled to "most cities" in Iowa "to enroll agent banks in the First of Omaha Service Corporation's BankAmericard plan."

Source: Ad, First National Bank of Omaha, *Northwestern Banker* (July 1968); deposition of J. William Henry, December 11, 1974, 6, *Fisher* Case File. Reprinted with permission from FNBO.

Interbank, but in April 1968 it joined BankAmericard instead. Bank of America assigned First of Omaha a territory encompassing Nebraska, Iowa, and the Dakotas, where First of Omaha would solicit customers, participating merchants, and agent banks. First of Omaha adopted the BankAmericard with great fanfare. In Nebraska, the bank's "BankAmericard Girls" wore blue, white, and gold uniforms and drove matching Volkswagen Beatles as they enrolled local merchants. Five male employees, not dressed in card-themed uniforms, traveled across the four-state region signing up agent banks to promote "First Charge/BankAmericard" in their communities. Meanwhile, the bank had also mailed 500,000 card applications and 250,000 unsolicited cards, one of which landed in Fred and Edna Fisher's mailbox. By the end of 1970, First Charge incorporated 227 agent banks, 8,000 merchants, and 675,000 consumer accounts.[5]

First of Omaha adopted BankAmericard's corporate architecture, which created legal divisions between the bank and the network to fix card lending in the issuing bank's home state. Under this agreement, First of Omaha performed all credit card lending functions: it checked consumers' credit, issued credit cards, extended credit when consumers made purchases or received cash advances, billed consumers, assessed interest, and accepted repayment from consumers. First of Omaha undertook these functions in its "BankAmericard Center," a system-wide term for a licensee bank's BankAmericard computer and operations division. The BankAmericard Center sat on the tenth floor of First of Omaha's downtown headquarters. Also located there was First of Omaha Service Corporation (Omaha Service), a subsidiary firm, which First of Omaha chartered to manage the BankAmericard network. The service corporation maintained the day-to-day functioning of the network, providing merchants and agent banks with the logistical support and BankAmericard materials they needed—forms, supplies, and equipment—to operate the program. It also solicited merchants in Nebraska and agent banks in neighboring states, like the Coralville Bank and Trust Company in Coralville, Iowa, where the Fishers banked.[6]

Omaha Service was a legal fiction—a way to artificially divide banking and non-banking aspects of card plans. Bank employees performed all service corporation work. The blue, white, and gold clad BankAmericard Girls signed up merchants for Omaha Service, but they were employed by First of Omaha. Asked if he could distinguish between the firms, bank executive Jim

Fig. 6: This figure depicts the division of roles and responsibilities within the BankAmericard network in the late 1960s.

Source: Bank of America, "Agent Bank Agreement," January 10, 1969, plaintiff's exhibit 4; BankAmerica Service Corporation, "Participant Letter License Agreement," June 10, 1969, plaintiff's exhibit 7; Contract between First National Bank of Omaha and First of Omaha Service Corporation, ca. 1968, defendant's exhibit G, *Fisher* Case File; "Bank Credit Card Service Organization and the Bank Service Corporation Act," *Federal Reserve Bulletin* 53, no. 11 (November 1967): 1912–1913.

Doody conceded that "to a person who came to the bank and wanted to see the Service Corporation[,] it would be impossible to locate."[7]

The legal fiction was necessary because it fixed credit card lending at the bank in Omaha, Nebraska, even as bank employees, under the guise of the service corporation, built card infrastructure across state lines. As it expanded its plan across the Midwest, First of Omaha charged cardholders Nebraska's installment credit rates, which before 1974 were 18 percent on balances below $500 and 12 percent thereafter. In their agreements with the bank, consumers accepted that "I may, by use of my BankAmericard, issue drafts upon you for acceptance by you at Omaha, Nebraska," and "I further

Table 2. Division of Functions between First of Omaha and Omaha Service.

First of Omaha (legally in Omaha)	Omaha Service (location variable)
•Check credit and issue cards	•Solicit merchant members
•Accept sales and cash advance drafts	•Solicit agent banks
•Keep transactions records of service corporation's merchant members	•Provide BankAmericard materials to merchants and agent banks
•Sell sales drafts to service corporation at its request	•Assist the same in operating program
	•Solicit consumer applications and mail credit cards
	•Collect merchant enrollment fees
	•Acquire (i.e., pay for) improper sales and cash advance drafts

Source: Contract between First National Bank of Omaha and First of Omaha Service Corporation, ca. 1968, defendant's exhibit G, *Fisher* Case File.

agree to pay my BankAmericard account to you at Omaha, Nebraska." From the perspective of banking law, such pronouncements were sound and sensible. First of Omaha was located in Omaha. Omaha Service, however, ranged more widely. It performed services for merchants and agent banks in Iowa, South Dakota, and beyond. To function, First of Omaha's BankAmericard program required those services as much as anything happening in Omaha. Lending, in an abstract, legal sense, may have taken place in Nebraska, but the card program—the infrastructure that made lending possible—existed in all these states. As state officials and consumers fought for low credit prices, they used the ambiguity between the bank and the service corporation to hold First of Omaha accountable to local laws.[8]

Minnesota: Enforcing Local Credit Laws

Licensee banks like First of Omaha began to construct cross-border card programs at the height of consumer mobilization over high credit prices. In Minnesota, political conflict over card rates emerged within national debates about the Truth-in-Lending Act and the Uniform Consumer Credit Code. In the late 1960s, Minnesota's usury laws were in exactly the state of confusion and haphazard accretion that the UCCC's drafters hoped to resolve. In 1957, lawmakers reenacted the state's 8 percent general usury rate. State law set distinct statutory rates for small loan companies, thrifts, credit unions, bank installment loans, and auto loans. Minnesota exempted most business loans, as well as federally insured home loans, from the 8 percent limit. Moreover, Minnesota's courts had long observed the time-price doctrine, exempting the sale of goods on credit from rate limits because such transactions reflected a difference in price rather than a loan of money. When the legislature took up the UCCC in the late 1960s, lawmakers "really d[id]n't know what the law is" regarding retail revolving credit. They also did not know what to do about the out-of-state bank cards that were pouring into Minnesota. Yet lawmakers knew enough to worry that the state's restrictive and uncertain rate rules were limiting the development of the bank card industry in their state.[9]

Because of Minnesota's low rate ceilings, the convenient credit revolution was bypassing local banks. In the 1950s, several banks in Minneapolis had run competing charge account plans, including the state's largest bank holding company, the Northwest Bank Group, known locally as "Banco." The plans had relied on merchant discounts for revenue. Yet competition among the banks, without the cooperation later developed in Chicago and elsewhere, meant none generated sufficient volume to turn a profit. Banco and its competitors sold their card plans in 1960. Over the next decade, firms like Bank of America shifted the emphasis of bank card plans from merchant discounts to consumer financing. In the late 1960s, a few Minnesota banks moved into the card field. In 1968, the Marquette National Bank of Minneapolis (Marquette) joined BankAmericard and began to solicit agent banks, merchants, and consumers. Banco and several other banks chartered the Central States Bank Card Association, which they planned to tie into the Interbank network. The only hang-up was Minnesota's low interest ceiling. To accommodate their new card plans, bankers lobbied the state legislature to establish card rates at 18 percent in its 1969 session. They expected ready success.[10]

Lawmakers, wrapped in the UCCC debate, were not in an accommodating mood. They defeated the rate increase, and bedlam ensued. Banco's Central States Bank Card Association, which had not yet issued cards, sat frozen. "The things that are legal aren't feasible, and the things that are feasible aren't legal," Banco chairman John Moorhead complained. Many Minnesota banks, including Banco, turned to agent bank agreements to offer card plans.

By September, a Minnesota Bankers Association representative explained to state lawmakers that "bank credit card operations are increasingly being conducted from banks outside the state." This situation was likely to become permanent, the representative continued, once Minnesota banks became locked into agent bank agreements, signing up local merchants for the card plans of out-of-state banks. By the early 1970s, the card revolution was bypassing Minnesota's banks: In 1973, 1.84 percent of all national bank loans were card receivables, but in Minnesota, only 0.18 percent were.[11]

As these figures indicate, a few Minnesota banks continued their card programs despite the legislature's unwillingness to raise permitted rates, taking various degrees of legal risk as they sought to make their card plans profitable—or at least viable. The state's installment loan statute allowed banks to charge 12 percent interest, and Minnesota authorities accepted Marquette's decision to charge consumers this rate on their outstanding BankAmericard balances. Within these constraints, Marquette built a sizable program. The bank claimed 110 agent banks, 7,000 merchants, and 50,000 cardholder accounts across Minnesota and the Dakotas. Taking a greater risk, the small St. Cloud National Bank and Trust Company charged its Master Charge customers an 18 percent annual rate on their outstanding balances. Minnesota department stores charged similar rates on revolving accounts under the time-price doctrine, as did Interbank banks operating in other states. These prices drew closer scrutiny from Minnesota authorities, though St. Cloud's executives believed the rates were permitted under federal law.[12]

With the legal environment ambiguous, many Minnesota banks offered cards through agent bank agreements, providing Minnesota consumers cards issued by out-of-state banks. The arrangement between the National Bank of Omaha—a rival of First of Omaha—and the Olmstead County Bank and Trust Company of Rochester, Minnesota, was typical. The Olmstead bank contracted with local Minnesota merchants to honor Master Charge cards and retained 1 percent of charge sales generated by these merchants, along with their annual membership fees. The Olmstead bank further agreed to "use its best efforts to obtain the names of persons who might be eligible to become Master Charge Card holders" and to forward those names to Omaha National Bank. Omaha National Bank ran its own credit check and mailed a Master Charge card to each qualifying consumer, for which the Olmstead bank received a $1 finder's fee. The front of the cards featured the name of the Olmstead bank, rooting the plan in Rochester and suggesting that the cards were issued in Minnesota. But the Omaha National Bank issued them in Nebraska, where, according to cardholder contracts, it extended all credit and retained all income. The Nebraska bank charged Minnesota consumers 1.5 percent a month, a rate legal in Nebraska but of dubious legality in Minnesota.[13]

The Republican attorney general—and gubernatorial candidate—Douglas Head recognized the problem and the political salience of high credit prices. In October 1969, Head ordered his staff to determine whether in- and out-of-state bank card plans violated Minnesota's 8 percent usury law. In doing so, he joined a bipartisan movement to hold card firms accountable to local price restrictions, one advanced by both Democrats and Republicans who sought to appeal to consumer-voters.

In July 1970, Head sued the St. Cloud National Bank as a card-issuing bank *located in Minnesota,* to test the legality of St. Cloud's 18 percent rate. The parties delayed, hoping, in the words of St. Cloud's attorney, that "the Legislature would resolve this matter" in the 1971 session. Instead, the legislature authorized *retailers* to charge 12 percent on their revolving charge accounts, a compromise between retailers, who also sought 18 percent rates, and consumer and labor groups, who fought to keep the rate at 8 percent. The compromise did not address bank cards. Although St. Cloud's executives maintained that they "were not subject to the limitations of the usury law . . . in view of federal regulation," the bank lowered its Master Charge rate to 1 percent a month. The bank's attorney also pleaded with the attorney general's office not to proceed with the litigation, drawing on the antimonopoly ideals that had driven early bank card plans. "Our little bank," the attorney wrote, "is deeply concerned with the survival of the smaller merchants and we are satisfied they cannot ultimately compete with the [retail] giants, absent some kind of credit help such as we are trying to give them." The state dropped the case on the stipulation that the bank, which at the time had fewer than 3,000 cardholders, keep its rate at 12 percent. As in Oregon, accepting local authority won out over fighting for federal privileges.[14]

The state's second action was more complicated—and ultimately more consequential. The attorney general's office sued the Olmstead County Bank and the Omaha National Bank, beginning a fight against out-of-state card issuers that would end at the Supreme Court. The question was whether a national bank *located in Nebraska* could charge Minnesota consumers Nebraska rates. At first glance, it looked like a hard case for Minnesota to win. The attorney general's office recognized that Section 85 of the National Bank Act allowed national banks to charge interest according to the laws of their home state. Credit card loans originated in Omaha, statements were mailed from Omaha, and consumers remitted payments to Omaha: National Bank of Omaha's card contracts clearly explained these facts to consumers. Courts usually upheld such contracts, Minnesota's attorneys noted. But there were exceptions. "Courts are hesitant to apply the Rule where it would work a gross injustice," the attorneys argued. Such injustice would occur if the parties were in substantially unequal bargaining positions or if the entire transaction was merely a pretense to evade the usury laws of one state. In these circumstances—circumstances Minnesota's attorneys believed matched their case—local courts were more likely to intervene to protect local citizens.[15]

Before a sympathetic Minnesota court could hear these arguments, however, the attorney general had to convince such a court that it had jurisdiction over a Nebraska bank. Just as national bank loans, for the purposes of applying state usury laws, existed in their home states, so too did national banks have the privilege of being sued only in their home states (ostensibly so they wouldn't have to cart their business records all over the country whenever they engaged in a legal dispute). Localism cut both ways. National banks could give up this right, although Minnesota's attorneys could not imagine that any bank would do so. If these legal propositions held—if card loans legally happened in Nebraska and the Omaha bank could only be sued there—they had decidedly unsavory consequences for Minnesota citizens. "Any Minnesota resident would be required to begin an action in Nebraska for the penalties under a usurious contract." As agent bank agreements became more common in Minnesota, state residents increasingly received unsolicited, high-interest cards from out-of-state banks. Using these cards was convenient. Exercising legal rights would not be.[16]

In their briefs to the Minnesota court, the state's attorneys tried to make the case about credit infrastructure, not just card lending. They asked the court to look beyond the loan contract and consider the entirety of the Master Charge plan. "The Omaha National Bank chose to enter this State and set up an elaborate banking relationship for one motive: profit," they argued. The court should thus consider all aspects of that elaborate relationship when considering jurisdiction. Minnesota state law required out-of-state corporations doing business in Minnesota to register with the secretary of state and accept legal service there. "Doing business," meant contracting with Minnesota citizens and performing some portion of the contract in Minnesota. The Master Charge plan, Minnesota's attorneys contended, met these conditions. The Minnesota court was sympathetic, but, compelled by federal statute and Supreme Court precedent, it dismissed the Omaha National Bank from the suit. It did so reluctantly: "The policy reasons advanced by the State of Minnesota for a different interpretation of that federal statute are quite convincing . . . and may very well justify a reversal." Although the attorney general's office chose not to pursue Omaha National Bank in federal court (in Nebraska), it still hoped to clarify the law. It maintained the case against the Olmstead Bank in order to determine whether the state could take action against agent banks that facilitated high-interest credit card plans, only ending its suit—without resolution—in August 1973.[17]

Following the dismissal, state legal assistant Mary Gallagher filed a lengthy memo evaluating Minnesota's efforts to hold Omaha National Bank accountable to Minnesota law and reflecting on the larger issues of credit prices and credit citizenship raised by the case. "Few holders of Master Charge cards are obviously poor or necessitous," Gallagher began. "They may nonetheless be in the usurer's clutches, since it is difficult to achieve a 'credit rating,' to pay for airline tickets and the like by check, and in general to operate as advertisements urge us to in a 'credit society' without a credit card like Master Charge." As Gallagher recognized, bankers were pushing their private payments infrastructure to the center of middle-class American life. To fully participate in the nation's credit society, consumers needed cards. Over the past half decade, Minnesota consumer groups, labor groups, and their political allies had fought to define the terms of credit access. They sought and attained safe, inexpensive credit in the state legislature. Minnesota's attorneys, in turn, fought to cement those rights in state courts. State officials had to carry on fighting, Gallagher reasoned. Citizens might take on the banks themselves, but at the risk of their credit standing. "On behalf of such borrowers, and there are many, who hesitate to endanger their status as high-quality debtors," Gallager argued, "the state must bring the action." The state of Minnesota would get its chance again. But first, borrowers with little left to lose would carry the fight to issuing banks' home states.[18]

Iowa and the *Fisher* Cases

Minnesota's case against the Olmsted and Omaha banks failed to clarify how financial federalism's geographically bounded system of state interest rate regulations applied to out-of-state banks and their cross-border card plans. Not long afterward, another series of cases picked up in Iowa that would advance the question, though not in ways that favored consumers or the states that sought to protect them. These cases were instituted on behalf of Fred and Edna Fisher, and their story will begin to answer Justice Blackmun's question.

As were their colleagues in other states, Iowa policymakers were deeply concerned about expensive revolving credit. Beginning in 1969, Iowa's legislature considered the Uniform Consumer Credit Code, which received local support from J. C. Penney and other retailers and bank card organizations, such as the Mid-America Bankcard Association. Lawmakers found the code exceedingly complicated; they moved slowly. Seeking quicker resolution, Iowa's Republican attorney general, Richard Turner, followed the example set in Wisconsin, where the state sued J. C. Penney to demonstrate that revolving credit plans were not time-price sales and thus had to abide by state interest rate restrictions. Turner sued Sears, Standard Oil, and Younker Brothers, a regional department store chain. He alleged all three had violated the state's 9 percent general usury limit with their revolving charge plans. In September 1973, the state's supreme court followed *J. C. Penney*, holding that revolving credit was not a time-price sale and setting retail credit rates at 9 percent. The ruling created momentum for the Iowa Consumer Credit Code, which, when enacted in June 1974, set revolving credit prices for both retail and bank cards at 18 percent for the first $500 and 15 percent on all exceeding balances.[19]

This legislative resolution, though, was in the future. The Fishers' story begins in February 1969, when they received in the mail a BankAmericard from the First National Bank of Omaha, which neither Fred nor Edna had requested. Their local bank, the Coralville Bank and Trust, was an agent bank in First of Omaha's BankAmericard program, and it seems to have given First of Omaha the Fishers' names as likely card prospects. They were. The Fishers quickly used their BankAmericard: Edna made purchases at two department stores and a local record shop. She favored the pop of Johnny Mathis and Ed Ames, and the country of Roger Miller and Johnny Horton.

Fred used the card at local restaurants and a nearby Chrysler-Plymouth dealer. Edna, who signed her name "Mrs. Fred J. Fisher" on her card, also received a $250 cash advance at the Coralville Bank. For several months the Fishers paid the minimum balance on their BankAmericard account until February 1970, when they started to miss their payments. First of Omaha began collection calls in July. The Fishers made a few more payments, but by March 1971, the bank determined their remaining debt of $490.18 was uncollectible. Then the lawsuits began.[20]

The issue was not the Fishers' bankruptcy—we do not know the outcome of their debt—but instead First of Omaha's lending practices. The bank charged the Fishers 1.5 percent per month on their outstanding balances (18 percent annually), a rate permitted in Nebraska but not yet in Iowa where the Fishers lived and used their card. First of Omaha also failed to comply with the Truth-in-Lending Act's disclosure rules. The Fishers' attorney, Everett Meeker, accepted the case on contingency, meaning he would be paid only if the Fishers prevailed. He also took advantage of new civil procedure rules to file the suit as a class action, on behalf of Fred Fisher *and all others similarly situated*. The First National Bank of Omaha had 56,940 cardholders living in Iowa. If Meeker won judgments for all of them, he stood to become a rich man (First of Omaha estimated its potential liability at $43 million). The Fishers had also received and used a card from the First National Bank of Chicago, which was charging them Illinois's 18 percent interest on their Iowa purchases. Meeker, an entrepreneurial litigator, sued the Chicago bank too.[21]

Like Minnesota's attorneys, Meeker believed his best chance was to try the Fishers' cases locally, in a court in Iowa, and Meeker brought both suits in federal court there in September 1971. (Although we'll focus on First of Omaha, early results in the First Chicago case were much the same.) In the same way that Minnesota's attorneys had urged the local court to consider the "elaborate banking relationship" that constituted the card plan, Meeker asked the Iowa court to examine the credit infrastructure that existed in Iowa when determining jurisdiction. Meeker zeroed in on the specific link between First of Omaha and its subsidiary Omaha Service. He sued the bank since it had issued the Fishers' card and assessed them allegedly usurious interest. But Meeker argued that the two firms were legally indistinguishable. Since Omaha Service was registered with Iowa's secretary of state to do business in Iowa and could be sued there, the bank, if his logic held, could be as well. Predictably, First of Omaha fought this argument and immediately petitioned to dismiss the case for improper venue.[22]

Meeker's argument focused on the slippery legal fictions that structured regulatory place and space in bank card systems. Questioning First of Omaha executive Jim Doody, Meeker asked if there was anything "that would indicate that the service corporation is different from the bank?" Doody pointed out that the "forms, with the First Service Corporation name on it" were different. "But," Meeker pressed, "to a person who came to the bank and wanted to see the Service Corporation[,] it would be impossible to locate a Service Corporation as such?" Yes, Doody agreed. Put another way—and to paraphrase legal scholar Felix Cohen—when asked "Where is a service corporation?" Doody conceded that nobody had ever seen a service corporation. It did not, in any tangible sense, exist.[23]

Meeker countered Doody's legal metaphysics by invoking the realness of the Fishers' location. If the service corporation had no concrete place, Fred and Edna Fisher certainly did. They lived and shopped and banked in Iowa. Under financial federalism, they expected their transactions would be regulated by Iowa. When First of Omaha mailed the Fishers an unsolicited card— on the letterhead of the Fishers' Iowa bank—First of Omaha relied on the place-based social contract to embed their card plan in Iowa. Fred Fisher, Meeker explained, "is now and always has been an Iowa resident. The card was accepted by plaintiff in Iowa and used in Iowa. It was used to make a loan at an Iowa bank and to make purchases from merchants in Iowa." Ultimately, Meeker argued, "How can a state regulate banking within its borders if it cannot bring an action against the bank in its own state?" State officials across the Midwest were asking the same question.[24]

Meeker's focus on Omaha Service—a strategy that would work in later cases—was astute, but although the Iowa court was receptive to his arguments, First of Omaha largely prevailed. "The court is in sympathy with the argument that the venue privilege imposes a hardship on the consumer." It agreed that Omaha Service was "merely an adjunct of the First National Bank of Omaha." Moreover, by making "contracts to be performed in whole or in part in Iowa," Omaha Service could be sued in the state. Meeker, however, had not sued Omaha Service. And Omaha Service had not made high-interest loans to Fred and Edna Fisher. First of Omaha had. The bank retained its venue privilege. Indeed, the court concluded, First of Omaha's use of a subsidiary corporation to conduct the parts of its BankAmericard business that could not be strictly construed as happening in Nebraska indicated that the bank intended to maintain a legal separation between its lending to the Fishers and the elaborate infrastructure that made that lending possible. The service corporation's tangible existence was irrelevant; its legal existence was what counted. Still, instead of dismissing the case, as First of Omaha requested, the judge transferred it to federal court in Nebraska. The same result obtained in Meeker's suit against First of Chicago, sending that case to federal court in Illinois.[25]

The movement of the cases out of Iowa did impose a hardship on the Fishers and on Meeker—Meeker made embarrassing filing errors because he did not know the local rules of the Nebraska courts—but Meeker was persistent. He carried the Fishers' grievances from their home in Iowa to the home states of First of Omaha and First of Chicago. At these sites, too, Meeker claimed that the banks were shipping usurious rates into Iowa; again he met frustration. The U.S. District Court for the Northern District of Illinois ruled that Illinois law governed all loans made by First of Chicago, "whether such loans are made in Illinois or elsewhere." Meeker traveled further still, appealing the cases to the federal Court of Appeals, for the Seventh and Eighth Circuits, respectively, which held sway over Illinois and Nebraska. Again, both courts ruled for the defendant banks, determining that they could charge the rates allowed by their home states. The Supreme Court declined to hear appeals, denying Meeker the opportunity to carry the Fishers' case to Washington. Everett Meeker was forced to go home.[26]

The Fishers' cases complicated new attempts by Iowa policymakers to hold First of Omaha accountable to local law. In June 1974, the Iowa legislature enacted the Iowa Consumer Credit Code (ICCC). The code raised revolving credit limits to 18 percent for the first $500 and 15 percent on all exceeding balances. These rates were comparable to, but still distinct from, the 18 percent for the first $999.99 and 12 on all exceeding balances charged by First of Omaha under then current Nebraska law. The ICCC also charged the state's attorney general with administering the act, empowering the office to enforce these provisions on the state's behalf. In November, Richard Turner sued Omaha Service and the Central National Bank and Trust Company, an Iowa agent bank for First of Omaha's BankAmericard plan. The case was a whirlwind. An Iowa state court signaled its intention to issue an injunction, preventing First of Omaha from "assessing or collecting" interest in excess of Iowa rates. Before the judge could sign the order, Omaha Service moved the case to federal court. The federal court, in turn, sent the case back to state court, which finally found that the banks were violating the ICCC and issued an injunction. It then reversed itself because of the precedent established in *Fisher v. First Nat. Bank of Chicago* and granted summary judgment in favor of First of Omaha. With his head likely still spinning, Turner appealed to the Iowa Supreme Court. But now new cases advanced in Minnesota.[27]

Minnesota and *Marquette*

As the Fishers' cases were moving through the courts, the bank card market continued to develop in Minnesota. Following its settlement with the state in 1972, the St. Cloud National Bank sought to "test the viability of the plan at twelve percent," but it soon discontinued its Master Charge program. This left Marquette National Bank of Minneapolis as the only card-issuing bank in Minnesota. Marquette, too, could not profitably maintain its Bank-Americard program under the state's 12 percent interest rate ceiling. In 1973, the bank began charging cardholders a $10 annual fee. The move was unprecedented: banks had always offered their cards as a "free" service to consumers, in contrast to elite travel cards like American Express. Most bank executives believed consumers would never accept an annual service charge. When the fee went into effect, Marquette lost 40 percent of its cardholders. Its card program also began to generate profits. By 1975, Marquette issued 80 percent of bank cards in Minnesota, with the rest coming from out-of-state banks. The state's low interest rates had taken a clear toll on bank card growth: in 1975, 2.38 percent of all national bank loans were for credit card accounts, whereas only 0.29 percent of Minnesota national bank loans were.[28]

In stark contrast, Nebraska bankers took advantage of their state's high rates, so that in 1975, card loans—spread across the Midwest—accounted for 5.11 percent of Nebraska national bank lending. First of Omaha led the way and executives were eager to continue expansion. The *Fisher* cases had been a boon to the bank. Although the suits remained unresolved, executive Jim Doody recalled, competing national banks had stopped soliciting customers in Iowa. On the advice of their attorney—who told Doody, "Don't worry . . . we're going to win"—First of Omaha redoubled its solicitation efforts. The bank used the conflict between state and federal law to break down the barriers to a national card market. "We were taking the state by storm," Doody explained, "and, buoyed by these developments, we decided to expand into Minnesota, which, like Iowa, also had a low usury ceiling." When First of Omaha turned its attention to Minnesota, Omaha Service again solicited agent banks, merchants, and consumers to join the BankAmericard plan. As in Iowa, First of Omaha planned to charge consumers 18 percent on the first $999.99 of their outstanding card balances, and 12 percent on any remainder. With these rates, First of Omaha could offer their cards for "free."[29]

Seeing its market in jeopardy, Marquette turned to the state for protection. In early 1976, the Minnesota legislature took up the Bank Credit Card Act, which formalized the 12 percent rate for bank card plans and allowed banks to charge up to a $15 annual fee "for the privilege of using a bank credit card." The law also provided tools to fight out-of-state card issuers. It applied to "any national banking association doing business in this state." Any bank operating in compliance with the law could seek injunctive relief when "injured competitively" by a bank violating the statute. As the state senator introducing the proposal explained to his colleagues, the law represented an "attempt to limit the influx of credit cards . . . from other states by requiring that . . . they must do what is required by our laws." Lawmakers understood that they were managing a trade-off between consumer protection and local bank profits: they should not "feel we are passing any 'big piece' of consumer legislation because we are not," "Baldy" Hansen, Labor and Commerce Committee chair told his colleagues. Although the committee did not do the math, consumers who carried an average balance of less than $166.67 would have been better off under First of Omaha's plan. Nevertheless, consumer and labor groups, who wanted to preserve low-cost credit, supported the law, as did financial institutions, which wanted state protection from price competition. Both sides shared an interest in preserving Minnesota's sovereignty over local interest rates and with it the legislative forum to renegotiate the balance between consumer and creditor interests in the future.[30]

When Minnesota's Bank Credit Card Act went into effect, Marquette promptly sued First of Omaha and Omaha Service, seeking to stop the Nebraska bank from issuing cards in Minnesota. But the Minnesota state court simply sent the case to federal court. Although the *Fisher* appeals had not yet been decided, Marquette's attorneys feared a federal court would be more sympathetic to the argument that First of Omaha's card program was governed by Nebraska law. Marquette's attorneys then took a novel step: they dropped their suit against First of Omaha, the bank, and sought injunctive relief only against Omaha Service. In doing so, they followed the course charted by Everett Meeker, focusing on the credit infrastructure that made card lending, not the loans themselves, possible. Marquette's attorneys took Meeker's strategy one step further. Although Meeker had tried to keep his case in Iowa by piercing the legal veil between First of Omaha and Omaha Service, his ultimate goal was recovering damages from First of Omaha. The bank, after all, had the money. Marquette wanted to halt First of Omaha's card solicitation. Stopping Omaha Service achieved that end. Omaha Service was licensed to do business in Minnesota and could be sued in state court. The case transferred there.[31]

For a time, this proved a winning strategy. Articulating the core tenets of financial federalism, the Minnesota court stated, "Since the founding of our republic, Congress, by its legislation, has allowed states to set their own interest rates." Yet, it continued, "the defendants are arguing that they have a right to export Nebraska's high interest rate into the State of Minnesota." The court permanently enjoined Omaha Service from issuing cards in Minnesota. The injunction effectively barred First of Omaha, which actually issued the cards, making the bank a de facto defendant. On appeal, a majority of the Minnesota Supreme Court argued that a "bank engaged in the interstate business of credit card financing should not be able to avoid the provisions of Minnesota law." The court, though, could not accept the procedural maneuvering employed by Marquette's attorneys. The majority reluctantly concurred with the *Fisher* rulings that First of Omaha was subject only to Nebraska law. Justice George M. Scott dissented. "Should a simple credit card transaction between a local citizen and a local merchant be construed as a bank loan by the Nebraska bank to a Minnesota citizen, as *Fisher* proclaims without question?" Scott demanded. "Minnesota," he added, "should reject such an extension as a misinterpretation of the National Bank Act and exercise its own judgment." It should, according to Scott, retain its policy prerogative over in-state interest rates.[32]

The Iowa Supreme Court, which heard Richard Turner's appeal of the Omaha Service case in June 1978, took just this position. The federal courts' rulings in the *Fisher* cases, the court contended, moved beyond the principle of "competitive equality" between national and state banks. Federal courts were "not arguing for equality but for superiority over All other lenders." Further, the Iowa court determined, the events that led to the *Fisher* cases had occurred before Iowa enacted its consumer credit code, which established explicit rates for credit card loans. "To follow the *Fisher* decisions," the Iowa court continued, would "ignore the express public interest this state has in protecting its citizens from excessive finance charges." The Iowa Supreme Court thus commanded the trial court to enjoin Omaha Service from charging excessive interest in Iowa. At the last moment, the court stayed its order pending the resolution of *Marquette,* which the U.S. Supreme Court agreed to hear in August 1978.[33]

The Iowa court's ruling was not unanimous, and here dissent drew on a growing Law and Economics movement, whose practitioners criticized regulation, like usury laws, that interfered with the free play of competitive markets. When viewed through the lens of legal economic reasoning, the arguments advanced by First of Omaha's opponents could look a little ridiculous. "The majority seems to have adopted the State's argument that allowing defendants to charge a higher rate of interest gives them an advantage over other lenders," Justice Clay LeGrand observed in dissent. "Really the contrary is true. Certainly there is no difficulty today in obtaining credit cards; the problem is to avoid getting them." First of Omaha, LeGrand continued, "should be at a disadvantage when they overprice their commodity credit in a highly competitive market." Yet by calling the bank card market "highly competitive" LeGrand invoked an ideal. He did not describe reality. Despite the best hopes of the Truth-in-Lending Act, card firms still did not compete on price. They would not for decades to come. As a simplification and as a symbol, competition held great power. Consumers and their allies, however, knew markets did not deliver low rates automatically: they had to fight for them. Across the decade, they had done so, in state after state. Using the tools of financial federalism, they had bargained with local bankers to construct card systems that were safe, low cost, and—for banks—modestly profitable. Consumers, however, could not negotiate with out-of-state banks.[34]

Whether charging high interest rates offered a competitive advantage was peripheral to the more fundamental issue of whether a Nebraska bank could charge high rates to Minnesota consumers. When the Supreme Court agreed to hear *Marquette* in 1978, it chose to address the challenges mobile bank cards and credit card infrastructure posed to a federalist financial regulatory system built on immobile state boundaries. The key legal question centered on the meaning of the word "located" as written in Section 85 of the National Bank Act of 1864, which mandated that a national bank assess interest based on the laws of the state in which it is "located." Was, the court contemplated, First of Omaha's BankAmericard program "located" in some state, and if so, where was it? When the law was written, this would have been self-evident: in 1864, a bank had a concrete location. Bank cards complicated this question. The program could have been "located" in Minnesota, where a Minnesota citizen used a First Omaha BankAmericard to purchase goods from a Minnesota merchant, as Judge Scott's dissent suggested, and therefore subject to Minnesota's usury laws. Initially, several justices shared this interpretation. Arguing that the court should take the case in May 1978, Justice Blackmun wrote that the *Fisher* ruling distorted the National Bank Act's "original purpose of preventing discrimination *against* national banks," instead making the law "a sword for discrimination *in favor of out-of-state* national banks."[35]

This sword threatened to carve the very heart out of financial federalism, negating local control over consumer credit markets inscribed in the National Banking Acts and maintained under the New Deal regulatory order. Through the legislative and legal challenges that culminated in Minnesota's Bank Credit Card Act, Marquette had reached an accommodation with its local financial constituents. The bank's BankAmericard customers were, through the state's democratic process, also its regulators. The case threatened to undermine local political negotiations by shifting regulatory decisions to places where Minnesota consumers, bankers, and state officials had no say. "A law enacted by the Nebraska legislature will determine the interest rates charged to respondent's Minnesota customers," lawyers representing Minnesota's AFL-CIO argued in a brief to the court. Yet "a consumer interest group in Minnesota has no voice in the legislatures of other states." The ramifications of the court's decision would not be limited to Nebraska, Minnesota, and Iowa. If the court found for First of Omaha, the state of Minnesota argued, it would "permit national banks to roam the country's market places free of the regulatory limitations which restrain the local competition." The specter of roving financial institutions, and with them the steady erosion of local rulemaking power through regulatory arbitrage, was antithetical to a regulatory system that confined banks to their home states.[36]

First of Omaha's attorney, William Morrow, had been sure of his firm's legal strategy as it expanded into low-usury states, but for the arguments before the Supreme Court he brought in a ringer, former U.S. solicitor general and experienced Supreme Court litigator Robert H. Bork. Bork stood before the court as a representative of the Law and Economics movement, and he scoffed at Marquette's competitive arguments. "This entire case—this entire attempt to change the structure of the National Banking System turns out to be a fight over alternative advertising techniques," Bork joked. "The Marquette Bank would have done better to take their case to an advertising agency than to a law firm." Jokes aside, the case hinged on the card plan's location. Here Bork offered a different line of reasoning than First of Omaha had previously employed. He began with the bank's basic premise, that all aspects of the credit transaction, its extension and repayment, happened by mail in Omaha. The card program was "located" there. Bork then reversed the language of export and extraterritoriality mobilized by Minnesota's courts and Marquette's attorneys. "Nebraska is not exporting interest rates," Bork argued. "It is more accurate to say that Minnesota is exporting its law to a Nebraska bank." By regulating credit prices within its borders, Minnesota pushed its rules, through card networks, into bank offices in other states. Bork's oral argument—which "made" Justice Byron White "a def[inite]"—swayed the Supreme Court.[37]

In a unanimous decision, the court chose business over consumer politics, nationwide markets over local regulatory control. Speaking for the court, Justice William Brennan offered: "If the location of the bank were to depend on the whereabouts of each credit card transaction, the meaning of the term 'located' would be so stretched as to throw into confusion the complex system of modern interstate banking." Yet for Fred and Edna Fisher, and for many other bank card users, the meaning of a bank's location was already confused. While the court fixed the "location" of a bank at the physical place stipulated by its charter, credit cards and the interfirm infrastructure that enabled them spread transactions further afield, erasing boundaries between states. State rules still mattered, just those of the states where cards were issued. The highest federal court tacitly sanctioned a geographic divergence. Local relationships—whether between a bank and its customers or a state and its citizens—might no longer have any fixed relationship to consumer credit. Nebraska usury laws could govern Minnesotans.[38]

Brennan's ruling was decisive and suggests the question of whether states like Minnesota or Iowa ever had viable arguments, or was the ten-year legal and legislative battle to hold out-of-state banks accountable to local laws just a long, expensive waste of time. First of Omaha had always made its terms clear to cardholders. The small type explained that lending took place in Omaha and was subject to Nebraska laws. A Minnesota consumer, Bork argued, could just as easily travel to Omaha and take out the same loan. What difference did it make if the consumer engaged in the transaction through the mail? Yet Minnesota consumers *had not* traveled to Nebraska. Nebraska had traveled to them—through unsolicited cards and mailed solicitations, through agent bank agreements and merchant contracts, and ultimately through the elaborate financial infrastructure First of Omaha and Omaha Service established throughout the Midwest. State efforts to protect consumers stood in the way of the efficient, interstate bank card markets that made credit so convenient. It was not a foregone conclusion that the court would choose national convenience over local democratic control.

Brennan's ruling was an end, but not the end. Eight months later First of Omaha and Marquette were back in court. This time, First of Omaha had sued Marquette, arguing that by lobbying for Minnesota's Bank Credit Card Act and then suing to enforce it, Marquette had intended to prevent price competition in violation of the Sherman Antitrust Act. First of Omaha further argued that Marquette's actions constituted malicious prosecution, abuse of legal process, and that they violated First of Omaha's rights of equal protection provided by the Fourteenth Amendment and secured through the Civil Rights Act of 1871. First of Omaha was piling it on and sending a message: the state usury regimes negotiated by consumer and labor groups, local financial elites, and state policymakers under—in short, the place-based social contract—would not stand in the way of bank card growth. First of Omaha lost the case—a federal district court determined that "a bank's ability to charge a certain rate of interest . . . is not in the nature of the rights protected by the Civil Rights Act [of 1871]"—but it had already won the war.[39]

In 1978, *Marquette*'s full consequences were not yet evident. Indeed, the case received little attention, which puzzled Justice Lewis Powell Jr. "Why has the banking industry taken so little interest in this case?" he asked Bork during oral arguments. Perhaps a dispute between midwestern banks was beneath the industry's notice. More likely, most card-issuing banks still focused on their local markets. Banks remained confined within states. Bankers imagined their consumer markets as local, tied to their branch networks. The most ambitious envisioned regional card markets. Card networks remained a collective enterprise—a cooperative venture linking local card plans. Few bankers recognized that consumer attention was shifting, from the bank to the network. BankAmericard (soon Visa) and Master Charge were transforming, as LeGrand surmised, into vectors of commodity credit. It would take an aggressive bank, with a national vision, to use *Marquette* to its full potential—not just to move regulation across state borders, but to move the card-issuing bank into a state that would not regulate rates at all. The prospect of national banks roaming the country's market places would soon become reality.[40]

In August 1977, legislators in Missouri were engaged in the time-honored tradition of tweaking their state's consumer credit laws. The state's small loan law permitted a 26.62 annual rate on loans of up to $500 and 10 percent on remaining amounts. The problem was a clause that prohibited lenders from circumventing the law by making multiple small loans under $500 rather than consolidating these into a larger loan at a lower rate. Banks operating credit card plans found that the law interfered with their ability to offer cash advances to cardholders with existing credit balances. Each cash advance looked like an additional small loan. As with similar state-level legislation, the governor had a file full of reasoned letters from local bankers urging the technical change. "The [Banking] Commissioner can't effectively enforce the law and lenders can't comply with it, because neither can determine whether a given rate is legal," one correspondent wrote.[41]

One letter, though, imparted new urgency. "I have been informed that First National City Bank of New York is in the process of putting together a massive nationwide solicitation of cardholders for the Visa Credit Card," St. Louis attorney Hugh McPheeters wrote. "I understand . . . that Citibank will use the same rate and fee structure it charges to its New York customers, as it is authorized to do by recent case law." The case McPheeters cited was Fisher's against the First National Bank of Omaha. "It is ironic that this business can be solicited by banks in other states which are not even bound by our rate limitations, while our law makes it illegal for Missouri banks to do so if they already have a . . . relationship with the same customer."[42] McPheeters was well-informed. And right to be worried.

9

Profits Anywhere

Dispatches

The end of financial federalism began in August 1977. The first dispatches came from Idaho. Bankers and state officials there were surprised that New York's Citibank had invited Idaho consumers to obtain a Visa card from the far-off New York bank. The next day, newspapers reported similar offers in Illinois, then Michigan. Georgia, California, and Missouri soon followed. When reporters pressed for details, Citi's spokespeople declined to elaborate on the bank's plans. With little concrete information, rival bankers and breathless financial journalists estimated that Citi had sent eight, twenty, even forty million card offers to consumers in at least twenty-five states, breaking with the geographically restrained marketing practices proscribed by the nation's state-based banking system. Some bankers brushed off the new, nationwide competition. A Long Beach, California, banker expressed confidence in his firm's "strong customer loyalty." Bankers in Idaho noted that out-of-state customers, having few ties to the card-issuing bank, were often delinquent and unprofitable. But most bankers who commented on Citi's marketing blitz recognized a fundamental change. "Citibank," a Chicago banker predicted, "is trying to establish a retail system on a nationwide basis." They saw the same future Citibank did, a technology-driven marketplace where the bank card, not the physical bank, was the locus of consumer financial services. Many saw their graves.[1]

Citibank's secretive campaign bypassed the geographic boundaries that structured American banking and the physical bank offices on which these restrictions relied. When bankers first rushed into the card market in the late-1960s, they invested cards with a vision of the industry's future with the physical bank at its center. Cards, they thought, would generate profits from unregulated revolving credit while forging new, profitable relationships with consumers and merchants inside the bank. By the early 1970s, this hopeful vision had fallen to hard reality. With the rush of competition, few banks gained the first-mover advantages they anticipated. High fraud and charge-offs dashed hopes for ready profits. New federal and state regulations forced bankers to charge fixed credit prices, even as rising market interest rates drove up their cost of funds. Consumers used cards for convenience, paying their balances every month without incurring interest. Credit cards became a uniform, low-margin product, identified more with the national network than with the local bank. Most bankers narrowed their aspirations for card technology. They scratched out profitability in competitive local markets. As industry optimism stalled, some financial executives, among them Citibank's Walter B. Wriston and BankAmericard's Dee W. Hock, imagined new futures for card technology, not as undifferentiated revolving credit but as a hub for the full suite of consumer financial services. Cards would not bring customers into the bank; instead, cards would *be* the bank, and with them would come a means of upending the New Deal regulatory order's fixed geographic markets.[2]

Citibank—the First National City Bank of New York before 1976—was materially and ideologically positioned to disrupt the card industry and the wider financial regulatory system. Led by Wriston, a fervent advocate of unbridled markets, the bank pressed hard at the edges of the regulatory structure, seeking and prizing any profitable gaps. Wriston and Citibank initially gratified their ambitions abroad, where the bank operated in less and differently regulated markets and where Citi bankers became adept at exploiting regulatory and tax differences across borders. Citi also led its American peers in developing new sources of lendable funds, through eurodollar markets and certificates of deposit, which the bank gathered and channeled toward consumer lending in the United States and sovereign and corporate lending around the world. In the mid-1970s, when Citibank was earning more than 70 percent of its profits abroad, robust competition from ascendant foreign banks ended easy revenues in international markets. The time was ripe for Citi, largely confined to New York City by federal and state regulation, to turn its attention, unregulated capital, and border-crossing experience back to the United States. Building on the certainty offered by the *Fisher* decisions, Citibank embarked on an ambitious, nationwide consumer banking plan, redefining the scope of the card networks and sparking renewed competition—and regulatory attention—in the process.[3]

Citibank moved aggressively as the United States' financial regulatory system continued to list between the New Deal's rigid financial structure and the new flexibility bankers were constructing alongside it. Prompted by the credit crunches of the late 1960s, the Nixon administration initiated yet another searching examination of the nation's financial system, yet again premised on injecting competition into financial markets, and yet again concluding without significant reform. Mired in postwar credit politics, Congress remained incapable of reinforcing the old system or bringing a new one into being. Mired in the Watergate scandal, Nixon had no political capital to spend. While debates stalled, bankers moved. They used credit cards and related technologies, like point-of-sale (POS) terminals and automatic teller machines (ATMs), to chip away at financial federalism's geographic restrictions. In doing so, bankers opened vexing regulatory questions: What was a bank branch? Where did consumer transactions occur? Which government unit would ultimately decide? Congress considered these questions but did not act. Federal agencies, state governments, and courts at both levels made their own ways as best they could, ultimately—and inadvertently—nudging banks toward cards as the most promising path toward geographic expansion. Citi pushed the boundaries furthest of all. The bank risked everything to bestride the national consumer market. It proved a daring and dangerous bet.

Anywhere at a Profit

Founded as a small merchant bank in 1812, the City Bank of New York—as Citibank was then called—was not predestined for financial glory. During the Panic of 1837, it very nearly failed. At its nadir, merchant and industrialist Moses Taylor took control. Taylor used City Bank as a treasury for his expanding commercial empire, making the bank a safe, liquid repository for business deposits. Taylor bolstered this reputation by securing a national charter in 1865. By 1891, when control passed to financier James Stillman, the National City Bank was prominent, if not predominant. Like Taylor, Stillman managed the bank in support of his wider business interests. Closely tied to powerful industrialists, most importantly the Rockefeller family, Stillman molded National City into a leading investment and overseas bank. In the 1910s, Stillman transformed National City from a specialized firm serving corporate clients to a comprehensive bank offering diversified financial services. Charles "Sunshine Charlie" Mitchell went further, expanding National City's branch network throughout New York City, offering prosperous consumers savings deposits and small personal loans. In the roaring 1920s, the firm spread brokerage offices, under the National City Company, across the country to sell stocks and bonds. Before "financial supermarkets" there were "financial department stores." National City was the prototype. By June 1929, National City controlled over $2 billion in aggregate resources and was "without question the world's leading financial intermediary."[4]

The Great Depression brought National City's diversified financial empire crashing to the ground. Sunshine Charlie, the embodied spirit of unbridled financial optimism, became one of the crash's prime scapegoats. He resigned to protect what little reputation National City had left. Through the Depression, the bank shored up its corporate-international-consumer strategy, even as the New Deal financial reforms stripped away its investment banking business. During World War II, National City executives restored the bank's reputation by funding the war effort. When Wriston joined the bank in 1946, National City had invested almost half its assets in government securities. It "was less a bank than a bond portfolio," Wriston's biographer wrote. Citi had been chastened, but it was also ready to rebuild.[5]

Tall, lanky, hawk-faced, and sharp, Wriston came to National City by way of an elite upbringing and wartime stints at the State Department and Army Signal Corps. Wriston's father, Brown University president and prominent New Deal critic Henry Wriston, instilled an unwavering belief in rugged individualism and an unwavering antagonism toward federal regulatory authority. The younger Wriston started at National City as a branch auditor but by the late 1940s was arranging complex oil tanker financing for Greek shipping magnate Aristotle Onassis. Combining government subsidies, shell corporations, and international flags of convenience, Wriston's dealings with Onassis provided early lessons in the ways an astute banker could profitably evade and manipulate the financial regulatory structure. Wriston soon headed the bank's Transportation Department, before being tapped to revive Citi's flagging Overseas Division under future president (1959–67) and chairman (1967–70) George S. Moore. International banking was the ideal place for Wriston. Although the federal government discouraged geographic expansion within the United States, policymakers encouraged banks to grow abroad. Under the Bretton Woods Agreement, which made the dollar the center of the global currency system, American banks projected U.S. political and economic power. Citibank adjusted slowly to this new reality. When Wriston arrived in the Overseas Division in the mid-1950s, "the London branch," he recalled, "was losing money," and "the Paris branch . . . was losing money, but elegantly." Spurred by government favor and anticipating the revival of global trade, Moore and Wriston reorganized and expanded the bank's international operations. The Overseas Division would provide Citi with a steady infusion of funds, profits, and ideas as the bank continued to press against the regulatory order within the United States.[6]

Citi executives focused on international operations in the 1950s because, in common with peers like David Rockefeller's Chase Manhattan, Citibank struggled to raise funds and increase profits domestically. Seeking higher returns, Citibank's corporate clients shifted their idle cash out of the bank's interest-free demand deposits into treasury bills and other short-term investments. As the bank's senior management reported to shareholders in 1959, "our principal problem . . . has been to meet greater loan demand in a period when our deposits have shown little gain." Wriston led Citi's efforts to generate more lendable funds. First, the Overseas Division began collecting dollar deposits through Citi's London branch in 1959. These offshore dollars (eurodollars) provided an unregulated pool of money that Citi lent abroad and channeled back into its domestic loan portfolio. Second, with Wriston's backing the bank developed the negotiable certificate of deposit (CD), a high-denomination, high-interest security that U.S. investors could buy and sell. With eurodollars and the CD, Citibank's deposit base no longer constrained its lending capacity. It could raise funds at will. Unlike regulated demand deposits, however, these new funds were expensive and variable. Their prices rose and fell with market interest rates, solving the funding problem while compounding the squeeze on profits and introducing new interest rate risk. The more Citi relied on high-cost liabilities, the narrower the spread between its borrowing and lending rates became. Citi, like its rivals, met the profit squeeze by aggressively expanding its balance sheet, pursuing additional deposit-and-loan business to compensate for the declining profitability of that business.[7]

By the 1960s, Wriston and a like-minded cohort of Citi executives, including Moore and protégé John Reed (CEO, 1984–2000), sought to do more than maximize the bank's net interest income. Building on a report produced by the consulting firm TEMPO, Citi executives revisited the diversification strategies pursued by Stillman and Mitchell in the 1920s. Wriston and his colleagues imagined Citi as more than a bank; they were fashioning it into a global financial services company. TEMPO's core recommendation, Moore recalled, was "to perform every financial service anywhere in the world [that] you can do at a profit, and that you can do legally." Moore and Wriston made the phrase Citibank's unofficial moto.[8]

At Citibank, the transformation into a global financial services company entailed three overlapping priorities: international diversification, information technology, and consumer markets. Moore, Wriston, and Reed had all spent formative time in the Overseas Division. They knew the bank's international operations enabled experimentation. During the 1950s, Citi expanded its global branch network to serve the bank's multinational corporate clients. It eventually boasted more than two hundred international branches, far more than its U.S. competitors. Under Wriston's leadership, the Overseas Division began offering financial services tailored to local markets free of Citibank's domestic restrictions. In Australia, for example, Citi acquired a specialist consumer finance firm in the late 1960s and transformed it into a nationwide consumer financial services business. Likewise, in the early 1970s, Citi built on experience making large, syndicated eurodollar loans to expand into investment banking through London and Tokyo subsidiaries. Using branches in the Channel Islands, Nassau, and Singapore, meanwhile, Citi executives became adept at arbitraging regulatory and tax differences across borders, finding ways to lend in one market while booking transactions in less regulated or less taxed countries. Unhindered by the New Deal regulatory order, the Overseas Division became Citi's main profit center.[9]

At home and abroad, Citi bankers viewed the bank's future through the lens of information technology. Computers, executives believed, would streamline costs, enable new accounting and risk management systems, and eliminate the reams of paperwork that clogged the bank's back offices. Most bankers shared these views. The TEMPO study encouraged Citi executives to go a step further: to use technology to make an end run around the New Deal regulatory order. The bank, the study's authors argued, should "use technology" to "do something that by the time the regulators wake up to the fact, it's too late." This aggressive advice aligned with Wriston's own predilections. "Wriston," his biographer Phillip Zweig wrote, "never did anything by hand that could be done by machine." Case in point: A friend remembered giving Wriston and his wife potted flowers for their anniversary, which Wriston proceeded to plant with a backhoe. John Reed joined Wriston in this enthusiasm, if not the overzealous use of construction equipment. Reed modernized the bank's global back-office systems before being elevated to head its domestic consumer business.[10]

Reed's appointment signaled Citibank's renewed emphasis on the U.S. consumer market. Although Citibank had a legacy of consumer banking, geographic restrictions confined the bank to New York City as affluent consumers spread to the suburbs. New York State's branching laws prevented Citibank from expanding outside New York's five boroughs before 1960, and then only in neighboring Nassau and Westchester Counties. New Jersey remained off limits, and so did Connecticut, where Wriston lived. Still, Citibank expanded its branch network considerably. Between 1960 and 1966, the bank added 43 branches within city limits and an additional 36 branches in the suburbs, primarily to generate low-cost consumer deposits to fund corporate lending. The bank also expanded its consumer lending portfolio, adding home mortgages, check credit, and eventually credit cards. Through the 1970s, however, the consumer strategy disappointed the bank's ambitions. Brick-and-mortar growth was slow and geographically confined, branches were expensive to operate, and competition in New York was fierce.[11]

Citi's early forays into the card market aligned with its growth priorities and underlined its persistent regulatory difficulties. In 1965, Citibank announced plans to acquire Hilton's Carte Blanche travel card program, which would enable Citi to manage a global card plan and build relationships with the business elites who used these cards. The Justice Department blocked the merger on antitrust grounds and also prevented Chase from acquiring Diners Club. The Antitrust Division argued that if New York's two largest

banks purchased ongoing card plans, they would attain unassailable positions in the credit card market. It would be better, the Justice Department's
attorneys reasoned, if Citi and Chase started from scratch, noting that Citibank "is especially qualified to enter the credit card business on a national
and international scale on its own," adding, "such entry is likely if the proposed merger is enjoined." Chase had tried to enter the card business de
novo in the late 1950s. Its executives were not eager to try again. Citibank, on
the contrary, accepted the Justice Department's invitation.[12]

After the Justice Department decision, Citi executives turned to consumer
credit, launching "the Everything Card" in August 1967. The Everything
Card embodied 1960s card mania. To build transaction volume, Citi mailed
more than one million cards to consumers gleaned from the bank's lending
rolls. Wriston, Citibank president from 1967, imagined the Everything Card
as an alternative to the BankAmericard and the basis for a rival network.
Other bankers weren't interested. Hemmed in, the Everything Card gained
little traction outside New York. Localism, Wriston believed, was not a viable
strategy. "All of these cards are going to be taken at the point of sale by people
who are not Rhodes scholars," Wriston vented. In other words, clerks could
only keep tabs on a few card brands—they would not recognize the Everything Card in Florida or California. Citi needed to join a national system. In
1968, the bank dropped Everything and joined Interbank, adopting the Master Charge brand then used by several California banks. The move convinced
other Interbank members, among them Marine Midland in upstate New
York, to unite nationally under Master Charge. Citi then built out its local
network, using agent banks to recruit merchants and cardholders in New
Jersey and Connecticut. When Congress banned unsolicited card mailing in
1970, Citibank was one of sixty New York banks competing in the local card
market, though Citi was also the nation's leading Master Charge issuer.[13]

Growth and restraint—the cycles that shaped Citi's card business—also
channeled Wriston's bolder efforts to transform Citibank into a full-service
financial conglomerate. In 1968, as it transitioned from Everything to Master Charge, Citi created the First National City Corporation (Citicorp), a new
holding company parent for the global bank. The regulatory system's industry silos sharply limited the lines of business Citi, as a commercial bank,
could pursue. A holding company, however, could own a commercial bank
along with a variety of non-bank businesses. Congress had tried to bar this

door before. The Bank Holding Company Act of 1956 prohibited holding companies that owned *two or more* banks from owning non-banking businesses. The act's framers, however, had excluded one-bank holding companies. Congress's target had been A. P. Giannini's giant conglomerate, Transamerica. The law left smaller holding companies intact and created a slim legal gap. Wriston plunged Citibank into this loophole, creating a corporate parent for the bank and with it gaining colossal new financial powers. Wriston, seeking to minimize regulatory scrutiny, downplayed the transformation. "Our goal," Wriston explained to shareholders, "is to preserve and strengthen our competitive position in the financial services business, which we are convinced can best be achieved by becoming a congeneric corporation, that is, a corporation which brings together allied activities which had a common relationship." What could be less threatening than a "congeneric corporation?"[14]

Behind its opaque language, Citi torched the regulatory system's industry silos. On Inauguration Day 1969, it announced plans to purchase the Chubb Corporation, a major property and casualty insurer. The regulatory machinery sprang into action. Both Wright Patman and the newly minted Nixon administration introduced one-bank holding company legislation to close the loophole. The bills initially hinted that existing subsidiaries would be grandfathered in. Citi moved faster, buying or chartering a flurry of diverse businesses as legislation coalesced. Wriston targeted firms— mortgage companies, tax preparation services, computer leasing firms, and the like—based far from New York. He planned to enlarge the bank's footprint and use congeneric subsidiaries to cross-sell other Citicorp services. The Justice Department remained an aggressive watchdog, blocking the Chubb acquisition. The 1970 Bank Holding Company Act, in turn, required holding companies to divest all non-banking businesses acquired since June 30, 1968. In Citibank's case, that meant all of them. In the future, the Federal Reserve would rule on Citicorp's acquisitions. Still, the straightjacketing of Citicorp was a temporary setback. Since the 1970 Bank Holding Company Act obliterated the distinction between holding companies that owned one bank and those that owned many, Citicorp started buying banks.[15]

Wriston's singular focus on profits anywhere placed him in a vanguard of U.S. executives who sought to recast the corporation from an institution responsible to diverse stakeholders, to a vehicle aimed unerringly at returning value to shareholders. Wriston startled the banking and investment community in October 1971 when he announced that Citi would grow earnings by an aggressive 15 percent a year (it had averaged 7 percent over the previous decade). Observers had expected Wriston to emphasize the bank's social and societal commitments, but he had other plans. Echoing University of Chicago economist Milton Friedman's recently articulated doctrine "the social responsibility of business is to increase its profits," Wriston told investors, "We see no contradiction between our commitment to increasing earnings-per-share growth and our responsibility to make a constructive contribution to society." Pitching an upward evaluation of Citi's stock price, Wriston explained the bank's strategy of embracing technology and pursuing new markets "as rapidly as possible." Behind the scenes, Citi's federal supervisors grew nervous that reckless earnings growth might endanger the bank. "Mr. Wriston is thought of as one person who 'breaks the mold,'" a Fed analyst wrote to Fed chairman Arthur Burns a year after Wriston's announcement. Citi's growth, as near as Fed staff could tell, was driven by leverage, exacerbated by the bank's habit of funneling profits to the holding company instead of retaining them as capital. "Without attempting to pass any refined judgment on the question of what is 'adequate' equity capital," the Fed analysts concluded, "we believe that the highly-leveraged position of FNCB [the bank] and FNCC [the holding company] raise important policy questions that will be difficult to solve." Wriston would not wait for the solution.[16]

Even as Wriston sought to convert his bold earnings target into tangible profits, geographic and regulatory barriers limited the headway Citi could make in the United States, and in the early 1970s the bank continued to grow abroad. When Wriston announced his growth target in 1971, the bank generated 42 percent of its earnings abroad. By 1976, that figure had reached 72 percent. But Citi's success brought new competition from foreign banks, both in eurodollar markets and for Citi's corporate customers in the United States. Citi's unimpeded international expansion was over. With international markets increasingly competitive and corporate business declining, Citibank renewed its attention on consumers and technology in the mid-1970s. Wriston would later explain this strategy quoting the famous bank robber Willie Sutton: Citibank turned to the consumer market because "that's where the money is."[17]

Networks over Banks

To access consumers, Citi executives turned to the card market, which remained unsettled after nearly a decade of rapid change. In the 1960s, bankers had imagined cards as distinct, locally branded products, that would
forge relationships with merchants and consumers, drawing them into the
banks. Revolving credit was a small part of the hoped-for card revolution. Yet
politics intervened. Consumer and labor groups objected to aggressive card
marketing and high credit prices. With Congress's 1970 unsolicited mailing
ban and state-level interest rate ceilings, these groups structured the card
market to provide safe and low-cost credit. The unsolicited mailing ban
proved a boon to bankers. It curbed banks' breakneck competition. It also
allowed bankers and card network builders to refine their technological systems and business practices—to focus on network management and maintenance, not just manic growth. All sought to make cards profitable, but they
faced a difficult road. In most states, new usury laws fixed the prices bankers
could charge. Since they could not adjust credit rates, bankers worked to reduce operating costs and increase transaction volume. Meanwhile, the bank
card networks improved transaction procedures and promoted the national
card brands, BankAmericard and Master Charge. Over time, consumer and
operational pressure narrowed the scope of cards, from locally distinct, bank-
specific products toward uniform, undifferentiated vehicles of commodified
revolving credit—from plastic capitalism to a plastic cage.[18]

Refining credit card interchange posed the most pressing challenge: from
the very beginning, operating national credit systems through geographically fragmented markets failed catastrophically. In theory, interchange was
a straightforward process. When a consumer used a BankAmericard issued
by the National Bank of Commerce in Seattle to purchase goods from a merchant enrolled by the First National Bank of Omaha, she initiated a series of
transactions. The merchant deposited the charge slip with the Omaha bank.
The Omaha bank credited the merchant's account, less the discount, and
then forwarded the charge slip to Seattle. The Seattle bank reimbursed the
Omaha bank and added the charge to its customer's bill. Presto! This was the
theory anyway. In practice, the Omaha bank sorted and tallied its daily charge
slips and immediately pulled funds from the Seattle bank through the Federal Reserve System. Before it could bill its cardholder, the Seattle bank had

to wait for First of Omaha to sort the relevant charge slips and physically mail them to Seattle. The Omaha bank, though, had already been paid; it had little incentive to prioritize the Seattle bank's charge slips over its own local transactions. Lack of processing capacity compounded the problem. As BankAmericard licensees rushed to build transaction volume, a sea of paper inundated their rudimentary systems. Merchant banks routinely processed charge slips destined for interchange last, tying up the consumer bank's funds. Merchants were paid but cardholders could not be billed. The waylaid funds, which bankers called "the float," existed physically in cigar boxes, and then in warehouses, full of unprocessed charge slips. All that stalled-out paper represented tens of millions of dollars in float drifting between banks, idle money that cost money.[19]

As early as 1968, BankAmericard licensees recognized that the architects of their network had failed to develop a functional system of rules and incentives. The float was just the beginning. Vexing questions emerged as consumers, merchants, and bank employees operated and experimented with national card infrastructure. What happened when the Seattle bank's customer wanted to return items she purchased in Omaha? Which bank was responsible for absorbing fraud losses? What interest rate applied on out-of-state transactions? Simple questions created administrative nightmare. Bank of America had signed individual agreements with each participant bank; to change network procedures, Bank of America had to renegotiate hundreds of contracts. Worse, member bankers did not believe Bank of America executives were committed to addressing their concerns. Bank of America and the licensee banks had a shared interest as network *participants* in extending the network. Yet Bank of America, as the network *owner,* also collected a half percent toll on every system transaction, eating into participant bank profits (or contributing further to their losses). Licensee bankers knew as well that Bank of America would pursue nationwide expansion at the first opportunity. "We all knew," banker Dee Hock recalled, "that BofA would swallow our banks like a snake swallows a mouse if branch banking law didn't prevent it." Participant banks worried that Bank of America would use the network they helped build to bring competition to their local markets.[20]

Member banks rebelled, staging a palace coup led by Hock, who was head of card operations at the National Bank of Commerce in Seattle. Before joining the Bank of Commerce, Hock had been an itinerant credit executive, largely self-educated and contemptuous of the hierarchal structures—managerial, governmental, social—typical of mid-century American life. At a meeting of licensee banks in 1968, Hock agreed to lead the reorganization of the Bank-Americard network. He devised a system of decentralized, regional committees to identify problems in operations, fraud, credit granting, and technology. Under Hock's leadership—and largely against Bank of America's wishes—BankAmericard transitioned from a network owned and controlled by Bank of America to a not-for-profit cooperative owned collectively by the participating banks. The new organization, National BankAmericard, Inc. (NBI), resembled Interbank's (Master Charge) decentralized, cooperative-competitive structure. Hock never acknowledged this similarity; he preferred to view NBI as the sui generis embodiment of his anti-hierarchical management philosophy. More important, Hock's organization of NBI ensured that both bank card networks existed as distinct institutions, owned and controlled by their member banks but with interests and identities distinct from the banks.[21]

Hock recognized that he had split the atom of network ownership and network control, that under his leadership NBI would take on an institutional life of its own. Hock made NBI a vehicle for his techno-futurist enthusiasm: He, like Wriston, believed information technology would massively disrupt existing financial and regulatory structures. Unlike Wriston, Hock's unit of analysis was the network, not the bank. Electronic data, Hock imagined, was the future of personal finance. By moving data among individuals and institutions, networks like NBI would facilitate the "exchange of value," not just the extension of credit. Even paired down to the possibilities achievable with early 1970s technology, Hock's vision entailed radical, fundamental change. There was no reason that value qua data should be held in banks. Organizing and expanding NBI, Hock worked to make the network paramount. Though he had the good sense to keep his most radical ideas mostly to himself.[22]

Through the early 1970s, both the networks and the banks focused their managerial energy on overcoming the operations problems that plagued card plans. Both NBI and Interbank constructed massive technical systems to speed card authorization (making cards more convenient for consumers and less susceptible to fraud) and interbank processing (diminishing the float, managing abnormal transactions, and allocating fraud costs). The

American Bankers Association, through its Bank Card Standardization Task Force, crafted uniform procedures for banks and networks and a uniform experience for consumers and merchants. As the networks focused on operations, so did individual banks. Once Congress's unsolicited mailing ban halted the industry's madcap competition, many bankers turned inward, focusing on mundane but critical activities such as analyzing personnel and work-flow procedures, developing in-house data processing, and whittling their cardholder lists. Bankers cultivated portfolios of active card users who paid their bills and did not commit fraud. They pruned the rest. Total cards outstanding declined from 1970 to 1972.[23]

As the industry caught its breath, bankers' collective ambitions—their vision of cards as a "road to the future" in David Kennedy's words—narrowed, squeezed by regulations that promoted uniformity, stifled revenues, and increased costs. The Truth-in-Lending Act loomed over the industry. Paul Douglas and other advocates believed that product differentiation in consumer credit markets often sowed confusion and harmed consumers. Uniform price disclosure, by contrast, enforced uniformity. State usury laws that grew out of Truth-in-Lending likewise imposed uniform credit prices. At the same time, new federal laws, enacted in response to the unsolicited mailing boom, added costs. The Fair Credit Reporting Act (1970), which William Proxmire yoked to the unsolicited mailing ban, required creditors to explain to consumers why they were denied credit. Consumers' complaints about card billing errors yielded the Fair Credit Billing Act (1974), which required card issuers to investigate and report on billing complaints. By 1976, Fed analysts explained to Chairman Burns that "credit cards have been the principal subject of by far the majority of the consumer credit legislation proposed and/or enacted since 1970." Credit cards continued to animate consumer politics more than any other financial issue.[24]

Consumer regulations also created a legal infrastructure that further drove cards toward uniformity. The Truth-in-Lending Act authorized plaintiffs to seek twice the finance charge if a creditor violated the law. In the early 1970s, plaintiffs' attorneys and consumer groups lined up to file class action complaints, seeking millions of dollars in damages. The Fishers' attorney, Everett Meeker, joined the queue. Threats of legal action stymied innovation. Nervous bankers reconsidered offering new services through cards. Even if regulators approved their disclosure procedures, bankers feared, they might not satisfy a consumer-friendly court. Plaintiffs also brought antitrust suits, claiming that card networks were elaborate schemes to fix the price of credit. Banks all tended to charge the same rates—the maximum rates allowed under state law (they would have charged more if they could have). Damage requests grew with each successive case. Hundreds of millions soon became billions. Bankers believed they would prevail, and they most often did. But the avalanche of consumer lawsuits chilled experimentation. "I don't think about fraud any less than I used to," one Pittsburgh banker observed in 1971, "but I think about class actions just as much."[25]

Regulation and pressure for operational efficiency narrowed bank cards down to uniform, undifferentiated vehicles for commodified revolving credit, trends compounded by card networks' national branding. Although bankers had imagined cards as a lure to draw consumers into their banks, the networks eroded banks' local identity and the links between the card plan and the physical bank. Bankers participated in this process. To achieve national and global acceptance, cards needed a trusted, recognizable brand. Local trademarks did not travel. Following Citibank's lead, Interbank members, which had operated local brands like Marine Midland's Midland Charge Plan and Continental's Town & Country Charge, gradually united under Master Charge. The networks soon launched competing national marketing campaigns touting the benefits of Master Charge or BankAmericard, while individual banks scaled down local advertising. Bankers still linked their bank to the network, promoting, for instance, "Continental Master Charge." Such distinctions were lost on most consumers. National branding focused consumer attention on the network instead of the card-issuing bank.[26]

Indeed, consumers increasingly saw only the network. They carried a Master Charge, not a Marine Midland Master Charge; they used a BankAmericard, not a First of Omaha BankAmericard. Although banks recruited merchants and consumers, processed transactions, and extended credit locally, the shift in emphasis from the bank to the network obscured these ties between the network and the community bank. When bank card managers looked at their cardholder lists, they saw this vividly. First of Omaha carefully built a customer base in Nebraska and in neighboring states though agent banks. By February 1973, a bank employee testified, First of Omaha had "credit cards in the hands of residents of all states in the United States except Alaska and Hawaii." When consumers moved, their bank cards still worked.

Their bills still came. Some consumers valued having a card from a local bank. It could speed authorization at the checkout counter, sparing the clerk the trouble of calling long distance. Aside from this small convenience, balanced for many consumers against the trouble of reapplying for credit, there was little obvious advantage in maintaining local ties.[27]

The shift from distinct local plans into commodified revolving credit is mostly visible in retrospect. In the early 1970s, bankers remained cautiously optimistic. Following a short recession in 1970, the card market began to grow again. As bankers trimmed their cardholder lists and focused on operations, cardholders used their cards more often. Master Charge and Bank-Americard systems generated $13.8 billion in purchases and cash advances in 1973, up from $10.5 billion the previous year. They also combined for nearly 60 million cardholders and more than a million participating merchants. According to the comptroller of the currency, card debt held by national banks had increased an average of 22 percent a year from 1970 to 1973, reaching almost $500 million. Bank cards were firmly entrenched as an important component of aggregate American purchasing power. Credit card debt, likewise, was rapidly becoming an area of significant policy concern.[28]

Market Structure in the 1970s

As the bank card industry developed, the ongoing problems of inflation and financial instability compelled the Nixon administration, the congressional Banking Committees, and the bank regulatory agencies to carry on with their seemingly irresolvable financial reform debates. In the late 1960s, prices were rising more than 5 percent a year. In response, the Federal Reserve raised its discount rate in December 1968 and again in April 1969, to a post–World War II high of 6 percent. It sought, in the words of Fed chairman William McChensey Martin, to "disinflate without deflating." The Fed's high rates encouraged savers to pull money from low-yielding bank accounts and seek higher returns wherever they could. Flexibility and inflexibility could not peacefully coexist. Disintermediation, and with it a renewed credit crunch, again threatened the financial system. Congress's paint-and-plaster expansion of Regulation Q ceilings to a wider range of deposit rates failed to keep capital flowing in its proper channels. Tight money disrupted flows of credit to social priorities like housing, small business, and local government.

Congressional liberals enacted the Credit Control Act in December 1969 and urged Nixon to restrain inflationary borrowing, especially by large corporations. Similar calls reverberated in the press. Nixon recognized the economic-cum-political consequences of clogged credit, but he and his economic staff resisted financial controls. Market competition, they determined, would succeed where regulated competition was clearly failing.[29]

To develop his administration's pro-competitive financial agenda, Nixon followed his former boss, Dwight D. Eisenhower, and called for a major study of the financial system in 1970. Like Eisenhower's Commission on Money and Credit (CMC), Nixon's Commission on Financial Structure and Regulation (chaired by industrialist Reed O. Hunt and known as the Hunt Commission) sought to inject competition into the financial system by peeling back layers of industry silos, price controls, and geographic restrictions. Nixon's advisers wanted the commission to focus first on the thrift industry, to "get savings flowing into mortgages and housing" and into the suburbs, where Nixon enjoyed political support. David Kennedy, formerly of Continental Illinois and now Treasury secretary, also lobbied for a close examination of the commercial banking industry. More banks were adopting the holding company structure to expand into new financial fields. Some regulation of commercial banks was necessary, Kennedy acknowledged in a January 1970 memo to Nixon, "yet excessively narrow boundary lines kill innovation." Kennedy sought to stop Congress from drawing new boundaries and to push back old ones where he could.[30]

Whereas Eisenhower's CMC had advanced an ambitious, idealistic agenda and subsequently gathered dust, the Hunt Commission crafted what members hoped were viable legislative proposals. Reflecting a growing academic and elite consensus that associated New Deal regulation with regulatory capture, the commission sought "to move as far as possible toward freedom of financial markets and equip all institutions with powers necessary to compete in such markets." Instead of industry silos, the commission proposed "specialization by choice, not by statute." Administration personnel were enthusiastic when the initial report was released in December 1971, but they recognized that the political climate was not yet suitable for reform. Small bankers and their influential trade associations blocked the way. Small bankers remained committed to a theory of competition that would preserve and protect numerous competitors from the market power of large firms. "The idea of competition in the report is used in its purest sense," policy adviser Richard Erb explained, devoid of considerations about market power. "As read by the small town banker, competition turns out to be the big city bank encroaching on his territory." Lacking the political capital to move the program forward, the administration waited. Following Nixon's sweeping victory in the 1972 election, it moved, introducing a legislative package focused on broadening the powers of financial institutions and eliminating the price controls on deposit interest rates.[31]

When the package arrived before a skeptical Congress in February 1973, members learned that the hypothetical "big city bank" was already using cards and related technologies to encroach on the small bankers' territory. Proxmire's Senate Banking Committee pivoted from considering cards as a consumer protection problem to examining how card technology was reshaping the financial regulatory structure. Or obliterating it. Bankers, the Hunt Commission's members recognized, were using cards to rub out the lines of financial federalism. "The issuance of bank credit cards has allowed commercial banks to extend consumer credit into areas not serviced by their branches," the commission observed in its 1971 report. Sharing his personal views before Proxmire's committee, Hunt went further. "What is your view about branching across state lines?" Proxmire asked. "I think we have already done it. What is a credit card?" Hunt replied. Presumably, it was a bank in miniature. With bankers using financial technologies to innovate around the rules, Hunt insisted, efforts to preserve the existing mix of siloed, geographically constrained firms were futile. Hunt predicted a future of nationwide, homogeneous financial firms offering a full suite of services. Already individual banks were charting paths in that direction. Would technological innovation spell the end of the nation's diversity of firms? "I think that a few years ago that the credit card didn't exist," Hunt observed, but now the erosion of industry silos and small, specialized firms, "is moving awfully fast."[32]

As the Senate Banking Committee considered the administration's proposals, boosters within the banking industry promoted a reconceptualization of card plans that aligned with Hunt's prediction. Instead of a commodified revolving credit service that drew customers *into* the physical bank, proponents reimagined cards as a diverse service platform that extended outward *from* the bank. *"No longer is the 'piece of plastic' strictly a charge card,"* the chairman of the

American Bankers Association's Charge Account Bankers Division declared in September 1973. Instead, "the so-called 'bank charge card' (now held by 53,000,000 persons)" was becoming "a 'bank card' which provides entry to a wide spectrum of banking and financial services via electronics." John J. Reynolds, former head of Citi's Everything Card and now president and CEO of Interbank, offered credit executives a similar vision: "The charge card . . . can be the heart of an emerging personal finance 'supermarket'" where "instalment loans, personal checking and accident insurance increasingly will be part of the product mix available through the card." The ABA and the networks promoted the "bank card" as a universal ideal, achievable by small and large banks alike through the card networks. Yet the bank card idea also held a latent tension: small banks depended on the networks for technology, but large banks were developing proprietary systems to promote their cards independent of the networks. The question of who would control the bank card's future—banks or networks—remained open.[33]

The new bank card concept depended in part on an emerging cluster of technologies grouped under the catchall term "electronic funds transfer" (EFT). Like the bank card, EFT was a contested concept. These new technologies would, some contemporaries believed, make existing institutional arrangements, for example, the Federal Reserve's check clearing system, more efficient. EFT might also change relationships between institutions, enabling private firms to take over some of the Fed's intermediary functions. It also promised to reshape relationships between financial firms and their customers. Point-of-sale terminals could authorize card transactions electronically at the checkout counter. Automatic teller machines allowed bank customers to access account information, make deposits, and withdraw cash—services formerly performed by bank employees inside bank branches. In the mid-1970s, large banks invested heavily in both technologies. Because they made banking functions available outside the bank, consumer-focused EFT systems raised fundamental questions about what, in the computer age, constituted a bank in the first place. Hunt had asked Proxmire, "What is a credit card?" He could have easily asked, "What is an ATM?"[34]

EFT played a minor role in debates over the Hunt Commission's recommendations, and enthusiasm for reform soon eroded as Nixon's presidency descended into the murky reaches of Watergate. The commission's study would burn as a beacon for financial reformers, culminating in the Depository

Institutions Deregulation and Monetary Control Act of 1980. In the early 1970s, though, financial industry interests opposed competition in its purest sense. The bill passed the Senate but failed in the House. Acknowledging the questions bank cards and EFT technologies raised about the financial structure, Congress took tentative action, establishing the National Commission on Electronic Funds Transfer (EFT Commission) in October 1974. Before it could act, Congress needed information and advice.[35]

Congress's appeal for time confirmed Wriston's conviction that technological innovation would outpace regulatory action. As bankers, card networks, and equipment manufacturers rushed to develop consumer-focused EFT technologies, the federal agencies had to regulate in Congress's stead. Decisions came quickly. In late 1974, James E. Smith, comptroller of the currency, confronted a variance in state laws on a fundamental question: were customer-bank communication terminals (CBCTs), a term that encompassed both POS terminals and ATMs, bank branches? Washington State said they were not and allowed state-chartered banks to install them; Nebraska said they were and restricted state banks from doing so. In both states, national banks sought Smith's permission to install CBCTs, forcing Smith to decide whether, as a matter of national policy, they could do so. He was hesitant, but he decided that "regulators have some responsibility . . . to act as a bit of a proxy for free and open competition." In December 1974, Smith ruled that CBCTs were not branches. National banks could install them, regardless of state branching laws. In issuing his ruling, Smith sought to downplay fears that large banks would blanket the nation with terminals and undermine the position of smaller competitors. "I think that CBCT's will be a cheap and effective competitive weapon for smaller banks," Smith predicted, citing the industry's credit card experience. Card networks enabled banks of all sizes to compete, Smith argued. There was no reason to expect CBCTs would be different.[36]

By allowing national banks to install CBCTs, Smith reinterpreted what constituted a branch bank under national banking law. The controlling statute, the McFadden Act (1927), was inherently vague. In its definition, a bank branch included "branch bank, branch office, branch agency, additional office, or . . . branch place of business," but it provided nothing more specific. The contemporary congressional debates shed little additional light. Even in the 1920s, Smith explained, the lawmakers who wrote and approved McFadden embraced competing theories. For some, a branch was a physical place. For others, it was a cluster of banking functions. Under either theory, CBCTs were not quite branches. "A CBCT obviously is not an 'office,'" Smith determined. There was, he averred, no furniture. CBCTs also offered a limited suite of services. Customers could not open accounts, apply for loans, or engage in other fundamental banking functions. "The CBCT therefore is more closely analogous to a mail box or a telephone." Like credit cards, any transaction executed through a CBCT happened, via electronic transmission, in a bank office. Smith urged banks not to follow his mail and phone analogy too far, spreading CBCTs as far as these utilities could reach. Rather, he asked bankers to wait on their home states, proceeding at the pace of local law, not jumping ahead of it.[37]

With Congress's EFT Commission on hold because President Gerald Ford had not yet appointed any members, large commercial banks jumped at Smith's ruling. In January 1975, Chicago's Continental Illinois introduced the Continental Banking Card—"the card that means convenience banking"—which allowed checking account holders to access the bank's new automatic banking centers. Through the terminals, consumers could make deposits, withdrawals, and loan payments; transfer funds between accounts; and receive cash advances through their Continental Master Charge cards—all without waiting for a human teller. At first, Continental placed the terminals inside its downtown office. But in June, the bank began installing them off-site, expanding its banking footprint without building physical branches. Illinois was a unit banking state. Continental was allowed only one bank office. Four days after Continental installed its first off-site terminal, the state's commissioner of banks sued both the bank and Comptroller Smith, charging them with violating Illinois branching laws. A federal judge enjoined Continental from building further terminals but allowed existing terminals to operate pending a final ruling.[38]

Citibank initially encountered less opposition as it developed its proprietary card and CBCT network in New York. The Citicard, which the bank issued to its 800,000 checking account customers beginning in October 1973, at first enabled cardholders only to check their balances at bank terminals and to speed check cashing at the teller window. New York's Banking Board regulated CBCTs as branches. Since the state allowed citywide branching, Citi faced little regulatory opposition. In April 1975, Citibank introduced cash-dispensing ATMs in New York City. At this early stage, the bank's Citi-card and Master Charge products remained distinct, with Citicards linked to checking accounts and Master Charge cards offering credit. The bank was also developing CBCT technology on the credit side, including a POS net-work for the merchants enrolled in the Master Charge program. The sales counter terminals, bank executives explained, would speed transactions and help cut down on card fraud.[39]

And they could probably do more than that. As Comptroller Smith, mem-bers of Congress, and federal judges all debated what constituted a bank, Wriston and Reed were increasingly convinced that plastic cards might be all the bank consumers needed. If true, they speculated, then a full-service Citicard—with integrated checking, credit, and other functions—could re-place the bank's brick-and-mortar network and circumvent the fusty geo-graphic regulations that had long ruled American banking. Following the geography of its Master Charge network, Citi tested this theory by installing POS terminals in northern New Jersey shopping centers. In addition to ap-proving Master Charge transactions, the terminals enabled merchants to confirm that Citicard-holders' checks would not bounce. With a few adjust-ments, New Jersey's banking commissioner and members of the New Jersey Bankers Association were sure, the terminals could easily accept deposits and distribute cash. "There is no doubt that these machines are bank branches," a New Jersey Bankers Association representative declared, "and hence an illegal branching across state lines." In July 1975, the New Jersey legislature banned all CBCTs. The banking commissioner looked forward to a court battle with Citi.[40]

At the center of the state-level controversies over CBCTs was the question, put directly to the parties in the Chicago case by Judge Hubert L. Will, "What is a minimum bank?" Courts struggled to parse this question. As CBCT cases multiplied across the country, bankers argued that the terminals were not banks at all. Following the same logic developed in interstate credit card cases and deployed by Comptroller Smith, bankers claimed that terminals merely communicated information to a bank's computer, located in a legal banking office, the same way a customer might by phone or through the mail. Courts rejected this analysis. Terminals were simply too physical. Something bank-like had to be happening inside of them. "How many things must be done before you have a bank?" Judge Will wondered. In December

1975, his court ruled that terminals "could not accept deposits, cash checks, make loans, or cash advances, or transfer funds between accounts." However, "they could be used for cash withdrawals from existing accounts and for the payment of installment loans." An appeals court overturned even these concessions in May 1976, banning all functions at remote terminals in Illinois. Mayor Richard J. Daley secured a city ordinance allowing the machines, but without state approval Chicago's banks had to wait and see if the Supreme Court would hear their case.[41]

In the meantime, several similar cases advanced around the country, the most important of which pitted the Independent Bankers Association of America against Comptroller Smith in the D.C. Circuit. The comptroller argued that CBCTs were not branches because they lacked the furnishings of a branch and because transactions were ultimately executed electronically within the bank. The court found this claim "without merit." It nullified the comptroller's ruling, a decision upheld on appeal in March 1976. "This court must decide whether the National Bank Act gives the Comptroller the power to initiate this technological revolution in banking or whether this initiative falls within the province of the states," the appeals court held. "The question we face is more of federalism and statutory interpretation than of sound banking practice or competitive equality. The Comptroller's decision to classify CBCT's as non-branches may be technologically a step in the right direction," yet "that is not for us to decide." As long as financial federalism reigned, bank branching policy remained a political decision for states, not a regulatory decision for the federal banking agencies. States would determine whether CBCTs were branches. Citibank could operate CBCTs in New York but not in New Jersey. Continental could not operate them at all.[42]

In the mid-1970s, federal judges struggled to apply 1920s law and their own lived experience to a mobile, electronic, technological revolution in banking. The resulting case law, which guided bank executives as they worked to develop new, consumer-focused strategies, offered little consistency or certainty. In the *Fisher* and *Marquette* cases, midwestern courts found that card transactions happened, for the purposes of applying local law, in a bank's office. In the CBCT cases, similar transactions, initiated with similar cards, happened at the terminals, not within the bank. Following Citicorp's annual meeting in Chicago in April 1978, Wriston expressed his industry's collective bafflement. "I don't know what a branch is," he confessed. "Under the modern concept of electronic funds transfer, you're no longer talking about bricks, mortar, and bodies." Citi executives may have wanted to follow the concept to its ultimate conclusion, placing CBCTs across the Hudson in New Jersey and perhaps farther afield, but they discerned a logic in the era's tortured judicial reasoning. Within financial federalism, cards, not terminals, were the way to expand consumer banking.[43]

Convenience Users and Credit Utility

Although regulatory conflict over technology and market structure roiled the banking industry, these struggles had little immediate impact on cardholders' experiences or policy concerns. Consumers and their advocates continued to favor safe, easy-to-understand, inexpensive credit. They lobbied for state-level interest rate restrictions and favorable lending terms. They expected state attorneys general to enforce state laws on their behalf. In Congress, consumer advocates sought and gained protection from the billing errors that plagued card issuers' computer systems. Although new card-based services, like photo identification and check guarantees, likely appealed to individual consumers, undifferentiated revolving credit remained the paramount service consumers expected from plastic cards. Banks had promised convenient credit; that's what consumers wanted. In effect, the unsolicited mailing campaigns had rooted universal bank cards in the pocketbooks and wallets of middle-class consumers. With more than 65 million bank cards in circulation by 1973, bank cards had become an indispensable component of consumer purchasing power.[44]

As cards became a central feature of middle-class economic identity, those excluded from credit access, especially women, racial minorities, and poor Americans, increasingly asserted rights to credit through the political process. As historians Lizabeth Cohen and Louis Hyman document, the National Organization for Women (NOW) led a grassroots campaign against discriminatory practices that often prevented women from maintaining credit identities independent of male breadwinners. During this organizing, which led to the Equal Credit Opportunity Act (1974) and its subsequent amendments (1976), NOW encouraged women to share their stories of credit exclusion. Many made credit cards central to their claims. "It's not the MASTER CHARGE card that concerns me as much as receiving my rights as a [*sic*] EQUAL citizen," one letter writer, Helaine Blythe, declared. Blythe had it half right: the Master Charge *was* equal citizenship under plastic capitalism. Daily participation in the credit economy depended on admission to private credit networks. Bankers and other card issuers guarded the entrances. When demanding admittance, women often articulated the very features bankers promised: universal access and convenience. "BankAmericard, as you know, is one of the handiest credit cards," Susan Burkhalter wrote her bank after being denied a card. "I see no reason why I should not have [one]." Women also stressed their intention to only use cards responsibly, not profligately. They wanted cards "for emergencies" or "'in between' checks for necessities." They understood that creditworthiness was the currency of credit citizenship.[45]

Consumer claims for credit access resonated in an economy where card use continued to expand, yet policymakers feared that credit card borrowing was driving the period's unyielding inflation. A short recession in 1970, followed by federal wage-price controls from August 1971 to January 1973, slowed price increases. Once controls ended, however, prices began to rise faster—above 6 percent a year in 1973 and topping 11 percent in 1974. With card networks blaring slogans like "Relax . . . you've got Master Charge" and "BankAmericard: Think of it as Money," the press named bank cards a prime culprit. Consumers used cards to buy ahead of rising prices, increasing demand that reinforced inflationary pressure. For their part, Federal Reserve officials worried that card lending undermined monetary policy. "Revolving-line consumer credit," a Fed analyst wrote in August 1974, "grows in relative importance during periods of aggregate credit restraint." As tight money made other forms of credit more expensive or vaporized them completely, consumers doubled down on cards. In the mid-1970s, bank card borrowing made "striking" gains, accounting for a quarter of consumer debt increases. Yet policymakers remained uncertain about whether credit cards, or any form of consumer credit, caused inflation. No one seemed to know for sure. Correlation—between rising card borrowing and rising prices—was all there was to go on.[46]

Although Fed policymakers and the national media worried that consumers were borrowing too heavily, bankers saw the opposite problem. In the early 1970s, bankers began to complain about a new category of cardholder, the "convenience user." These consumers employed their credit cards as charge cards: they made purchases and paid off their balances each month without accruing interest. Convenience users practiced thrift and responsibility; they used convenient credit and did not get into debt. Yet because they did not pay interest, they did not generate profits. Whereas charge account bankers in the 1950s had levied high merchant discounts to profit strictly from convenience spending, bankers had since redesigned their card plans to balance merchant-discount and revolving-credit income. Convenience users enjoyed a month or more of free credit, while bankers had to pay interest for funds that earned no interest. With inflation driving up the cost of money, these liabilities were ever more expensive.[47]

One way to overcome the convenience user problem was to simply charge cardholders a fee, as travel cards had always done, ensuring that even convenience users paid for card services. Most bankers, however, did not see fees as a viable option. Since the 1960s mass-mailing campaigns, banks had marketed their cards as "free." Could banks go back on this promise? Vigorous competition between banks and the apparent uniformity of revolving credit meant that no bank wanted to be the first to impose a fee. With many card-issuing banks offering the same service, consumers would simply choose another bank. Worse, bankers feared, consumers would take their deposit accounts and other business with them. For years, bankers agonized over fees. There was never a clear path out of the industry's feeless equilibrium. Outside of specific regulatory contexts like Minnesota, where the state's low local interest cap encouraged the Marquette National Bank to adopt an annual charge, no bank was willing to take the plunge. Marquette also proved the rule: its fee quickly drew competition from out-of-state bankers.[48]

Where other bankers dared not go, Citibank strode boldly ahead. In early 1976, Citi instituted a 50-cent monthly service fee on cardholders who used the card but did not incur interest. Until that time, the bank had, in accordance with New York law, granted its Master Charge customers twenty-five interest-free days from their billing date to repay their balances, before charging the statutory rates of 18 percent for the first $500 and 12 percent on subsequent amounts. "We feel that this small fee is well within reason," a Citibank executive explained to the *New York Times* in April. "This revision is necessary to offset our rising costs and to improve our level of customer service." Most bankers looked at their card plans in the aggregate, balancing total expenses against total revenues. Citi executives expected each cardholder to be individually profitable for the bank. The fee may have seemed sensible, but bank customers took the opposite view. As one Citibank chronicler recalled, "Angry cardholders stormed into branches and threw their cards in the tellers' faces, forcing Citibank to take special security measures." Customer anger was understandable. Cardholders felt that by paying their bills every month, they were using cards responsibly. They were not succumbing to temptation. They were not going into debt. They were not spending extravagantly. It hardly occurred to them that convenience came with a cost, that they were committing the most intolerable act of all: they weren't making Citibank any money.[49]

Consumers were outraged; Citi's fellow bankers were thrilled. Banks still struggled to make cards profitable. High operating expenses, expensive funding costs, and continued problems with fraud and consumer delinquencies all weighed on bank card issuers. Large banks tended to fund their card programs directly through money markets, using instruments like large denomination certificates of deposit, commercial paper notes, and even eurodollar borrowing. Rising interest rates, which ratcheted up with inflation, narrowed the spread between the cost of funds to banks and the interest they could charge. "With the way the usury laws are," one Pennsylvania banker complained, "it's very difficult to make a profit." Bankers eagerly studied Citibank's policy. Many saw it as the industry's future. "I would be very surprised if the industry doesn't follow Citibank's lead," one California banker observed; another added, "Some change (in pricing) is inevitable." Other bankers criticized the move. Thomas Wilcox, a former Citi executive who left for California's Crocker National Bank after losing the top post to Wriston, remained committed to evaluating his new bank's plan holistically: "We think our Master Charge should be considered in light of its ability to bring other retail business to our bank. We can consider it a loss leader." Wherever bankers stood on card fees, they all watched Citi's experiment closely. And though many hoped fees would stick, they would also take some delight if failure brought the aggressive bank down a peg.[50]

The consumer furor, however, was more intense than Citi executives anticipated. So was the regulatory and legal response. Representative Frank Annunzio (D-IL), chairman of the House Banking Committee's Consumer Affairs Subcommittee, played for headlines. "Just like the spider who lured the fly into its parlor and then trapped it in its web," Annunzio vented, "the bank has lured customers into its credit card program with glossy promises and is now trying to collect extra fees." Annunzio introduced legislation to ban bank card fees and threatened hearings. The congressman barked. Consumer lawsuits bit. As a result of a class-action suit brought by three Citi cardholders, a district court ruled such service charges illegal under New York law and ordered Citibank to repay all collected fees. Commenting on the case, John Reed snarled, "These people knew it was a free ride—people like to beat the system." One of those people, plaintiff Richard Oster, received his 50-cent refund and "a lot of satisfaction." The outcome embarrassed the bank. It also firmly locked Citi cards into New York's strict interest rate regime—the full consequences of which would become apparent later on.[51]

Citibank Goes National

Even as the bank wrangled over convenience fees, Wriston and other Citibank executives remained true to their faith that technology, and card technology especially, would propel Citi beyond the geographic confines of the New Deal regulatory order. The bank pressed out in all directions, yet every move into new businesses and territories brought conflict with federal regulators. Federal law still prohibited interstate banking. The Federal Reserve and Justice Department sought to enforce those provisions; Citi executives worked to creatively evade them. Citibank won many of these battles. The results, though, often amounted to small, expensive-to-maintain breeches in the regulatory structure. Through its Nationwide Financial Services unit, Citicorp operated more than one hundred limited-service offices in southern and western states, which provided consumer loans but could not accept deposits. In cities like San Francisco and Miami, meanwhile, Citi opened Edge-Act subsidiaries, special-purpose branches that could only engage in international transactions. These and other financial nodes marked significant incursions, but none matched Wriston's ambition. Cards, though, could redraft the regulatory map. In an interview with *American Banker,* Reed made the bank's ambitions plain. "My own personal belief is that almost everything we have traditionally distributed through branch system can be delivered on the card." And cards could go anywhere, enabling Citi to traverse federal and state branching boundaries and build a truly nationwide card-based consumer bank.[52]

Visa inadvertently opened the gate for Citibank's interstate expansion. In late 1976, National BankAmericard Inc. (NBI) announced plans to drop the BankAmericard name in favor of consolidating the network's domestic and international operations under a new name: Visa. Executives designed the name change to distance NBI from Bank of America, the original issuer of the BankAmericard, providing a unified brand for the thousands of card-issuing members of NBI's global payment network. Dee Hock chose the name because, as he explained, the "adoption of the single name 'Visa,' surmounts language and cultural barriers and is the final step in assuring instant recognition and acceptance around the world." Hock also intended the rebranding to shift consumer attention away from the individual card-issuing banks and toward the power and utility of the network. To inform consumers of the change, NBI planned a national advertising campaign, forewarning cardholders to expect a new Visa card from their local bank—and presenting the artful executives at Citi with a unique opportunity.[53]

Before 1976, the competing card networks did not allow their members to issue more than one card brand. A Master Charge issuer like Citi could not also issue BankAmericards. Forcing banks to choose between networks, Hock believed, left open the possibility that additional networks might emerge. By contrast, allowing banks to issue cards under both networks, called "duality," raised high barriers to entry at the network level. Hock saw duality as a short step to a grueling antitrust fight or, worse, nationalization of the card networks as public utilities. For merchants who accepted both BankAmericard and Master Charge, however, the ban on duality meant they had to maintain accounts with separate banks. Agent banks in small towns sided with their merchants. Hock's position constituted a restraint of trade at the bank level, they argued, demanding the freedom to offer card services of their choosing. After years of private litigation and an expanding Justice Department inquiry, NBI relented.[54]

Citibank immediately joined NBI, as did many of its rivals. Citi did so with different motives. The bank did not intend to target only its existing New York market; instead, in August 1977, Citi began mailing tens of millions of preapproved Visa applications to consumers across the country. The bank bought up lists of potential cardholders from direct mailers and phone companies and ran them through new, national credit bureaus. In what newspapers dubbed "Citi's Credit Card Blitz," the bank capitalized on the confusion caused by NBI's rebranding and pushed aggressively into markets previously controlled by other NBI banks.[55]

By sending preapproved applications instead of actual cards, Citi dodged the 1970 unsolicited mailing ban and soon inundated the nation with Citibank Visas. Rival bankers were not sure what to make of Citi's strategy. Some assumed Citibank planned to target their merchant customers. Local banks had fought for generations against New York's financial dominance. Businesses, unlike consumers, could easily go to New York or San Francisco for loans. Was this a new strategy to target business customers? Other bankers recognized Citi's consumer focus. "They must feel the barriers against interstate banking will soon give way," one Idaho banker observed, "and they may be trying to establish a broad customer base right now." Citi executives did and were. The bank's competitors responded with incredulity and outrage, rooted in timeworn assumptions about the link between consumer borrowing and financial geography. Successful card plans depended on local embeddedness, on the close connections between the issuing bank and its community. Bankers who struggled to generate profits locally could not imagine issuing cards across the country. "Competing banks," the *Los Angeles Times* reported, "contend that no matter how many new cardholders Citibank gets, it will end up losing money on most of them." A Seattle banker put the sentiment bluntly: "They are foolish to do it." Other NBI issuers responded with flat anger. Missouri bankers, who had advance word of Citi's plans, were irate that Citibank dared encroach on their market. "The only thing bad about the credit-card business," fumed St. Louis banker William Travis, "is that some banks are getting too greedy." Citi's greed paid off. Many consumers, assuming Citi's offer was part of the Visa name change, promptly mailed the bank their acceptances—four million of them.[56]

Citibank's break with accepted financial geography went further than simply mailing cards across state lines. First of Omaha and other midwestern banks had already built regional card plans by crossing into neighboring states, but they did so while building the BankAmericard network from the ground up. First of Omaha employees recruited hundreds of agent banks, and through them thousands of merchants, introducing and embedding the BankAmericard plan in local communities. Omaha executives negotiated with local policymakers. Omaha lawyers fought extended legal battles, including the *Fisher* cases that by 1977 gave Citi relative certainty that its cards would be regulated in New York. First of Omaha's experience was, in theme if not precise detail, the experience of card-issuing banks across the country. Although Wriston liked to portray *markets* as neutral, natural phenomena, the *bank card market* in any given place only existed because of the long, hard, expensive work put in by local bankers. Now Citibank swept in to reap the rewards, appropriating the infrastructure which local banks had created to make the card market in the first place. Citi signed up no agent banks. It enrolled no merchants. It came for the consumers, offering them the same commodified revolving credit they could get at their local bank. And local bankers took Reed and Wriston at their word: Citi intended to offer these consumers much more in the future.

Dee Hock imagined the adoption of Visa as a significant step toward making the private network paramount, so that the information exchange that facilitated economic life could occur without the involvement of either the banks or the government. Instead, Citibank commandeered Hock's network, harnessing the system that thousands of Visa-née-BankAmericard banks had built over the previous decade and transforming it into a conduit for Citi's ambitions. Citibank executives understood better than their rivals the consequence of undifferentiated revolving credit. While local card-issuing banks saw cardholders as their customers, cardholders did not necessarily see themselves that way. The cards issued through BankAmericard and Master Charge carried these logos prominently, reorienting consumers' focus away from the issuing bank and toward the national network—the name on the card that gave it its purchasing power. These card systems initially relied on local banking relationships to build their merchant and customer bases, but they also eroded these boundaries as BankAmericard and Master Charge became national, even international, institutions, synonymous with mobility and surmountable distance—exactly what Visa was meant to capture. Bank-Americard customers, Citi bankers believed, were unaware of the local bank connections that linked them to the payment networks. "The consumer," a Citibank executive explained to congress in September 1977, "has been telling us through his behavior that he does not view the card as a 'local' geographically constrained product." By appropriating the network, Citi would no longer be a local geographically constrained bank.[57]

In the face of Citibank's aggressive salvo, what could its rivals do fight back? "If other banks exercise their muscle," Continental's head of cards explained, "we can't just sit idly by." And they did not. "Regional banks," the *Wall Street Journal* reported, "say the heavy national promotion has forced them to step up their own marketing to compete." Just as in the heady days of the unsolicited mailing boom, in the late 1970s banks unleashed a rush of competition, one no longer confined by the extent of their branch and agent-bank networks. Continental Illinois mailed 550,000 solicitations to select New Englanders, including one to the chairman of the First National Bank of Boston, much to his shock. The Barnett Banks in Florida, which had expanded statewide on the back of their BankAmericard franchise in the late 1960s, defensively mailed 350,000 Visa offers, urging Florida consumers, "don't take Visa cards from strangers." Bankers compounded the competitive pressure through duality. Banks which had formerly issued only BankAmericard *or* Master Charge cards now tried to hook customers on a second brand. With credit offers raining down, the nation's headline writers competed pun for pun: in Chicago, "Consumers [were] Charging through a Credit Card Blizzard"; in Los Angeles "Credit Cards [were] Dealt in Game for Big Money." By January 1979, Visa and Master Charge banks were approving almost 75,000 new cards a day. Bank credit card debt had grown by 15 percent a year from 1974 to 1977, but over the next two years it leapt up at a 30 percent annual rate. In the process, bank cards surpassed retail credit plans as the dominant form of revolving credit.[58]

The explosion of card solicitations revived long-standing concerns that cards drove inflation by increasing consumer demand for goods, enabling anticipatory buying, and fueling inflation psychology. Price increases slowed in 1976 to a still significant 5.7 percent a year but accelerated again in 1977 and 1978 as the card boom raged. "We wonder whether the proliferation of credit cards is actually plastic inflation," a House Banking Committee staffer told the *Los Angeles Times*, adding, "We have a time bomb situation here." For recently inaugurated Jimmy Carter, renewed card expansion was a minor current in the sea of economic problems facing his administration. As cards flooded the market, Carter's staff revisited federal credit controls as one means to stem the tide. In spring 1980, the administration would make a daring effort to shift the course of plastic capitalism.[59]

In the meantime, Citibank's mass-solicitation strategy was wildly successful and tremendously expensive. Purchasing third-party lists of likely cardholders and screening them through credit bureaus exposed the bank to bad

debt and fraud losses. Credit bureaus, like the card networks, had embraced
technology to create national systems by consolidating local credit agencies,
yet their screening methods remained far from perfect. Like tides, Reed observed, each wave of solicitations echoed back again in a wave of fraud and
charge-offs. Citi's consumer loan losses increased from $54.5 million in 1977
to $93.9 million in 1978. Charge-offs hurt the bottom line, but the real dan-
ger was interest rate risk. While the bank's millions of Master Charge and
Visa customers paid rates held flat by New York law, money markets around
the globe set Citibank's cost of funds. "Consumer lending on a fixed-rate basis, which tends to penalize our earnings in high-interest-rate environments
such as today's," the bank reported in 1978, "will contribute to earnings
growth when rates decline." Or, more accurately, *if* rates decline. Unfortu-
nately for Wriston and Citibank, over the next two years interest rates went in
the opposite direction. When Citibank started its solicitation campaign in
1977, the bank's cost of funds stood at 6.21 percent. By 1978, they rose to 9
percent. And Citi executives saw them only going up from there.[60]

Through the 1970s, the bank card industry developed along the geographic
lines that had long ruled American banking. Local banks served local markets, embedding card plans in community relationships that bound consumers, merchants, and their banks together. Bankers built their nationwide
networks on these relationships. Even ambitious banks, like First of Omaha,
that pursued aggressive regional growth in the 1960s and 1970s did so
through agent bank agreements. They built local credit card markets from
the bottom up. Consumers, though, had little knowledge of the institutional
and relational infrastructures that made the card systems work. As networks
developed stand-alone identities distinct from card-issuing banks, the ties
that bound cards to space and place faded from view. Wriston and Reed,
schooled in Citibank's international operations and eager to use technology
to sprint past laggard regulators, stood ready to take advantage.

  Wriston and Reed were well-positioned to drive change, but their views
about the transformative power of financial technology were hardly unique.
Rather, they reflected a growing consensus among business leaders and policymakers that information networks were eroding the traditional geographies of finance. In the Carter administration, deregulation-minded officials
were warming to similar views. "Our present banking laws are based on a

world in which most customers had to queue up at their local bank, or local branch, to make deposits and withdrawals or to borrow money," Lyle Gramley, a former Fed staffer and member of Carter's Council of Economic Advisers, mused in October 1979. "The advent of electronic funds transfer technology in recent years," he continued, "had called into question the whole concept of physical location as a relevant, or desirable, basis of banking regulation." Federal courts, however, had restrained the very EFT technologies Gramley invoked, foreclosing one technological path for bypassing place-based regulation and pushing bankers toward another. The regulatory structure continued to shape bank strategy even as bankers chose among technologies with which to work around it.

Gramley also recognized that in Congress, where physical location remained the basis for political representation, lawmakers were unlikely to accept a world where local authority over finance was not protected. Congressional leaders, among them William Proxmire, were increasingly amenable to market-based deregulation. Yet they also sought to maintain finance's place-based social contract through legislation like the Community Reinvestment Act (1977), which required banks to meet the credit needs of the communities in which they operated, including low-income neighborhoods. Proxmire and the Carter administration would pursue some federal financial deregulation under the aegis of combatting inflation, but Citi executives and their peers would need to pursue place-based deregulation by a different road.[61]

10

Credit Control

A Ton of Bricks

Citibank's massive nationwide marketing campaign changed the composition and structure of American consumer credit markets. As in the 1960s, bankers rushed to compete, now no longer constrained by the geographic reach of their branch networks. Shaken by the volatile 1970s economy and hounded by seemingly untamable inflation, consumers grasped cards as a lifeline to purchasing power and the previous generation's prosperity. Within a year, bank card debt surpassed department store and similar retail borrowing for the first time. It would never turn back. Politicians and policymakers watched these developments closely, nowhere more so than within the Carter administration. From his first days in office, Carter and his economic staff struggled to confront the nation's economic challenges, especially the ominous combination of high unemployment and persistent inflation, known popularly as "stagflation." At first policymakers tried to solve both problems at once, vacillating between expansion and contraction, and between the managed Keynesianism of the past and new policy ideas, like deregulation, gaining traction in the present. In late 1978, however, Carter and his advisers decided to prioritize inflation. Carter invested the contest with a deep moral urgency, embodied most forcefully in his "Crisis of Confidence" speech the following summer. Yet the ongoing expansion of credit card lending flew in the face of Carter's calls for restraint. After much deliberation and a few false starts, Carter took direct steps to curtail what one sympathetic commentator called the "credit card craze." In March 1980, Carter exercised powers granted by the Credit Control Act (1969) and authorized the Federal Reserve to institute controls on credit card lending.[1]

Ongoing credit market turmoil and an emphatic consumer response combined to make the policy unexpectedly effective. In mid-1979, Carter had appointed Paul A. Volcker Jr., president of New York Federal Reserve Bank, as chairman of the Federal Reserve. Volcker soon began his well-known experiment in monetary policy, strictly managing the supply of money and allowing market interest rates to skyrocket. The policy violently disrupted global credit markets. It hiked costs for card firms tremendously, yet state usury laws prevented lenders from passing higher interest rates on to consumers. Lenders were desperate to cut back on credit extensions but fearful of losing the market share they had so recently attained. Consumers who accepted and used cards remained deeply uneasy about their reliance on plastic purchasing power. When Carter announced controls in stern moral language, consumers responded. Credit buying slammed to a halt, and not just on cards but across the economy. The policy, as one administration veteran recalled, "hit like a ton of bricks." The nation's gross national product fell at a dramatic 8 percent annual rate in the second quarter of 1980, the fastest drop since the Great Depression. The policy quickly became a victim of its own success. So did Carter. The rise of modern conservatism, the ongoing Iranian hostage crisis, and the administration's failure to address the nation's persistent energy dependence all contributed to Carter's loss to Ronald Reagan in 1980. But the sharp economic decline that year, caused by the credit control policy, was the paramount cause of Carter's defeat.[2]

Carter's credit control policy mirrored the 1960s political response to mass unsolicited card mailing. In both cases, politicians reacted to breakneck credit marketing by enveloping card plans in the New Deal's restraining web of financial rules. Indeed, Carter's policy built directly on these earlier regulatory efforts. The Credit Control Act and the state-level price controls that gave credit restraints their bite were products of the initial countermovement against unrestrained card plans. By 1980, however, the balance of forces had shifted. An unrelenting campaign to discredit New Deal economic controls had borne fruit. Proponents of unrestrained markets, like Paul Volcker, commanded the policy high ground. Meanwhile, consumer credit, an auxiliary engine of consumer purchasing power—ignited by New Deal credit policies, stoked by private lenders seeking profits in consumer markets, and revved by consumers claiming access to credit citizenship—propelled the economy with unprecedented force. While state policymakers and some congressional Democrats remained committed to controlling and channeling credit, the ideological and material balance had shifted. Instead of driving a new countermovement against unconstrained credit, Carter's crusade was outflanked, cut off, and routed.

Rejection of Credit Controls

Jimmy Carter focused his 1976 election campaign on themes of economic recovery and national renewal. During the campaign, the unemployment rate remained stubbornly above 7 percent, the federal government continued to run a substantial deficit, and inflation, which would become the true economic bugbear of his administration, fluctuated between a 5 and 6 percent annual rate. As a candidate, Carter lambasted incumbent Gerald Ford's economic performance, repeatedly citing the "misery index"—the sum of the inflation and unemployment rates—as the leading indicator of Ford's failings. Carter also assumed the mantle of Washington outsider. He espoused a "populist" faith in the honesty and integrity of the American people. Government, in light of Vietnam and Watergate, had not lived up to its founding ideals. To regain Americans' trust, it needed a fresh, values-driven approach. Carter's varied career as a naval officer, small-town businessman, Baptist missionary, and state governor cemented his outsider appeal. The Georgian offered himself as the embodiment of national spiritual revival. Voters hoisted him into the nation's highest office.[3]

Once in the White House, Carter struggled to turn his populism into effective economic policy. Two conflicting currents propelled Carter's politics: a faith-driven compassion that aligned with Democratic social priorities like racial and economic justice, and a deep-seated fiscal conservatism that made Carter reluctant to open the national pocketbook to pay for them. As he later reflected, "The Southern brand of populism was to help the poor and the aged, to improve education and to provide jobs. At the same time the populists tried not to waste money, having almost an obsession about the burden of excessive debt." Constrained by contrary impulses, Carter could not chart a decisive course on economic policy. Moreover, the administration's economic ambivalence extended throughout the economic policy staff. The stagflation of the 1970s, coupled with the increasing prominence of free-market ideology among academic economists, undermined the Keynesian ideas that had guided policy in the postwar era. Carter's staff, caught adrift in changing seas, adopted a pragmatic approach. Advisers like Alfred E. Kahn and Charles L. Schultze, chairs, respectively, of the Council on Wage and Price Stability and the Council of Economic Advisers (CEA), relied on Keynesianism where it seemed effective. They also gradually committed to deregulation and adopted thinly veiled antagonism toward organized labor. Carter wanted to move the Democratic Party beyond the political-economic orthodoxies of the New Deal and the Great Society, especially as they seemed to crack under the weight of slowing productivity growth and the transition from a manufacturing- to a service-based economy. But the path forward was dimly lit and treacherous.[4]

Carter and his economic team zigzagged between tightening and expansion, matching the changing course of the economy. The economic recovery that was underway in 1976 continued into 1977, ushering in a period of strong economic growth. Growth, however, brought inflationary pressure. Carter instituted voluntary wage and price controls and limited pay raises for federal workers in early 1978. These policies fizzled. In October 1978 the administration undertook "phase two" of its anti-inflation strategy, which called for budgetary restraint and a more rigorous attempt to stem wage and price increases. By then Carter had determined that inflation was "our most serious domestic problem." He urged Americans to join the government in fighting inflation through their daily economic decisions.[5]

While Carter's economic team debated inflation-fighting measures, Citibank launched its nationwide Visa campaign, spurring a dramatic upsurge in card use and fears of credit-induced inflation. As cards saturated the market, inflation surged. By early 1979, the consumer price index was increasing at double-digit annual rates. Americans appeared to be losing confidence in the administration's ability to combat rising prices, frustrating White House officials. In early 1979, senior economic staff scrambled to craft policies that might slow inflation's steady climb. Within this environment, credit controls emerged as one tool which might stem credit-fueled consumption. Under authority granted by the Credit Control Act (1969), Carter could authorize the Federal Reserve to regulate "the extension of credit in an excessive volume." Advisers argued that taking this step would send a strong signal that the administration *"will act* on the inflation crisis where it has the power to do so." They emphasized credit cards as a prime target for controls. In March 1979, Treasury secretary W. Michael Blumenthal informed Carter, "some consumers may be overextending their debt positions to an extent that is not desirable," counseling further, "Your advisers also agree unanimously that action should be taken to limit the most liberal terms of consumer credit." Carter agreed to pursue "preliminary discussions" regarding limitations on consumer credit. Through April and May, the economic staff examined the viability of a credit control policy.[6]

With Carter's mandate to pursue "preliminary discussions," CEA economists began examining options for a credit control policy. Initially, proponents recommended shortening repayment periods, which would force consumers to make larger monthly payments. Higher monthly payments, the core feature of World War II and Korean War controls, increased the price and thus reduced the demand for credit. Yet such controls had to be monitored and enforced. As economist Lyle Gramley noted, "Installment credit has grown tremendously in importance since the last time that controls were used." Staff estimated that there were likely 50,000 consumer lenders in the market, meaning that instituting controls "would involve monumentally heavy costs." Further, the increasing fungibility of credit, linked especially to the expansion of card plans, also frustrated Carter's economic team. "As the credit instrument has become divorced from the asset purchased," one report lamented, "consumer credit has become a more generalized source of purchasing power." This meant that "restraint imposed in one area would lead to expansion from other sources." Credit controls, Carter's advisers determined, were "essentially unworkable." In May 1979, they abandoned the idea.[7]

The essential unworkability of controls resulted from the size and scope of consumer credit markets, a fact which raised further questions for Carter's economic staff. Controls had long been premised on the idea that consumer credit was pro-cyclical, that it exacerbated swings in the economy by adding momentum during the upswing and compounding decline in the downswing. The upswing momentum was inflationary, economists believed. Controls could impose moderation. Yet too much debt overall might drag on the economy once recovery was underway. Overindebted consumers could not spend the economy into recovery. Carter's policy staff observed steadily increasing consumer debt and steadily declining national savings. They worried. In memos examining these concerns in spring 1979 one staff economist, K. Burke Dillon, reported that though "the total outstanding debt of borrowers has increased substantially in relation to disposable income," this increase "has been offset by the lengthening of maturities." Consumers owed more, but they were able carry their debts longer and pay less each month. There was, Dillon argued, no "true increase in the debt repayment burden." Consumers' purchasing power was not declining. Future aggregate demand was not in jeopardy. Dillon's analysis may have reassured administration economists, but it would have provided little comfort to consumers who did not experience lengthening maturities and total debt outstanding as cold economic facts but as real and growing burdens in an unsettled world.[8]

The Confidence to Fight Inflation

The economic concerns that prompted Carter's staff to debate consumer indebtedness and credit controls also animated deeper currents that flowed through the administration in early 1979. A decade of high inflation had eroded American incomes and undercut consumer prosperity. The long energy crisis choked and stalled the nation's perpetual optimism. Throughout the decade, opinion shapers and public intellectuals challenged the preeminence of affluence in American society—not from the upslope, as critics like John Kenneth Galbraith and Vance Packard had in the 1950s—but from the trough. Historian R. Christopher Lasch and sociologists Daniel Bell and Robert N. Bellah figured prominently in these debates. Their widely read books grappled with themes of renewed self-restraint and religiosity, of re-embrace of national traditions and communal values, and above all of abhorrence for degenerative self-indulgence. Americans, they feared, were abandoning traditional goals of family, work ethic, and spirituality in favor of hedonistic, individualistic consumption. "Social scientists, worried that self-indulgence would undermine the fabric of American society, expressed concern about the dangers of profligate spending," historian Daniel Horowitz argues. These concerns were not new, of course, but they took on new urgency as Americans' certainty in their nation's strength cracked and crumbled.[9]

Themes of self-restraint resonated profoundly with Carter. After two and a half years battling inflation and fighting for a sustainable national energy policy, which he termed the "moral equivalent of war," Carter concluded that the nation's problems transcended economics and energy. "Americans," Carter recalled, "were rapidly losing faith in themselves and in their country." The president's chief pollster, Pat Caddell, guided Carter to this conclusion. Caddell had read widely about consumption and confidence. He had seen, he believed, the concerns of Lasch, Bell, and Bellah emerge vividly in his own polling data. Sharing his views with Carter in an April 1979 memo entitled "Of Crisis and Opportunity," Caddell put it bluntly: "America is a nation deep in crisis." In his seventy-five-page report he examined the deep national malaise eroding citizens' confidence in their government and themselves. Among its causes, Caddell cited non-voting, the "Me" generation, consumer behavior, and lack of purpose. He lamented that "the public . . . is spending as if there is no tomorrow," and further, "Live for today, financed by greater and greater debt has replaced the stable rock of steady, prudent future planning in America." Caddell urged Carter to project a new national vision. The crisis, he wrote, "presents you the opportunity, so rare in American history, to reshape the structure, nature, and purpose of the United States in ways which your predecessors only dreamed." Carter took Caddell's advice very seriously. The two began reading from a shared list that included Lasch, Bell, and Bellah's works.[10]

The themes of consumption and self-indulgence presented by Caddell carried deep implications for the administration's two most pressing domestic concerns: inflation and energy. In early July 1979, with gas lines again snaking into service stations, Carter reevaluated his approach to both issues. That month, the president had been scheduled to address the nation for the fifth time on the energy crisis. Instead, he abruptly scrapped the speech and headed to Camp David for a period of reflection that would redefine his presidency. Following ten days of consultations with numerous advisers, including politicians, business and labor representatives, religious and community leaders, and economists and energy experts, Carter delivered a speech that defined a new direction for his administration. Officially known as the "Crisis of Confidence" speech, though better known as the "Malaise" speech, Carter drew on Caddell's memo to offer a bold critique of the nation's direction and purpose. Borrowing the phrase "a crisis of confidence" from Lasch's *Culture of Narcissism,* Carter told Americans that their inability to unite on energy reflected deeper problems: "It is a crisis that strikes at the very heart and soul and spirit of our national will." Carter lamented Americans' lost national purpose. "Too many of us now tend to worship self-indulgence and consumption. Human identity is no longer defined by what one does, but by what one owns." Americans could feel this too. "We've discovered that owning things and consuming things does not satisfy our longing for meaning." Carter also offered hope, buttressed by faith in the inexhaustible resources of the American people. He warned his audience, estimated at over 100 million, that although there were no short-term solutions, with unity and sacrifice, the nation's crisis of confidence—and with it the crises of energy and inflation—could be overcome.[11]

The speech won immediate support from viewers and the media, but Carter quickly squandered the momentum. After the speech, the White House received a surge of letters and phone calls, 85 percent of which lauded the president's bold message. Americans embraced Carter's call to action. They too were troubled by the pervasiveness of consumerism and self-interest they saw in themselves and their fellow Americans. But then Carter reoriented his administration, requesting the resignation of his entire cabinet. He declined most resignation offers. However, he showed a few top advisers, including Treasury Secretary Michael Blumenthal, the door. The apparent disorder reignited concerns about Carter's ability to manage his administration. The moves elicited comparisons to Nixon's "Saturday Night Massacre," overshadowing Carter's message and diminishing its impact. Carter squandered the opportunity and was left with crisis.[12]

The cabinet shakeup created high-profile gaps in the president's economic team, which had to be plugged quickly for the administration to address the problem of inflation. First, Carter had to replace Blumenthal at the Treasury, which he did by selecting William G. Miller, then chairman of the Federal Reserve. This left a crucial vacancy at the Fed, one that Carter filled with the rangy economist Paul Volcker. Volcker was president of the New York Federal Reserve Bank, the branch responsible for executing the Fed's monetary policies through purchases and sales of treasury securities. Volcker came to the New York Fed after a long career straddling banking and public service. He had assisted Chase's David Rockefeller on the Commission on Money and Credit in the 1960s and helped convince Richard Nixon to decouple the dollar from gold in the 1970s. At the New York Fed, Volcker established a clear record as an inflation hawk, favoring policies to constrain the growth of the money supply and fight inflation at all costs. Volcker's appointment highlighted Carter's increasingly firm stance against inflation, though the administration's record still left some observers unconvinced. In a magnificent bit of underestimation, the *New York Times* called Volcker's appointment "largely symbolic."[13]

Sensing the need for decisive action to curb inflation, Volcker steered the Federal Reserve in a new direction, embarking on a dramatic policy shift in October 1979. The change Volcker instituted was, in some respects, highly technical, but the shock waves it unleashed reverberated through the global financial economy for a generation. Until then, the Fed had managed inflation by manipulating interest rates. In theory, by increasing rates, the Fed made it difficult for banks to attract deposits and other funds (in part because of Regulation Q price restrictions). Higher rates reduced banks' reserves and thus their capacity to make new loans, slowing, in turn, the growth of the money supply and with it the rate of inflation. Traditional monetary policy also kept interest rates stable and under the Fed's control. Volcker, though, believed that inflationary psychology was too deeply entrenched. Bankers were not taking the Fed's actions seriously enough. They kept lending, and so the money supply kept growing.[14]

On October 6, 1979, Volcker called a secret meeting of the Federal Open Market Committee, the policymaking arm of the Federal Reserve, to discuss a new direction. Volcker opened the meeting with a call for decisive action: "We can't walk away today without a program that is strong in fact and perceived as strong in terms of dealing with the situation." He proposed that the Fed stop managing interest rates and move instead to control the growth of the money supply directly. Volcker argued for tightening the Fed's supervision of bank reserves, which would directly curtail overall bank lending. In doing so, the Fed would allow interest rates to "fluctuate over a wider range." Such a transition in policy, Volcker hoped, would lead to "a change in the psychological atmosphere" that "will give us more bang for the buck." Not all Fed members fully embraced the new direction. Governor Nancy Teeters, for one, felt "queasy about it." But the final vote was unanimous in favor of money aggregates. Volcker emphatically demonstrated his seriousness to break inflation and inflationary psychology. By ceding control of interest rates, the Fed willingly accepted a galloping increase in credit prices.[15]

Credit Controls Renewed

Volcker's determination to turn the monetary screws until inflation was finally wrung from the economy marked an epochal shift in postwar economic management. In the short term, however, rising interest rates did little to stem inflation. Instead, the price of money and the price of goods climbed apace. When the Bureau of Labor Statistics released the producer price index in mid-February 1980, it showed a 19.2 percent annualized jump for the previous month, the highest such increase in five years. Vacationing with his family in Florida, CEA chairman Charles Schultze was summoned back to Washington to devise a new inflation strategy. Rising producer prices, the administration feared, would soon reach consumers. With the election only nine months away, Carter's staff urged the president "to increase the visibility of our anti-inflation effort." Credit controls, which had been scrapped in May 1979, reemerged amid a bundle of possible policies aimed at taking strong, effective action on inflation.[16]

Outside the White House, surging inflation and Volcker's strident monetary policy created a growing constituency for targeted credit controls. By abdicating direct control over interest rates, the Fed allowed rates to surge across the board, squeezing home and construction financing, auto loans, business investment—every economic activity that relied on credit. Seeking relief, some proponents of controls, such as William Proxmire, Senate Banking Committee chair, pressed the Fed to direct credit to productive uses rather than damming the flows entirely. Others, such as economist John Kenneth Galbraith, urged limits on consumer borrowing, which was driving the national "inflationary psychosis" and consumer "dis-saving." Volcker opposed controls, which would interfere with the Fed's monetary policies and the natural workings of the market. As Volcker argued, credit controls would "severely complicate the situation," adding as late as February 1980, "I'm no enthusiast of using direct controls" since "they can be counterproductive" and "lead to anticipation of inability to raise money and thereby actually increase demand." In other words, consumers, fearing impending credit scarcity, would leverage their credit for all it was worth.[17]

Administration economists believed consumers were already using credit to buy ahead of inflation, and they again began to evaluate a credit control policy. In late February, Treasury staff reiterated concerns about credit-driven anticipatory buying, arguing that credit controls "would directly carry the message to the American public of the need for restraint." Revisiting the Credit Control Act, the Treasury again suggested imposing higher monthly payments to stymie demand. CEA staff again rejected this route as unworkable. Instead, Burke Dillon consulted with the Fed, which would ultimately administer whatever controls were chosen, to find a new path for the CCA. Volcker's public stand against controls complicated negotiations, generating concern that the Fed might not go along with the administration. While the text of the CCA enabled the president to "*authorize* the [Fed] to regulate and control any or all extensions of credit," it did not mandate that the Fed do so. Volcker, though, recognized that he needed Carter's support, given the rising congressional opposition to his tight money policies. After two meetings with Carter and his economic team in late February, Volcker assented to the administration's credit control plan.[18]

Under Volcker, the Fed developed a much different vision of what the CCA could accomplish, one indicative of the shifting reliance on market forces to allocate scarce economic resources. Instead of mandating credit terms that increased the price of credit, and in turn decreased the demand, Carter's economic team decided to increase the cost of lending, thus decreasing the supply. To do so, CEA and Fed economists planned to effectively tax new consumer lending by requiring lenders to deposit a percentage of all new loans in non-interest-bearing accounts with the Federal Reserve. For each dollar lent to consumers, lenders would set aside 10, 15, or 20 cents—depending on what the Fed decided would be most suitable. Instead of making loans subject to mandatory deposits, policymakers hoped, lenders would redirect credit toward more profitable, and less inflationary, activities. The policy relied on the nation's patchwork of state usury laws to ensure lenders would not simply pass high costs on to consumers through higher interest charges. With state price ceilings in place, lenders would have to internalize the costs of controls, creating a strong incentive for them to reduce the availability of credit. "It will" Dillon explained, "simply make consumer lending even less profitable than it is now."[19]

Carter's staff had a strategy. Now they needed a conspicuous target. They quickly built their plan around the most visible form of consumer borrowing: credit cards. Since the 1950s, cards had symbolized profligate spending and irresponsibility. Citi's nationwide marketing blitz and the acceleration of card solicitations that followed only reinforced the association of cards, credit buying, and rising prices. Placing controls on cards, administration officials believed, would curtail inflationary spending. It would also send a clear message that Carter meant to beat inflation. Targeted controls also appealed to traditional Democratic constituencies, particularly organized labor. Unions wanted wage-driven prosperity, not credit-driven consumerism. By pushing up interest rates across the board, Volcker's policies dampened "productive" mortgage and auto lending markets, which directly supported unionized employment. Under the still resonant logic of the New Deal regulatory order, blocking the channel to cards would send more credit flowing toward these other forms of lending, increasing supply, lowering prices, and making it possible for consumers to continue supporting unionized industrial work.[20]

In early March, Carter's economic team convened at Camp David to assess the potential response to the credit control policy and other anti-inflationary initiatives under consideration. Administration staff invited hundreds of representatives from various constituencies, including business, the elderly, African Americans, consumers, organized labor, and ethnic groups. Most groups, including African American, elderly, and ethnic leaders, voiced strong support for credit controls. Business leaders, predictably, expressed "*universal opposition.*" Bankers were incensed. If left alone, they argued, credit markets would adjust without administration interference. Volcker's tight money policies had already driven up the cost of consumer lending. Banks, pinned against state usury ceilings, were scaling back their card programs. Controls would only make matters worse, they argued, for their banks and the larger economy. Two days before the meetings, Citibank took out full-page ads in the *New York Times, Washington Post*, and *Wall Street Journal* denouncing credit controls. "There may be policy makers who believe this to be in the national interest but it is doubtful that many citizens will find it to be in theirs," the bank opined. Despite this opposition, on March 12 Carter gave the final go-ahead on the program. He announced it to the nation two days later.[21]

Carter's March 14 announcement of the credit control policy had much in common with his "Crisis of Confidence" speech nine months earlier. Carter began by detailing inflation's causes, most importantly "our failure in government and as individuals, as an entire American society, to live within our means." He called for discipline, strong medicine, and stern measures. For government's part, Carter promised to balance the 1981 budget. The state had not provided an example of frugality and fiscal responsibility. As a consequence, Carter lamented, there would be "cuts in good and worthwhile programs—programs which I support very strongly." Citizens, too, had not done their part. "Consumers have gone in debt too heavily." Like a disappointed father or a remonstrating pastor, Carter implored Americans to shift from spending to saving. "In the fight against inflation, what is at stake is more than material wealth or material comfort," he argued. "What is at stake is whether or not Americans—as a nation and as a people—will retain control of our own destiny." Though full of Carter's patented moralism, discussion of the Credit Control Act was relatively brief. In a scant two sentences, Carter explained that he was implementing the act, that the Federal Reserve would "establish controls for credit cards and other unsecured loans," and that loans for homes, cars, and other durable goods would not be covered by the policy. Although his description of controls was limited, Carter's message was clear: Americans were living beyond their means, and credit cards were partially to blame.[22]

What was less clear, however, was how the policy would actually work. The Federal Reserve rolled out the full details a few hours after Carter's speech. The policy placed restrictions on credit cards, as well as "check credit overdraft plans, unsecured personal loans and secured credit where the proceeds are not used to finance the collateral," which offered potential substitutes or workarounds. The Fed required lenders who extended unsecured consumer credit, and who had $2 million or more of such credit already outstanding, to deposit 15 percent of all *new* credit extended with the Federal Reserve in non-interest-bearing accounts. Under this plan, for each dollar newly lent to consumers that earned interest, lenders had to set aside 15 cents that did not. Because lenders still had to pay depositors or money markets for funds that languished at the Fed, this special deposit significantly increased the cost of consumer lending. Instead of providing guidance on how to allocate these new costs, the Fed left it to lenders to determine the best way to administer controls.[23]

Headline writers understandably skipped the finer details of the Fed's policy. Instead, national media emphasized that credit card borrowing would become much more expensive, if it was available at all. Under the front-page headline "Credit Card Interest Rates to Rise," the *Los Angeles Times* warned consumers that "banks, department stores, and others issuing credit cards will reduce the amount of credit available" and "individual citizens may find it virtually impossible to get new cards." Other papers similarly made card restrictions central to their coverage of Carter's anti-inflation policies, magnifying the president's message of credit restraint. In light of the administration's past unsuccessful bouts with inflation, some observers argued that the White House was offering up yet another slate of misguided policies. Credit controls, *Washington Post* editor Robert J. Samuelson argued, amounted to a knee-jerk reaction from policymakers bent on satisfying citizens' calls to "do something." They failed to attack inflation's underlying causes. "Anyone who believes credit cards have much to do with the nation's inflation," quipped Samuelson, "probably also thinks you can get to China with a pick and shovel." Nevertheless, even Samuelson's criticism put cards at center stage, where consumers could work out for themselves the relationship between credit and inflation.[24]

Carter's policy elicited a searching examination of plastic capitalism. Consumers embraced the president's call for more judicious use of credit, voicing support in the media and at the cash register. "Isn't our present dilemma caused by the 'now' syndrome," one writer asked in the *Washington Post*, "wanting things now instead of waiting until we can afford them?" Others forwarded new credit offers to the White House, suggesting that the card companies had given Carter "another *kick* in the pants." Inflation adviser Alfred Kahn remembered these letters years later. "Some people sent me credit cards, wrote irate letters to the effect that Sears Roebuck was still soliciting credit card accounts." Carter's moralizing tapped deeper currents. The democratization and expansion of cards during the previous decade contrasted sharply with oft-espoused ideals of thrift and moderation. So did the increasing use of consumer debt to fund daily consumption. As the 1970s economic crisis undercut Americans' ability to consume without resorting to credit, Carter's credit crackdown offered consumers the opportunity to realign their financial practices with their values.[25]

Card issuers recognized that the links between credit, anticipatory buying, and inflation continued to threaten their legitimacy, and some publicly supported the control policy. In a television ad set in front of the Capitol in Washington, D.C., Interbank president Russell Hogg urged consumers to use their Master Charge cards "only for necessities and emergencies."

American Express voiced support for Carter's policies while distancing their
cards from demon credit. "The American Express Card . . . offers no revolving, open-end credit," one ad noted. "You are expected to pay your bill in full
every month. Since this helps you live within your means," the ad continued,
"you don't get in over your head," mirroring Carter's call to "live within our
means." Perhaps Amex executives believed their customers identified with
the president's message. If so, they made a safe bet. In April 1980, the American Retail Federation commissioned a survey to gauge consumer attitudes
about credit controls and inflation. Conducting more than 1,500 interviews,
researchers found that 63 percent of respondents believed controls were necessary. Almost as many intended to reduce credit purchasing in the months
ahead. Other sources corroborated these findings. A New York Times/CBS
News poll taken in April found that 58 percent of Americans claimed to be
using cards less than they had during the previous year; only 5 percent
claimed to be using them more.[26]

Faced with a potent mix of social momentum and policy ambiguity, consumers rapidly retreated from credit purchasing, with dramatic economic
consequences. In March and April, major national retailers saw double-digit
declines in credit buying. Sears's earnings fell by 60 percent from the previous year, and J. C. Penney's earnings shrank 58.9 percent. Revolving credit,
which had grown continuously over the previous decade, stalled then fell.
Consumers pulled back from installment borrowing as well, so that total
consumer debt decreased by $1.8 billion in April, marking the first signifi-
cant decline since the mid-1970s recession. The fall continued in May, to the
tune of $2.6 billion. Overall, the U.S. economy experienced the largest post-
war decline in consumer debt in the second quarter of 1980, as consumers
did what they could to rein in credit spending. Although economists initially
dismissed controls as largely symbolic, some began to find that Americans
were making a real effort to alter their buying habits. "It may have been symbolic, but it was quite shocking," said S. Lee Booth, senior vice president and
economist for the National Consumer Finance Association, "It made a lot of
people rethink their credit practices."[27]

Carter's advisers met consumers' withdrawal from credit spending with a
mix of pleasure and dread. Controls, they saw, were working. And they may
have gone too far. Preparing for a May meeting of the economic team, Schultze worried that "many consumers believe the use of credit cards is now illegal

or unpatriotic." He asked if the administration ought to counter these notions. Carter had not wanted to face down high inflation during an election year—he certainly did not want a crumbling economy. The meeting did little to allay Schultze's fear. A subsequent memo notified Carter that Volcker was looking into whether consumers were overreacting to the controls. As Volcker explained to the House Banking Committee two months later, "We, in fact, took the mildest action that we could conceive of, but there was clearly a physiological message."[28]

In retrospect, consumers were, if not overreacting, at least responding very strongly to controls. Their behavior partially stemmed from social concern over credit card proliferation. The White House and the Federal Reserve also failed to explain clearly how the government was administering controls and what they were meant to accomplish. Although Carter firmly asserted that Americans had lived beyond their means and that cards were a notable culprit, the public did not readily grasp the mechanics of the Fed's non-interest-bearing special deposits. Rather, they knew the president had instituted a control policy aimed at credit cards. As evidence of consumers' retreat from card spending mounted, the administration decided to back off. They claimed a moral victory over inflationary psychology while continuing to urge Americans to practice moderation. In May, Volcker amended the policy, reducing the special deposit from 15 percent to 7.5 percent. The Fed enabled lenders to offer credit more easily. Still, Carter did not encourage Americans to go shopping. "We must not," he warned, "permit the ravages of recession to damage the progress that we've made."[29]

"Out of Proportion to the Mere Goal of Credit Restraint"

Credit industry executives had predicted such ravages when consulted about the control policy in early March 1980. At that time, firms were already responding to Volcker's revolutionary monetary policies and the escalating cost of money. As their costs ratcheted up, banks, retailers, and other lenders could not pass higher prices onto borrowers. State usury limits blocked the way. In early February 1980, more than a month before the CCA went into effect, members of the Federal Open Market Committee (FOMC) noticed lenders withdrawing from consumer credit markets. "More and more banks are cutting back on the availability of consumer credit and are increasing the

price and other factors," its vice chairman Frederick H. Schultz told other
board members. "We're also seeing that with . . . retail establishments; Sears
and Penneys and others have recently made those kinds of announcements."
Lenders pursued a variety of strategies to cope with the Fed's tight money
policy. Some simply lent less, allowing only the most creditworthy customers
to borrow. For cards, however, reducing access was not always an option.
Cardholders had prearranged lines of credit that could not be easily altered
or revoked, especially if the issuer hoped to retain the customer in the future.
Banks had recently invested heavily in building their card businesses; they
would not now cut off customers and sacrifice hard-won market share. In a
bid to eke out extra income without exceeding state usury ceilings, card issuers restructured their finance charges. Some banks began charging Visa and
Mastercard customers interest from the day they made purchases instead of
allowing the customary thirty-day grace period. Others gave up and tried to
offload their card portfolios entirely. On March 7, a week before credit controls were implemented, FOMC member Thomas M. Timlen nonchalantly
observed, "There is also a good deal of concern regarding losses on consumer credit cards, but that's news to no one."[30]

When business leaders consulted with the Carter administration in the
lead up to the CCA's implementation, they expressed "*Universal Opposition*"
to credit controls. They argued that "market forces are seen as working" to
restrain consumer credit "and would handle the problem." And they pointed
out that "credit controls would shift the blame of denial of credit to the President when, because of market forces, credit institutions would have to deny
credit anyway." This last observation proved especially prescient.[31]

As the executives predicted, credit controls exacerbated the problems that
began with Volcker's policies. Many firms complied with controls in ways
that complimented the administration's objectives. Citibank and Chase
Manhattan stopped issuing new Visa and Master Charge cards altogether,
even refusing requests from current customers. Manufacturers Hanover
and Bank of America promised to "more rigidly scrutinize new card appli-
cants" to limit credit extensions. Further, Bank of America, along with major
retailers Sears and Montgomery Ward, raised the required minimum
monthly payments on credit card accounts in order to get customers to repay
their balances faster. Such changes in repayment policy, however, violated
many state consumer protection laws, which barred lenders from abruptly

manipulating repayment terms. Concerned that variations in state law would cause enforcement to "vary 50 different ways," the Fed used its authority under the Credit Control Act to override local statutes, allowing lenders to increase consumers' monthly payments as they saw fit. The landscape of state usury legislation gave the CCA much of its potency, but the Fed was willing to dispense with other local protections when those laws conflicted with its objectives.[32]

Limiting credit access and accelerating repayment periods served the administration's credit control goals; many actions taken by banks and other lenders emphatically did not. For many banks, controls provided an opportunity to rescue their card businesses from the Fed's tight policy and their own credit-issuing excesses. Though bankers howled at federal intervention, many of the nation's largest banks were at the same time losing millions on their credit card portfolios, suffering under the combined weight of tight monetary policy and restrictive usury ceilings. Carter thus gave bankers carte blanche to re-price their card plans and point to the president as the culprit: this is exactly what they did. Across the nation, banks added annual fees, retroactively raised interest rates, booted marginally profitable customers, and undertook a variety of other measures to make their cards profitable under the guise of federal interference. After examining the changes announced by eighty-nine bank card issuers, a House Banking Subcommittee found that "*some creditors took actions that appear to be so drastic as to be out of proportion to the mere goal of credit restraint.*"[33]

Bankers' imposition of annual fees illustrates the point. According to the subcommittee's findings, more than half of banks examined began charging an annual fee, $14 a year on average. Banks had long coveted annual fees as a way to profit from "convenience users," those who paid their card balances each month without paying interest. Rigorous competition, however, kept banks from instituting fees for fear that customers would walk to the mailbox and find a better offer. When Marquette National Bank imposed an annual fee on its Minnesota customers, the First National Bank of Omaha quickly offered a higher interest, no fee, alternative. When Citibank instituted a monthly service charge for convenience users in 1976, cardholders threw their cards in tellers' faces. Fees, once impossible, rapidly became standard. Carter took the blame. "The annual fees and higher interest rates brought on by President Carter's credit-tightening moves of three months ago may be here to stay," the *Christian Science Monitor* reported in June 1980. The Union National Bank of Wichita, Kansas, explained its new annual fee by informing customers, "Now UNB and other banks are forced, through changes in regulations, to also charge for this service." The Credit Control Act, spurred by the mass-solicitation strategies bankers employed to get their cards into consumer hands, also bailed these banks out, allowing them to restructure credit card pricing. By 1981, annual fees became the industry standard, helping to transform bank cards into permanent profit centers.[34]

"Is It Easier for You to Go Shopping?"

Carter had asked the nation to examine its dependence on plastic money, but he would soon lose the 1980 presidential election and his bully pulpit. Consumers, convinced by Carter's message if unsure of the CCA's implementation, cut credit spending just as banks and retailers curtailed consumer lending. Consumer debt fell faster than it ever had in the postwar period. The economy, dependent on consumer borrowing, contracted sharply. From April to June, the nation's gross national product plummeted at an 8 percent annualized rate. Unemployment, which stood at 6.3 percent when controls were implemented, jumped to 7.8 percent by July, falling only to 7.5 percent by November. The economic news was not all bad; overall interest rates declined, with the prime rate falling from 19.5 percent in April to 11 percent in July. Inflation also fell precipitously. Though Carter later blamed Volcker's tight monetary policy for the election year downturn, credit controls prompted consumers to put the brakes on spending and push the economy into recession.[35]

Carter, true to form, couched the dour economic news in terms of shared sacrifice. His opponent, Ronald Reagan, offered a different vision of the country's future. The former actor and California governor crafted his campaign in opposition to Carter's "Crisis of Confidence" speech and the moralizing tone of the incumbent's presidency. Reagan spoke enthusiastically about American greatness—not that which had passed but that which had yet to come. In accepting the Republican nomination, Reagan told his audience, "The American people . . . who created the highest standard of living, are not going to accept the notion that we can only make a better world for others by moving backwards ourselves." He further enjoined Americans,

"We do not have inflation because, as Mr. Carter says, we have lived too well."
Americans had not lived beyond their means; their means, like those of their
nation, were infinite.[36]

Carter fought tenaciously. On October 28 just seven days before the election, he led Reagan in the most recent Gallup poll. That night, the candidates
squared off in their only televised debate, an event that showcased the candidates' contrasting visions. When asked about inflation, Carter responded,
"We have demanded that the American people sacrifice, and they've done
very well," expounding on successful efforts of conservation and responsible
spending. Reagan countered, charging that Carter "has blamed the people
for inflation . . . he has then accused the people of living too well and that we
must share in scarcity, we must sacrifice and get used to doing with less."
Reagan then repeated the line from his nomination speech: "We don't have
inflation because the people are living too well," instead, "We have inflation
because the Government is living too well." Reagan drove the message
home most forcefully in his closing statement, when he asked memorably:
"Are you better off than you were four years ago? Is it easier for you to go
buy things in the stores than it was four years ago?" The first line is often
quoted. The second connects national well-being directly to purchasing and
consumption—convenient consumerism facilitated by convenient credit.
These questions emphasized a new vision of society's goals and signaled the
death knell of Carter's presidency.[37]

Reagan nailed Carter to a cross of plastic. The sharp economic decline that
had followed the credit control policy placed Carter's presidency in an untenable position. Though Volcker was cooling the economy before the CCA went
into effect, and would have continued to do so had controls not been employed, publicly the White House, not the Federal Reserve, plunged the economy into freefall with its March 14 action. Though voters may not have
entered the booth with the Credit Control Act top of mind, the CCA's effect
on unemployment and the broader economy made it a central factor in voters' dissatisfaction with Carter's economic performance. Although the Iranian hostage crisis, the Panama Canal Treaty, and the rise of cultural
conservatism all influenced the outcome of the election, a New York Times/
CBS News poll of more than 10,000 voters found that "the biggest issue in
their minds was the nation's economy." In presidential elections, the economy has consistently been the most important factor affecting voter response.

By confronting the nation's credit dependence, Carter played into Reagan's hands. "Is it easier for you to go buy things in the stores than it was four years ago?" For the millions of credit-wielding consumers who responded in the negative, the cause may not have been clear, but the answer certainly was. Reagan's rhetoric made the experience of credit concrete. He went on to win a landslide victory, claiming 489 electoral votes to Carter's 49, a result that transformed national politics and federal economic policymaking.[38]

Reagan's administration heartily embraced the free market as a panacea for the nation's economic and psychic woes. In doing so, Reagan rejected the notion of limits. He offered citizens a vision of America that would satisfy all their desires. "Morning in America," though, proved expensive, often paid for through increased reliance on consumer credit. As a card industry news-letter rejoiced in April of 1981, "Consumers have rebounded from the gov-ernment's curb on credit spending imposed one year ago this month and now they're using credit cards at a faster clip than ever." After growing a mere 2.6 percent during 1980, outstanding credit card balances expanded at a moderate pace during the 1981–82 recession, 10.8 and 8.9 percent a year respectively. With recovery in full swing and card solicitations on the rise, outstanding balances jumped 19.1 percent in 1983, then a full 27 percent in 1984. For card firms, Morning in America was bright indeed.[39]

In the years that followed, Carter's economic team deflected responsibility for the control policy and the economic decline it unleashed. "The whole thing," Charles Schultze recalled to one interviewer, "was literally a comedy of errors." Only inflation adviser Alfred Kahn admitted supporting controls, though he recognized that they "really helped plunge us into recession." "No-body," he continued, "contemplated that the response would be so enormous." In one sense, the reaction was unexpected because the pressures underlying it were deep and slow-building. American consumers had long been unset-tled by their ever-greater reliance on credit to access material prosperity. In the early postwar years, this credit remained largely local, embedded in interper-sonal relationships. Consumers drew on credit at a time of economic expan-sion and wage growth. Their debts increased in line with their incomes. Credit was a manageable, knowable risk. Still they distrusted it. In the 1960s and 1970s, credit became increasingly impersonal—a card mailed from a far-away bank. It seemed to become more expensive, as inflation drove lenders to seek the highest allowable interest rates. It became more binding, as firms spread debt repayment over longer periods. Instead of using credit in the warm summer of prosperity, consumers depended on credit to maintain their slipping purchasing power. Inflation ate away their incomes. Surveys show they loathed it. Their collective goal was to "not be in debt." Carter's control policy gave consumers a chance to align their practices with their ideals. They mailed cards to the White House by the dozen.[40]

Consumers, of course, were only one part of the story. Controls gave bankers a chance to extricate themselves from the consequences of years of frantic card competition. Since the late 1960s, bankers had been torn between a hopeful quest for card-driven profits, built on visions of a future where cards were at the center of consumer finance, and a fearful defense of their existing markets, where cards were a necessary evil. Both impulses dictated relentless marketing, especially once Citibank expanded the geographic range of card competition. The frenzied promotions of the late 1970s exposed bankers to new challenges, the most pressing of which was interest rate risk. In their zeal for promotion, many banks had shifted from funding card receivables with price-controlled consumer deposits to relying on variable and expensive market-rate liabilities. Because consumer and labor groups had succeeded in extending state usury laws to cover card plans in the late 1960s and early 1970s, bankers faced rigid price ceilings with no cost floor. Volcker's tight money policies, and then Carter's credit controls, put firms, like Citibank, with large card portfolios in a sudden and vicious bind. Yet, while banks' aggressive card marketing had made cards conspicuous political targets, credit controls provided bankers political cover to forge paths to stable profitability. Annual fees, for instance, allowed banks to profit from convenience users who dutifully paid their balances on time. But it would take more dramatic moves to circumvent state regulation altogether.

As contests over consumer credit moved back to the states, where local lawmakers would reassess their states' usury laws and debate banks' new annual fees, concern for managing the flow of credit evaporated within the executive branch. Administration officials fully committed to ceding credit allocation to financial markets. Over the next generation, as wages—the prime driver of postwar purchasing power—continued to stagnate for most Americans, credit cards and other forms of consumer borrowing provided necessary fuel for America's consumption engine, filling the gap between the promise of American prosperity and its realization. The veneer of material prosperity made Reagan's soaring rhetoric believable, and his successors in the White House made ensuring wide credit access their paramount goal. For a brief time, Jimmy Carter tried to chart a different, more conservative path, suggesting that Americans ought to try and live within their means. Americans, experiencing the economy's shift toward finance firsthand, agreed. But by then it was already too late.[41]

11

Breakdown

Laboratories of Financialization

When they devised the administration's credit control policy in early 1980, members of Jimmy Carter's economic team relied on state usury laws to force banks and other card issuers to internalize the costs of federal controls, rather than passing them on to consumers. Many banks circumvented cost internalization by imposing new, unregulated annual fees, but still, usury laws gave controls their bite. Too much for Carter, as it turned out. In the wake of controls, consumer advocates again turned to state legislatures to roll back banks' annual fees and reimpose the low-cost, convenient credit regime they had secured through state regulation. They had every reason to expect success.[1]

Yet at the same moment that Carter's team was building a control program on a state regulatory foundation, Citibank, whose massive solicitation campaign had brought cards into the political spotlight, was planning to make state usury regulations irrelevant. In March 1980, Citi announced that it would relocate its card operation from New York to South Dakota, a state with no applicable usury laws. From there, aided by the Supreme Court's 1978 *Marquette* decision, Citi could export South Dakota's rates to cardholders across the country. Citibank had already leapt over the geographic restrictions on interstate banking by mailing cards nationally in the late 1970s; now it gained new leverage to rewrite the terms of the place-based social contract. Before 1980, bankers were one constituency among many negotiating over how ideals of economic fairness and imperatives of profitability would be reflected in state-regulated credit markets. After Citibank showed state policymakers and its banking peers that bank capital could move, state debates shifted to focus on local jobs and tax revenue, realigning the political calculous and putting bankers in the driver's seat. A state-driven deregulation of the credit card industry followed, clearing the way for banks to recast cards, from instruments of convenient credit to tools of long-term debt.

The state-level deregulation of credit card interest rates transformed the structural incentives of consumer credit markets by shifting interest rate risk from financial institutions onto consumer households. With rate caps in place, banks bore the costs when market interest rates rose, and as a result they rationed credit, granting access to borrowers—white, male, affluent, straight—deemed most creditworthy. In the 1960s, bankers and their political allies had argued that eliminating rate caps would expand the boundaries of financial citizenship by making credit more widely available. Mobilized consumers rejected these arguments. They preferred low-cost, safe credit. In concert with state-level allies, they shaped market rules to deliver on these preferences. By the late 1970s, however, deregulatory arguments had gained traction. Across the political landscape, business lobbying groups undermined and delegitimized the consumer movement and the New Deal regulatory project. More narrowly, William Proxmire and other congressional leaders, who pursued equal credit opportunity in the name of expanding credit citizenship, gradually embraced financial deregulation as a means of spreading the benefits of financial participation to previously marginalized and excluded groups. Yet the scope of congressional deregulation in the early 1980s remained limited, amounting to a recognition that banks and other financial firms had already undermined federal deposit controls by innovating around them. States retained the power to impose credit price ceilings, and the broader structures of financial federalism and industry silos largely remained in place. State rules continued to decisively shape consumer credit markets, and it was state-level deregulation that decisively transformed them. Banks in states without price ceilings massively expanded national credit card markets by charging higher prices and lending to more and riskier borrowers. Gresham's law of plastic, where expensive, heavily marketed credit pushed out lower cost, more highly regulated alternatives, prevailed.[2]

South Dakota: Reimagining Regulatory Space

In early 1980, Citibank was in an untenable position. Over the previous two and a half years, the bank had built a nationwide portfolio of Visa card accounts, more than four million in all. CEO Walter Wriston and protégé John Reed had staked the bank's future on the U.S. consumer market, with cards—banks in miniature—as the centerpiece of their plans. Yet despite the wide geographic reach of Citi's cards, under financial federalism, the bank's millions of accounts remained regulated in New York, a state firmly committed to controlling the price of consumer credit. New York's limits on revolving credit prices were low by national standards. The state allowed Citi and its peer institutions to charge 18 percent on the first $500 of revolving credit outstanding and 12 percent on any amount above that. State court rulings, meanwhile, barred Citi from charging monthly or annual fees. If consumers paid their bills on time, they enjoyed the convenience of credit without the expense. Usury limits also shielded consumers from fluctuations in the market price of credit. The cost banks paid for loanable funds could rise or fall with market interest rates, but the price they could charge consumers remained fixed. Put another way: state usury limits forced banks to internalize the risk of rising market interest rates, and this interest rate risk disincentivized banks from extending too much credit through card plans. As market interest rates climbed in the 1970s and spiked after Paul Volcker began the Fed's monetarist experiment in October 1979, interest rate risk became an outright danger.

Citibank and its competitors could not have predicted this outcome when they began competing aggressively for new card accounts in the late 1970s. Bankers had significantly improved back-office efficiency, and in the 1970s operating costs declined by 40 percent. Bankers still struggled to squeeze profits from card plans, but doing so was increasingly possible. State usury laws limited the amount of interest most banks could charge to around 18 percent, but the total income from credit purchases, which also included fees paid by merchants accepting banks' cards, exceeded most banks' expenses and costs of funds. In 1979, Visa reported that the average income for bank cards had equaled 19 percent of outstanding balances in June 1978. Subtracted from this were processing costs, at 7.7 percent, and fraud and credit losses, at 1.7 percent. With a cost of funds averaging 7 percent, banks

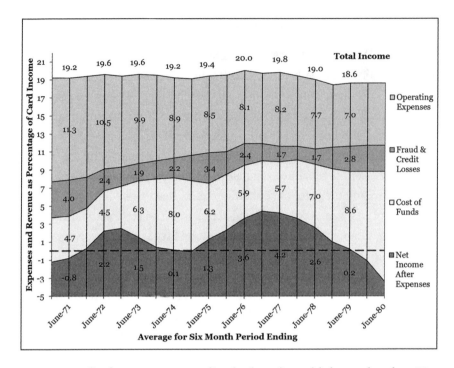

Fig. 7: Annualized return on outstanding bank credit card balances, based on Visa System quarterly member reports. The graph shows the steady decline in operating expenses during the 1970s and the decisive importance of cost of funds in determining card plan profits—or losses. The first six months of 1980 were Visa's forecast.

Source: Visa USA Inc., "Credit Controls and Bank Credit Cards: Analysis and Proposals," 794.01 (L) Voluntary Credit Restraint March 1980, Federal Reserve Bank of New York Archives.

cleared a net income of 2.6 percent on their outstanding card balances. But by 1979, those profits were under pressure. Fraud and credit losses increased because of wide and sometimes unwise card distribution. The real worry, however, came from interest rate risk as the cost of funds rose ever higher. In the third quarter of 1977, when Citi began its nationwide Visa campaign, its internal cost of funds stood at 6.21 percent, a rate that compares favorably with industry figures. A year later that number stood at 9 percent and the bank's internal forecasts estimated that it would rise to over 10 percent by the third quarter of 1979. At this rate, and taking into consideration the high cost of administering card accounts, the bank was losing money on every credit card transaction it financed.[3]

Citibank was in dire straits. It had invested enormous financial resources to build a nationwide card-based bank; its executives had publicly marked out the consumer market as the key to Citi's growth: the firm's reputation was at stake. There was too much on the line to back out. In early 1980, Citi executives began looking for a political solution, reaching out to New York's governor and legislators to see if a repeal of the usury limit was politically possible. But Citi's executives knew their political environment and knew they lacked leverage to overturn the state's strong commitment to consumer protection. The usury limit, noted one Citibank executive "is a popular issue that even conservatives find themselves [siding with consumers]," adding, "people see it as [akin to] motherhood and so on." Thus, even as they tested the political waters, Citi executives explored other means of circumventing regulatory constraints, favoring a strategy that would give them both local leverage and a clear way out of New York. Citibank's lawyers had puzzled out a way forward. They had the *Marquette* decision.[4]

The 1978 *Marquette* decision turned on the meaning of the word "located" as written in the National Bank Act (1864), specifically, any national bank "may . . . charge on any loan . . . interest at the rate allowed by the laws of the State . . . where the bank is *located*." That word meant one thing to the parties in the case, the First National Bank of Omaha and Marquette National Bank of Minneapolis, which were located in fixed places. It meant something else to Citibank executives, whose global experience taught them that the "location" of a bank's operations depended on the legal fictions of a bank charter, not the physical infrastructure of a bank building. With *Marquette,* Citi executives saw an opportunity to save the card business and perhaps the bank itself by relocating its card operation to a high-usury state. From there, Citi could project higher interest rates back into New York and to its credit card customers across the country. The bank would substitute a spatial solution for a political one, escaping the challenges of local regulation by simply moving to a more favorable location.[5]

Such a move was legally possible under conditions set out in the Bank Holding Company Act of 1956, but only if another state explicitly invited the bank in. In early 1980 Citibank's lawyers set to narrowing a list, first to states with usury ceilings at 22 percent or higher, then to states with legislatures still in session, and finally to states other than California (it was inconceivable that Bank of America's home state would welcome Citi). The final list was short: Missouri and South Dakota. With a large labor pool and an established communications infrastructure, Missouri seemed the obvious choice. The 2,000 jobs Citi promised guaranteed the bank a thoughtful hearing from the state's governor and legislators. The local banking community was not as welcoming. St. Louis bankers were still irate that Citi had blanketed "their market" with Visa solicitations; they blocked the move.[6]

That left South Dakota, a state not generally known as a center of banking and finance. In fact, when Citi executives began phoning the governor's office, the state was in dire financial straits. South Dakota had long suffered from the decline of family farming in the face of globalized agribusiness. For seven years running, its nonagricultural workers were the lowest paid in the nation, contributing to an out-migration of young South Dakotans seeking better opportunities. The money policies under Volcker's Fed wrought further havoc for South Dakota's local banks. With their cost of money rising as Volcker wrung inflation out of the economy, South Dakota bankers were bumping up against the state's already high usury limit in their efforts to make local loans, squeezing out small borrowers and virtually halting local economic activity. Looking back, then governor Bill Janklow recalled, "The economy was, at that time, dead."[7]

Before Citibank arrived, South Dakota bankers were working on their own solution to the problems imposed by interest rate limits. If the state lifted the regulatory constraints on lending, these men believed, they could resurrect the local economy. At their annual policy meeting in November 1979, the South Dakota Bankers Association considered recommending a 2 percent increase in the state's usury limit to keep pace with the rising cost of money emanating from the Fed. To the surprise of those attending, Thomas Reardon of the Western Bank of Sioux Falls proposed a more dramatic move— that the state exempt all regulated lenders from the state's usury limit, a proposal that would allow South Dakota banks to charge any interest the market would bear. Following a "short and compelling argument" from Reardon and a quick second from his brother-in-law, the CEO of Pierre National Bank, the motion carried. Although some bankers were stunned, the association rallied support from the governor and the legislature, and South Dakota's anti-usury bill passed by a wide margin in January 1980.[8]

This action, of which Citibank had no knowledge, clearly demonstrated the power of South Dakota's local banking community, authority rooted in financial federalism and bankers' role in the place-based social contract. When Citi approached Janklow in February 1980 about relocating to South Dakota, the first place Janklow turned was the South Dakota Bankers Association. The bankers were deeply concerned about competing against Citibank. They were also encouraged by the possibility of local jobs and the banking services Citi could provide them. Though Citibank initially promised only a few hundred positions—holding out hope that New York would raise its rate caps to stave off the bank's threatened move—the potential economic impact of Citi's entire card division was estimated at between $63 and $68 million. "Citibank's credit card operations are exactly the type of business that will not only maintain but enhance the quality of life we all enjoy in South Dakota," Janklow told state lawmakers as they considered Citibank's offer the following month. "They won't pollute our air or water. They won't place large strains on our highway system. . . . They won't exert any additional pressures on state or community services." Furthermore, Janklow was convinced, economic growth need not come from Citibank alone; with *Marquette* and a new appreciation for federal banking law provided by Citi's executives, the governor saw the potential to bring an entirely new industry to his state.[9]

Still, to approve the deal South Dakota's bankers wanted protection, and Janklow, the state legislature, and Citibank's lawyers gave it to them. According to the bill drafted by Citi's attorneys, card-issuing banks, like Citi, hoping to relocate to South Dakota would need to seek the approval of the state's banking commission, a board controlled by local bank executives. The "Citibank bill" further limited out-of-state banks to one location and read, "Such single banking office shall be operated in a manner and at a location which is not likely to attract customers from the general public in the state to the substantial detriment of existing banks in the state." In practice, this meant that Citi's "bank" was a nondescript office building in an industrial park by the airport, not a cheerful storefront downtown. Citibank's South Dakota subsidiary could thus focus exclusively on card operations. Citi's lawyers designed the law's competition provisions, in part, to appeal to the bank's federal regulators, who worried about the competitive effects of full-service Citibank branches on the local banking market. The offer proved compelling. On March 12, 1980, the Citibank bill cleared both houses of the state's legislature by a combined vote of 97 to 3. State officials wasted little time trying to bring other banks to the prairie: by the end of March, South Dakota's director of banking and finance was calling on bankers in New York, Pennsylvania, and Illinois, eager to explain the new opportunities available in South Dakota.[10]

New York: Holding on for Dear Life

As they negotiated with Missouri and South Dakota officials, Citibank executives did not forsake New York. In February 1980, the bank's top officers sought a deal that could restore the card business's profitability and keep it in the state. But brash actions by the bank had cooled the political climate. First, in an effort to stem the bank's immediate losses, Citi exercised a loophole in national banking law that allowed it to charge one percentage point higher than the Federal Reserve's discount rate, which the Fed had raised to 13 percent. Citibank now charged cardholders 14 percent on balances over $500, instead of the state mandated 12. In making the change Citibank had snubbed local authority, alienating potential allies. Other New York banks, likewise suffering tremendous strain, continued to abide by state rate rules. The day after Citi raised its rates, Wriston appealed personally to Governor Hugh L. Carey, advising Carey that Citibank might move its card operation out of New York if the legislature did not raise the state's usury limit. On the same day, other Citi executives launched a coordinated media campaign, advertising the bank's negotiations with other states and describing the likely loss of local jobs and credit access that would result if the legislature failed to act. But the politicians were not yet ready to bend to the bank's threats. The governor's office was eager to explore options other than raising or removing the state's usury laws. The speaker of the State Assembly, Stanley Fink, was "very pessimistic" about the possibility of raising rates.[11]

Citibank was playing hardball, but it was not the only bank seeking to change New York's interest rate laws. As market rates continued to rise in early 1980, New York's financial community lined up for interest rate relief. The New York Bankers Association lobbied Carey for increases in credit card and other lending rates. Meanwhile, as Citi became more adamant about relocating, community stakeholders worried about the broader economic consequences of losing Citi's card operation. On Long Island, where some New York City banks had located their card operations (fittingly, in retrofitted shopping centers), business leaders and the local press were especially concerned. "As a businessman," one landlord concluded, "it appears asinine to me that New York State is willing to suffer so great an economic loss." Finally convinced of the issue's urgency, Carey asked state banking superintendent Muriel Siebert to develop legislative plans for addressing New York's usury problem. In June, Carey submitted legislation, prepared by the banking department in consultation with bankers and consumer groups, that would raise rate ceilings on mortgages and card accounts. Carey pushed hard for the legislation, and it cleared the Republican-led state senate. Legislators in the Democratic assembly, however, refused to raise rates. The banking bill, Fink argued, was "everything good for the banks and nothing good for the consumer." The assembly refused to vote on the measure.[12]

Assembly members were committed to protecting consumers from high credit prices. They also continued to operate under the expectation, ingrained by the financial system's geographic regulations, that banks did not move. Wriston knew better. Soon after the legislation failed, Wriston wrote Carey, expressing gratitude for his administration's work on the bill and urging Carey to continue to help "the Legislature recognize the disparity between the banking and regulatory laws of this State and our sister states." Wriston and Carey both knew the bill's failure would send New York banks down the path forged by Citi. Some had visited South Dakota in April and May. Others were testing the waters in nearby Delaware and Connecticut. "Many of the major banks are presently looking to other states," Wriston warned, "to obtain the relief we desperately need." Indeed, many states saw in New York's banks the economic development *they* desperately needed. In July, Siebert publicized a letter written by the mayor of Wilmington, Delaware, urging New York's banks to consider Wilmington as a possible home for their consumer credit operations. Siebert accused rival states of circling New York's banks "like vultures."[13]

Throughout the summer, the New York press speculated about bank moves, while lawmakers fretted. Several wrote Carey, urging him to call a special legislative session to change the usury law. They worried about potential damage to New York's economy, pointing to Citibank's relocation specifically and predicting dire consequences if the law was not changed. "The specter of further joblessness stares us in the face," a Republican state senator wrote. To forestall these losses, Carey called the legislature into special session in November 1980. When New York lawmakers finally returned to Albany, Carey proposed more dramatic measures, asking legislators to remove interest rate ceilings on consumer loans entirely, "letting the free market set the rate according to the laws of supply and demand." With so many local jobs at risk, the legislature largely accepted the governor's proposals.[14]

Consumers were outraged as bankers, sensing their leverage, pried in further. "You have been instrumental in screwing the citizens of New York," wrote one irate consumer. "Successful blackmail begets further attempts," wrote another. Bankers reinforced this message through thinly veiled threats. Edward W. Duffy, chairman of Marine Midland Bank, thanked the governor for his leadership reminding Carey of the "very adverse" consequences of not securing the bank-friendly legislation. "Marine Midland has its roots in New York State and we intend to continue to headquarter as many of our operations within the State *as possible*," Duffy assured. Richard LaBlond, vice president of Chemical Bank, likewise told the governor, "New York banking law should be competitive with other jurisdictions and we are anxious to continue to maintain operations here *as long as we can operate competitively*." LaBlond's Chemical Bank colleagues had toured Sioux Falls earlier in the year. And although it was on its way out, New York's usury repeal likely benefited Citibank more than any other firm. The new law allowed Citi to raise rates while federal regulators evaluated its relocation application, saving the bank $100 million in Wriston's estimation.[15]

Delaware: "The Luxembourg of the United States"

Citibank was not the only large New York bank upside down on its card business in early 1980. In the months after Citi announced its plans to relocate its card program to Sioux Falls, executives from several New York banks visited the state; they also cast about closer to home. Chase Manhattan looked south seeking a new home for its 2.4 million Visa accounts. Recognizing that they would need support from local bankers to secure a relocation deal, Chase executives reached out to Delaware's banking community in spring 1980. Delaware had a long history of favorable chartering policies and a business-friendly corporate law environment (40 percent of NYSE listed companies held Delaware charters in 1981). Like South Dakota's, the state's economy had suffered under the shifting fortunes of postwar capitalism.

Whereas South Dakota depended on agriculture, Delaware relied on the chemical and auto industries. The state's leaders stared down the barrel of deindustrialization. In Delaware, the relocation movement reached its apogee, and consumer groups at last mounted a credible, if brief, resistance.[16]

Delaware's negotiations with Chase took more work and proceeded more slowly than Citi's shotgun wedding with South Dakota. Delaware's banking community was lukewarm to Chase's initial overtures: its bankers, like their counterparts in other states, worried about inviting the nation's third-largest bank into their small market. Still, executives at the Bank of Delaware, some of whom had previously worked at Chase, saw the potential impact and pursued a deal. Through the spring, they worked to keep Chase interested, to enlist the support of local business elites, and to finally bring the banking and political community on board. They found allies in local business leaders, especially DuPont CEO Irving I. Shapiro. Though not noted at the time, Shapiro was a member of Citicorp's board of directors. He likely understood what Delaware stood to gain by luring in the bank card industry. Business leaders eventually convinced Delaware's bankers to consider the proposal. As in South Dakota, Delaware's tight-knit community of business and financial elites gave Chase executives a streamlined path to the halls of local power. The quiet campaign culminated at a June 11, 1980, meeting at the Wilmington Club, where Delaware's business and banking leaders gave their blessing. Governor Pierre S. "Pete" du Pont agreed to pursue the matter. By July 1980, the mayor of Wilmington felt negotiations had moved far enough to write the letters to New York's banks that so enraged Muriel Siebert.[17]

Delaware's Intergovernmental Task Force became the locus of negotiations and of an expanding vision of financial deregulation as state development strategy. Working through the summer to court New York's banks, task force members fielded mundane but critical questions about the local labor market and telecommunications capabilities. They also listened to New York's bankers. The Bank Holding Company Act, they discovered, opened opportunities beyond cards and rates exportation. At meetings with Morgan Guaranty Trust Company, a wholesale bank that served corporations, governments, and other large clients, Delaware's developers learned that New York banks chafed under the state's high taxes. Because banks were theoretically immobile, they were easy to tax. New York State taxed bank profits at 25.8 percent. As state officials crafted a law to invite banks into the state, they broadened it to include tax breaks, quietly developing their plans in the fall and winter of 1980 as the du Pont administration waited for the next legislative session to begin.[18]

To drive deregulatory growth, the task force crafted the Financial Center Development Act (FCDA), a bill designed to pull banks into Delaware. First, the bill plagiarized South Dakota's provisions inviting holding companies into the state while restricting their subsidiaries' ability to compete with local banks. The bill also abolished all usury restrictions on consumer loans and specifically allowed firms to charge annual fees on credit card accounts. In addition to the usury provisions, Delaware sweetened the pot by including a regressive bank franchise tax, meant to appeal not only to card-issuing banks but to all banking firms that used the state as an offshore haven. Delaware banks paid only 8.7 percent of all profits to the state, much less than New York's 25.8 percent. The bill maintained the 8.7 percent tax rate up to the first $20 million in profits, then lowered the rate to 2.7 percent on all subsequent profits. At the time, the state's largest bank had profits of only $13 million a year. Chase and Morgan Guaranty would likely generate much more. The law did require relocating financial institutions to employ at least 100 people in Delaware within a year, making the quid pro quo as clear as day.[19]

Governor du Pont and his allies feared that the controversial provisions would meet resistance in the state legislature; they also feared that if Delaware did not act quickly, other states might seize the deregulatory momentum. In January 1981, when du Pont placed the Financial Center Development Act before the legislature, he already had commitments from Chase and Morgan Guaranty that they would establish Delaware subsidiaries. These commitments were contingent, du Pont explained, on lawmakers acting quickly; the deal expired on February 4, 1981. If the bill succeeded, du Pont declared, Delaware would become "the Luxembourg of the United States." Legislators and local media received the proposal with cautious optimism. The Delaware House took up the bill first and quickly passed it with little opposition. Local media remained skeptical but supportive. "The most repeated argument for the bills," a local columnist wrote, "was that some state eventually would pass laws making it a mecca for the banking industry, and it might as well be Delaware."[20]

When the bill went to the state senate, it met more strident consumer opposition led by the Consumer Federation of America (CFA). National consumer groups had been caught off guard by Citibank's negotiations with South Dakota. Over the previous year they had resisted and rolled back the rate increases and annual fees induced by Volcker's monetary policies and the Credit Control Act. They were now prepared to challenge the new trend of interest rate exports. "The bill may be good for Delaware in attracting more business," James Boyle, CFA director of government relations explained to Delaware senators during a special hearing, "but you will be acting to supersede the laws of many other states." Opposition legislators introduced eighteen hostile amendments aimed at including more consumer protections and forcing the bill back to the House, "where opposition ha[d] reportedly grown since overwhelming passage" two weeks prior. After seven hours of debate, the lure of jobs and the banks' looming deadline won the senate over. "If Delaware doesn't do it," the *Wilmington Evening Journal*'s political correspondent wrote, "the carpetbankers from New York will find another pushover state legislature somewhere else."[21]

With the guidance from New York's bankers, Delaware followed South Dakota down a path that promised to import jobs and tax revenues, and export high interest rates and tax savings. Echoing remarks by South Dakota's William Janklow, du Pont explained to Delaware's lawmakers, "These are non-polluting jobs that pay well." The press recognized that these would also be white-collar jobs intended for white workers, reflecting the continued racial tension and inequality in Delaware's economy. On the same day the Delaware Senate passed the FCDA, its House rejected a bill honoring Martin Luther King Jr. with a state holiday. Still, Delaware's investment paid quick dividends. In Maryland, at the same moment Delaware lawmakers debated the Financial Center Development Act, Maryland lawmakers banned the new annual fees card-issuing banks had instituted since Carter's implementation of the Credit Control Act. The First National Bank of Maryland, determined to keep the fees which had finally made its card plan profitable, announced they were simply moving to Delaware. The symbolism of Delaware's new economy was soon imprinted in the built environment: the First National Bank toured a recently abandoned National Cash Register plant in Millsboro, a building that would ultimately serve as the home of First Omni Bank's card program. Bankers repurposed the infrastructure of the industrial economy for the new age of financialization.[22]

Relocation and Financial Structure

For South Dakota and Delaware policymakers, bringing card-issuing banks into their states was initially about generating jobs and tax revenues, not reshaping the nation's financial regulatory structure. Their intentions, though, were irrelevant. States had exercised an important restraining influence under the New Deal regulatory order. Local usury laws in particular, by shifting interest rate risk to card-issuing banks, acted as a structural check on consumer debt accumulation. Interest rate risk compelled banks to keep repayment periods short and consumer credit limits low. Credit cards provided convenience, not indebtedness; usury limits enforced this bargain. Now, state interest rates and credit laws played a new role in the consumer credit system, enabling banks to shape credit policy in small places like South Dakota and Delaware and then export those policies to their cardholders across the country. The system still functioned, yet the flow of power had reversed. There is little evidence that the lawmakers in Delaware or South Dakota thought very much about the national financial system when they invited banks to enjoy deregulated interest rates in their states. Neither state had significant bank card industries before 1980. Consumer and labor groups, which had secured interest rate caps on revolving credit and other protections, better understood what local deregulation might mean for national consumer credit markets. State regulators with more card experience, even those friendly to banks, worried that the system was breaking down. "If our states keep passing laws to steal banking jobs from other states, it could have an adverse effect on the entire banking system," Muriel Siebert warned.[23]

Citibank's move to South Dakota required federal regulatory approval. With protections against local competition in place, Citi's greatest support came from South Dakota's banking community. These bankers' prestige and profits—not to mention their political influence—were intertwined with the economic prosperity of their state. Citi, they hoped, would help attract additional "desirable commerce and clean industry." Consequently, they testified at public hearings held by the comptroller of the currency and wrote letters of support to the Federal Reserve. "Though it is not customary for a banking institution to write in support of a potential competitor," wrote a Sioux Falls banker to the secretary of the Fed's Board of Governors, "we . . . feel the proposal has great future potential for Sioux Falls and South Dakota and do support it wholeheartedly." By supporting Citi's move and mediating between the bank, the federal government, and their communities, South Dakota bankers reaffirmed their status of local economic leadership even as they helped Citibank relocate.[24]

Federal regulators at the Comptroller of the Currency and the Federal Reserve, committed to the idea that competition, not controls, would best serve consumers, approved Citibank's move and with it a new regulatory geography, still reliant on states, even as individual state decisions could be projected nationally. Now a New York citizen, shopping at a New York retailer, using a credit card from a nominally New York bank, could be subject to the lending laws not of the state of New York but to those of South Dakota— where they could not vote, hold office, or stand to sue. Being able to "locate" in South Dakota, or any other non-usury state, enabled Citibank to orchestrate a deft regulatory arbitrage, projecting the local decisions of South Dakota legislators onto its cardholders across the country. The bank broke the connection between finance and local democracy that enabled consumers to enforce the place-based social contract.

South Dakota and Citibank laid the groundwork for a new era in American consumer finance. With no applicable usury ceiling, Citi could set its credit card rates at will and project the laws of one small state onto every Citi card transaction, circumventing local regulations by locating transactions in South Dakota. Further, because Citibank's South Dakota subsidiary could not compete for local deposits, "the bank's principal source of funds" would, Citi reported in its national bank application, "be obtained through money market instruments." These money markets were global, reflecting Citibank's mastery of cross-border money movement. As the comptroller explained, "Funding of the proposed bank . . . will be managed through the global money market activities of the parent, Citicorp." The point is not that Citi drew on global money markets to finance its card portfolio: that had always been the bank's strategy. The difference was that before 1980, Citi held the risk of market volatility. Because of New York's usury limits, it could not pass that risk on to cardholders. With those limits removed in South Dakota, Citi would intermediate directly between global capital markets and consumer borrowers, transferring risk and volatility from one to the other. This was the essence of financialization.[25]

Through its use of *Marquette*, the bank had brought its mastery of regulatory arbitrage to bear on the domestic market, stretching the seams of federalism as it had the sovereignties of nation-states. With locations across the globe, Citi finessed differences in tax structure and regulatory requirements to great profitability throughout the 1970s. As the Securities and Exchange Commission later found, Citibank subsidiaries in London and Frankfurt regularly booked transactions through subsidiaries in Nassau and the Chanel Islands, skillfully avoiding British and German currency regulations, capital requirements, and taxes. Citi executives had, through these means, long stretched the meaning of the term "located." As one commentator noted, "The real significance of Citibank's activities . . . relates not so much to the question of illegality or wrongdoing as to the ease with which deals can be booked to any part of the world that happens to be convenient and the possibilities presented thereby for regulatory circumvention." And, of course, profit.[26]

Citibank's relocation reverberated through statehouses, transforming the regulatory incentives for the bank card market. By the end of 1981, nine banks had committed to opening offices in Delaware. Forced to react to such moves, forty-four states either loosened or lifted their usury laws by 1983. Even states whose lawmakers and administrators had fought hard against high rates throughout the 1970s made an abrupt about-face. By 1984, Iowa governor Terry Branstad was busy luring out-of-state banks. "Effective July 1, 1984, there will no longer be a finance charge limit on bank credit cards," Branstad wrote the president of Washington's Rainier Bancorp, adding, "This assures Rainier Bancorp. a competitive position in credit card operations regardless of fluctuating interest rates." As Branstad's memo made explicit, the elimination of state usury limits effectively removed the interest rate risk that had constrained card plans. Without them, unrestrained banks could begin pumping capital into consumer credit and credit card debt. This undoubtedly opened credit markets and made credit available to underserved consumers. It also gave primacy to bankers in a political debate where unrestrained markets and consumer protection were at odds, at a moment when increasing credit availability replaced rising wages as the foundation of economic citizenship and purchasing power.[27]

Wriston and his political allies called this a victory for the market, yet in the card industry, the market reigned in theory, not in practice. In the first decade of the new consumer credit regime, the benefits market advocates promised did not materialize. Credit was widely available but prices were high, and they remained high for a long time—long after a truly competitive market should have brought them down. "Credit card interest rates have been exceptionally sticky relative to the cost of funds," economist Lawrence M. Ausubel later observed. "Moreover, major credit card issuers have persistently earned from three to five times the ordinary rate of return in banking during the period 1983–1988." Ausubel attributed these outsized profits to "a class of [irrational] consumers who do not intend to borrow on their accounts but find themselves doing so anyway." But in an economy where wages for middle-class Americans were stagnating, millions of "rational" convenience users likely became irrational revolvers against their will. "The data provide indirect empirical confirmation of the presence of consumers who act as though they do not intend to borrow but who continuously do so," Ausubel observed.[28]

Card-issuing banks rationally took advantage. With New York's usury ceiling lifted, Citibank raised its card rates in December 1980 from 18 percent on the first $500 and 12 percent thereafter to 19.8 percent for all balances, plus a $15 annual fee. Chase increased its rates to 18 percent for all balances and also charged a $15 annual fee. The new rate laws in New York, Delaware, and South Dakota allowed Citi and other banks to raise rates at any time, as long as they notified consumers. In January 1982, following a similar move by First National Bank of Chicago, Citibank raised its fee to $20. When policymakers and consumers objected to rate hikes, bankers blamed federal deregulation. In the first major financial deregulatory action of the postwar era, Congress phased out the New Deal's federal price controls on deposit interest rates (Regulation Q) beginning in 1980. The phaseout, bankers argued, meant they had to pay higher rates on consumer deposit accounts, costs they had to pass on through higher consumer interest rates. Never mind that the largest banks financed their card plans primarily through global money markets. Even as market interest rates fell over the decade, and with them consumer deposit rates, banks kept credit card rates high. Large banks continued to aggressively market cards. Once ensconced in South Dakota, Citibank resumed nationwide card solicitations. Its rivals followed suit. Yet while banks competed aggressively for new card accounts, they did not compete on price. "Credit-card rates will be the last to fall," bankers declared as other interest

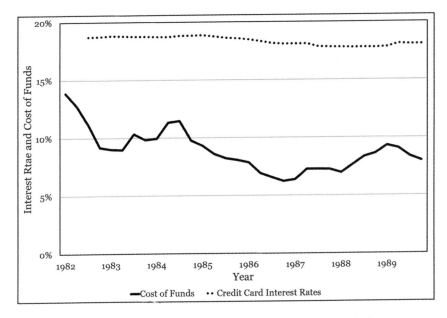

Fig. 8: Sticky credit card interest rates, 1982–1989. In 1991, economist Lawrence Ausubel found that although market interest rates declined through the 1980s, credit card interest rates remained "sticky," fixed at a high level that suggested a lack of meaningful price competition despite the elimination of state-level price controls.

Source: Reconstruction of graph in Lawrence M. Ausubel, "The Failure of Competition in the Credit Card Market," *American Economic Review* 81, no. 1 (1991): 54. Credit card interest rates are from *Federal Reserve Bulletin*, "Terms of Consumer Installment Credit (Table 1.56)," FRASER. Cost of funds is one-year Treasury bill yield plus .75 percent, from *Federal Reserve Bulletin*, "Interest Rates (Table 1.35)," FRASER."

rates declined in 1984. They were in a position to know; credit prices in 1985, and for the rest of the decade, proved them right.[29]

Banks poured money into the credit card market. They did so first through tried-and-true methods of balance sheet expansion, pulling in money from capital markets and lending it out again through cards, growing their liabilities and assets in the process. Bankers also developed new financial strategies to ensure that the credit spigot stayed open. Securitization, where banks bundled loans and resold them on secondary markets, had long been used in mortgage markets and was experiencing a boom in the early 1980s. By the middle of the decade, a few investment banks experimented with credit card securitization, but the strategy was slow to catch on. Explaining why relatively few credit card securities had been offered, two analysts argued that "the attractive gross margins available on credit cards means that there is no shortage of lending capital in this sector thus removing one of the most fundamental pressures for the development of this market." Bankers were happy to accumulate card loans on their books and were even buying other banks' card portfolios at significant premiums.[30]

By 1986, the market's magic act was wearing thin and Democratic politicians began to pressure bankers to match their rhetoric with action. "There is no . . . competition in the credit card industry," Representative Charles E. "Chuck" Schumer (D-NY) declared in a *Washington Post* op-ed, demanding to know why card rates never seemed to fall. Schumer, brandishing data from the Federal Reserve Bank of New York, showed that card loans were the most profitable line of bank lending. Bankers claimed they were merely recouping losses their card plans had sustained in the 1970s and early 1980s. Such claims, Schumer pointed out, simply confirmed that banks were maintaining artificially high prices, since truly competitive markets would have little sympathy for past losses. Schumer, though, did not call for new regulations. Instead, his office published a list of small banks offering lower rates, relying on consumer initiative to balance the market. Schumer's list revealed how politics had narrowed. Politicians could not demand price or credit controls; they could only prod markets to work more perfectly.[31]

The state regulatory changes initiated by Citibank favored large financial institutions over their smaller competitors, and they help explain why—in addition to Ausubel's irrational consumers—card competition did not work to pull down rates. Banks that offered less expensive cards could not afford to market those cards heavily, whereas banks like Chase and Citi could blanket consumers with credit promotions. Consumers, whether rationally or irrationally, were in the market for accessible credit. It was more convenient to take the credit offered. Put another way: search costs were high, which was why Schumer published his list of low-cost lenders. This fact ultimately undermined the last state holdouts, which had tried to keep their usury regimes into the mid-1980s. Massachusetts maintained an 18 percent interest ceiling and did not allow annual fees. Local banks still offered low-cost cards. Following a now well-worn promotion strategy, out-of-state banks—and Citibank in particular—flooded Massachusetts with promotions beginning in 1983. Like Gresham's law in reverse, expensive credit pushed out inexpensive credit; Citi and its peers could justify high marketing expenses while

Massachusetts banks could not. Eventually Massachusetts's banks lost patience and threatened to move if the state legislature did not raise rates. It was cheaper to fight for deregulation than to fight for market share. Credit cards, which banks introduced in the 1950s to help small businesses compete against monopolistic department stores, became a bludgeon of corporate market power.[32]

The Profits and Perils of Plastic Capitalism

Credit card banking was a windfall for South Dakota and Delaware, one which bound the states' fortunes to the card industry. In South Dakota, cards accounted for just .28 percent of all national bank loans in 1980. In 1986, before Citibank began securitizing its card portfolio, 82 percent of national bank loans in South Dakota were for card accounts. At the time, that represented 15 percent of all national bank card loans outstanding and 7 percent of all revolving credit outstanding. South Dakota workers processed these transactions. As Janklow explained in a 2004 interview, "In my last couple years in office, 16 percent of all the people in the state were employed in the financial services industry." Census data do not quite bear out Janklow's claim. Nevertheless, financial industry job growth was significant, expanding from 4.7 percent of the workforce in 1980, to 7.4 percent two decades later. The state's increase in tax revenue was also impressive. From 1978 to 1988, bank franchise tax receipts increased from $719,156 to $22,015,968, or from .43 percent of the state's overall tax revenue to 5.54 percent.[33]

The expansion in tax revenue reflected a subtle but telling shift in the state's relationship to banking institutions worked by the Citibank bill. In 1957, during the height of the New Deal regulatory order, the state instituted a bank franchise tax, applicable to all banks operating in South Dakota. The law mandated that each bank pay 6 percent of its gross revenues in taxes, 73.33 percent of which would be remitted to the county in which the bank operated and 26.66 percent would go to the state government. This system kept banks' tax revenues within the communities they served, strengthening the ties between banks and their local economic constituents. The Citibank bill amended the bank franchise tax. Banks entering the state to operate credit card businesses paid 95 percent of the tax to the state, and only 5 percent to the county in which they operated. Credit card banks owed their

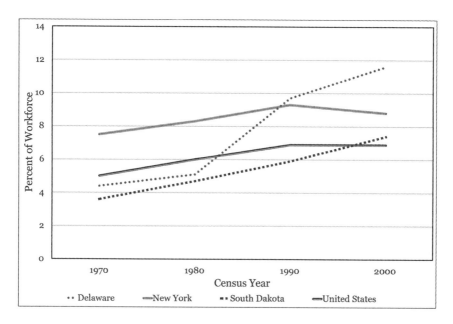

Fig. 9: Finance, insurance, and real estate employment in Delaware, New York, South Dakota, and the United States, 1970–2000. New York saw some increase in financial industry employment through 1990 before experiencing a relative decline thereafter, while South Dakota and especially Delaware saw significant increases in their financial industry workforces. These figures, though, mask significant differences in the kinds of jobs located in each state.

Source: U.S. Decennial Census, accessed through Social Explorer.

loyalty to South Dakota, not to the communities where they resided. Though both methods of taxation fell under the bank franchise tax, internal state documents distinguished between the local "bank franchise tax" and the state "bank card tax," marking the state's special interest in the success and profitability of its new credit-issuing residents.[34]

Delaware experienced even greater financial industry growth. From June 1981 to June 1985, bank assets in Delaware increased from $4.7 billion to $22.5 billion. This booming growth also held for individual firms. At the end of June 1982, Chase Manhattan's Delaware subsidiary had just over $100 million in assets. Three years later, it had grown to $2.8 billion, and by 1988, Chase had $6.3 billion in assets. By 1986, Delaware led the nation in card loans. This all meant more revenue for the state. In 1988, the state collected $36.9 million in bank franchise taxes. In 1989, more than 21,000 people worked for banks.[35]

Table 3. Bank Assets and Franchise Tax Collections in Delaware, 1979–1989 (in millions)

Total bank assets	Bank franchise tax collections	Chase Manhattan assets
1979 $4,402	$2.5	
1980 $4,677	$2.1	
1981 $4,732	$2.5	
1982 $6,439	$2.2	$103
1983 $11,064	$4.1	
1984 $16,242	$9.5	
1985 $22,522	$17.8	$2,821
1986	$23.0	
1987 $39,389	$32.4	
1988 $56,420	$36.9	$6,312
1989	$53.6	

Source: State of Delaware, Office of the State Bank Commissioner, "Consolidated Statement of All Banks and Trust Companies in Delaware, 1979–1988, RG 1325 and RG 1340 (microfiche), Delaware State Archives; Bank Franchise Tax and Banking Employment, RG 1325–147, State Reports, Delaware State Archives; State of Delaware, *Annual Report of the State Bank Commissioner*, 1982–1988.

Note: In 1979 and 1980, the fiscal year ended on December 31, for all other years June 30. Table includes all available data.

In South Dakota and Delaware, the rapid growth of the financial services industry gratified the ambitions of policymakers, but it also created anxieties that the footloose firms might one day skip out. Critics voiced these fears early and often. During summer 1980, at the comptroller's hearing in Sioux Falls, one local banker wondered, "If it leaves its traditional home . . . because it is miffed at the State Legislature . . . how much would it take to have Citicorp pull out of South Dakota?" Members of Delaware's Intergovernmental Task Force assured lawmakers and citizens that the mobile banks would stay put. "They don't move quickly," economic development secretary Nathan Hayward III assured the state senate. "This is not going to be a one-night stand or even a torrid weekend." Quickly or not, banks now moved, and the threat weighed on state policymakers. Other observers worried that once their state's economy was bound to the banking industry, state policy might become captive to the interests of the industry rather than its citizens.

"All of the down-home testimony South Dakotans can muster won't stand a chance against the lobbying power of an operation like Citibank," a *Sioux Falls Argus Leader* columnist warned in December 1980.[36]

Although state policymakers had shown little concern for the national financial structure when they invited banks to their states, they soon faced enormous pressure to pursue regulatory innovation. Through the early 1980s, Citibank, Governor Janklow, and local development groups like the Sioux Falls Chamber of Commerce worked to make South Dakota "the Frontier of Modern Banking" by finding and widening gaps in the regulatory structure. In 1983, at Citi's insistence, the legislature allowed state-chartered banks to acquire insurance companies. These companies, in turn, could market insurance nationally but—copying the anti-competitive language from the Citibank bill—not in South Dakota. The legislation, which breached the Glass-Steagall Act's barriers dividing commercial banking and insurance, earned the state the dubious designation of "South Dakota, Inc." "We have no intentions of becoming the Liberian or Panamanian registry for banks," Janklow insisted. His actions, however, evidenced a transparent desire to make South Dakota a haven for swashbuckling financial firms. Citi moved quickly to acquire the American State Bank of Rapid City, through which it planned to initiate a national insurance operation regulated under South Dakota law. The Federal Reserve finally had enough, belatedly chastising Janklow and South Dakota "for placing job expansion concerns above considerations for the soundness of the national banking system." More pointedly, Paul Volcker, who sat quietly by as Citibank found usury freedom in South Dakota, objected to Citi's move into insurance as "smart-ass" banking at its worst. Citibank was hardly cowed; it would orchestrate the complete demise of Glass-Steagall through its acquisition of Travelers Insurance a decade and a half later.[37]

As financial institutions fragmented and spread, so did financial labor. In New York, the absolute number of financial industry workers declined, but the Empire State retained the managerial workforce that now exercised greater power across a wider space. South Dakota and Delaware lured financial industry jobs, but mostly low-paid clerical positions. In essence, banks followed a strategy long employed in manufacturing, disciplining state policymakers by relocating low-wage production work. The products were now financial rather than physical. Policymakers responded to these incentives.

In the 1990s, South Dakota lawmakers began to worry that other card-friendly states, notably Nevada and Delaware, might offer Citibank a more favorable tax climate. Though quick to assure citizens that Citi had made no threats to leave, the House Republican leader Jerry Lammers warned that "by a stroke of the pen, Citibank could, if it wished to do so." The legislature quickly instituted a new sliding tax scale, sharply discounting all bank income above $500 million. Citibank was the only South Dakota bank approaching this revenue figure, and the tax break came in a year when a budget shortfall forced the state to raise taxes elsewhere. "What has happened," one concerned citizen understandably wondered, "to our general sense of fairness that taxes should be borne most by those that can most afford to pay them?" The legislation achieved the desired results. Two years later, Mastercard—headquartered in New York City—sponsored a study of employment and regulation in the card industry, which included an index of "State Attractiveness of Credit Card Firms." The study ranked South Dakota at the top (Delaware was third). When the Sioux Falls *Argus Leader* celebrated the news with a table of state employment and wages, an astute reader crunched the numbers. South Dakota's credit card employees earned less than in every other state save one. "Thanks *Argus*," the reader wrote in exasperation, "for showing me being friendly doesn't pay!"[38]

The bank has not left. Walking in Wriston's footsteps, CEO Charles Prince came to Sioux Falls in April 2006 to honor Citi's twenty-fifth anniversary in the state. At the celebration, Prince recalled the leaders who, in Citibank's hour of darkest need, found a solution to the bank's credit card problem. "A solution that was good for South Dakota—and that's terrific!—but frankly can be seen to have saved Citibank. Think of that," Prince continued reverently, "saved Citibank." Prince sought to chart the path forward for his gargantuan and often troubled bank. He urged his listeners to expand the bank's already dominant card business. And in the short term, Prince succeeded. Citi's net income from the U.S. Cards division rose an impressive 41 percent in 2006, to $3.9 billion. But the crash also came quickly. As the global financial crisis began to unfold, the bank's card income fell and then collapsed. Citi lost $523 million on its North American credit card accounts, underscoring the massive growth in consumer indebtedness that its relocation to South Dakota helped create. Outstanding revolving consumer debt had doubled

from 1980 to 1985, again by 1990, again by 1995, and again by 2005, topping
out in May 2008 at more than $1 trillion. The removal of usury limits, and
with them interest rate risk that restrained credit card accounts, made credit
card debt an outsized component of the newly financialized economy.[39]

Banks turned a regulatory system meant to stymie their growth to their
advantage, enabling the booming expansion of consumer debt after 1981.
Indeed, a financial regulatory system founded on a bank's location proved
incompatible with a new era of mobile financial instruments, which bankers
used to extend state regulation, through the national banking system, onto
the citizens of other states. "A law enacted by the Nebraska legislature will
determine the interest rates charged to respondent's Minnesota customers,"
lawyers for Minnesota's AFL-CIO argued in their *Marquette* brief, yet "a consumer interest group in Minnesota has no voice in the legislatures of other
states." What was true for card accounts was also true for a variety of other
financial products, including mortgages and money market checking accounts that also moved across state lines. Once banks, aided by state allies,
embraced the possibilities of relocating beyond regulatory frontiers, the politics of economic development mingled with those of financial regulation,
threatening states reluctant to accede to bank interests. Freewheeling financial products reshaped a regulatory landscape that had limited the political
power of financial institutions by limiting their mobility. Barriers to their
mobility continued to fall.[40]

For Walter Wriston, the bank regulatory system's polycentricity was not a
flaw but a feature, one the bank's executives had long appreciated in their
international operations. Writing to Senate Banking Committee member
Charles Percy, Wriston stated his position clearly: "If a complicated structure
is a concomitant of less regulation and more competition, then I am for it."
Wriston meant competition between financial institutions, but his bank's
actions also led to competition between states for bank jobs and tax revenue.
Yet Citibank's use of regulatory barriers led other states to tear them down,
to the detriment of Citi's partners in South Dakota who continued to push
regulatory innovation, first to bring more banks in and then to ensure its
banks didn't leave.[41]

For Americans, this meant a diminished voice in the local political economy of consumer credit, even as regulatory geography continued to structure the bank card industry. In 1991, the Supreme Court extended *Marquette*

to include late fees and other card account charges. By 2003 almost three-quarters of credit card loans in the United States originated from states, including South Dakota and Delaware, containing just 4 percent of the country's population. Importantly, Citibank's relocation did not make state interest rate regulation irrelevant; rather, it made the interest rate regulation of a few states national policy. Opponents of interest rate limits might argue that they and other price caps impede market efficiency, and that through the removal of interest rate and other pricing restrictions, American consumers benefited from greater credit availability. Financialization, though, is about more than just credit access. Whether consumers should be able to shield themselves from high interest rates, annual fees, and overdraft charges is also always a political question. The extraterritoriality of bank credit cards reshaped this question in favor of the banking industry, ultimately leading to the instability of political and economic citizenship in America's age of finance.[42]

Table 4. Top Ten States in National Bank Credit Card Outstandings

1980	1986
New York	Delaware
California	South Dakota
Illinois	California
Texas	New York
Pennsylvania	Illinois
Ohio	Ohio
Michigan	Nevada
Florida	Florida
Washington	Washington
Georgia	Maryland

Source: Comptroller of the Currency, *Annual Report of the Comptroller of the Currency*, "Outstanding Balances, Credit Cards and Related Plans of National Banks," 1980 and 1986, FRASER.

Table 5. Bottom Ten States in National Bank Credit
Card Outstandings

1980	1986
Delaware	Hawaii
Hawaii	Wyoming
South Dakota	North Dakota
Vermont	Vermont
Wyoming	Maine
North Dakota	Montana
Montana	Alaska
Maine	Mississippi
New Hampshire	West Virginia
Alaska	District of Columbia

Source: Comptroller of the Currency, *Annual Report of the Comp-troller of the Currency*, "Outstanding Balances, Credit Cards and Related Plans of National Banks," 1980 and 1986, FRASER.

Epilogue

WHEN YOU BOUGHT THIS BOOK—if you bought it—you likely used a bank card, either a debit card that transferred monetary data from your bank account, or a credit card that obliges you to repay your balance every month or pay some interest. *Plastic Capitalism* has focused on bank credit cards and the networks bankers constructed to circumvent the place-based regulatory order, which had long restrained their industry. Bank debit cards, in turn, layered atop these earlier innovations, but with the flow of influence reversed. In the 1960s, banks created BankAmericard (Visa) and Master Charge (Mastercard) to offer nationwide consumer credit. In the 1990s, Visa and Mastercard convinced reluctant banks to adopt and promote debit cards. Since then, the collective effort to popularize debit in the United States has shifted an increasing share of consumer transactions onto the card networks and away from other payment media, especially cash and checks. About 60 percent of purchases now occur via card payment, with debit outpacing credit nearly 2 to 1 (though the aggregate value of credit card transactions remains higher). Private card networks are the essential infrastructure of consumer payments. Our money, as data, moves on private rails.[1]

As with the emergence of bank credit cards, the transition to debit relied on business strategy and political negotiation. Visa and Mastercard had to convince bankers that debit cards would still generate sufficient revenue through transaction fees and enhanced consumer relationships, without the interest income from revolving credit. The networks also had to convince— or coerce—retailers, who resisted the high cost of debit transactions. When they emerged in the 1950s and gained momentum in the 1960s, bank credit cards had offered retailers an obvious value proposition: retailers could sell on credit without the risk or cost of managing their own in-house credit plans. They paid for the privilege and did so on the promise that consumers, borrowing to buy, would spend more. Debit, by contrast, merely offered an expensive substitute for cash and checks. The credit trap—when all merchants offered credit, they all bore the cost without gaining any competitive advantage—was reborn as a debit trap. To compel adoption, in the 1990s Visa and Mastercard applied the full weight of their market power: retailers accepting any of their cards had to accept all of them—credit and debit. Retailers and their trade groups howled. They also sued.[2]

Merchant resistance to high transaction costs falls out of this book's narrative in the 1960s, when consumer politics moved to center stage. Retailers and their allies had also—with less success than consumers—used the available political and legal tools to shape the card market. As cards became the dominant media for consumer payments, retailers mobilized with greater urgency. In the late 1990s and early 2000s, they launched a series of antitrust lawsuits aimed at Visa's and Mastercard's transaction fees. Although the card networks originated in efforts by small banks to help small firms compete against giant department stores, in the interchange fee cases, Walmart—the epitome of monopolistic corporate retailing—was the networks' chief antagonist and retailers' leading champion. Plastic capitalism encouraged concentrated capitalism. Legal scholar Adam Levitin called the contest the "Super Bowl of Antitrust," Goliath versus Goliath. The question of who will bear the costs of plastic payments remains unresolved, having moved more recently from the courts to Congress. An amendment to the 2010 Dodd-Frank Act, the core financial reform legislation that grew out of the 2008 financial crisis, required the Federal Reserve to regulate debit transaction fees. The lawmakers who secured those rules now seek to extend them to credit card fees.[3]

With the majority of transactions occurring via electronic payment, retailers—even Walmart—have little choice but to participate in card networks; likewise, as card-based payments have become predominant, consumers who lack access to cards are excluded from full participation in consumer society. We can think about *payments citizenship* under the larger rubric of *financial citizenship,* the idea that to fully realize economic and social opportunity, consumers need access to affordable financial services. Cards, in this sense, play a double role, at once markers of class status and access keys to essential economic infrastructure. The divisions caused by the latter function are especially apparent online, where internet commerce has been built on the back of card-based payments. More recently, payments citizenship has migrated from the digital realm to the physical with the rise of no-cash policies at retailers and restaurants (a trend preceding the Covid-19 pandemic and accelerated by it). No-cash policies reflect employer distrust of often low-paid service employees and an effort to exclude low-income clientele, who are more likely to pay in cash. Some local governments have challenged the practice, seeking to democratize payments by requiring retailers to accept hard currency. These policymakers recognize that poor and minority consumers continue to pay more to access basic financial services. In the case of electronic payments, predatory inclusion manifests alternatively as high interest costs on credit cards or as account maintenance and overdraft fees for debit cards linked to checking accounts. The fruits of financial innovation have accrued to the privileged at the expense of the marginalized.[4]

The tremendous growth of high-interest credit card debt and the super-abundant profits generated by credit card issuers also demonstrate the extent to which the fruits of financial innovation have accrued to card issuers at the expense of cardholders. Before the early 1980s, consumers and their political allies used state interest rate caps to restrain credit card profits and minimize financial risk for consumer households. Usury laws capped topline credit costs, holding card issuers to a locally negotiated standard of fair credit prices. More importantly, rate caps placed interest rate risk squarely on card-issuing banks, discouraging them from ensnaring consumers in long-term, high-interest debt.

Without interest rate risk to restrain them, banks and other card issuers pumped capital into credit card markets. As they did so, the largest issuers adhered to Gresham's law of plastic: they crowded out low-cost card plans with aggressively marketed high-cost alternatives. The most aggressive firms—Citibank, J. P. Morgan Chase, Bank of America, and MBNA—cornered the bank credit card market. Over time, bad plastic money got worse for many consumer households. Bankers and other lenders paired sophisticated credit scoring and underwriting practices, which identified and targeted the consumers most likely to rack up debts, with strategies like lengthening repayment periods, which encouraged indebted consumers to repay high-

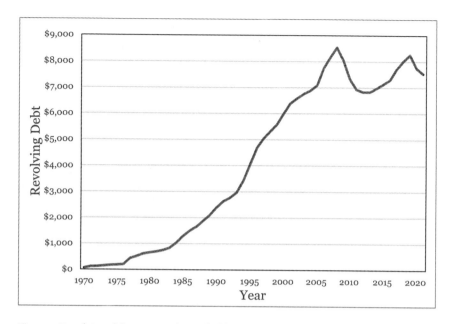

Fig. 10: Revolving debt per U.S. household, 1970–2021.

Source: Board of Governors of the Federal Reserve System, "G.19, Consumer Credit, Historical Data," https://www.federalreserve.gov/releases/g19/HIST/cc_hist_sa_levels.html; World Bank, "Population, Total for United States (POPTOTUSA647NWDB)," FRED; United States Census Bureau, "HH-4, Households by Size: 1960 to Present," https://www.census.gov/data/tables/time-series/demo/families/households.html.

interest debts over longer periods of time. Bankers also partnered with affinity organizations, like universities, and marketed cards to credit-hungry undergraduates, complete with their school's burly-yet-cuddly mascot emblazoned on the card. Collectively, these strategies—and others designed to encourage consumers to borrow to buy more—fueled a massive expansion of credit card debt. In 1980, revolving debt per household in the United States amounted to $658.32. By 2000, the figure had jumped to $5,989.86, peaking at $8,542.29 at the start of the 2008 financial crisis. Adjusted for inflation, those figures amount to roughly $2,500 (1980), $10,500 (2000), and $12,000 (2008) in January 2023 dollars. Through this process—and through parallel processes of financial extraction—household finances became more fragile, consumers became more stressed, and the economy became more unstable.[5]

All that debt, in turn, has been remarkably profitable for credit card issuers, defying theoretical expectations that market competition—infusions, say, of good plastic money—would bring card profits down. In 1991, economist

Lawrence Ausubel marveled at the extraordinary profitability of bank card plans. Thirty years later, a 2021 Federal Reserve report found that "credit card earnings have almost always been higher than returns on all bank activities."[6] Despite the intervening global financial crisis, the government bailouts of the financial system, and the post-crisis consumer reforms, high-interest lending remains a remarkably lucrative business.

Together, the financial intermediation of daily economic life (via private card networks), the consequent requirement to engage with private payment systems (as a buyer and a seller), and the continuous extraction of value by financial intermediaries (at the moment of sale and over time) all point to a process that scholars now call "financialization." As a term of art, financialization, like its cousin neoliberalism, can be vague, amorphous, and unsatisfying. In simplest terms, financialization refers to the increasing prevalence of financial profit-making as the dominant mode of profit generation for firms and other owners of capital. Scholars understand this rise of finance as at once a political solution to distributional challenges of the 1970s, when building social claims for economic equity crashed against a secular decline in economic growth, and as an intellectual response among owners of capital to waning corporate profits in the same period. These macro processes led, in turn, to the financialization of daily life, that is, the shift of financial risk from corporations and the state onto households, paired with the multiplication of financial products designed to profitably help households manage those new risks.[7]

Though I have mostly avoided using the term in the preceding pages, I wrote *Plastic Capitalism* to tell a new story about the processes that drove financialization. The aim was to put financiers at the center of the action, to show how they used financial technologies and business strategies to innovate around market rules and, in doing so, to change the social and political conditions under which market rules were created and maintained. Looking at financialization in this way requires a long-term perspective. Momentum for financial change began earlier than scholars have tended to recognize, in the 1950s, when the postwar social contract appeared robust and the financial regulatory order looked stable and strong. Bankers initially developed regulatory circumvention strategies in alignment with the prevailing regulatory norms—here the political economy of small finance and the place-based social contract—and only slowly, incrementally, and contingently undermined them. This perspective, in turn, recasts the pivots on which financial-ization appeared to turn. Take the 1978 *Marquette* decision. Critics of credit card industry practices have long understood *Marquette*'s foundational role in allowing banks to shape the national credit card market from states with the weakest regulations. But such analyses tend to miss the ways that *Marquette* rested on bankers' earlier efforts to overlay standardized markets atop heterogeneous political spaces, using networks that were themselves con-structed to circumvent geographic limits on physical expansion. Likewise, *Marquette*, on its own, did little to fundamentally change consumer lending markets. It affirmed a status quo of regional bank card plans still tightly regulated by state law. The ruling became powerful only when banks began to relocate, to trade jobs for favorable—and exportable—financial rules.[8]

At the same time, this book has been about the long-running efforts by consumer and labor groups, in league with their political allies, to preserve and reinforce the market rules that enacted their vision of economic fairness and the appropriate role of credit in consumer society. These efforts flowed through the New Deal regulatory order, the dynamic system of financial fed-eralism, industry silos, and price controls that constrained financial firms and channeled their activities toward socially determined goals. Here, geo-graphic restrictions on banks played an especially important role. By confin-ing banks within individual states, the regulatory system compelled bankers to negotiate the price and terms of credit with local stakeholders. These ne-gotiations were never perfectly democratic. Bankers were well organized and politically influential. Minority groups, women, and low-income consumers all enjoyed less influence than white, affluent suburbanites. Nevertheless, the privileged consumers who shaped these debates had a clear idea that unrestrained finance would lead to unrestrained indebtedness and economic precarity. As bankers sought to escape financial regulations through unregu-lated revolving credit, these consumers used their power to forestall that fate. They harnessed the federalist political institutions to maintain and extend the New Deal's moral economy of credit. Eventually, however, once banks showed state policymakers that financial capital could move, consumers lost their grip on the regulatory levers. The future they had anticipated, feared, and fought, rushed headlong into being.

NOTES

Abbreviations

Newspapers

AB	*American Banker*
BG	*Boston Globe*
BS	*Baltimore Sun*
CSM	*Christian Science Monitor*
CT	*Chicago Tribune*
FPRAY	*Financial Public Relations Association Yearbook*
LAT	*Los Angeles Times*
NYHT	*New York Herald Tribune*
NYT	*New York Times*
SFAL	*Sioux Falls Argus Leader*
WP	*Washington Post*
WWD	*Women's Wear Daily*

Archives

Barclays Archives	Barclays Group Archives, Wythenshawe, Manchester, UK
Carter Library	Jimmy Carter Presidential Library, Atlanta, GA
FRBNY Archives	Federal Reserve Bank of New York Archives, New York, NY
HSBC Archives	HSBC Archives, Brooklyn, NY
Johnson Library	Lyndon B. Johnson Presidential Library, Austin, TX
Kennedy Library	John F. Kennedy Presidential Library, Boston, MA
NARA I	National Archives of the United States, Washington, DC
NARA II	National Archives of the United States, College Park, MD
Nixon Library	Richard Nixon Presidential Library, Yorba Linda, CA
Reagan Library	Ronald Reagan Presidential Library, Simi Valley, CA
Wisconsin Archives	Wisconsin State Historical Society, Madison, WI

Archival Collections

Anderson Papers	The Personal Papers of Thomas J. Anderson (RG 74-38, lot 2), Archives of Michigan, Lansing, MI
Blackmun Papers	Harry A. Blackmun Papers, Manuscript Division, Library of Congress, Washington, DC
Bolton Papers	Frances P. Bolton Papers, Western Reserve Historical Society, Cleveland, OH
Bork Papers	Robert H. Bork Papers, Manuscript Division, Library of Congress, Washington, DC
Braucher Papers	Robert Braucher Papers, Harvard University Law Library, Cambridge, MA
Brennen Papers	William J. Brennan Jr. Papers, Manuscript Division, Library of Congress, Washington, DC
Burns Papers	Arthur F. Burns Papers, Gerald R. Ford Presidential Library, Ann Arbor, MI
Carey Subject Files	Governor Hugh L. Carey Central Subject and Correspondence Files, New York State Archives, Albany, NY
Celler Papers	Emanuel Celler Papers, Manuscript Division, Library of Congress, Washington, DC
CRR	Records of Consumers' Research Inc., Rutgers University, New Brunswick, NJ
Douglas Papers	Paul H. Douglas Papers, Chicago Historical Society, Chicago, IL
Dunne Papers	John R. Dunne Papers, State University of New York, Albany, NY
Eccles Papers	Marriner S. Eccles Papers, University of Utah Libraries, Salt Lake City, UT (accessed through FRASER)
FDIC Exam Reports	Analysis of Examination Reports, Records of the Federal Deposit Insurance Corporation (RG 34), NARA II
Fisher Case File	Civil case file 72-0-156, *Fred Fisher, Etc. vs. First Natl. Bank of Omaha*, box 891, Records of the U.S. District Court for the District of Nebraska, National Archives of the United States, Kansas City, MO
Janklow Papers	William J. Janklow Papers, University of South Dakota, Vermillion, SD
Kennedy Papers	David M. Kennedy Papers, Brigham Young University, Provo, UT
MBS Records	House Financial Institutions Committee and Senate Commerce Committee, Subcommittee on Banking, Minutes, 1969–1970, Minnesota Historical Society, St. Paul, MN
Mondale Papers	Walter F. Mondale Papers, Minnesota Historical Society, St. Paul, MN
NJCL Papers	New Jersey Consumers League Papers, Rutgers University, New Brunswick, NJ
Northwest Papers	Northwest Bancorporation, Records of Member Banks, Minnesota Historical Society, St. Paul, MN
NOW Records	Records of the National Organization for Women, Arthur and Elizabeth Schlesinger Library, Radcliff Institute, Cambridge, MA

ONBCS	State v. Omaha National Bank, et al., box 3, Attorney General: Civil Case Files (Series 3), Minnesota Historical Society, St. Paul, MN
Patman Papers	Papers of Wright Patman, Lyndon B. Johnson Presidential Library, Austin, TX
Reed Papers	Philip D. Reed Papers, Hagley Museum and Library, Wilmington, DE
Reifler Papers	Winfield W. Reifler Papers, NARA II (accessed through FRASER)
SCSB Records	Select Committee on Small Business, United States Senate (RG 46), NARA I
St. Cloud Case File	Minnesota vs. St. Cloud National Bank and Trust Company, box 20, Attorney General: Civil Case Files (series 3), Minnesota Historical Society, St. Paul, MN
Teasdale Papers	Joseph P. Teasdale Papers (RG 3.48), Missouri State Archives, Jefferson City, MO
WHCF	White House Central File (common to post-Eisenhower Presidential Libraries)

Online Archives

APP	The American Presidency Project, ed. Gerhard Peters and John T. Woolley, http://www.presidency.ucsb.edu.
FRASER	Federal Reserve Archival System for Economic Research, Federal Reserve Bank of St. Louis, https://fraser.stlouisfed.org/.
FRED	Federal Reserve Economic Data, Federal Reserve Bank of St. Louis, https://fred.stlouisfed.org/.

Introduction

1. Citigroup, *Citigroup Annual Report 2006*, 23, https://www.citigroup.com/citi/investor/quarterly/2007/ar06c_en.pdf; "The Ultimate Player," *Conference Board Review* 44, no. 6 (December 11, 2006): 28–34; Arthur E. Wilmarth Jr., *Taming the Megabanks: Why We Need a New Glass-Steagall Act* (Oxford University Press, 2020), 181–184.

2. Citigroup, Citibank South Dakota N.A., *A State of Dreams. A World of Difference* (2006), author's possession; Citigroup, *Citigroup Annual Report 2006*, sec. 1, 3.

3. The Federal Reserve defines revolving debt as short- to intermediate-term debt held by individuals, excluding loans such as those for automobiles, education, and mobile homes, and those secured by real estate. Most is credit card lending, but the series includes other non-negligible categories. Board of Governors of the Federal Reserve System, "G.19, Consumer Credit, Historical Data," https://www.federalreserve.gov/releases/g19/HIST/default.htm; *Regulatory Requirements and Industry Practices of Credit Card Issuers*, 109 Cong. 30 (2005) (statement of Anthony Jenkins, Executive Vice President, Citi Cards); Dean Corbae and Pablo D'Erasmo, "Rising

Bank Concentration," Federal Reserve Bank of Minneapolis Staff Report No. 594 (March 2020), https://www.minneapolisfed.org/research/staff-reports/rising-bank-concentration; James Freeman and Vern McKinley, *Borrowed Time: Two Centuries of Booms, Busts, and Bailouts at Citi* (Harper Business, 2018), 297.

4. Neil Fligstein, "Innovation and the Theory of Fields," *AMS Review* 11 (2021): 287. I build here on Richard R. John's assertion that "political structure shaped business strategy" (*Network Nation: Inventing American Telecommunications* [Harvard University Press, 2010], 8), showing how business strategy in turn reshaped political structure. In this way, I challenge Richard H. K. Vietor's framework that divides the market structure and the political arena into "parallel contexts," a distinction between market strategy and political strategy that I do not see in practice (*Contrived Competition: Regulation and Deregulation in America* [Harvard University Press, 1994]). Rather, in alignment with Neil Fligstein, I focus on the ways individuals create, maintain, and dissolve markets through social institutions, with a primary emphasis on political institutions and formal rules (*The Architecture of Markets: An Economic Sociology of Twenty-First-Century Capitalist Societies* [Princeton University Press, 2001]). This focus on innovation as "strategic pragmatic action" provides a new perspective on the process of regulatory change, commonly called deregulation. For foundational studies on deregulation and the political movements behind it, see Martha Derthick and Paul J. Quirk, *The Politics of Deregulation* (Brookings Institution, 1985); Angus Burgin, *The Great Persuasion: The Reinvention of Free Markets since the Depression* (Harvard University Press, 2012); Kim Phillips-Fein, *Invisible Hands: The Businessmen's Crusade against the New Deal* (W. W. Norton, 2010); Jacob S. Hacker and Paul Pierson, *Winner-Take-All Politics: How Washington Made the Rich Richer—and Turned Its Back on the Middle Class* (Simon & Schuster, 2010); Judith Stein, *Pivotal Decade: How the United States Traded Factories for Finance in the Seventies* (Yale University Press, 2010); Benjamin C. Waterhouse, *Lobbying America: The Politics of Business from Nixon to NAFTA*, Politics and Society in Twentieth-Century America (Princeton University Press, 2014); Shane Hamilton, *Trucking Country: The Road to America's Wal-Mart Economy* (Princeton University Press, 2008).

5. Many contemporaries and later scholars would strongly object to applying the word "order" to the postwar financial regulatory structure; indeed, Richard Vietor graphically demonstrates the apparent regulatory, supervisory, and administrative chaos that reigned in the postwar years (Vietor, *Contrived Competition*, 256). Yet such arguments often find regulatory chaos in the service of regulatory retrenchment. Instead, following Hyman Minsky and Martin Wolfson, I contend that the broad priorities articulated here were widely understood—if not universally accepted—by market participants and policymakers (Wolfson, *Financial Crises: Understanding the Postwar U.S. Experience* 2nd ed. [Routledge, 1994], 219–221). Scholars of financialization and recent critics of deregulation also find order in the system (e.g., Greta R. Krippner, *Capitalizing on Crisis: The Political Origins of the Rise of Finance* [Harvard University Press, 2012], 60–63]). The New Deal regulatory order was also a political order, and in this sense I am building on the framework developed by Fraser and Gerstle (Steve Fraser and Gary Gerstle, *The Rise and Fall of*

the New Deal Order, 1930–1980 [Princeton University Press, 1989]; Gary Gerstle, *The Rise and Fall of the Neoliberal Order: America and the World in the Free Market Era* [Oxford University Press, 2022]). For histories of New Deal banking policy, see Susan Estabrook Kennedy, *The Banking Crisis of 1933* (University of Kentucky Press, 1973); Helen M. Burns, *The American Banking Community and New Deal Banking Reforms, 1933–1935* (Greenwood Press, 1974). Sociologists debate the extent to which American policymakers substituted credit for welfare (Monica Prasad, *The Land of Too Much: American Abundance and the Paradox of Poverty* [Harvard University Press, 2012]; Gunnar Trumbull, *Consumer Lending in France and America: Credit and Welfare* [Cambridge University Press, 2014]). I side with scholars who see New Deal and postwar credit policies as public welfare channeled through private firms toward deserving (i.e., creditworthy) groups (see Louis Hyman, *Debtor Nation: A History of America in Red Ink* [Princeton University Press, 2011]; Ira Katznelson, *When Affirmative Action Was White: An Untold History of Racial Inequality in Twentieth-Century America* [W. W. Norton, 2005]; Sarah L. Quinn, *American Bonds: How Credit Markets Shaped a Nation* [Princeton University Press, 2019]). The use of private actors as conduits for public benefits aligns with Brian Balogh's associational state (*The Associational State: American Governance in the Twentieth Century* [University of Pennsylvania Press, 2015]).

6. Federal Deposit Insurance Corporation, *1980 Annual Report of the Federal Deposit Insurance Corporation* (Government Printing Office, 1980), 290; Commission on Money and Credit, *Money and Credit: Their Influence on Jobs, Prices, and Growth* (Prentice-Hall, 1961), 155. A massive historical literature examines the migration of American industry in the postwar era, for example, Bruce J. Schulman, *From Cotton Belt to Sunbelt: Federal Policy, Economic Development, and the Transformation of the South, 1938–1980* (Oxford University Press, 1991); Thomas J. Sugrue, *The Origins of the Urban Crisis: Race and Inequality in Postwar Detroit* (Princeton University Press, 1996); Jefferson Cowie, *Capital Moves: RCA's Seventy-Year Quest for Cheap Labor* (Cornell University Press, 1999); Elizabeth Tandy Shermer, *Sunbelt Capitalism: Phoenix and the Transformation of American Politics* (University of Pennsylvania Press, 2013). The literature on suburbanization is larger still, including Kenneth T. Jackson, *Crabgrass Frontier: The Suburbanization of the United States* (Oxford University Press, 1987); Paige Glotzer, *How the Suburbs Were Segregated: Developers and the Business of Exclusionary Housing, 1890–1960* (Columbia University Press, 2020). The history of postwar U.S. banking focuses on individual firms, e.g., Harold van B. Cleveland and Thomas F. Huertas, *Citibank, 1812–1970* (Harvard University Press, 1985); John Dover Wilson, *The Chase: The Chase Manhattan Bank, N.A., 1945–1985* (Harvard Business School Press, 1986); Vietor, *Contrived Competition*, 234–309; though cf. Mark H. Rose, *Market Rules: Bankers, Presidents, and the Origins of the Great Recession* (University of Pennsylvania Press, 2018). Scholars have paid more attention to the post-1970s period, examining the runup to the global financial crisis: Ranald C. Michie, *Banks, Exchanges, and Regulators: Global Financial Markets from the 1970s* (Oxford University Press, 2020); Wilmarth, *Taming the Megabanks*.

7. Standard Oil Company of California, *Annual Statement to Stockholders* (1938), 11 (ProQuest ID: 88187630); Phillips Petroleum Company, *Twenty-First Annual Report* (1938), 3 (ProQuest ID: 88186889). Business histories of the credit card industry largely treat politics as exogenous or outside the scope of inquiry: David Evans and Richard Schmalensee, *Paying with Plastic: The Digital Revolution in Buying and Borrowing* (MIT Press, 1999); Lewis Mandell, *The Credit Card Industry: A History* (Twayne Publishers, 1990); Joseph Nocera, *A Piece of the Action: How the Middle Class Joined the Money Class* (Simon & Schuster, 1994); David L. Stearns, *Electronic Value Exchange: Origins of the VISA Electronic Payment System* (Springer, 2011). Popular and sociological accounts, meanwhile, to the extent that they consider politics at all, tend to portray politicians as captured by industry interests: Charles R. Geisst, *Collateral Damaged: The Marketing of Consumer Debt to America* (Bloomberg Press, 2009); Lloyd Klein, *It's in the Cards: Consumer Credit and the American Experience* (Praeger, 1999); Robert D. Manning, *Credit Card Nation: The Consequences of America's Addiction to Credit* (Basic Books, 2000); Matty Simmons, *The Credit Card Catastrophe: The 20th Century Phenomenon That Changed the World* (Barricade Books, 1995).

8. On financial innovation as regulatory circumvention, see Fligstein, "Innovation and the Theory of Fields"; William L. Silber, "The Process of Financial Innovation," *American Economic Review* 73 (2) (May 1983): 89–95. On the ways visions of the imagined future state of markets, once innovation has been adopted, shape the process of innovation, see Bernardo Bátiz-Lazo, Thomas Haigh, and David L. Stearns, "How the Future Shaped the Past: The Case of the Cashless Society," *Enterprise & Society* 15, no. 1 (March 2014): 103–131; Jens Beckert, *Imagined Futures: Fictional Expectations and Capitalist Dynamics* (Harvard University Press, 2016).

9. While concerned with business power, this book does not seek to affirmatively theorize it (Neil Rollings, "'The Vast and Unsolved Enigma of Power': Business History and Business Power," *Enterprise & Society* 22, no. 4 [December 2021]: 893–920). Contra Davis and Kim, who understand financialization as the "displacement of financial institutions by financial markets," this study emphasizes the preliminary and necessary process through which financial institutions carve out intermediary roles in formerly un-intermediated economic relationships (Gerald F. Davis and Suntae Kim, "Financialization of the Economy," *Annual Review of Sociology* 41 [2015]: 203–221).

10. For Pocketbook politics, see Meg Jacobs, *Pocketbook Politics: Economic Citizenship in Twentieth-Century America* (Princeton University Press, 2004). For third wave consumerism and U.S. consumer politics generally, see Lizabeth Cohen, *A Consumers' Republic: The Politics of Mass Consumption in Postwar America* (Alfred A. Knopf, 2003); Lawrence B. Glickman, *Buying Power: A History of Consumer Activism in America* (University of Chicago Press, 2009); Tracey Deutsch, *Building a Housewife's Paradise: Gender, Politics, and American Grocery Stores in the Twentieth Century* (University of North Carolina Press, 2010). Some of these writers, like Deutsch, engage intermittently with state politics, but it is never a sustained site of analysis.

11. The role of federalism in enabling democratic control over financial institutions aligns with Charles W. Calomiris and Stephen H. Haber's theorization of the po-

litical economy of financial governance (*Fragile by Design: The Political Origins of Banking Crises and Scarce Credit* [Princeton University Press, 2014]), and contrasts the simple narrative of regulatory capture (George J. Stigler, "The Theory of Economic Regulation," *Bell Journal of Economics and Management Science* 2, no. 1 [1971]: 3–21). On federalism in the postwar era, see Karen M. Tani, *States of Dependency: Welfare, Rights, and American Governance, 1935–1972* (Cambridge University Press, 2016); Brent Cebul, Karen Tani, and Mason B. Williams, "Clio and the Compound Republic," *Publius: The Journal of Federalism* 47, no. 2 (April 2017): 235–259.

12. On the influence of *Marquette*, see Samuel Issacharoff and Erin F. Delaney, "Credit Card Accountability," *University of Chicago Law Review* 73, no. 1 (Winter 2006): 157–182; Johnna Montgomerie, "The Financialization of the American Credit Card Industry," *Competition & Change* 10, no. 3 (September 2006): 301–319.

13. James A. White, "Consumers Are Charging through a Credit-Card Blizzard," *CT*, January 22, 1978.

14. Ad, BankAmericard, "Think of It as Money," *WP*, April 20, 1971; Bátiz-Lazo, Haigh, and Stearns, "How the Future Shaped the Past." Louis Hyman emphasizes the importance of department store credit cards to consumer experiences, but he misses the importance of bank cards to debates about consumer protection and banking market structure (*Debtor Nation*, esp. 98–99, 111–118, 145–148, 169–170). To avoid complex and contentious debates, this book generally accepts the dominant intermediation theory of banking, i.e., banks intermediate between savers and borrowers without creating new money in the process. I find the money creation theory of banking convincing however, and see the development of the card industry, especially in the later stages, as an effort by bankers to claim greater control over the creation and movement of money. For an overview of competing monetary theories, see Michael McLeay, Amar Radia, and Ryland Thomas, "Money Creation in the Modern Economy," *Bank of England Quarterly Bulletin* 2014 Q1: 14–27.

15. On the 1970s as a transformative decade, see Bruce J. Schulman, *The Seventies: The Great Shift in American Culture, Society, and Politics* (Simon & Schuster, 2001); Stein, *Pivotal Decade*. On the transition from industrial to service work, see Claudia Goldin, "Labor Markets in the Twentieth Century," in *Cambridge Economic History of the United States*, ed. Stanley L. Engerman and Robert E. Gallman. vol. 3. (Cambridge University Press, 2000), 549–623; Gabriel Winant, *The Next Shift: The Fall of Industry and the Rise of Health Care in Rust Belt America* (Harvard University Press, 2021). On concerns about American affluence, see Daniel Horowitz, *The Anxieties of Affluence: Critiques of American Consumer Culture, 1939–1979* (University of Massachusetts Press, 2004). Scholars chronicling the Carter presidency tend to ignore or minimize the credit control policy (Kaufman and Kaufman, *The Presidency of James Earl Carter* [University of Kansas Press, 1993]; Erwin Hargrove, *Jimmy Carter as President: Leadership and the Politics of the Public Good* [Louisiana State University Press, 1988]). Those interested in Reagan's ascent, often more interested in long-term social and cultural developments, also neglect credit controls, e.g., Gil Troy, *Morning in America: How Ronald Reagan*

Invented the 1980s (Princeton University Press, 2005); Sean Wilentz, *Age of Reagan: A History, 1974–2008* (Harper, 2008); Donald T. Critchlow, *The Conservative Ascendency: How the GOP Right Made Political History* (Harvard University Press, 2007).

16. Scholars tend to accept that the Volcker Shock fundamentally transformed domestic and global financial markets (for example, by precipitating the savings and loan crisis in the U.S. and the Latin American sovereign debt crisis), but detailed examination of this assumption is rare. For the Volcker Shock, see Iwan Morgan, "Monetary Metamorphosis: The Volcker Fed and Inflation," *Journal of Policy History* 24, no. 4 (2012): 545–571. For Volcker's influence generally, see David Harvey, *A Brief History of Neoliberalism* (Oxford University Press, 2007).

17. Lawrence M. Ausubel, "The Failure of Competition in the Credit Card Market," *American Economic Review* 81, no. 1 (1991): 50–81. Financialization is a burgeoning field. For key texts, see Krippner, *Capitalizing on Crisis;* Davis and Kim, "Financialization of the Economy"; Natascha van der Zwan, "Making Sense of Financialization," *Socio-Economic Review* 12, no. 1 (January 1, 2014): 99–129. My focus on the conflict between capitalism and democracy aligns with Wolfgang Streek, *Buying Time: The Delayed Crisis of Democratic Capitalism,* trans. Patrick Camiller (Verso, 2014).

Chapter 1. The New Deal Regulatory Order

1. Gary Richardson, "Categories and Causes of Bank Distress during the Great Depression, 1929–1933: The Illiquidity versus Insolvency Debate Revisited," *Explorations in Economic History* 44, no. 4 (2007): 593; Marriner S. Eccles to A. P. Giannini, October 12, 1934, folder 1, box 9, Eccles Papers, FRASER.

2. Raymond Moley, *After Seven Years* (Harper & Brothers, 1939), 155; A. P. Giannini, draft editorial, folder 8, box 20a, Eccles Papers, FRASER. Giannini's editorial was published as "A. P. Giannini Says: Average Man Pays His Debts," *San Francisco Examiner,* August 12, 1936; "Banks Should Make More Personal Loans," *Bankers Magazine* 131, no. 4 (October 1936): 351–352.

3. Blanche Bernstein, *The Patterns of Consumer Debt, 1935–1936* (National Bureau of Economic Research, 1940), 124; Board of Governors of the Federal Reserve System, *Consumer Instalment Credit,* part 1, vol. 1 (Government Printing Office, 1957), 201. Bernstein's figures for 1936 are for "non relief families," so the percentage of households holding installment debt at that time was likely somewhat higher.

4. Board of Governors of the Federal Reserve System, *All Bank Statistics: United States, 1896–1955* (Government Printing Office, 1959), 33, FRASER; Bray Hammond, *Banks and Politics in America from the Revolution to the Civil War* (Princeton University Press, 1957); Charles W. Calomiris and Stephen H. Haber, *Fragile by Design: The Political Origins of Banking Crises and Scarce Credit* (Princeton University Press, 2014), 153–189; Henry M. Dawes, "In Defense of Unit Banking," *Selected Articles on Chain, Group and Branch Banking,* ed. Virgil Willit (H. W. Wilson, 1930), 255; Louis Hyman, *Debtor Nation: A History of America in Red Ink* (Princeton University Press, 2012), 76–77; Mehrsa Baradaran, *The Color of Money: Black Banks and the Racial Wealth Gap* (Harvard University Press, 2017).

5. Anne Fleming, *City of Debtors: A Century of Fringe Finance* (Harvard University Press, 2018), 213–245. Fleming examines financial federalism in the narrower context of consumer protection, rather than, as I do here, the wider framework of financial structure, contra studies, like Krippner, focused solely on federal regulations (Greta R. Krippner, *Capitalizing on Crisis: The Political Origins of the Rise of Finance* [Harvard University Press, 2011]).

6. Eugene N. White, "Banking and Finance in the Twentieth Century," in *The Cambridge Economic History of the United States*, ed. Stanley L. Engerman and Robert E. Gallman (Cambridge University Press, 2000), 748–752.

7. Marriner S. Eccles, *Beckoning Frontiers: Public and Personal Recollections*, ed. Sidney Hyman (Alfred A. Knopf, 1951), 54–55, 175; Ira Katznelson, *When Affirmative Action Was White: An Untold History of Racial Inequality in Twentieth-Century America* (W. W. Norton, 2005).

8. Eugene N. White, "State-Sponsored Insurance of Bank Deposits in the United States, 1907–1929," *Journal of Economic History* 41, no. 3 (1981): 537–57; Edwin J. Perkins, "The Divorce of Commercial and Investment Banking: A History," *Banking Law Journal* 88, no. 6 (June 1971): 483–528; Helen M. Burns, *The American Banking Community and New Deal Banking Reforms, 1933–1935* (Greenwood Press, 1974); Susan Estabrook Kennedy, *The Banking Crisis of 1933* (University of Kentucky Press, 1973), 205–209, 211–212, 215–216, 218–219; Calomiris and Haber, *Fragile by Design*, 189–190.

9. Richard Vietor, *Contrived Competition: Regulation and Deregulation in America* (Harvard University Press, 1994), 246–252; Carter Glass, *Operation of the National and Federal Reserve Banking Systems*, S. Rep. 70–584, April 22, 1932, 10. Whether Glass's diagnosis was accurate is disputed; cf. Calomiris and Haber, *Fragile by Design*, 190–191; Paul G. Mahoney, *Wasting a Crisis: Why Securities Regulation Fails* (University of Chicago Press, 2015).

10. Krippner, *Capitalizing on Crisis*, 63; Veitor, *Contrived Competition*, 250; *Banking Act of 1935*, 74 Cong. 218, 330 (1935) (statements of Dr. Oliver M. W. Sprague, Harvard University, and Marriner S. Eccles, Governor Federal Reserve Board).

11. Memorandum, Marriner Eccles to Franklin Roosevelt, November 12, 1936, folder 6, box 5, Eccles Papers, FRASER; Perkins, "Divorce of Commercial and Investment Banking."

12. Jason Scott Smith, *Building New Deal Liberalism: The Political Economy of Public Works, 1933–1956* (Cambridge University Press, 2005); Elis W. Hawley, *The New Deal and the Problem of Monopoly: A Study in Economic Ambivalence* (Princeton University Press, 1966); Julian E. Zelizer, "The Forgotten Legacy of the New Deal: Fiscal Conservatism and the Roosevelt Administration, 1933–1938," *Presidential Studies Quarterly* 20, no. 2 (June 2000): 332–359; Arthur Schlesinger Jr. *Coming of the New Deal* (Houghton Mifflin, 1959), 496–503; Franklin D. Roosevelt, "Address to the Bankers' Convention at Constitution Hall, Washington D.C.," October 24, 1934, APP.

13. Marriner S. Eccles, "Reconstructing Economic Thinking," October 27, 1933, folder 5, box 74, Eccles Papers, FRASER; Winfield Reifler, "Housing Program," April 19, 1934, folder 5, box 1, Reifler Papers, FRASER; Mark Wayne Nelson, *Jumping the*

Abyss: Marriner S. Eccles and the New Deal, 1933–1940 (University of Utah Press, 2017), 145–156.

14. Calder, *Financing the American Dream*, 156–208; Hyman, *Debtor Nation*, 10–12, 20–42; Fleming, *City of Debtors*, 109–113; Vicki Howard, *From Main Street to the Mall: The Rise and Fall of the American Department Store* (University of Pennsylvania Press, 2015), 74–75, 87–89.

15. William Leach, *Land of Desire: Merchants, Power, and the Rise of a New American Culture* (Pantheon: 1993), 299–302; Calder, *Financing the American Dream*, 71–72; Meg Jacobs, *Pocketbook Politics: Economic Citizenship in Twentieth-Century America* (Princeton University Press, 2005), 18.

16. Christina D. Romer, "The Nation in Depression," *Journal of Economic Perspectives* 7, no. 2 (Spring 1993): 29–31; Martha Olney, "Avoiding Default: The Role of Credit in the Consumption Collapse of 1930," *Quarterly Journal of Economics* 114, no. 1 (February 1999): 319–335; Board of Governors of the Federal Reserve System, *Consumer Instalment Credit*, part 1, vol. 1 (Government Printing Office, 1957), 236–239; memo, Marriner Eccles to Jacob Viner, September 4, 1934, folder 2, box 41, Eccles Papers, FRASER; Eccles, *Beckoning Frontiers*, 144–147; Nelson, *Jumping the Abyss*, 133–175.

17. Gail Radford, *Modern Housing for America: Policy Struggles in the New Deal Era* (University of Chicago Press, 1996), 179–180; Hyman, *Debtor Nation*, 53–58; Winfield Reifler, "A Plan to Provide 'Consumer Credit' for Home Modernization," April 19, 1934, folder 5, box 1, Reifler Papers, FRASER; Eccles, *Beckoning Frontiers*, 148. Harnessing private interest to direct capital toward the public good was a longstanding strategy of the American political economy, e.g., Louis Hartz, *Economic Policy and Democratic Thought: Pennsylvania, 1776–1860* (Harvard University Press, 1948).

18. David M. P. Freund, *Colored Property: State Policy and White Racial Politics in Suburban America* (University of Chicago Press, 2007).

19. Hyman, *Debtor Nation*, 73–97; Reifler, "Plan to Provide 'Consumer Credit'"; Ronald C. Tobey, *Technology as Freedom: The New Deal and the Electrical Modernization of the American Home* (University of California Press, 1997), 107–108; memo, Ronald Ransom to Board Members (individually), December 9, 1946, folder 5, box 41, Eccles Papers, FRASER.

20. Marriner Eccles, "Comments on Public Works," November 1934, folder 5, box 9, Eccles Papers, FRASER (I attribute this document to Eccles based on similarity to 1933 speech quoted above); Chloe N. Thurston, *At the Boundaries of Homeownership: Credit, Discrimination, and the American State* (Cambridge University Press, 2018); Louis Hyman, "Ending Discrimination, Legitimating Debt: The Political Economy of Race, Gender, and Credit Access in the 1960s and 1970s," *Enterprise & Society* 12, no. 1 (Spring 2011): 200–232. For the parallel idea of "financial citizenship," see Andrew Leyshon and Nigel Thrift, "Geographies of Financial Exclusion: Financial Abandonment in Britain and the United States," *Transaction of the Institute of British Geographers* 20, no. 3 (1995): 312–341.

21. Eccles to Giannini, October 12, 1934, folder 1, box 9, Eccles Papers, FRASER; Sarah L. Quinn, *American Bonds: How Credit Markets Shaped a Nation* (Princeton University Press, 2019), 124–149.

22. Board of Governors of the Federal Reserve System, Meeting Minutes, June 25, 1941, FRASER; Eccles, *Beckoning Frontiers*, 350, 372–374; Franklin D. Roosevelt, "Message to Congress on an Economic Stabilization Program," April 27, 1942, APP; Hyman, *Debtor Nation*, 100.

23. Federal Reserve System, Meeting Minutes, June 25, 1941; Leon Henderson to Carl E. Perry, July 25, 1941, folder 3, box 41, Eccles Papers, FRASER; Roosevelt, "Message to Congress on an Economic Stabilization Program"; Rolf Nugent, *Consumer Credit and Economic Stability* (Russell Sage Foundation, 1939); Hyman, *Debtor Nation*, 100–102; Fleming, *City of Debtors*, 64–68, 81–82, 130–134.

24. Federal Reserve, *Consumer Instalment Credit*, part 1, vol. 1, 296, 305; Hyman, *Debtor Nation*, 114–118.

25. Federal Reserve, *Consumer Instalment Credit*, part 1, vol. 1, 296; Hyman, *Debtor Nation*, 114–118; Josh Lauer, "Plastic Surveillance: Payment Cards and the History of Transactional Data, 1888 to Present," *Big Data & Society* (January 2020): 5.

26. Hyman, *Debtor Nation*, 118–130; Howard, *Main Street to the Mall*, 123, 147–149.

27. Eccles, *Beckoning Frontiers*, 417, 426–433. More specifically, controls were lifted in 1947, reimposed in September 1948, and authority expired in 1949 (U.S., President and Council of Economic Advisers, *Economic Report of the President* [Government Printing Office, 1949], 16–17, FRASER).

28. Robert M. Collins, *More: The Politics of Economic Growth in Postwar America* (Oxford University Press, 2000), 16–22; Federal Reserve, *Consumer Instalment Credit*, part 1, vol. 1, 244–245; *Consumer Credit Control*, 80 Cong. 15 (1947) (statement of Marriner Eccles), 15; memo, Clark L. Fauver, February 11, 1949, folder 8, box 41; memo, Chad F. Calhoun, February 19, 1949, folder 11, box 41, Eccles Papers, FRASER.

29. *Consumer Credit Control*, 84 (statement of Gary M. Underhill, Executive Director, Consumer Bankers Association); Howell John Harris, *The Right to Manage: Industrial Relations Policies of American Business in the 1940s* (University of Wisconsin Press, 1982), 150.

30. U.S., President and Council of Economic Advisers, *Economic Report of the President* (Government Printing Office, 1950), 12; U.S., President and Council of Economic Advisers, *Economic Report of the President* (Government Printing Office, 1956), 94; Hyman, *Debtor Nation*, 127–129; Federal Reserve, *Consumer Instalment Credit*, part 1, vol. 1, 1–6; Michael R. Glass and Sean H. Vanatta, "The Frail Bonds of Liberalism: Pensions, Schools, and the Unraveling of Fiscal Mutualism in Midcentury New York," *Capitalism: A Journal of History and Economics* 2, no. 2 (Summer 2021): 427–472.

31. Henry H. Heimann, "Sound Credit, Our First Line of Defense," *Credit World* 39, no. 11 (August 1951): 4; Gary Gerstle, *The Rise and Fall of the Neoliberal Order* (Oxford University Press, 2022), 20–27; Calder, *Financing the American Dream*, 242–249, 251; Paul Mazur, *The Standards We Raise: The Dynamics of Consumption* (Harper & Brothers, 1953), 31, 100–101, 129, 144.

32. Federal Reserve, *Consumer Instalment Credit*, part 1, vol. 1, 162, 203, part 3, 24, 98, 138, 226–229; John Kenneth Galbraith, *The Affluent Society* (Riverside Press, 1958), 201; Daniel Horowitz, *The Anxieties of Affluence: Critiques of American Consumer Culture, 1939–1979* (University of Massachusetts Press, 2004); "Regulation of Consumer Instalment

Credit: Views of the Board of Governors," *Federal Reserve Bulletin* (June 1957), 647–648. In a later edition, Galbraith amended the quote to read, "Can the bill collector or the bankruptcy lawyer be the central figure in the good society?" a change that reflected unfolding negative consequences of credit-fueled prosperity for individual American households.

33. Eric Monnet, *Controlling Credit: Central Banking and the Planned Economy in Postwar France, 1948–1973* (Cambridge University Press, 2018), 1, 247–282; Stuart Aveyard, Paul Corthorn, and Sean O'Connell, *Politics of Consumer Credit in the UK, 1938–1992* (Oxford University Press, 2018).

34. David Michael Kennedy, "What the New Deal Did." *Political Science Quarterly* 124, no. 2 (2009): 253–254; Joseph A. Schumpeter, *Business Cycles,* vol. 2 (McGraw Hill, 1939), 1004, quoted in *Consumer Instalment Credit,* part 1, vol. 1, 240; Giannini, "Banks Should Make More Personal Loans." In this sense, private credit and public welfare were compliments within the New Deal financial order, though they would become substitutes after that order collapsed in the 1980s. Monica Prasad, *The Land of Too Much: American Abundance and the Paradox of Poverty* (Harvard University Press, 2012); Gunnar Trumbull, *Consumer Lending in France and America: Credit and Welfare* (Cambridge University Press, 2014).

Chapter 2. Charge Account Banking

1. G. L. Toole, "Development and Progress of a Bank Charge Account Service: Part I," *AB,* April 28, 1955; G. L. Toole, "Development and Progress of a Bank Charge Account Service: Part II," *AB,* May 16, 1955; Otto C. Lorenz, "21 Charge Account Bankers Show Profits for 3rd Quarter," *AB,* November 30, 1955; Otto C. Lorenz, "5 More Banks Enter Charge Account Profit Column," *AB,* August 25, 1959; brochure, Upper Darby National Bank, "Upper Darby National Bank: Charge-Rite Revolving Credit Plan," box 1294, Douglas Papers. A version of this chapter appeared as Sean H. Vanatta, "Charge Account Banking: A Study of Financial Innovation in the 1950s," *Enterprise & Society* 19, no. 2 (June 2018): 352–390.

2. My emphasis on postwar antimonopoly politics runs counter to Richard Hofstadter ("What Happened to the Antitrust Movement?" in *The Paranoid Style in American Politics and Other Essays,* ed. Richard Hofstadter [Alfred A. Knopf, 1965]). Instead, I follow Richard John's call for renewed focus on antimonopoly ("Robber Barons Redux: Antimonopoly Reconsidered," *Enterprise & Society* 13, no. 1 [March 2012]: 1–38). Financial historians view charge accounts as a failed path toward innovation (David Evans and Richard Schmalensee, *Paying with Plastic: The Digital Revolution in Buying and Borrowing* [MIT Press, 1999], 55–56; Louis Hyman, *Debtor Nation: The History of America in Red Ink* [Princeton University Press, 2011], 145–148; Lewis Mandell, *The Credit Card Industry: A History* [Twayne Publishers, 1990], 26–29; David L. Stearns, *Electronic Value Exchange: Origins of the VISA Electronic Payment System* [Springer, 2011], 18–19; Timothy Wolters, "'Carry Your Credit in Your Pocket': The Early History of the Credit Card at Bank of America and Chase Manhattan," *Enterprise & Society* 1, no. 2 [June 2000]: 322–324).

3. *Consumer Credit Control,* 80 Cong. (1947); Hyman, *Debtor Nation,* 100–127; Samuel Feinberg, "From Where I Sit: 'To Thine Own Self Be True,'" *WWD,* February 18, 1953; Thomas F. Conroy, "Credit Drive Urged to Expand Sales," *NYT,* January 10, 1946; "Retail Executive: Credit Sales Promotion Gains Ground," *WWD,* February 18, 1946.

4. Hyman, *Debtor Nation,* 114–125; 148–156; Vicki Howard, *From Main Street to the Mall: The Rise and Fall of the American Department Store* (University of Pennsylvania Press, 2015), 132–153; A. L. Trotta, "Bank Charge Account Plans," *Stores* (March 1953): 19; "Costs May Cause Stores to Merge," *NYT,* July 11, 1949.

5. "For the Smaller Businessman: Sales Promotions, Office Procedures, Credit & Collection Problems," *Credit World* 40, no. 9 (June 1952): 24; Frank W. Price, "Credit Operations in a Specialty Store, "*Credit World* 40, no. 12 (September 1952): 5; Feinberg, "From Where I Sit: To Thine Own Self Be True"; "Store Operations: Smaller Stores Given Methods to Meet Chains," *WWD,* June 30, 1950. For retail antimonopoly, see Laura Phillips Sawyer, "California Fair Trade: Antitrust and the Politics of 'Fairness' in U.S. Competition Policy," *Business History Review* 90, no. 1 (Spring 2016): 31–56; Marc Levinson, *The Great A&P and the Struggle for Small Business in America* (Hill and Wang, 2011).

6. "Store Operations: Smaller Stores Given Methods to Meet Chains"; *Shopping Centers-1959,* 86 Cong. (1959); Theodore Philip Kovaleff, *Business and Government during the Eisenhower Administration: A Study of the Antitrust Policy of the Antitrust Division of the Justice Department* (Ohio University Press, 1980), 11; *The Impact of Suburban Shopping Centers on Independent Retailers: Report of the Select Committee on Small Business,* 86 Cong. (1960); Levinson, *Great A&P.*

7. Toole, "Charge Account Service: Part I"; Federal Reserve, Board of Governors of the Federal Reserve System, *Consumer Instalment Credit,* part 1, vol. 1 (Government Printing Office, 1957), 36–37; Johnathan Levy, *Ages of American Capitalism: A History of the United States* (Random House, 2022), 524–527.

8. "Bank Starts First Credit Plan," *Newsday,* August 16, 1946.

9. "Manufactures Trust Co. Buys Flatbush National," *NYT,* May 8, 1946; ad, First National Bank and Trust Co. of Bay Shore, *Newsday,* October 22, 1946, 6; "Bank Starts First Credit Plan," *Newsday,* August 16, 1946; C. Kenneth Fuller, "A Bank's 'Charg-It' Plan for Merchants," *Burroughs Clearing House* (November 1950), 28. Prior accounts of Biggins's plan claim it operated within four blocks of the Flatbush bank, but I have found no contemporary evidence to support these claims. The Bay Shore bank had a long-standing correspondent relationship with Manufacturers Trust (though Biggins may also have licensed the program independently of his position with the bank).

10. "Charge It—With the Bank," *Business Week* (September 23, 1950), 58, 60; Toole, "Charge Account Service: Part I"; Hyman, *Debtor Nation,* 123–124.

11. "A Bank's Retail Charge Account Service," *Banking* 44, no. 12 (June 1952), 122; Edward M. Donohue, "Charge Account Financing by Banks," *Bulletin of the Robert Morris Associates* 35, no. 10 (June 1953): 333.

12. Donohue, "Charge Account Financing by Banks," 334; J. H. Peters, "From Where We Sit: Bank Credit via Charge Accounts," *Bankers Monthly* (June 1952), 4. For

embeddedness, see Mark Granovetter, "Economic Action and Social Structure: The Problem of Embeddedness," *American Journal of Sociology* 91, no. 3 (November 1985): 481–510.

13. Toole, "Charge Account Service: Part II"; David C. Hopper, "'Easy Charge' Credit Plan Proving Profitable for Jersey Bank, Aiding Other Departments," *AB*, September 27, 1956; Lizabeth Cohen, *A Consumers' Republic: The Politics of Mass Consumption in Postwar America* (Alfred A. Knopf, 2003), 278.

14. Donohue, "Charge Account Financing by Banks," 334; Peters, "From Where We Sit," 4.

15. Charles H. Landrain, "Charge Accounts Offer Banks Chance to Provide Valuable Service," *AB*, June 16, 1959; Otto C. Lorenz, "Will Revolving Check-Credit Vie with Charge-Account Banking?" *AB*, January 26, 1959; Toole, "Charge Account Service: Part I"; Elaine Tyler May, *Homeward Bound: American Families in the Cold War Era* (Basic Books, 1988). Typical applications asked first for the occupation of "Mr. or Miss," with space for "wife's occupation" below. Brochure, Upper Darby National Bank, "Upper Darby National Bank: Charge-Rite Revolving Credit Plan," box 1294; ad, Florida National Bank, "A NEW Source of Revenue for Orlando MERCHANTS," (n.d.), box 1298, Douglas Papers.

16. "Charge It—With the Bank"; "Bankers Move In on Charge Credit," *Business Week* (April 11, 1953), 42; "A Bank's Retail Charge Account Service," *Banking* 44, no. 12 (June 1, 1952): 122; "Bank Devises A Small-Store Charge-It Plan," *NYHT,* May 1, 1952; Dean J. Madsen, "The Charge Account Road to Bank Growth," *FPRAY* (1958), 284; G. L. Toole, "Community Service with Reciprocal Benefits," *FPRAY* (1958), 292; Toole, "Charge Account Service: Part I."

17. Fuller, "A Bank's 'Charg-It' Plan for Merchants," Otto C. Lorenz, "Wham! . . . In the Gold with Charge Account Banking," *AB*, February 26, 1957; "A.B.A. Charge Plan Panel Urges Caution in Adopting Method," *AB*, March 26, 1953; "3 Banks Map New Shopper Credit Service," *CT,* January 14, 1953; "Single Check Shopping," *WSJ,* February 9, 1953; William Henry Herrman, "Charge Account Banking" (master's thesis, Wharton School, University of Pennsylvania, 1960), 26–30; Donohue, "Charge Account Financing by Banks," 334.

18. Frederick L. Vesperman, *History of Charge Account Banking* (Charge Account Bankers Association, 1968) (though cf. "Charge Account Firm Sues Bank, Company Selling Like Services," *WSJ,* March 20, 1953; "LI Bank Says Ex-VP Stole Charge Plan," *Newsday,* March 24, 1953); Jens Beckert, *Imagined Futures: Fictional Expectations and Capitalist Dynamics* (Harvard University Press, 2016). On business associations as social, meaning-making institutions, see Lyn Spillman, *Solidarity in Strategy: Making Business Meaningful in American Trade Associations* (University of Chicago Press, 2012).

19. Otto Carl Lorenz and Harold Meade Mott-Smith, *Financial Problems of Instalment Selling: Practical Methods for the Determination of Capital and Discount Requirements, Earned Income, Yield, etc.* (McGraw Hill, 1931); "Otto C. Lorenz Dead, Was Associate Editor of 'American Banker,'" *AB*, January 26, 1960; Otto C. Lorenz, "From the Consumer Credit Desk: Charge Account Bankers Show Great Improvement," *AB*, April 28, 1955; Otto C. Lorenz, "Bank Retail Charge Account Service Volume

$726,098 for May, '53," *AB*, June 19, 1953; Otto C. Lorenz, "21 Charge Account Bankers Show Profit for 3rd Quarter," *AB*, November 30, 1955; Otto C. Lorenz, "From the Consumer Credit Desk: About Figures . . . and Surveys," *AB*, August 26, 1954.

20. J. C. Gilliland, quoted in Vesperman, *History of Charge Account Banking*, 5; Vesperman, *History of Charge Account Banking*, 5, 7, 10; "Urges Bankers Ease Credit to Spur Economy," *CT*, March 25, 1954; "Chge-Acct Bankers Form Association to Exchange Information," *AB*, March 23, 1954; Lorenz, "From the Consumer Credit Desk: Charge Account Bankers Show Great Improvement"; "Florida National Starts Charge Account Plan," *AB*, December 27, 1957.

21. Robert H. Cole, *Financing Retail Credit Sales through Charge Account Bank Plans*, Business Management Survey No. 5 (Bureau of Business Management, 1962), 36; Otto C. Lorenz, "Credit Engineering—For Bank Examiners," *AB*, May 29, 1956; Vesperman, *History of Charge Account Banking*, 22; "Five Charge Account Banks Earn Net Rate of 10%," *AB*, November 27, 1957; Otto C. Lorenz, "Charge Account Bankers Announce Gains for 2nd Quarter," *AB*, August 21, 1958.

22. Here and elsewhere, I convert monthly to annual interest charges by multiplying the former by 12. With monthly compounding, the true annual rate would be higher, but states often prohibited compound interest on consumer loans. Bank, press, and government sources from the period uniformly use the simple calculation. Computing the "true" rate of interest was complicated and contentious, as we will see in later chapters.

23. Herrman, "Charge Account Banking," 59. On state credit rules generally, see Barbara A. Curran, *Trends in Consumer Credit Legislation* (University of Chicago Press, 1965).

24. "Over $4.4 Million Outstandings in Charge Account Banking at Year End," *AB*, January 28, 1954; Toole, "Community Service with Reciprocal Benefits"; Donohue, "Charge Account Financing by Banks"; Harold G. Vatter, *The U.S. Economy in the 1950's: An Economic History* (W. W. Norton, 1963), 98–113.

25. Otto C. Lorenz, "Want More Persons to Use Bank Services?," *AB*, November 27, 1956; Otto C. Lorenz, "Charge Account Bankers Create Surplus Demand Deposits in Tight Money Market," *AB*, June 26, 1957. Contra the business and economics literature on two-sided markets, this chapter demonstrates that these markets are not merely coordinated though carefully balanced prices. Rather, they developed through more complex, embedded structures of interfirm and interpersonal relationships. Evans and Schmalensee, *Paying with Plastic;* Jean-Charles Rochet and Jean Tirole, "Two-Sided Markets: A Progress Report," *RAND Journal of Economics* 37, no. 3 (Autumn 2006): 645–667; Marc Rysman, "The Economics of Two-Sided Markets," *Journal of Economic Perspectives* 23, no. 3 (Summer 2009): 125–143.

26. Ad, Pan American Bank of Miami, "Mr. Merchant: Here's a New Avenue of Revenue!," (n.d.); ad, Florida National Bank, "A NEW Source of Revenue for Orlando MERCHANTS," (n.d.), box 1298, Douglas Papers; ad, Northwestern National Bank, "Introducing . . . NWCP: The Northwestern Charge Plan," (n.d., ca. 1960), box 8, Northwest Papers.

27. Donald H. Maffly and Alex C. McDonald, "The Tripartite Credit Card Transaction: A Legal Infant," *California Law Review* 48, no. 3 (1960): 459–500. The holder-in-due course doctrine, which limited consumer remedies in cases of dissatisfaction or fraud, was the subject of significant debate throughout the era (Robin P. Hartmann and H. William Walker, "The Holder in Due Course Doctrine and the Consumer," *Commercial Law Journal* 77, no. 4 [1972]: 116–127).

28. "Three Banks Introducing Charge-Plate Accounts for Chicago Merchants," *AB*, January 20, 1953; "Bankers Move In on Charge Credit"; ad, First National Bank and Trust Co. of Bay Shore, *Newsday*, October 22, 1946; "Denver Nat'l Adopts Retail Sale Charge Plan Service," *AB*, July 6, 1953; John R. Markley, "Charge Account Banking for an Atlanta Bank" (master's thesis, Emory University, 1959), 5, 41; Northwestern Banks, "Northwestern Charge Plan Fee Schedule and Refund Chart," box 8, Northwest Papers; "Charge Account Banking," *AB*, February 26, 1960.

29. Donohue, "Charge Account Financing by Banks"; L. S. Crowder, "Bank and Central Charge Plans," *Credit World* 41, no. 12 (September 1953): 32; Trotta, "Bank Charge Account Plans."

30. First National Bank and Trust of Kalamazoo, "First National Charge Account Service Shoppers Guide," First National Bank and Trust of Kalamazoo Clipping File, Kalamazoo Public Library; Northwestern Banks, "Directory of NWCP Members," box 8, Northwest Papers; "Clothing Stores Lead 'Handy-Charge' Outlets for South Bend Bank," *AB*, December 15, 1953; Norman Townshend-Zellner, "The Bank-Charge-Account Plan and Retail Food Marketing," *Agricultural Economics Research* 12, no. 4 (October 1, 1960): 85–104.

31. Trotta, "Bank Charge Account Plans"; "Florida National Starts Charge Account Plan"; D. A. Freeth, "What's Wrong with Midland Charge Plan?," March 1962, NA0339–1619, HSBC Archives; "Smaller Stores Find Favor in Charge Plans," *WWD*, January 25, 1954; Lloyd Schwartz, "Store Criticism Aimed at Bank Credit Drives," *WWD*, May 12, 1959; Samuel Feinberg, "From Where I Sit: Banks Cutting In on Retail Territory," *WWD*, June 17, 1959; "Hess Tells Consumer Bankers Retail Charge Service for Merchants Is Here to Stay," *AB*, October 23, 1953.

32. William F. Hoffman, "The Experience of Industrial Trust and Savings Bank in the Field of Charge Account Banking" (master's thesis, Ball State Teachers College, 1959), 105–107; *Review of Report of the Commission on Money and Credit*, 87 Cong. 293 (1961) (statement of J. Irwin Miller, Chairman of the Board, Cummins Engine Co.).

33. Robert H. Wilson, "Charge Account Banking—Advantages and Disadvantages," *FPRAY* (1959), 98; Clarence Mead, "Credit Cards on Main Street," *FPRAY* (1966), 203–205; "Almost 1,000 New Stores Join Charge Account Bank Plans since June 1954—Total Now 8,905," *AB*, October 29, 1954; Albert J. Wood, "A Charge Customer Is Worth Nearly Four Times as Much as a Cash Customer," *Credit World* 42, no. 3 (December 1953): 5.

34. Charles E. Groover, "Citizens Commercial, Flint, Mich., Offers New Service to Correspondent Banks," *AB*, May 29, 1956.

35. "Second Correspondent Charge Account Plan Successful, First NB&T, Kalamazoo, States." *AB*, May 1, 1959.

36. First National Bank and Trust of Kalamazoo, "First National Charge Account Service Shoppers Guide," First National Bank and Trust of Kalamazoo Clipping File, Kalamazoo Public Library.

37. Freeth, "What's Wrong with Midland Charge Plan?"; J. C. Gilliland, "Bank Charge Account Plans," *Credit World* 42, no. 2 (November 1953): 14–15; "Chge-Acct Bankers Form Association to Exchange Information"; David Hopper, "Key to Success—Training Merchants," *FPRAY* (1958), 288; Charles H. Landrain, "Getting Started and Building Momentum," *FPRAY* (1958), 296; Wilson, "Charge Account Banking—Advantages and Disadvantages," 99; Feinberg, "From Where I Sit: You Can Bank on It!", *WWD*, October 28, 1955.

38. Freeth, "What's Wrong with Midland Charge Plan?"; Donohue, "Charge Account Financing by Banks."

39. Otto C. Lorenz, "Charge Account Bankers Are Now Facing New Competition from Seaboard International," *AB*, November 24, 1959.

40. Robert L. Rudolph, "Charge Account Operations Successful in Miami," *AB*, July 24, 1956; Raymond H. Alm, "Charge Account Banking" (master's thesis, Stonier Graduate School of Banking, Rutgers University, 1962), 37–39.

41. "Bank Retail Charge Account Volume $986,098 for September, 1953," *AB*, October 30, 1953; "Charge Account Volume 1st Quarter '56 up 36% to $9.17 Million from Year Ago," *AB*, May 29, 1956; Otto C. Lorenz, "Charge Account Bankers Announce Gains for 2nd Quarter," *AB*, August 21, 1958.

42. Alm, "Charge Account Banking," 53–54; Cohen, *Consumers' Republic*, 123; Pan American Bank of Miami, "Apply for Your Pan American Bank Charge Plan Credit Card Now!"; Florida National Bank, "Apply for Your F.N.B. Charge Plan Credit Card ToDAY!," box 1298, Douglas Papers.

43. Hyman, *Debtor Nation*, 98; "Charge It, Please," *Time*, April 9, 1951, 102. The story was first recounted in "Dining on the Cuff," *Newsweek*, January 29, 1951, 73. It has been reproduced widely, including: Peter Z. Grossman, *American Express: The Unofficial History of the People Who Built the Great Financial Empire* (Crown Publishers, 1987), 261–262; Mandell, *Credit Card Industry*, 1–10; Evans and Schmalensee, *Paying with Plastic*, 53–54. The original spelling was Diners' Club. For simplicity, the modern spelling has been used throughout.

44. Matty Simmons, *The Credit Card Catastrophe: The 20th Century Phenomenon That Changed the World* (Barricade Books, 1995), 26. Lana Swartz, "Gendered Transactions: Identity and Payment at Midcentury," *Women's Studies Quarterly* 42, no. 1/2 (Spring/Summer 2014): 137–153.

45. Ad, Diners' Club, "Indispensable New Convenience," *LAT*, December 12, 1950; "Charge It, Please," 102; J.R. Carll Tucker, "Credit System Lures 40,000 Eaters-Out in 1st Year of Operation," *WSJ*, March 28, 1951; "Diners' Club Opens Offices on Continent," *LAT*, November 29, 1953; H. Eugene Dickhuth, "Diners' Club Gathering Popularity," *NYHT*, November 1, 1953.

46. Ad, Diners' Club, "Say 'Charge It,'" *NYT*, October 10, 1950; "Charge It, Please," 102; Joseph Kaselow, "Advertising Field: Credit Where Due," *NYHT*, January 3, 1954; ad, Diners' Club, "Indispensable New Convenience," *CT*, December 19, 1950.

47. Simmons, *Credit Card Catastrophe,* 23–24, 41, 46–47; John Linehan, "Diners' Club," *Barron's* (January 9, 1956), 15.
48. "Charge Everything," *Newsweek,* January 3, 1955.
49. "Diners' Club Pays in Stock," *LAT,* April 28, 1956; Quarterly Charge Account Banking Reports, *AB;* Vanatta, "Charge Account Banking," 21.
50. "Five Charge Account Banks Earn Net Rate of 10%, 11 Reach 6%, among 35 Making Quarterly Report"; Otto C. Lorenz, "Past Lessons in Charge Account Banking Show Pitfalls Which Must Be Avoided If Full-Scale Operation Is to Succeed," *AB,* November 20, 1958.
51. On small-firm ecosystems as a context for innovation, see Philip Scranton, *Endless Novelty: Specialty Production and American Industrialization, 1865–1925* (Princeton University Press, 1997).
52. "Hess Tells Consumer Bankers Retail Charge Service for Merchants Is Here to Stay," *AB,* October 21, 1953; Peters, "From Where We Sit," 4.

Chapter 3. Profits Squeeze

1. David Rockefeller, *Creative Management in Banking* (McGraw Hill, 1964), 20–22; Timothy Wolters, "'Carry Your Credit in Your Pocket': The Early History of the Credit Card at Bank of America and Chase Manhattan," *Enterprise & Society* 1, no. 2 (June 2000): 342.
2. Commission on Money and Credit, *Money and Credit: Their Influence on Jobs, Prices, and Growth* (Prentice-Hall, 1961); David Rockefeller and John F. Kennedy, "A Businessman's Letter to J.F.K and His Reply," *Life,* July 6, 1962, 30–34; "President Lauds Study on Financial Reforms," *LAT,* June 20, 1961; "Report Is Praised," *NYT,* June 20, 1961; Rockefeller, *Creative Management,* 5.
3. Raymond J. Saulnier, *Constructive Years: The U.S. Economy under Eisenhower* (University Presses of America, 1991), 19–21; John W. Sloan, *Eisenhower and the Management of Prosperity* (University of Kansas Press, 1991), 32–38; Dwight D. Eisenhower, "Annual Message to the Congress on the State of the Union," January 10, 1957, APP; Board of Governors of the Federal Reserve System, *Consumer Instalment Credit* (Government Printing Office, 1957).
4. Kim Phillips-Fein, *Invisible Hands: The Making of the Conservative Movement from the New Deal to Reagan* (W. W. Norton, 2009), 31, 61; Benjamin Waterhouse, *Lobbying America: The Politics of Business from Nixon to NAFTA* (Princeton University Press, 2014), 19; Karl Schriftgiesser, *The Commission on Money and Credit: An Adventure in Policy-Making* (Prentice-Hall, 1973), 3–21.
5. Joseph B. Treaster, *Paul Volcker: The Making of a Financial Legend* (John Wiley & Sons, 2004), 37; Perry Mehling, "An Interview with Paul A. Volcker," *Macroeconomic Dynamics* (December 5, 2001): 440; Hyman Minsky, "Financial Crisis, Financial Systems, and the Performance of the Economy," in *Private Capital Markets: A Series of Research Studies Prepared for the Commission on Money and Credit* (Prentice-Hall Inc., 1964); Robert M. Collins, *More: The Politics of Economic Growth in Postwar America* (Oxford University Press, 2000). For a transnational comparison,

see Gunnar Trumbull, *Consumer Lending in France and America: Credit and Welfare* (Cambridge University Press, 2014).

6. Commission on Money and Credit, *Money and Credit*, 2, 167, 177–178; Raymond W. Goldsmith et al., *Studies in the National Balance Sheet of the United States*, vol. 2 (Princeton University Press, 1963), 88–89, 114–115, 162–163.

7. American Bankers Association, *The Commercial Banking Industry: A Monograph Prepared for the Commission on Money and Credit* (Prentice-Hall, 1962), 4, 63 (emphasis added), 132–134; Board of Governors of the Federal Reserve System, *All Bank Statistics: United States, 1896–1955* (April 1959), FRASER, 31; Carl T. Arlt, "The Changing Character of Bank Deposits," in *The Changing World of Banking*, ed. Herbert V. Prochnow and Herbert V. Prochnow Jr. (Harper & Row, 1974), 59.

8. American Bankers Association, *Commercial Banking*, 72, 81–82; Commission on Money and Credit, *Money and Credit*, 164–165.

9. Arlt, "Changing Character of Bank Deposits," 46; American Bankers Association, *Commercial Banking*, 72, 76–81, 131–132; Chase Manhattan Bank, *Chase Manhattan Bank Annual Report to Stockholders for 1961*, 4 (ProQuest ID: 88194403); Commission on Money and Credit, *Money and Credit*, 167; David Rockefeller, *Memoirs* (Random House, 2003), 197. The profits squeeze prefigured the later problem of disintermediation (Gerald F. Davis, *Managed by the Markets: How Finance Reshaped America* [Oxford University Press, 2009], 112–115).

10. John Donald Wilson, *The Chase: The Chase Manhattan Bank, N.A., 1945–1985* (Harvard Business School Press, 1986), 43–45, 56–73; "Chase Manhattan Bank (National Association)," box 165, FDIC Exam Reports, NARA II; Commission on Money and Credit, *Money and Credit*, 165; Paul Heffernan, "Merger Confirms New Banking Era," *NYT*, January 16, 1955; "Celler Plans Inquiry," *NYT*, January 15, 1955; Coleman A. Harwell, "Long Fight on Monopoly in Business Waged by Estes in House and Senate," *WP*, May 15, 1956; Nancy Beck Young, *Wright Patman: Populism, Liberalism, and the American Dream* (Southern Methodist University Press, 2000), 227; American Bankers Association, *Commercial Banking Industry*, 9–21.

11. Wright Patman in *Review of Report of the Commission on Money and Credit*, 87 Cong. 110, 310 (1961) (statements of J. Irwin Miller, Chairman of the Board, Cummins Engine Co. and Leon Keyserling, President of Conference on Economic Progress).

12. Young, *Wright Patman*, 226–235, 237–240; American Banking Association, *Commercial Banking Industry*, 14; memo, John F. Kenney to Chairman of the Council of Economic Advisers et al., March 12, 1962, FI2 (executive), box 215, WHCF; John F. Kenney to Frazar B. Wilde, June 21, 1962, FI5 (executive), box 220, WHCF; memo, Douglas Dillon to John F. Kennedy, August 23, 1962, FI2 (executive), box 215, WHCF, Kennedy Library; Eugene N. White, "Banking and Finance in the Twentieth Century," in *The Cambridge Economic History of the United States*, ed. Stanley L. Engerman and Robert E. Gallman (Cambridge University Press, 2000), 779–780.

13. On generational change and the rise of market fundamentalism among the American business elite, see Kim Phillips-Fein, *Visible Hands: The Making of the Conservative Movement from the New Deal to Reagan* (W. W. Norton, 2009); Edward J. Balleisen, *Fraud: An American History from Barnum to Madoff* (Princeton University Press, 2017), 342–347.

14. Otto C. Lorenz, "26 Charge Account Banks Wind Up '57 with Net Profits," *AB*, February 25, 1958; Thomas P. Hughes, *Networks of Power: Electrification in Western Society, 1880–1930* (Johns Hopkins University Press, 1983), 15.

15. Bord of Governors of the Federal Reserve System, *Forty-Fifth Annual Report of the Board of Governors of the Federal Reserve System* (1958), 126–127, FRASER; Board of Governors of the Federal Reserve System, *Bank Credit-Card and Check-Credit Plans* (Government Printing Office, 1968), 86; Chase Manhattan Bank, *The Chase Manhattan Bank Annual Report, 1958* (ProQuest ID: 88193381), 27; Bank of America, *Bank of America National Trust and Savings Association Annual Report, 1958* (ProQuest ID: 88192321), 16; Chase Manhattan Bank, *The Chase Manhattan Bank Annual Report, 1957* (ProQuest ID: 88192043), 11; Thomas P. Hughes, "The Evolution of Large Technological Systems," *The Social Construction of Technological Systems: New Directions in the Sociology and History of Technology,* ed. Wiebe E. Bijker, Thomas P. Hughes, and Trevor F. Pinch (MIT Press, 1989), 51–82.

16. Wilson, *The Chase,* 57–67, 74–88; Wolters, "'Carry Your Credit in Your Pocket,'" 337–338, 342–345.

17. "Chase Manhattan Plans to Begin Charge Account Banking on Dec. 1," *AB*, October 17, 1958; brochure, Chase Manhattan Bank, "A Brand New Way to Shop without Cash"; brochure, Chase Manhattan Bank, "How Chase Manhattan Bank Charge Plan Benefits Retailers," box 1294, Douglas Papers; Rockefeller, *Creative Management,* 21; ad, Chase Manhattan Bank, "Send Them Back to School *in Style,*" *NYHT,* August 17, 1960, 9; ad, Chase Manhattan Bank, "Busy Mother of 4," *NYT,* September 1, 1959, 18.

18. Chase Manhattan Bank, *The Chase Manhattan Bank Annual Report, 1959* (ProQuest ID: 88191683), 24; Wolters, "'Carry Your Credit in Your Pocket,'" 340–341, 346; Clinton W. Schwer, "Chase Manhattan Observations," *Banking* (November 1959), 101; "Chase Manhattan Bank (National Association)," box 165, FDIC Exam Reports, NARA II. Wolters stresses that the commercial banking background of Chase executives compelled the retailer focus of their program. This seems likely; however, as the previous chapter demonstrated, a retailer focus was the *prevailing* strategy for bank card plans at the time. Wolters, "'Carry Your Credit in Your Pocket,'" 350.

19. Rockefeller, *Creative Management,* 21. Wilson, *The Chase,* 93–94; *The Chase Manhattan Bank Annual Report—1959,* 7; Wolters, "'Carry Your Credit in Your Pocket,'" 347–348; "A Brand New Way to Shop without Cash"; "How Chase Manhattan Bank Charge Plan Benefits Retailers," box 1294, Douglas Papers; "Chase Manhattan Bank (National Association)," box 165, FDIC Exam Reports, NARA II.

20. Wolters, "'Carry Your Credit in Your Pocket,'" 325; *Bank of America Annual Report—1958,* 9–10, 12, 18; "Bank of America National Trust and Savings Association," box 11, FDIC Exam Reports, NARA II.

21. James L. McKenney, *Waves of Change: Business Evolution through Information Technology* (Harvard Business School Press, 1995), 52, 66–67; Wolters, "'Carry Your Credit in Your Pocket,'" 325–332; *Bank of America Annual Report, 1958,* 18. Sterns, *Electronic Value Exchange,* 19–21.

22. Joseph Nocera, *A Piece of the Action: How the Middle Class Joined the Money Class* (Simon & Schuster, 1994), 23–26.

23. The available statistics make this a difficult claim to validate. Charge account advertisements are ambiguous. *American Banker's* statistics give service charge as a percentage of quarterly charge volume. For this to mean anything, you'd have to know what percentage of quarterly volume is subject to the charge, which is not provided. Looking at individual bank brochures (in Douglas Papers, box 1294), the Florida National Bank's F.N.B. Charge Plan charged "one cent per dollar . . . on the remaining unpaid balance," as did the Pan American Bank of Miami. Charge Rite, as of the early 1960s, charged 1.5 percent a month on outstanding balances. The Northwestern Banks NWCP Charge Plan promised to assess "a small additional charge on the unpaid balance," without ever saying how much that charge would be (box 8, Northwest Papers).

24. Charge Account Banking Statistics, *AB*, November 20, 1958 (19 of 33 banks); Wolters, "'Carry Your Credit in Your Pocket,'" 329; D. A. Freeth, "What's Wrong with Midland Charge Plan?," March 1962, NA0339–1619, HSBC Archives.

25. Charles Landrain, "Charge Account Bank Problems Can Be Solved by Study of Other Systems," *AB*, November 20, 1958; Bob Hershon, "Store Credit Men Call Credit Cards 'Added Headaches,'" *WWD*, October 14, 1960. For a similar logic in the rollout of Barclaycard in the UK, see memo, H. E. Darvill et al., to The Local Directors and Branch Managers, Barclays Bank Limited, January 21, 1966, 415/488, Barclaycard, 1966–1989, Barclays Archives.

26. Otto C. Lorenz, "Past Lessons in Charge Account Banking Show Pitfalls Which Must Be Avoided If Full-Scale Operation Is to Succeed," *AB*, November 20, 1958; "Bank America Achieves New Yearly Highs," *LAT*, January 18, 1961; Ronald Roy Horcher, "Charge Account Banking and Check Credit Systems" (master's thesis, Ohio State University, 1960), 23; Nocera, *Piece of the Action*, 27.

27. Nocera, *Piece of the Action*, 27; ad, Bank of America, "Bank of America Announces a Revolutionary New Service," *Fresno Bee*, September 18, 1958. Bank of America's card program was originally called the Bank of America Charge Account Plan.

28. Stanley A. Dashew and Josef S. Klus, *You Can Do It! Inspiration and Lessons from an Inventor, Entrepreneur, and Sailor* (Constellation Press, 2010), 159–174; Nocera, *Piece of the Action*, 28. For the role of federal contractors in Silicon Valley's development, see Bruce Cumings, *Dominion from Sea to Sea: Pacific Ascendency and American Power* (Yale University Press, 2009), 424–470. Thanks to Paris Spies-Gans for pointing me to Dashew's memoir.

29. Wolters, "'Carry Your Credit in Your Pocket,'" 324–333; Bank of America, *Bank of America National Trust and Savings Association Annual Report—1959* (ProQuest ID: 88193355), 19.

30. 'There Ought to Be a Law . . .," *Consumer Reports*, January 1960, 44; Wolters, "'Carry Your Credit in Your Pocket,'" 333–336, 348; Nocera, *Piece of the Action*, 31; Mandell, *Credit Card Industry*, 30; "Charge Account Banking: Getting Started and Building Momentum," *FPRAY* (1958), 296–297; "The Charge-It Plan That Really Took-Off," *Business Week*, February 27, 1965, 58.

31. Wolters, "'Carry Your Credit in Your Pocket,'" 333–335.

32. Wolters, "'Carry Your Credit in Your Pocket,'" 341–342, 350; Rockefeller, *Memoirs*, 168–169; Wilson, *The Chase*, 94–95.

33. "Otto C. Lorenz Dead,'" *AB,* January 26, 1960; Wolters, "'Carry Your Credit in Your Pocket,'" 333–336, 348; Mandell, *Credit Card Industry,* 30.

Chapter 4. Deluge

1. David M. Kennedy, "Required Reading: Credit Cards Provide Meaningful Approach to Banking Procedures," *AB* (n.d., ca. January 1967), folder 4, box 5, Kennedy Papers.
2. Richard R. John, *Network Nation: Inventing American Telecommunications* (Harvard University Press, 2010), 8. For the theory of "system style," see Thomas P. Hughes, *Networks of Power: Electrification in the Western Society, 1880–1930* (Johns Hopkins University Press, 1983). Histories of the card industry miss this connection to earlier interbank networks (David S. Evans and Richard Schmalensee, *Paying with Plastic: The Digital Revolution in Buying and Borrowing* [MIT Press, 2005]; Lewis Mandell, *The Credit Card Industry: A History* [Twayne Publishers, 1990]). For correspondent banking in the U.S, see John A. James and David F. Weiman, "From Drafts to Checks: The Evolution of Correspondent Banking Networks and the Formation of the Modern U.S. Payments System, 1850–1914," *Journal of Money, Credit and Banking* 42, no. 2/3 (2010): 237–65.
3. James J. Groome, "Plastic Credit," *Burroughs Clearing House* (December 1967), 22; "Chicago's Credit Card Crisis," *Business Week,* July 15, 1967, 35; Thomas J. Sugrue, *Sweet Land of Liberty: The Forgotten Struggle for Civil Rights in the North* (Random House, 2009), 414–422; "The Treasury Secretary Discusses Equal Employment Opportunity," *Banking* (October 1970), 52. On racial exclusion in postwar housing and credit markets, see Lizabeth Cohen, *A Consumers' Republic: The Politics of Mass Consumption in Postwar America* (Alfred A. Knopf, 2003), 170–172, 212–227, 355–356; Louis Hyman, *Debtor Nation: The History of America in Red Ink* (Princeton University Press, 2011), 137–145, 173–219; Mehrsa Baradaran, "Jim Crow Credit," *UC Irvine Law Review* 9, no. 4 (2019): 887–952.
4. U.S. Bureau of Economic Analysis, "Gross Domestic Product (GDP)," FRED; James T. Patterson, *Grand Expectations: The United States, 1945–1974* (Oxford University Press, 1996), 450; Lyndon B. Johnson, "Radio and Television Remarks upon Signing the Tax Bill," February 26, 1964, APP; Robert Frost, "Note of Confidence Sounded on Quality of Credit," *NYT,* July 11, 1965, F1; Board of Governors of the Federal Reserve System, "G.19, Consumer Credit, Historical Data," https://www.federalreserve.gov/releases/g19/HIST/default.htm.
5. Glenn Armon, "The Business Front: After the Morning After," *Barron's* (March 23, 1964), 11; Sidney P. Allen, "Credit Card Operation That's Hit the Jackpot," *Burroughs Clearing House* (September 1964), 50–51, 103–104; "The Charge-It Plan That Really Took Off," *Business Week* (February 27, 1965), 58; Harlan Paterson, "What Spells Success for Bank Charge Plans?," *Banking* (February 1964), 53; George A. Nikolaieff, "Bank in the Billfold," *WSJ,* December 1, 1965; "Credit-Card Plan Set in Arizona," *Banking* (June 1965), 73; "Personality: Guiding a Bank into New Fields," *NYT,* September 5 1965; *Burroughs Clearing House* (December 1966), cover.

6. "Banking: At the Crossroads," *Forbes* (June 15, 1968), 22–24; Mark H. Rose, *Market Rules: Bankers, Presidents, and the Origins of the Great Recession* (University of Pennsylvania Press, 2018), 13–38; Hyman Minsky, *Stabilizing an Unstable Economy* (Yale University Press, 1986), 87–91.

7. Mellon National Bank and Trust Company, *Annual Report, 1965*, 10 (ProQuest ID: 88197003); Crocker-Citizens National Bank, *Annual Report, 1966*, 4 (ProQuest ID: 88197219); "Bank Offers Credit Card," *Banking* (April 1966), 110; "Credit Card an 'Explosion' or a 'Business Revolution,'" *Banking* (December 1967), 88; Bernardo Bátiz-Lazo, Thomas Haigh, and David L. Stearns, "How the Future Shaped the Past: The Case of the Cashless Society," *Enterprise & Society* 15, no. 1 (March 1, 2014): 103–131; Wyatt Wells, "Certificates and Computers: The Remaking of Wall Street, 1967 to 1971," *Business History Review* 74, no. 2 (Summer 2000): 193–235; Amy Weaver Fisher and James L. McKenney, "The Development of the ERMA Banking System: Lessons from History," *IEEE Annals of the History of Computing* 15, no. 1 (1993): 44–57; James L. McKenney, *Waves of Change: Business Evolution through Information Technology* (Harvard Business School Press, 1995), 66–67; "Banking: At the Crossroads."

8. Armon, "After the Morning After"; Richard Rutter, "Personal Finance: The Era of the Credit Card," *NYT*, February 8, 1965; Alfred Bloomingdale, "Readers Say: Credit Cards," *Forbes* (October 15, 1966), 10.

9. Ad, Bank of America, "Important Message for California Shoppers," *LAT*, October 13, 1959; ad, Bank of America, "Your Wallet's Never Empty . . . When You Carry a BankAmericard!," *LAT*, August 24, 1959; ad, Bank of America, "Popping Up All Over Town," *LAT*, March 22, 1960; "Boundary-Jumping—Electronic-Style," *Forbes* (September 15, 1966), 39–40. On market segmentation by gender, see Cohen, *Consumers' Republic*, 312–315; Lana Swartz, "Gendered Transactions: Identity and Payment at Midcentury," *Women's Studies Quarterly* 42, no. ½ (2014): 137–53.

10. "Hilton Credit Cites Overseas Expansion," *NYT*, August 25, 1965; "New York Bank, Hilton Hotels Unit Set Merge Plan," *WSJ*, September 22, 1965; Brett Christophers, *Banking across Boundaries: Placing Finance in Capitalism* (John Wiley & Sons, 2013), 161–169; Harold van B. Cleveland and Thomas F. Huertas, *Citibank, 1812–1970* (Harvard University Press, 1985), 253–254, 260–268, 272–275, 277–297, 324–345; H. Erich Heinemann, "Diners' Club Stock Would Cost Chase $56.5 Million Cash," *NYT*, November 18, 1965; "Hilton Seeks to Sell 50% of Carte Blanche to New York City Bank," *WSJ*, August 25, 1965.

11. Heinemann, "Diners' Club Stock Would Cost Chase $56.5 Million Cash"; Richard Phalon, "City Bank Weighs Credit-Card Move," *NYT*, August 24, 1965; memo, Board of Directors, "UNI-SERV CORPORATION," April 6, 1965, box 2, series 2, Reed Papers; "Chase Drops Bid for Diners' Club," *NYT*, April 13, 1965; "Court Bars Sale of Carte Blanche," *NYT*, December 31, 1965; "Carte Blanche Sale to Bank Hit by U.S. Suit," *LAT*, December 31, 1965; "Saxon Puzzled by Suit to Bar Credit Card Deal," *WP*, January 2, 1966; "Chase Bank, Diners' Club End Merger Plan after Justice Unit Threatens Trust Suit," *WSJ*, April 13, 1966.

12. Federal Deposit Insurance Corporation, *Annual Report* (1966), xi.

13. Otto C. Lorenz, "Charge Account Banking Show Pitfalls Which Must Be Avoided If Full-Scale Operation Is to Succeed," *AB*, November 20, 1958; McKenney, *Waves of Change*, 67; Oral History, Alan H. Duncan, August 11, 1998, ref: 725/3, Barclays Archives; Kenneth V. Larkin, "Launching a National Card," *Pacific Banker & Business* (October 1966), 24; Paul Chutkow, *VISA: The Power of an Idea* (Harcourt, 2001), 69–70. Chutkow refers to a March 25, 1966, memo from Larkin to bank management as the origin of the expansion program. My account of the importance of software marketing to the later development of the BankAmericard network is inferred from the Barclays and Midland archives (HSBC Archives).

14. David L. Stearns, *Electronic Value Exchange: Origins of the VISA Electronic Payment System* (Springer, 2011), 27; Thomas W. Bush, "B of A Opens Its Credit Card Plan to Rival Banks," *LAT*, May 25, 1966; Larkin, "Launching a National Card"; Dee W. Hock, *One from Many: VISA and the Rise of the Chaordic Organization* (Berrett-Koehler, 2005), 60–61; Chutkow, *VISA*, 69.

15. "Bank Credit Card Expansion," *Bankers Monthly* (July 1966), 44; "Bank of America Plans Nationwide Licensing of Its Credit Cards," *WSJ*, May 25, 1966; Bush, "B of A Opens Its Credit Card Plan to Rival Banks"; "The Charge-It Plan that Really Took Off"; "Enlarging the Charge Card," *Business Week* (May 28, 1966), 42; "Boundary-Jumping—Electronic Style," *Forbes* (September 15, 1966), 39; Patrick E. Doyle, "Small Bank Opportunities in Charge Card Banking," *Bankers Monthly* (June 15, 1969), 29–34. Larkin, "Launching a National Card." Bank of America also recruited banks with large branch networks when it expanded the BankAmericard globally (Bernardo Bátiz-Lazo and Gustavo A. Del Angel, "The Ascent of Plastic Money: International Adoption of the Bank Credit Card, 1950–1975," *Business History Review* 92, no. 3 [Autumn 2018]: 509–33).

16. Mandell, *The Credit Card Industry*, 31; Sterns, *Electronic Value Exchange*, 27, 35–37; Arnold H. Lozowick, "Compatible Bank Credit Cards (Part I)," *Bankers Monthly* (June 15, 1967), 29.

17. Chutkow, *VISA*, 70.

18. Karl Hinke Oral History, July 29, 1981, in Frank H. H. King and Christopher Cook, *The Hongkong and Shanghai Banking Corporation Investment in Marine Midland Banks, Incorporated*, part 1, vol. 2, 457.

19. Martin B. Hickman, *David Matthew Kennedy: Banker, Statesman, Churchman* (Deseret Book, 1987), 92–102, 109–137, 129.

20. Hickman, *David Matthew Kennedy*, 138–140, 158–177, 183–185, 188–192, 211–214; Austin C. Wehrwein, "Personality: The Head of a Big-Little Bank," *NYT*, January 16, 1966; Alison Isenberg, *Downtown America: A History of the Place and the People Who Made It* (University of Chicago Press, 2004), 166–175, 188–192, 199–202, 207–229; Sugrue, *Sweet Land of Liberty*, 414–422; "The Treasury Secretary Discusses Equal Employment Opportunity"; Kennedy, "Required Reading."

21. Elrick and Lavidge, Inc., "Bank Charge Cards (Exploratory Research): Report for Continental Illinois National Bank and Trust Company of Chicago," 1966, box 29, David Kennedy Papers; "Bank Offers Credit Card."

22. Elrick and Lavidge, "Bank Charge Cards"; Hyman, *Debtor Nation*, 174–180.

23. Elrick and Lavidge, "Bank Charge Cards." For assumption of whiteness, see Josh Lauer, *Creditworthy: A History of Consumer Surveillance and Financial Identity in*

America (Columbia University Press, 2017), 67, 141–142, 236; S. Roxanne Hiltz, "Black and White in the Consumer Financial System," *American Journal of Sociology* 76, no. 6 (May 1971): 987–998. We lack demographic data on card distribution, but at least some Black Chicagoans received cards ("Inquiring Photographer," *Chicago Daily Defender,* December 13, 1966). A 1968 examination of Continental's plan did not use race as a category of analysis (Thomas X. Gatlin, *The Demographic Analysis of the Town and Country Bank Charge Card* [master's thesis, Northern Illinois University, 1968].)

24. "Banks Study Credit Cards," *CT,* June 24, 1966; "Four Biggest Illinois Banks Plan to Issue Credit Card," *WSJ,* June 24, 1966; "Credit Card Program Set by 10 Banks," *CT,* August 13, 1966; Kenneth Ross, "Explain Why Banks Take to Credit Cards," *CT,* October 16, 1966; Kenneth Ross, "Banks Report Credit Cards in High Gear," *CT,* October 25, 1966; Groome, "Plastic Credit," 22; Lozowick, "Compatible Bank Credit Cards (Part I)," 28–29, 32, 40; Harold S. Taylor, "The Chicago Bank Credit Card Fiasco," *Bankers Magazine* 151, no. 1 (Winter 1968): 49–52. Weit v. Continental Illinois Nat. Bank Trust Co., 467 F. Supp. 197 (N.D. Ill. 1978).

25. Kenneth Ross, "Bank Credit Cards Make Hasty but All-Out Debut," *CT,* January 9, 1967; Kennedy, "Required Reading"; "Banks Study Credit Cards"; Weit v. Continental Illinois Nat. Bank Trust Co., 467 F. Supp. 197, 200–224.

26. "Four Major Banks to Weigh Universal Credit Card Plan," *LAT,* May 24, 1966; "Four California Banks Form Credit-Card Plan Set for Mid-1967 Start," *WSJ,* October 24, 1966; Garrison A. Southard Jr., "California Master Charge Plan," *Bankers Monthly* (February 15, 1968), 40–42, 50, 53; "Explain New St. Louis Credit Card," *Northwestern Banker* (December 4, 1967), 1; Stephen P. Coha, "Credit Card Pace Accelerates," *Bankers Monthly* (October 15, 1968), 21–22, 24, 27.

27. Hinke Oral History, 455; Minutes of the Board of Directors, Marine Midland Corporation, December 3, 1958, NA0339/1834; "Remarks of Baldwin Maull, President, and Karl Hinke, Executive Vice President, Marine Midland Corporation before the St. Louis Society of Financial Analysts," February 26, 1963, NA0339/1620; Gerald C. Fischer, "Wall to Wall Banks: The Marine Midland Story," ch. 10, 11–13, HSBC Archives.

28. Bush, "B of A Opens Its Credit Card Plan to Rival Banks"; Hinke Oral History, 455; Minutes, Bankers Trust Board of Directors, November 19, 1968, box 4, series 2, Reed Papers; "BankAmericard to Be Used Here," *NYT,* November 4, 1968. Midland executives' fears were realized when Bankers Trust secured a BankAmericard license in November 1968.

29. Hinke Oral History, 455–456.

30. Donald Moffitt, "Credit-Card Competition," *WSJ,* May 24, 1966; Hinke Oral History, 454–459; Marine Midland Board Minutes, October 19, 1966, NA0339/1718, HSBC Archives.

31. Hinke Oral History, 457; Edward E. Bontems, "The Story of Interbank," *Bankers Monthly* (July 15, 1968), 39; "Midwest Card Joins Interbank," *Northwestern Banker* (January 1969), 14.

32. Hinke Oral History, 457–458; Bontems, "Story of Interbank"; Groome, "Plastic Credit," 21–22; ad, Interbank, *Bankers Monthly* (June 15, 1968), 9.

33. Board of Governors of the Federal Reserve System, *Bank Credit-Card and Check-Credit Plans* (Government Printing Office, 1968), 86; Andrew F. Brimmer, "Statement to Congress," *Federal Reserve Bulletin* (June 1970), 500; Board of Governors of the Federal Reserve System, *Annual Report of the Board of Governors of the Federal Reserve System* (1970), 238; "Half of All Banks Have BAC or Master Charge," *Banking* (April 1970), 126; N. E. Magnis Jr. and T. C. Franklin Jr., "The Newest Venture in Charge Card Banking," *Banking* (January 1970), 39–40; Thomas L. Bailey, "The Unique Role of the Bank Card Association," *Banking* (October 1970), 34–35; Andrew Brimmer, "New Horizons in Credit Card Banking: Remarks before the Seattle Clearing House Association at the Rainier Club, Seattle, Washington," September 23, 1969, Statements and Speeches of Andrew F. Brimmer, FRASER.

34. Coha, "Credit Card Pace Accelerates"; Moffitt, "Credit-Card Competition"; Groome, "Plastic Credit," 21; "Focusing on the Credit Card Conference," *Banking* (January 1968), 78.

35. Sugrue, *Sweet Land of Liberty,* 414–422; Elrick and Lavidge, "Bank Charge Cards"; Taylor, "Chicago Bank Credit Card Fiasco," 51; Kennedy, "Required Reading."

36. Taylor, "Chicago Bank Credit Card Fiasco," 50–52; Ross, "Banks Report Credit Cards in High Gear"; Ross, "Bank Credit Cards Make Hasty but All-Out Debut"; Joanne Knoch, "Banks Tell First Year of Credit Cards-Hectic," *CT,* September 24, 1967.

37. Taylor, "Chicago Bank Credit Card Fiasco"; Illinois Legislative Investigating Commission, "The 'Todd' Story," *Credit Card Fraud in Illinois* (September 1972), 55–60.

38. Letter quoted in Kennedy, "Required Reading"; *The Doctrine and Covenants of the Jesus Christ of Latter-day Saints,* 19:35; Hickman, *David Matthew Kennedy,* 190.

39. Kennedy, "Required Reading" (emphasis added); Taylor, "Chicago Bank Credit Card Fiasco"; Knoch, "Banks Tell First Year of Credit Cards-Hectic"; *Unsolicited Bank Credit Cards,* 90 Cong. 12–14 (1967) (statement of Andrew Brimmer, Member, Board of Governors, Federal Reserve System).

40. Continental Illinois Bank, *Annual Reports,* 1962–1972, esp. *Mid-Year Report to Shareholders,* June 30, 1967 (ProQuest ID: 88199101); Joanne Knoch, "Banks Confident Pain of Credit Cards Past," *CT,* September 25, 1967; Kennedy, "Required Reading"; Taylor, "Chicago Bank Credit Card Fiasco"; David D. Jordan, "Curbs of Credit Cards Issued by Banks Being Sought by Patman in House Bill," *WSJ,* August 28, 1967; Federal Reserve, *Bank Credit-Card and Check-Credit Plans,* 73.

41. "Bank Credit Card Report," *Bankers Monthly* (December 15, 1967), 30; *Unsolicited Bank Credit Cards,* 90 Cong. 14 (statement of Andrew Brimmer).

42. "Bank Credit Card Report"; William Clark, "Bank Credit Cards May Pose Problems," *CT,* October 26, 1966; John Kirk and Theodore Fischer, "Credit Card Survey Ready," *Banking* (September 1967), 98; John L. Gibson, "Word of Caution: Keep an Eye on Costs," *Bankers Monthly* (August 15, 1967), 23; Robert W. Pullen, "Bank Credit Card and Related Plans," *New England Business Review,* December 1966, 2; Paul O'Neil, "A Little Gift from Your Friendly Banker," *Life* (March 27, 1970), quoted in Joseph Nocera, *A Piece of the Action: How the Middle Class Joined the Money Class* (Simon & Schuster, 1994), 59; Groome, "Plastic Credit." Reliable data show that mid-sized banks often mailed 100,000 cards at a time, with larger banks sending upwards of 1 million. By the end of 1970 more than 1,000 banks issued

cards, and other card issuers like retailers and oil companies likewise engaged in mass, unsolicited mailing.

43. Robert E. Nichols, "B of A's Peterson Cautions Banks on 'Credit-Card Race,'" *LAT*, March 17, 1967; Clark, "Bank Credit Cards May Pose Problems"; "The Bank Credit Card," *Banking* (May 1967), 100; *Bank Credit-Card and Check-Credit Plans*, 90 Cong. 24 (1968) (statement of Thomas L. Bailey, Vice President, Marine Midland Banks, Inc.); William Howard Jr., "Bank Consumer Credit: Present and Future," *Bankers Monthly* (August 15, 1967), 21.

44. O'Neil, "Little Gift from Your Friendly Banker."

45. Groome, "Plastic Credit," 22; Elenor Gould Murphy and United States Bureau of Labor Statistics, *Economic Forces in the United States: In Facts and Figures: Its People, Its Labor Force, Its Economy*, Bulletin of the United States Bureau of Labor Statistics, No. 1384 (Government Printing Office, September 1963), FRASER, 53; Sylvia S. Small and United States Bureau of Labor Statistics, *Black Americans: A Chartbook*, Bulletin of the United States Bureau of Labor Statistics, No. 1699 (Government Printing Office, 1971), FRASER, 37–51.

46. Walter R. Miller Jr., "Challenge of Change in Consumer Credit," *Bankers Monthly* (June 15, 1968), 19.

Chapter 5. Regulating Revolving Credit

1. State of Washington, *1967 Session Laws of the State of Washington* (reg. sess., 40 leg.) vol. 1, ch. 234, 1130–1147; State of Washington, Attorney General, "Banks and Banking—Sale—Regulation of Bank Credit Card Transactions," *Attorney General Opinions 1968* No. 6; Daryl Lembke, "Washington State Adopts Limitation," *LAT*, November 8, 1969.

2. Meg Jacobs, *Pocketbook Politics: Economic Citizenship in Twentieth-Century America* (Princeton University Press, 2007), 252; Scholars have documented federal-level efforts to secure *credit access* but have neglected contemporaneous state-level contests to secure low *credit prices* (Louis Hyman, *Debtor Nation: A History of America in Red Ink* (Princeton University Press, 2011), 173–219; Lizabeth Cohen, *A Consumers' Republic: The Politics of Mass Consumption in Postwar America* (Alfred A. Knopf, 2003), 370–386; Felicia Ann Kornbluh, *The Battle for Welfare Rights: Politics and Poverty in Modern America* (University of Pennsylvania Press, 2007), 114–131.

3. William Warren, "The Case for Re-Examination of Consumer Credit Laws," September 23, 1964, box 50, Braucher Papers; Robert L. Jordan and William D. Warren, "The Uniform Consumer Credit Code," *Columbia Law Review* 68, no. 3 (1968): 392. Gunnar Trumbull, *Consumer Lending in France and America: Credit and Welfare* (Cambridge University Press, 2014), 152–158, 181–182. For a recent critique of the information model of consumer protection, see Oren Bar-Gill and Elizabeth Warren, "Making Credit Safer," *University of Pennsylvania Law Review* 157, no. 1 (2008): 1–102.

4. Hyman, *Debtor Nation*, 137–145, 173–219; Mehrsa Baradaran, "Jim Crow Credit," *UC Irvine Law Review* 9, no. 4 (2019): 887–952; Walter D. Malcolm, "The Uniform Consumer Credit Code," *Business Lawyer* 25, no. 3 (1970): 945.

5. Board of Governors of the Federal Reserve System, *Consumer Instalment Credit* (Government Printing Office, 1957); Robert Collins, *More: The Politics of Economic Growth in Postwar America* (Oxford University Press, 2000), 45; David Caplovitz, *The Poor Pay More: Consumer Practices of Low-Income Families* (Free Press of Glencoe, 1963); Hillel Black, *Buy Now, Pay Later* (William Morrow, 1961).

6. Edward L. Rubin, "Legislative Methodology: Some Lessons from the Truth-in-Lending Act," *Georgetown Law Journal* 80, no. 2 (December 1991): 233–308; Paul H. Douglas, *In the Fullness of Time: The Memoirs of Paul H. Douglas* (Harcourt Brace Jovanovich, 1972), 64–65, 350, 372, 530; Ken McLean, Oral History, September 11, 2009, 33, William Proxmire Collection, Wisconsin Archives, http://content.wisconsinhistory.org/cdm/ref/collection/proxmire/id/1930; Paul H. Douglas to Morton I. Goldman, March 21, 1960, Banking and Currency Committee, box 249; speech, Douglas before the National League of Insured Savings Associations, May 10, 1960, Douglas Statements 1960, box 1297; Douglas to Winnie Christmas, August 9, 1961, Douglas Correspondence 1961, box 1299, Douglas Papers. Disclosure, a regulatory approach for requiring consistent and reliable information, was a regulatory strategy New Dealers used to made markets, like those for investment securities, function more effectively, and which was widely used in consumer-oriented regulatory policy in the 1960s and 1970s.

7. Douglas, *Fullness of Time*, 525–531. Rubin, "Legislative Methodology," 243.

8. Cohen, *Consumers' Republic*, 347–355; Paul H. Douglas to Theodore Sorensen, December 6, 1962, LE/FI 8–LE/FI 10, box 475, WHCF, Kennedy Library; John F. Kennedy, "Special Message to the Congress on Protecting the Consumer Interest," March 15, 1962, APP; Lyndon Johnson, "Special Message to the Congress on Consumer Interests," February 5, 1964, APP.

9. Martha Derthick, "Crossing Thresholds: Federalism in the 1960s," in *Keeping the Compound Republic: Essays on American Federalism,* ed. Martha Derthick (Brookings Institution, 2001), 138–152.

10. Barbara A. Curran, "Legislative Controls as a Response to Consumer-Credit Problems," *Boston College Industrial and Commercial Law Review* 8, no. 3 (Spring 1967): 409; Barbara A. Curran, *Trends in Consumer Credit Legislation* (University of Chicago Press, 1965).

11. For a $100 loan, at 6 percent annual interest, spread over twelve equal monthly installments, the consumer would pay a total of $3.28 in interest, because over time they would pay down the principal, applying the 6% charge to a dwindling principal balance.

12. Curran, "Legislative Controls," 410; *Truth in Lending Bill,* 87 Cong. 2–3 (statement of Sen. Paul H. Douglas).

13. *Consumer Credit Labeling Bill,* 86 Cong. 1–2 (statement of Sen. Paul H. Douglas); *Truth in Lending—1967,* 90 Cong. 1 (statement of Sen. William Proxmire).

14. A. Willis Robertson to Paul H. Douglas, December 12, 1961, Douglas Correspondence 1961, box 1299; Robertson to Douglas, March 17, 1964, Douglas Correspondence 1964, box 1307, Douglas Papers; "Truth-in-Lending Drive Is Urged by Proxmire," *WP,* December 30, 1966.

15. "'Truth-in-Lending' Bill's Chances Improve with New Senate Banking Panel Makeup," *WSJ*, January 13, 1967; memo, Harry H. Wilson Jr, to Lyndon Johnson, June 14, 1966; memo, Joseph W. Barr to Califano, Sanders, and Obrien, October 25, 1967; Joe Califano to Lyndon Johnson, August 15, 1967, LE/FI 5, box 49, WHCF, Johnson Library.

16. *Truth in Lending—1967*, 90 Cong. 274 (statement of Bronson C. La Follette, Attorney General, State of Wisconsin); Hyman, *Debtor Nation*, 148; Mary Elizabeth Curry, *Creating an American Institution: The Merchandising Genius of J. C. Penney* (Garland Publishing, 1993), 306, 312; J. C. Penney Company, Inc., *J. C. Penney Company, Incorporated Annual Report—1968*, 14 (ProQuest ID: 88200657); Sears, Roebuck and Co., *Sears, Roebuck and Company Annual Report—1968*, 16, 19 (ProQuest ID: 88199402).

17. Curran, *Trends in Consumer Credit*, 102; Hogg v. Ruffner, 66 U.S. (1 Black) 115, 118–119 (1861).

18. *Consumer Credit Protection Act*, 90 Cong. 682–683, 749–751, and 803; Sarah Newman to Susanne Zwemer, June 14, 1967, NJCL Papers; memo, Barefoot Sanders to Lyndon B. Johnson, January 25, 1968; memo, Sanders to Johnson, January 26, 1968; memo, Sanders to Johnson, January 30, 1968; memo, Sanders to Johnson, February 1, 1968; memo, Joseph Barr to Johnson, February 7, 1968, LE/FI 5, box 50, WHCF, Johnson Library; Douglas, *In the Fullness of Time*, 535.

19. Memo, Joe Califano to Lyndon Johnson, August 15, 1967, LE/FI 5, box 49; memo, Jack T. Conway to Walter P. Ruether, February 20, 1968, LE/FI 5, box 50, WHCF, Johnson Library; *Consumer Credit and the Poor*, 90 Cong. 1 (1968) (statement of Sen. William Proxmire). For Proxmire's views on usury regulations, see William Proxmire, in *Consumer Credit in the United States: Report of the National Commission on Consumer Finance* (Government Printing Office, December 1972), 221.

20. Frank E. Moss to Paul H. Douglass, April 26, 1960, Douglas Correspondence 1960, box 1295, Douglas Papers; "Consumer Credit Protection Act," PL 90–321 § 123; William Rehnquist, "Foreword," in Walter Armstrong, *A Century of Service: A Centennial History of the National Conference of Commissioners on Uniform State Laws* (West Publishing, 1991), 1; *Consumer Credit Labeling Bill*, 6.

21. Lawrence Bugge, "Preface," in Armstrong, *Century of Service*, 3; Allison Dunham, "A Project for a Uniform Law on Consumer Credit," January 10, 1964 (though I think that may be 1965), box 50, Braucher Papers.

22. National Conference of Commissioners on Uniform State Laws, *Uniform Consumer Credit Code: Official Text with Comments* (West Publishing, 1968), xix.

23. Federated Department Stores, Inc., "Comments on First Tentative Draft: Uniform Consumer Credit Code," September 19, 1966, box 48; memo, J. C. Penney and Co., "Draft No. 6 of the Uniform Consumer Credit Code," January 1968, box 34; memo, John Rolph, III, "The American Bankers Association to National Conference of Commissioners on Uniform State Laws, Special Committee on Retail Instalment Sales, Consumer Credit, Small Loans and Usury," September 16, 1966, box 48, Braucher Papers.

24. Marion Benfield, "Money, Mortgages, and Migraine—The Usury Headache," *Case Western Reserve Law Review* 19, no. 4 (June 1968): 819; William Warren, "The Case for Re-Examination of Consumer Credit Laws," September 23, 1964, box 50;

Walter D. Malcolm to William Wemple, August 17, 1968, box 33; Walter Malcolm, "Malcolm Comments on Warren-Jordan Preliminary Draft of September 25, 1965—Coverage, Disclosure and Other Provisions," box 36, Braucher Papers.

25. National Conference of Commissioners on Uniform State Laws, *Uniform Consumer Credit Code*, 33–39, 45–46; memo, Leslie Dix to Special Committee on Retail Instalment Sales, Consumer Credit, Small Loans and Usury of the National Conference of Commissioners on Uniform State Laws, January 11, 1968, box 34; Walter Malcolm to William Wemple, August 27, 1968, box 33; City of New York Mayor's Council on Consumer Affairs, "Statement to be presented at a public hearing of The National Conference of Commissioners on Uniform State Laws, in Chicago on January 18, 1968," box 34, Braucher Papers.

26. *Consumer Credit Regulation (Proposed Uniform Consumer Credit Code)*, 91 Cong. 106, 177 (statements of William Pierce, President, National Conference of Commissioners on Uniform State Laws, and Robert W. Johnson, reporter-economist of the Uniform Consumer Credit Code); Kornbluh, *Battle for Welfare Rights*, 114–131; Keeanga-Yamahtta Taylor, *Race for Profit: How Banks and the Real Estate Industry Undermined Black Homeownership* (University of North Carolina Press, 2019), 5–6.

27. Memo, Fred Willman to All Democratic State Representatives, April 19, 1972, "Doyle—WCA General" folder, box 2, Consumer Credit Division: Litigations and Investigations Part 4 (2002/089), Wisconsin Archives.

28. Walter Malcolm, "The New Maximum Charges," April 1, 1969, box 46, Braucher Papers; *Consumer Credit Regulations (Proposed Uniform Consumer Credit Code)*, 142 and 147; "Statement of Paul H. Douglas Before the Legislature of the Commonwealth of Massachusetts on the Uniform Consumer Credit Code," January 29, 1969; memo, Alfred Buerger to Members and Ex-Officio Members, June 19, 1969, box 33, Braucher Papers.

29. "Statement by the AFL-CIO Executive Council on the Uniform Consumer Credit Code," February 17, 1969, Committee on Consumer Credit, 1968–1970, box 2, House of Representatives: Committee Records (RG 76-80), Archives of Michigan; "A Consumer Credit Code . . . *for Lenders*," *Consumer Reports* (March 1969), 121–126; "A Code to Legalize Usury," *WP*, February 10, 1969; *Consumer Credit Regulations (Proposed Uniform Consumer Credit Code)*, 5, 17, and 143; Sidney Margolius, "Labor Led Voters to Clamp Lid on Washington Credit Charges," *AFL-CIO News*, December 7, 1968; John Oravec, "Convention Urges Action: Consumers' Need Termed 'Pressing,'" *AFL-CIO News*, October 11, 1969.

30. Alfred Buerger to Members and Ex-Officio Members, June 19, 1969, box 33; memo, Nathaniel Butler to U3C Special Committee, September 1969, box 47; memo, Allison Dunham to Consumer Credit Committee, October 23, 1968, box 33; Robert Braucher to Robert J. Klein, April 28, 1969, box 33, Braucher Papers; "Consumer Code: Another View," *WP*, March 2, 1969.

31. Memo, Nathaniel Butler to U3C Special Committee, September 1969, box 47; Walter Malcolm to Albert Jenner Jr., December 31, 1969, box 47, Braucher Papers.

32. State officials, in this sense, acted as bureaucratic entrepreneurs (Daniel P. Carpenter, *The Forging of Bureaucratic Autonomy: Reputations, Networks, and Policy Innovation in Executive Agencies, 1862–1928* [Princeton University Press, 2001]).

33. John Doyle, "Charges for Revolving Credit and Charge Accounts, Subject for Scrutiny, Wisconsin Supervisor Suggests," *Personal Finance Law Quarterly Report* 12 no. 2 (Spring 1958): 65–68; John Doyle, "Conference with Assistant Attorney General Roy Tulane," April 8, 1958; Bronson La Follette to William Nuesse, December 31, 1965; John Doyle, "Revolving Charge Account Plans Held Usurious in Wisconsin," (n.d., ca. October 1970), Consumer Credit Division: Litigations and Investigations Part 1 (1998/151), box 3, Wisconsin Archives.

34. Minutes, "Conference on Revolving Credit and Charge Account Plans," April 3, 1968, Consumer Credit Division: Litigations and Investigations Part 1 (1998/151), box 3, Wisconsin Archives.

35. Bronson La Follette to William Nuesse, December 8, 1967, Consumer Credit Division: Litigations and Investigations Part 1 (1998/151), box 3, Wisconsin Archives; "Revolving Credit," *Northwestern University Law Review* 55, no. 3 (July–August 1961): 335; State v. J. C. Penney Co., 48 Wis. 2d 125, 179 N.W.2d 641 (1970).

36. John Boyle to Joseph Riley, April 25, 1969, box 14, NJCL Papers; "Wisconsin Supreme Court Service Charge Decision against J. C. Penney Starts Chain Reaction," *Personal Finance Law Quarterly* 25, no. 1 (Winter 1970): 26–27; Rollinger v. J. C. Penney Co., 86 S.D. 154, 157, 192 N.W.2d 699 (1971), overruled by Smith v. Tobin, 311 N.W.2d 209 (S.D. 1981); Sliger v. R. H. Macy & Co., 59 N.J. 465, 283 A.2d 904 (1971); Maine Merchants Ass'n, Inc. v. Campbell, 287 A.2d 430 (Me. 1972); Johnson v. Sears Roebuck & Co., 14 Ill. App. 3d 838, 303 N.E.2d 627 (1973); Sidney Margolius, "Major Gains Noted in Battle to Ease Credit Charge Rates," *AFL-CIO News*, April 24, 1971; "Alabama Labor Sues Banks for Credit Gouge," *AFL-CIO News*, August 21, 1971.

37. Membership roster, Advisory Committee on the Uniform Consumer Credit Code, box 38; Minutes, Wisconsin Legislative Council Uniform Consumer Credit Code Advisory Committee, April 19, 1971 and June 21, 1971; Lawrence Kenney to Arlene Miller, October 16, 1970; Lawrence Kenney to Ken Clark, June 25, 1971; Minutes, Wisconsin Legislative Council Uniform Consumer Credit Code Advisory Committee, April 19, 1971, and May 17, 1971; Jack B. Reihl to Lawrence Kenney, January 23, 1974, box 38, Wisconsin State AFL-CIO Records, Wisconsin Archives; Eugene Harrington, "Compromise Bill on Credit Ready," *Milwaukee Journal*, February 13, 1972; State of Wisconsin, *Wisconsin Session Laws 1971*, ch. 239 § 422.201, 689–691.

38. Memo, Fred Willman to All Democratic State Representatives, April 19, 1972; "W.I.B.A.: Our Role in 1057A," n.d.; "WCA—Banks," box 2, Consumer Credit Division: Litigations and Investigations Part 4 (2002/089), Wisconsin Archives.

39. State of Minnesota, Senate, Report Committee on Commerce Subcommittee on Consumer Credit and Banking, Interim Activities and Recommendations, December 11, 1968; Alfred Burger to Harold Reed Jr., September 13, 1968; Minutes, Meeting of Subcommittee on Consumer Credit and Banking of the Senate Committee on Commerce, October 23, 1968, and November 14, 1968; Robert Braucher to Walter Malcolm, November 7, 1968, box 39, Braucher Papers; "Minutes, Banking Subcommittee of the Senate Commerce Committee," March 5, 1970, MBS Records; Jim Fuller, "Interest Ceiling Cools Banks to Credit Cards," *Minneapolis Tribune*, August 10, 1969.

40. Robert Sullivan to Alfred Buerger, May 13, 1969, box 39; James Bush to Robert Braucher, September 26, 1969; James M. Bush to Robert Braucher, September 12, 1969; Statement of Arizona AFL-CIO to Arizona Interim Legislative Study Committee on UCCC and Creditors Rights, September 11, 1969, box 38, Braucher Papers; Kimberly Graber, "Arizona Usury Laws," *Arizona State Law Journal* 1981, no. 1 (1981): 132.

41. John L. C. Black, "State Variations of the Uniform Consumer Credit Code: The Case for Legislative Restraint," *Denver Law Journal* 48, no. 2 (1972): 244; memo, Jim Starr to Members on the Special Committee to Study the Uniform Consumer Credit Code," April 16, 1969, Committee on Consumer Credit, 1968–1970, box 2, House of Representatives: Committee Records (RG 76-80), Archives of Michigan.

42. William D. Warren, "Consumer Credit Law: Rates, Costs, and Benefits," *Stanford Law Review* 27, no. 3 (February 1975): 966. By 1980, twenty-three states permitted a flat 18 percent rate on revolving credit, and another thirteen states allowed 18 percent on a portion of the balance and a lower amount thereafter. Seven allowed more than 18 percent, and seven capped rates below 18 percent (Visa USA Inc., "Credit Controls and Bank Cards," March 1980, 794.01 (L) Voluntary Credit Restraint March 1980, FRBNY Archives).

43. Memo, Fred Willman to All Democratic State Representatives, April 19, 1972, "Doyle—WCA General" folder, box 2, Consumer Credit Division: Litigations and Investigations Part 4 (2002/089), Wisconsin Archives. For predatory inclusion, see Taylor, *Race for Profit*.

Chapter 6. Confronting Cards in Congress

1. Richard Halloran, "Rep. Don Quixote," *WP*, June 22, 1969; Rep. Wright Patman, "Chairman Patman Suggests Moratorium on Bank Credit Cards—'A Dangerously Unsound Banking Practice'—Questions Legality," 113 *Cong. Rec.* 21545–21546 (1967); memo, Lee Morse to Chairman Patman, February 15, 1968, "Banks and Credit Cards" folder, box 611, Patman Papers.

2. Hyman Minsky, *Stabilizing an Unstable Economy* (Yale University Press, 1986), 87–91; L. Randall Wray, "The 1966 Financial Crisis: Financial Instability or Political Economy?," *Review of Political Economy* 11, no. 4 (1999): 415–425.

3. Greta R. Krippner, *Capitalizing on Crisis: The Political Origins of the Rise of Finance* (Harvard University Press, 2011), 59–73.

4. Proxmire's concerns for expanding credit access and fostering financial innovation were a necessary precursor for his mobilization of these arguments in support of market liberalization in the late 1970s (Krippner, *Capitalizing on Crisis*).

5. *The Plastic Jungle*, 91 Cong. 107 (1969) (statement of Rep. Arnold Olsen). For the emergence of consumer politics, see Lizabeth Cohen, *A Consumers' Republic: The Politics of Mass Consumption in Postwar America* (Alfred A. Knopf, 2003), 345–397.

6. Joseph S. Clark Jr. to Paul H. Douglas, June 15, 1957, box 248, Douglas Papers; Commission on Money and Credit, *Money and Credit: Their Influence on Jobs, Prices,*

and Growth (Prentice-Hall, 1961), 160; John F. Kennedy, "Remarks to the Members of the Commission on Money and Credit," June 19, 1961, APP.

7. Minsky, *Stabilizing an Unstable Economy*, 87–91; Albert M. Wojnilower, Benjamin M. Friedman and Franco Modigliani, "The Central Role of Credit Crunches in Recent Financial History," *Brookings Papers on Economic Activity* 1980, no. 2 (1980): 277–339, esp. 287.

8. Ernest Bloch, "Two Decades of Evolution of Financial Institutions and Public Policy," *Journal of Money, Credit and Banking* 3, no. 2 (1971): 555–570; Krippner, *Capitalizing on Crisis*, 67–71.

9. H. Erich Heinemann, "Credit Cards," *NYT*, August 1, 1967; *Consumer Credit Protection Act*, part 1, 90 Cong. 118 (1967) (statements of Betty Furness, Special Assistant to the President for Consumer Affairs, and Rep. William B. Windall); "U.S. Business: Midwest Banks Find Credit Cards Pose Problems," *NYT*, August 6, 1967; David D. Jordan, "Curbs on Credit Cards Issued by Banks Being Sought by Patman in House Bill," *WSJ*, August 29, 1967; "What the Banks Have to Sell," *WSJ*, September 8, 1967.

10. Morse to Patman, February 15, 1968, Patman Papers; *Unsolicited Bank Credit Cards*, 90 Cong. 1–4, 25–26 (1967) (statement of Rep. Wright Patman).

11. *Unsolicited Bank Credit Cards*, 4, 6–7, 26–27 (statements of Furness and Rep. Florence P. Dwyer).

12. C. R. Stevens to Betty Furness, October 21, 1967, in *Unsolicited Bank Credit Cards*, 57; *Unsolicited Bank Credit Cards*, 34, 58 (statements of Furness and Rep. Tom S. Gettys); Lendol Glen Calder, *Financing the American Dream: A Cultural History of Consumer Credit* (Princeton University Press, 2001), 217.

13. *Unsolicited Bank Credit Cards*, 59–60 (statement of Rep. Seymore Halpern); Milton Lipson, "Law Enforcement and the Credit Card," Symposium of International Association of Chiefs of Police, September 30, 1969, "Crime 6–1 Check and Credit Card Fraud" folder, box 28, 91 Cong., SCSB Records.

14. *Unsolicited Bank Credit Cards*, 8, 12–13, 22, 61, 78 (statements of Andrew F. Brimmer, Member, Board of Governors, Federal Reserve System, and K. A. Randall, Chairman, Federal Deposit Insurance Corporation).

15. *Unsolicited Bank Credit Cards*, 8, 16 (statement of Brimmer); Patman, "Regulation of Credit Card Mailings," 116 *Cong. Rec.* 30875 (1970); Rep. Joseph Karth (MN), Bill 90, H.R. 13829, "To Restrict the Mailing of Unsolicited Credit Cards," 113 *Cong. Rec.* 32946 (1967); memo, Philip B. Byrne to Senator Mondale, November 13, 1967, "Credit Card Abuses" folder, 153.L.12.9B, Mondale Papers; Sen. Walter Mondale (MN), "Restriction on Mailing of Unsolicited Credit Cards," 113 *Cong. Rec.* 36845 (1967).

16. Board of Governors of the Federal Reserve System, *Bank Credit-Card and Check-Credit Plans* (Government Printing Office, 1968), 4, 27, 42–43, 55, 59.

17. *Bank Credit-Card and Check-Credit Plans* (hearings), 90 Cong. 1 (1968) (statement of Sen. William Proxmire).

18. Louis Hyman, *Debtor Nation: The History of America in Red Ink* (Princeton University Press, 2011), 173–219; David A. Skeel, *Debt's Dominion: A History of Bankruptcy*

Law in America (Princeton University Press, 2003), 131–159; *Bank Credit-Card and Check-Credit Plans* (hearings), 32 (statement of Royal E. Jackson, Chief of the Bankruptcy Division, Administrative Office, U.S. Courts).

19. *Bank Credit-Card and Check-Credit Plans* (hearings), 15–16, 22, 32, 65, 83 (statements of Furness, Proxmire, Jackson, Eric E. Bergsten, Professor of Law, University of Iowa, and Thomas L. Bailey, Vice President, Marine Midland Banks, Inc.).

20. Abbye Atkinson, "Rethinking Credit as Social Provision," *Stanford Law Review* 71, no. 5 (2019): 1093–1162.

21. Stewart Macaulay, "Private Legislation and the Duty to Read—Business Run by IBM Machine, the Law of Contracts and Credit Cards," *Vanderbilt Law Review* 19 (1966): 1051; Donald H. Maffly and Alex C. McDonald, "The Tripartite Credit Card Transaction: A Legal Infant," *California Law Review* 48, no. 3 (August 1960): 479–488; *Bank Credit-Card and Check-Credit Plans* (hearings), 73 (statements of Proxmire and William F. Willier, Professor of Law, Boston College).

22. The bank's "control group" included only 731 "selective" mailings, of which 139 were activated—hardly a conclusive study when placed against the tens of millions of cards sent out by banks each year.

23. *Bank Credit-Card and Check-Credit Plans* (hearings), 4, 8, 16, 22–24 (statements of Andrew Brimmer, Member, Board of Governors, Federal Reserve System, and Bailey).

24. Sen. William Proxmire, "S. 721—Introduction of Bill to Establish Ground Rules for the Issuance of Credit Cards," 115 *Cong. Rec.* 1947–1952 (1969); Proxmire, "Consumer Credit Legislation: The Future," *Banking* (April 1969), 47, 106, 108; Josh Lauer, *Creditworthy: A History of Consumer Surveillance and Financial Identity in America* (Columbia University Press, 2017), 217–229; Wallace F. Bennett to Bryce N. Harlow, July 8, 1969, FI5 (general), box 41, WHCF, Nixon Library.

25. U.S. Bureau of Labor Statistics, "Unemployment Rate (UNRATE)," FRED; Minsky, *Stabilizing an Unstable Economy,* 90, 284; U.S., President and Council of Economic Advisers, *Economic Report of the President* (Government Printing Office, 1970), 34–39, 101–104; Justin Douglas, "Translating the Blueprint for Financial Deregulation: The American Bank Lobby's Unyielding Quest for Legislative Profits, 1968–1982," *Enterprise & Society* 20, no. 2 (June 2019): 290.

26. Krippner, *Capitalizing on Crisis,* 63–71; Eric Monnet, *Controlling Credit: Central Banking and the Planned Economy in Postwar France, 1948–1973* (Cambridge University Press, 2018), 250–254; *Expanding the Mortgage Market,* 91 Cong., S. Rep. No 91–516 (1969); David M. Kennedy to Richard Nixon, December 22, 1969, FI5 (executive), box 41, WHCF, Nixon Library; Richard Nixon, "Statement on Signing a Bill Affecting Interest, Credit, and Lending," December 24, 1969, APP; *Lowering Interest Rates, Fight Inflation, Help Housing, Small Business, and Employment,* 91 Cong. 10, H. Rep. No. 91–755 (1969).

27. Rep. Leonor Sullivan (MO) "Congresswoman Sullivan Introduces Bill for Standby Powers to Regulate All Forms of Credit, Including Business Credit," 115 *Cong. Rec.* 35615 (1969); William Proxmire, quoted in "Credit Craze? Senators Push for Action to Tighten Credit-Card Controls," *CSM,* December 16, 1969.

28. Sidney M. Milkis, "The Federal Trade Commission and Consumer Protection: Regulatory Change and Administrative Pragmatism," *Antitrust Law Journal* 72, no. 3 (2005): 911–41; Cohen, *Consumers' Republic*, 346; "FTC Proposes to Ban Unsought Credit Cards Mailed by Some Issuers," *WSJ*, May 14, 1969; *Unsolicited Credit Cards*, 91 Cong. 33 (1969) (statement of Paul Rand Dixon, Chairman, Federal Trade Commission). On the ways autonomous agencies used leverage to direct the policy process, see Daniel P. Carpenter, *The Forging of Bureaucratic Autonomy: Reputations, Networks, and Policy Innovation in Executive Agencies, 1862–1928* (Princeton University Press, 2001).

29. Cohen, *Consumers' Republic*, 346; Judith Stein, *Pivotal Decade: How the United States Traded Factories for Finance in the Seventies* (Yale University Press, 2010), 24, 26. Christopher Lydon, "Richardson To Go Easy on Changes," *BG*, January 22, 1967; Cornelius J. Noonan, "State Enforcing New Consumer Law," *BG*, March 29, 1968; "Testimony by Robert L. Meade, Director of Legislative Affairs, President's Committee on Consumer Interests before the Federal Trade Commission," September 10, 1969, "Crime 6–1 Check and Credit Card Fraud" folder, box 28, 91 Cong., SCSB Records.

30. Alan Bible to Federal Trade Commission, August 11, 1969; "Statement by W. J. Bittles, Jr., General Manager Retail Marketing—Shell Oil Company," September 10, 1969; Robert C. Pier, President, New England Bankcard Association to Federal Trade Commission, August 14, 1969; Charles R. McNeill to Federal Trade Commission, August 13, 1969; "Statement of Earl E. Pollock on Behalf of Midwest Bank Card System, Inc., at Federal Trade Commission Hearing on Unsolicited Credit Cards," September 10, 1969, "Crime 6–1 Check and Credit Card Fraud" folder, box 28, 91 Cong., SCSB Records; Andrew Brimmer, "New Horizons in Credit Card Banking: Remarks before the Seattle Clearing House Association at the Rainier Club, Seattle, Washington," September 23, 1969, Statements and Speeches of Andrew F. Brimmer, FRASER.

31. H.R. 858 folder, box 7; H.R. 1092 folder; H.R. 1232 folder, box 9; H.R. 6487 folder; H.R. 6488 folder, box 25; H.R. 9778 folder, box 43; H.R. 14527 folder, box 66, 91 Cong., Legislative Files, Committee on the Judiciary, House of Representatives (RG 233), NARA I; *Plastic Jungle* 1, 3–8 (1969) (statements of Rep. Robert N. C. Nix and Rep. Wright Patman); *Protecting Postal Patrons from Obscene Mail*, 89 Cong. (1965); *Obscene and Pandering Advertising Mail Matter*, 90 Cong. (1967); *Postal Revenue and Offensive Intrusion of Sexually Oriented Mail*, 91 Cong. (1969); *Plastic Jungle*, 8, 10, 18, 21, 107 (statements of Reps. Glenn Cunningham, Benjamin Rosenthal, and Arnold Olsen). On consumer surveillance, see Lauer, *Creditworthy*, 212–229.

32. Walker B. Lowman, "Federal Pandering Advertisements Statute: The Right of Privacy versus the First Amendment," *Ohio State Law Journal* 32, no. 1 (Winter 1971): 149–150; Rowan v. Post Office Dept., 397 U.S. 728 (1970); *Plastic Jungle*, 28 (statement of Rep. William D. Ford).

33. *Plastic Jungle*, 61, 64, 74–75, 88, 92, 94 (statements of Robert Meade, Legislative Director, Office of Special Assistant to the President on Consumer Affairs, Seymour Rotker, executive assistant to the district attorney, Bronx County, NY, David A. Nelson, General Counsel, Post Office Department, and Earl E. Pollock, attorney for Midwest Bank Card System, Inc.).

34. *Unsolicited Credit Cards,* 91 Cong. (1969).

35. "Session Blocked, Proxmire Sets Hearing for Tomorrow," *BS,* December 6, 1969; Ken McLean, Oral History, September 11, 2009, 38–39, William Proxmire Collection, Wisconsin Archives, http://content.wisconsinhistory.org/cdm/ref/collection/proxmire/id/1930; Robert J. Samuelson, "Credit Card Foes Clash at Hearing," *WP,* September 9, 1969; John D. Morris, "Credit Card Industry Is Mobilizing against Curbs," *NYT,* September 10, 1969; "Credit Card Regulation Gets White House Nudge," *WP,* November 20, 1969.

36. *Unsolicited Credit Cards,* 63–65, 67 (statement of Robert Meade, Legislative Director, Office of Special Assistant to the President on Consumer Affairs); *Plastic Jungle,* 61 (statement of Robert Meade).

37. Memo, Virginia Knauer to Wilfred Rommel, November 26, 1969; Paul W. McCracken to Wilfred Rommel, December 2, 1969; note to Jon Rose, December 5, 1969; press clip "The President's Committee on Whose Interests," *WP,* December 11, 1969; memo, Jonathan Rose to Peter M. Flanigan, December 11, 1969, FI5 (executive), box 41, WHCF, Nixon Library.

38. *Unsolicited Credit Cards,* 70 (statement of Proxmire); "Senators Hear Stolen Credit Card Is Worth $100," *NYT,* December 8, 1969; "Senators Told: Criminals Use Credit Cards," *BG,* December 8, 1969; "Stolen Credit Card Price of $100 Told," *CT,* December 8, 1969; "$100 Reported Tag on Stolen Credit Cards," *LAT,* December 8, 1969; Robert J. Samuelson, "Credit Card Ban Seen Expanded," WP, April 13, 1970.

39. *S. 721—"Unsolicited Credit Cards"* (Executive Session) (HRG-1970-BCS-0026), 91 Cong. 2, 6–7 (statements of Ken McLean, professional staff member, and Sen. Wallace Bennett); "Elementary and Secondary Amendments of 1969," 116 *Cong. Rec.* 3037 (1970).

40. *S. 721 [Unsolicited Credit Cards]* (Executive Session) (HRG-1970-BCS-0027), 91 Cong. 5 (Bennett).

41. *S. 721 [Unsolicited Credit Cards],* 91 Cong. 39, 70 (statement of Sen. Proxmire).

42. "Unsolicited Credit Cards," 116 *Cong. Rec.* 11827–11845 (1970); Rep. Halpern and Rep. Bingham, "Regulation of Credit Card Mailings," 116 *Cong. Rec.* 30889–30890 (1970).

43. "Unsolicited Credit Cards," *Congressional Quarterly Almanac* 26 (91 Cong., 2d Sess.), 621–624; Sen. Proxmire, "Bank Records and Foreign Transactions; Credit Cards; Consumer Credit Reporting—Conference Report," 116 *Cong. Rec.* 35939 (1970); Rep. Sullivan (MO), "Conference Report on H.R. 15073, Bank Records and Foreign Transactions; Credit Cards; Consumer Credit Reporting," 116 *Cong. Rec.* 36572 (1970); H. Rep. 91–1587, at 28 (1970) (Conf. Rep.); Rep. Windall, "Conference Report on H.R. 15073, Bank Records and Foreign Transactions; Credit Cards; Consumer Credit Reporting," 116 *Cong. Rec.* 36572 (1970); Newsletter, "U.S. Senator William Proxmire Reports to you from Washington," November 1970, Proxmire Collection, Wisconsin Archives, http://content.wisconsinhistory.org/cdm/compoundobject/collection/proxmire/id/4972/show/4804/rec/16.

44. *Unsolicited Credit Cards,* 110, 114 (Thomas L. Bailey, Vice President, Marine Midland Banks); Office of the Comptroller of the Currency, "Outstanding Balances,

Credit Cards and Related Plans," *Annual Report of the Comptroller of the Currency,* 1970 to 1980; "Everything Up but Delinquencies," *Banking* (August 1976), 50; Robert A. Bennett, "Citibank's Credit Card Blitz," *NYT,* July 23, 1978.

45. Memo, David M. Kennedy to Richard Nixon, December 22, 1969, FI5 (executive), box 41 WHCF, Nixon Library.

Chapter 7. Risk Shifting

1. Elihu Blotnick, "How to Counterfeit Credit Cards and Get Away with It," *Scanlan's Monthly* 1, no. 4 (June 1970): 21–28, box 471, CRR; Illinois Legislative Investigating Commission, *Credit Card Fraud in Illinois* (September 1972), 55–60.

2. H. W. Dugdale to Alfred A. Buerger, September 7, 1966, folder 247, box 15, Bolton Papers; Richard G. Kleindienst to William Proxmire, October 5, 1970, Headquarters Case Files, case file 36-HQ-00, serial 33, box 41, classification 36 (Mail Fraud), Records of the Federal Bureau of Investigation (RG 65), NARA II.

3. For the sociology of law and illicit markets, see Richard Swedberg, "The Case for an Economic Sociology of Law." *Theory and Society* 32, no. 1 (2003): 1–37; Jens Beckert and Matías Dewey, *The Architecture of Illegal Markets: Towards an Economic Sociology of Illegality in the Economy* (Oxford University Press, 2017).

4. On government's role as risk manager, see David A. Moss, *When All Else Fails: Government as the Ultimate Risk Manager* (Harvard University Press, 2004).

5. Miraglia, "My $10,000 Credit Card Binge," *Life,* October 26, 1959, 53–54; "Credit Card Companies Put Squeeze on Cheats, Improve Fiscal Health," *WSJ,* October 30, 1962; Anthony R. Scaiza, "Strictly on the Cuff," *Barron's* (November 12, 1962).

6. Blotnick, "How to Counterfeit Credit Cards," 22; Kenneth B. Wilson, "A $20 Million Dollar Racket," *Supervision* (ca. 1967), "Legislative Files, Unsolicited Credit Cards" folder, box 418, Anderson Papers; James Snyder, "A Multimillion-Dollar Racket Sweeps the United States—Guard Your Credit Cards," *Parade,* October 22, 1967; Lipson, "Crime and the Credit Card." On the relation of legitimate and illegitimate markets, see Wendy A. Woloson, "'Fence-ing Lessons': Child Junkers and the Commodification of Scrap in the Long Nineteenth Century," *Business History* 61, no. 1 (2019): 38–72.

7. People v. Buckley, 202 Cal. App. 2d 142, 147, 20 Cal. Rptr. 659, 662 (Ct. App. 1962); Blotnick, "How to Counterfeit Credit Cards," 22; *The Plastic Jungle,* 91 Cong. 107, 108 (1969) (statement of Rep. Arnold Olsen); U.S. v. Kellerman, 431 F.2d 319, 322 (2d Cir. 1970); Illinois Legislative Investigating Commission, *Credit Card Fraud in Illinois.*

8. Blotnick, "How to Counterfeit Credit Cards," 23; Richard Rosenfeld and Aaron Levin, "Acquisitive Crime and Inflation in the United States, 1960–2012," *Journal of Quantitative Criminology* 32, no. 3 (September 2016): 436, 443 (Rosenfeld and Levin define acquisitive crime as "crimes committed for monetary gain"); William Estes, "Check Frauds Heading for Another Record," *LAT,* March 19, 1967; World Bank, "Inflation, Consumer Prices for the United States (FPCPITOTLZGUSA)," FRED.

9. U.S. v. Kelem, 416 F.2d 346 (1969); U.S. v. Chason, 451 F.2d 301 (1971); U.S. v. Madison, 458 F.2d 974, 974 (2d Cir. 1972); Illinois Legislative Investigating Commission, *Credit Card Fraud in Illinois*, 9–10.

10. Milton Lipson, "Law Enforcement and the Credit Card," Symposium of International Association of Chiefs of Police, September 30, 1969; Seymour Rotker to William D. Dixon, September 11, 1969, "Crime 6–1 Check and Credit Card Fraud" folder, box 28, 91 Cong., SCSB Records; Harold S. Taylor, "The Chicago Bank Credit Card Fiasco," *Bankers Magazine* 151, no. 1 (Winter 1968): 50; James A. Kaufman to Donald E. Holbrook, April 5, 1967, "Legislative Files: Unsolicited Credit Cards" folder, box 418, Anderson Papers; *Enforcement Report of the Postal Inspection Service*, November 1970 and December 1970, "Enforcement Report" folder, box 20, Office of the Postmaster General, Records of the Post Office Department (RG 28), NARA I; U.S. v. Mikelberg, 517 F.2d 246, 253 (5th Cir. 1975).

11. Lipson, "Law Enforcement and the Credit Card"; Illinois Legislative Investigating Commission, *Credit Card Fraud in Illinois*, 119–336; Clayton M. Christensen and Michael E. Raynor, *The Innovator's Solution: Creating and Sustaining Successful Growth* (Harvard Business School Press, 2003); John K. Galbraith, *The Affluent Society* (Riverside Press, 1958), 201; Vance Packard, *Status Seekers: An Exploration of Class Behavior in America and the Hidden Barriers that Affect You, Your Community, and Your Future* (D. McKay, 1959), esp. 122–123; Robert K. Merton, *Social Theory and Social Structure*, 1968 enl. ed. (Free Press, 1968), esp. 195–203.

12. Donald H. Maffly and Alex C. McDonald, "The Tripartite Credit Card Transaction: A Legal Infant," *California Law Review* 48, no. 3 (August 1960): 459–500; Blotnick, "How to Counterfeit Credit Cards," 22; Douglas Wick to Frances Bolton, November 13, 1964, box 15, Bolton Papers.

13. U.S. v. Fordyce, 192 F. Supp. 93, 94, 96 (S.D. Cal. 1961); Williams v. United States, 192 F. Supp. 97 (S.D. Cal. 1961); United States v. Jones, 182 F. Supp. 146 (W.D. Mo. 1960); Brockman Adams, quoted in Douglas Wick to Frances Bolton, September 17, 1962, box 15, Bolton Papers; Barack v. United States, 317 F.2d 619 (9th Cir. 1963); H. Rawlins Overton to Emanuel Celler, June 12, 1963, box 15, Bolton Papers.

14. Frances Bolton to Emanuel Celler, June 4, 1962; Celler to Bolton, June 14, 1962; Douglas Wick to Bolton, July 25 1962; Wick to Bolton, October 18, 1963; Norman F. Page to Bolton, February 19, 1963; Arthur J. Prink to Bolton, August 17, 1964; James E. Bromwell to Bolton, November 8, 1963; John B. Simpson to Wick, November 7, 1963; Wick to Bolton, March 18, 1966, box 15, Bolton Papers.

15. Ramsey Clark to Emanuel Celler, February 15, 1966, box 15, Bolton Papers.

16. H. W. Douglas to Alfred A. Buerger, September 7, 1966; Ramsey Clark to Emanuel Celler, February 15, 1966, Frances Bolton to Douglas Wick, February 21, 1966; Bolton to Wick, March 30, 1966; Bolton to C. L. Phillips, July 29, 1966, box 15, Bolton Papers.

17. Elizabeth Hinton, *From the War on Poverty to the War on Crime: The Making of Mass Incarceration in America* (Harvard University Press, 2016); Jonathan D. Cohen, "'Put the Gangsters Out of Business': Gambling Legalization and the War on Organized Crime," *Policy History* 31, no. 4 (2019): 533–556.

18. Lipson, "Crime and the Credit Card," 12, 24; Lipson, "Law Enforcement and the Credit Card."

19. "L.A. Unit to Fight Credit Card Fraud," *LAT,* November 6, 1966; William Estes, "Credit Card Theft Growing Problem," *LAT,* July 10, 1966; Tom Renner, "The Hot Credit Card Racket," *Newsday,* February 1, 1966; Tom Renner, "Bonanza for Hoodlums," *Newsday,* February 2, 1966; Tom Renner, "Curbing the Chiselers," *Newsday,* February 3, 1966.

20. Lyndon Johnson appointed Jack Weinstein to the federal bench just after the model law was published. Asked about the report, Weinstein wrote, "My files for the period are destroyed and I remember nothing of the circumstances. I'm sorry I can't help. I don't even remember who asked me to do the draft—I think I received a small honorarium." Email, Jack Weinstein to Sean Vanatta, October 16, 2014, in author's possession.

21. Milton Lipson to Calista Cooper Hughes, January 27, 1967, "Credit Cards" folder; Alfred Buerger to Edward J. Speno and Alexander Chananau, February 29, 1968, S2234-A folder, Dunne Papers; Jack B. Weinstein and Tom J. Farber, *State Credit Card Crime Act* (American Express Company, 1967), 6, Columbia University Law Library. The Card Crime Act's circumscribed criminal rights contrast sharply with Weinstein's record as a federal judge. Edward J. Rymsza, "Hon. Jack B. Weinstein Judicial Profile," *Federal Lawyer* 63 (2016): 24–25. The Dunne Papers were being processed and re-boxed when I viewed them, so only folder titles have been provided.

22. Guy Capel to John R. Dunne, September 19, 1967, S2234-A folder, Dunne Papers.

23. "Dunne Asks New Law on Credit Card Thefts," *Newsday,* July 21, 1966; "Propose Curb On Credit Card Racket in NY," *Newsday,* February 22, 1967; Renner, "Hot Credit Card Racket"; Renner, "Bonanza for Hoodlums"; Renner, "Curbing the Chiselers"; telephone conversation with John R. Dunne, September 9, 2013, notes in author's possession; Dunne to Thomas V. LaFauci, February 16, 1967; John Scott Fones, "Credit Card Bill Press Conference," February 27, 1967, "Credit Cards" folder, Dunne Papers; Peter Z. Grossman, *American Express: The Unofficial History of the People Who Built the Great Financial Empire* (Crown Publishers, 1987), 272; Alan Eysen, "Dunne Fears Credit Card Bill Doomed," *Newsday,* March 31, 1967; "Legislator Wants Stiffer Laws Governing Credit Card Crimes," *Newsday,* November 22, 1967. Michigan lawmaker Thomas J. Anderson read an article by Renner in the *Kiwanis Magazine,* which inspired him to advance card fraud legislation before being contacted by Capel. Tom Renner, "Crime and the Credit Card," *Kiwanis Magazine* (Summer 1966), 21; State of Michigan, *Public and Local Acts of the State of Michigan Passed at the Regular Session of 1967,* Act no. 255, 484–485; Guy Capel to Thomas Anderson, July 17, 1967, "Legislative Files: Unsolicited Credit Cards, 1968–1969" folder, box 418, Anderson Papers.

24. John P. Heinz, Robert W. Gettleman, and Morris A. Seeskin, "Legislative Politics and the Criminal Law," *Northwestern University Law Review* 64, no. 3 (July–August 1969): 277; People v. Swann, 213 Cal. App. 2d 447, 28 Cal. Rptr. 830 (Ct. App. 1963); John F. McCarthy to Ronald Reagan, August 8, 1967, Bill file, Senate Bill 1055, Chapter 1395 (1967), California State Archives; Guy Capel to John R. Dunne, June 27, 1967; Guy Capel to John R. Dunne, June 1, 1967; Guy Capel to John R.

Dunne, September 19, 1967, S2234-A folder, Dunne Papers; Thomas W. Bush, "New California Law Tightens Penalties for Credit Card Thefts," *LAT,* September 6, 1967.

25. "Minutes of Meeting of Model Penal Code—Special Advisory Board," March 9–10, 1962, box 5616, American Law Institute Collection, Biddle Law Library, University of Pennsylvania; Robert R. McMillan to John R. Dunne, February 9, 1968; Lynn J. Ellins to J. Robert Thomas, January 31, 1968, S2234 folder, Dunne Papers; letter of Richard Denzler, Temporary Commission on Revision of the Penal Law and Criminal Code, June 3, 1968, bill jacket (vetoed), L. 1968 Veto 304, New York State Archives; Nelson Rockefeller, "To Amend the Penal Law, in Relation to Illegal Use of Credit Cards," *Public Papers of Nelson A. Rockefeller* (State of New York, 1968), 501; Commonwealth of Massachusetts, *Acts and Resolves Passed by the General Court of Massachusetts during the Session of 1969,* ch. 832, 795–798; Bill file 1969 S482, New Jersey State Archives; State of New Hampshire, *Journal of the Honorable Senate of the State of New Hampshire January Session of 1969* (statement of Sen. John Bradshaw), 578.

26. Bernard S. Meyer to Allard Lowenstein, February 7, 1969, H.R. 164 folder, box 1, 91 Cong., Legislative Files, Committee on the Judiciary, House of Representatives (RG 223), NARA I.

27. H. Erich Heinemann, "Credit Cards," *NYT,* August 1, 1967; John Kirk and Theodore Fischer, "Bank Charge Card Creates Climate for Change," *Banking* (April 1968), 88; Phillip L. Zweig, *Wriston: Walter Wriston, Citibank, and the Rise and Fall of American Financial Supremacy* (Crown Publishers, 1995), 230, 540; Seymour Rotker to William D. Dixon, September 11, 1969, "Crime 6–1 Check and Credit Card Fraud" folder, box 28, 91 Cong., SCSB Records.

28. Citibank, "Re: Report on Security Department," November 27, 1968, in John J. Reynolds to Emanuel Celler, May 13, 1969; Celler notes on conversation with Citibank executives, May 7, 1969, "Post Office—Credit Cards" folder, box 328, Celler Papers.

29. Thomas Wilcox to Emanuel Celler, September 19, 1969; W. J. Cotter to Emanuel Celler, May 28, 1969, "Post Office—Credit Cards" folder, box 328, Celler Papers; John Kirk, "Losses Are Still in the Cards for Bankers!," *Banking* (December 1970), 84.

30. "Probe Starts Today in Credit Card Thefts," *Newsday,* January 31, 1969; Val Adams, "Banker Says Postal Employes Are Paid to Steal Credit Cards," *NYT,* February 1, 1969; *Plastic Jungle* 233 (1969) (statement of John R. Dunne, New York State senator).

31. Richard Denzler to Robert R. Douglass, March 14, 1969, Bill file, Chapter 115 (1969–1970 Regular Session), New York State Archives; "Tough Credit-Card Bill Signed," *Newsday,* March 27, 1969.

32. Adams, "Banker Says Postal Employes Are Paid to Steal"; Tom Renner, "Credit Card Liability Limit Urged," *Newsday,* February 1, 1969; "Memorandum in Support of an Act to Amend the General Business Law in Relation to Limitations on Liability for Use of Lost or Stolen Credit Cards," n.d. (ca. March 1969), S5174 folder; "Memorandum in Support of an Act to Amend the General Business Law in Rela-

tion to the Issuance of Unsolicited Credit Cards," n.d. (ca. March 1969), S5175 folder, Dunne Papers; Fred Bruning, "Lefkowitz on Husbands' Side," *Newsday*, November 11, 1969; "Credit Card Law Signed," *NYT*, May 25, 1970.

33. Bill file, Senate Bill 97, Chapter 1019 (1971), California State Archives; James F. Carrig, California State Banking Department, "Enrolled Bill Report," October 4, 1971, SB97 (1) folder, box L269, Legislative Unit, Ronald Reagan Gubernatorial Papers, Reagan Library; Heinz, Gettleman, and Seeskin, "Legislative Politics and the Criminal Law," 303–305; Illinois Legislative Investigating Commission, *Credit Card Fraud in Illinois*, vii–viii.

34. *Plastic Jungle* 88 (1969) (statement of Seymour Rotker, Executive Assistant to the District Attorney, Bronx County, Bronx, NY).

35. 116 Cong. Rec. 35939 (1970) quoted in brief for the Respondent, U.S. v. Maze, 1973 WL 172278 (U.S.), 18–19 (U.S., 2004); 1970 amendment to the federal Truth in Lending Act, 15 U.S.C. 1644.

36. Karl Polanyi, *The Great Transformation* (Beacon Press, 1957 [1944]).

37. Richard G. Kleindienst to William Proxmire, October 5, 1970, Headquarters Case Files, case file 36-HQ-00, serial 33, box 41, classification 36 (Mail Fraud), Records of the Federal Bureau of Investigation (RG 65), NARA II.

38. Richard G. Kleindienst to William Proxmire, October 5, 1970, Headquarters Case Files, case file 36-HQ-00, serial 33, box 41, classification 36 (Mail Fraud), Records of the Federal Bureau of Investigation (RG 65), NARA II. On the use of the federal mail fraud statute as a tool for confronting new varieties of fraud, see Edward J. Balleisen, *Fraud: An American History from Barnum to Madoff* (Princeton University Press, 2017), 128–140, 155–173; U.S. v. Maze, 414 U.S. 395, 405–408, 94 S. Ct. 645, 646, 38 L. Ed. 2d 603 (1974).

39. Adams v. U.S., 312 F.2d 137, 140 (5th Cir. 1963).

40. Kloian v. U.S., 349 F.2d 291, 293 (5th Cir. 1965); U.S. v. Reynolds, 421 F.2d 178 (5th Cir. 1970); U.S. v. Thomas, 429 F.2d 408 (5th Cir. 1970).

41. U.S. v. Kellerman, 431 F.2d at 322.

42. Kloian v. U.S., 349 F.2d; U.S. v. Chason, 451 F.2d 301 (2d Cir. 1971); *Enforcement Report of the Postal Inspection Service*, January-December 1970, "Enforcement Report" folder, box 20, Office of the Postmaster General, Records of the Post Office Department (RG 28), NARA I; memo, Will Wilson to Director, November 2, 1970; memo, Director to Assistant Attorney General, Criminal Division, November 6, 1970, Headquarters Case Files, case file 36-HQ-00, serial 33, box 41, classification 36 (Mail Fraud), Records of the Federal Bureau of Investigation (RG 65), NARA II; US v. Kelly, 467 F.2d 262 (7th Cir. 1972); U.S. v. Ciotti, 469 F.2d 1204 at 1206 (3d Cir. 1972); People v. Swann, 213 Cal. App. 2d.

43. U.S. v. Maze, 414 U.S. at 396; brief for the United States, U.S. v. Maze, 1973 WL 172277 (U.S.), 5 (U.S., 2004).

44. U.S. v. Maze, 468 F.2d 529, 534, 536 (6th Cir. 1972), aff'd, 414 U.S. 395, 94 S. Ct. 645, 38 L. Ed. 2d 603 (1974).

45. United States v. Lynn, 461 F.2d 759 (10th Cir. 1972); William T. Warner to Michael Rodak, March 8, 1973, 72–1168, box 565, U.S. Supreme Court Appellate Case Files, Supreme Court (RG 267), NARA I; preliminary memo, J. Harvie Wilkinson III, 17

April 1973, 72–1168 folder, box 179, Blackmun Papers; William T. Warner oral argument, "United States v. Maze," Oyez, November 14, 1973, https://www.oyez.org/cases/1973/72–1168.

46. Draft memo, Harry A. Blackmun, November 13, 1973; Harry A. Blackmun conference notes, November 16, 1973, 72–1168 folder, box 179, Blackmun Papers; U.S. v. Maze, 414 U.S. at 402.

47. Warner oral argument, "United States v. Maze"; Commonwealth of Kentucky, *Acts of the General Assembly of the Commonwealth of Kentucky, Regular Session* (1970), ch. 83, 356–365; U.S. v. Maze, 414 U.S. at 416.

48. U. S. v. Mikelberg, 517 F.2d.; Brian F. Caminer, "Credit Card Fraud: The Neglected Crime," *Journal of Criminal Law and Criminology* 76, no. 3 (1986), 755.

49. James B. Rule, *Private Lives and Public Surveillance* (Allen Lane, 1973), 223–268.

Chapter 8. The *Marquette* Decision

1. Harry A. Blackmun, case notes, September 6, 1978, 77–1265 folder, box 285, Blackmun Papers.

2. For similar legal efforts in the nineteenth century to use federal law to blunt state regulation, see Charles W. McCurdy, "American Law and the Marketing Structure of the Large Corporation, 1875–1890," *Journal of Economic History* 38, no. 3 (1978): 631–49.

3. Scholars have not examined the interfirm relationships that undergirded national bank card systems. David L. Stearns documents the computer systems that processed transactions (*Electronic Value Exchange: Origins of the VISA Electronic Payment System* [Springer, 2011]). Dee Hock, president of BankAmericard Inc. and later VISA documents the corporate and organizational culture (*One from Many: VISA and the Rise of the Chaordic Organization* [Berrett-Koehler, 2005]). David S. Evans and Richard Schmalensee are concerned with payment systems economics (*Paying with Plastic: The Digital Revolution in Buying and Borrowing* 2nd ed. [MIT Press, 2005]).

4. Jerry G. South, "Credit Cards: A Primer," *Business Lawyer* (January 1968): 330–331, "Correspondence" folder, ONBCF; Tiffany v. National Bank of Missouri, 85 U.S. 409, 413, 21 L. Ed. 862 (1873); United States, Comptroller of the Currency, *Comptroller's Manual for National Banks: Laws, Regulations, Rulings* (Government Printing Office, 1968), Ruling 7310; State of Oregon, Attorney General, *Biennial Report and Opinions of the Attorney General of the State of Oregon 1966–1968* 33, no. 6250 (March 8, 1967), 160; memo, John S. Cushman to Arne Schoeller, November 25, 1969, "Bank Credit Cards" folder, *St. Cloud* Case File.

5. Stephen Szmrecsanyi, *The First National Bank Story* (First National Bank of Omaha, 1996), 61–65, 116; "Single Check Shopping," *WSJ*, February 9, 1953; "Chge-Acct Bankers Form Association to Exchange Information," *AB*, March 23, 1954; First National Bank of Omaha, "1969 Certificate of Sales Volume," May 18, 1970, plaintiff's exhibit 49, *Fisher* Case File.

6. Bank of America, "Agent Bank Agreement," January 10, 1969, plaintiff's exhibit 4; BankAmerica Service Corporation, "Participant Letter License Agreement," June

10, 1969, plaintiff's exhibit 7; contract between First National Bank of Omaha and First of Omaha Service Corporation, ca. 1968, defendant's exhibit G, deposition of Marvin L. Jablonski, December 11, 1974, 4; deposition of James Doody, December 11, 1974, 3–5; deposition of J. William Henry, December 11, 1974, 5, 9–10, *Fisher* Case File; "Bank Credit Card Service Organization and the Bank Service Corporation Act," *Federal Reserve Bulletin* (November 1967), 1912–1913.

7. Deposition of James Doody, December 11, 1974, 3–5, *Fisher* Case File.

8. BankAmericard promotional mailer, First National Bank of Omaha, ca. 1969, plaintiff's exhibit 48; BankAmericard application, First National Bank of Omaha, November 1974, plaintiff's exhibit 41.5, *Fisher* Case File.

9. State of Minnesota, *Session Laws of the State of Minnesota, Enacted by the Legislature at the Session Commencing January 8, 1957 and at the Extra Session Commencing April 30, 1957*, ch. 347, 418–419; Minutes, Banking Subcommittee of the Senate Commerce Committee, March 5, 1970, MBS Records; Jim Fuller, "Interest Ceiling Cools Banks to Credit Cards," *Minneapolis Tribune*, August 10, 1969, "Bank Credit Cards" folder, *St. Cloud* Case File; State of Minnesota, Senate, "Report, Committee on Commerce, Subcommittee on Consumer Credit and Banking: Interim Activities and Recommendations, July 1967–December 1968," December 11, 1968, box 39, Braucher Papers.

10. "Northwest National Bank Credit Card Materials, ca. 1960" folder, box 8, Northwest Papers; "Twin Cities Banks Sell Credit Plans," *NYT*, September 17, 1960; "Form 'Central States' Card," *Northwestern Banker* (October 1968), 78.

11. Fuller, "Interest Ceiling"; "Statement of Dean F. Scott Before the Interim Subcommittee, House Financial Institutions Committee," September 22, 1969, MBS Records; United States, Office of the Comptroller of the Currency, *Annual Report of the Comptroller of the Currency* (1973), 253–254.

12. "The Bank Credit Card with a $10 Annual Fee," *Business Week*, March 3, 1973, 23, box 471, CRR; Memo, John R. Kenefick to George Reilly, October 13, 1971, "Correspondence" folder; memo, Richard A. Emerick to Douglas Head, December 1, 1969, "Bank Credit Cards" folder, *St. Cloud* Case File; Fuller, "Interest Ceiling."

13. R. V. Sullivan to Steven. M. Gunn, December 16, 1971; Omaha National Bank, Agent Bank Agreement, ca. 1968, "Research" folder, ONBCF.

14. Memo, Douglas M. Head to Jerome D. Truhn, October 31, 1969; Memorandum of Law, Douglas M. Head, Jerome D. Truhn, and John R. Kenefick, October 5, 1970, "Correspondence" folder, ONBCF; "3 Banks Are Sued Under Usury Law: Minnesota Charges Limits Exceeded on Credit Cards," *NYT*, July 31, 1970; memo, Fred J. Hughes to John R. Kefenick, October 12, 1971, "Pleadings" folder, *St. Cloud* Case File; Douglas Cray, "Revolving Credit Plans under Fire," *NYT*, August 15, 1971; Fred J. Hughes to John Kenefick, October 6, 1971; Fred J. Hughes to John Kenefick, October 6, 1971, "Correspondence" folder, ONBCS; memo, George Reilly to John Kenefick, October 18, 1971; memo, John Kenefick to George Reilly, October 13, 1971; Stipulation for Dismissal, State v. St. Cloud National Bank & Trust Co., "Pleadings" folder, *St. Cloud* Case File.

15. Memo, John R. Kenefick to Douglas Head, November 24, 1969, "Research" folder, ONBCF.

16. Memo, John R. Kenefick to Douglas Head, November 24, 1969; memo, Arne Schoeller and John R. Kenefick to Douglas Head, December 15, 1969; memo, Steven M. Gunn to file, November 23, 1971; C. R. Servoss to Janice Eckstrand, October 13, 1971, "Research" folder, ONBCF.

17. Memorandum of Law, Douglas M. Head, Jerome D. Truhn, and John R. Kenefick, October 5, 1970; Complaint, Douglas M. Head and John R. Kenefick, July 29, 1970, "Correspondence" folder; memo, O. Russell Olson, June 30, 1971, "Pleadings" folder; John R. Kenefick to John Troyer, July 22, 1971; Curtis D. Forslund to John Troyer, December 6, 1972, "Correspondence" folder; Notice of Dismissal by Plaintiff, August 8, 1973, ONBCF. These questions were also central to the Uniform Consumer Credit Code, which bared nonconforming out-of-state lenders from using its remedies.

18. Memo, Mary Gallagher to William Kuretsky, August 9, 1973, "Research" folder, ONBCF.

19. Memo, John S. Cushman to Arne Schoeller, November 24, 1969, "Bank Credit Cards" folder, St. Cloud Case File; Minutes, Financial Institutions Subcommittee of the Standing Committees on Commerce, October 22, 1969; memo, Burnette E. Koebernick to All Members of the Financial Institutions Subcommittee, November 5, 1969, "Financial Institutions" folder, box 14, Minutes and Supporting Materials, 1967–1970, Interim Study Committee, Legislative Service Bureau, Iowa State Archives; "Sears, Iowa Retailer, Indiana Standard Face Usury Charge in Suit," WSJ, November 4, 1970; State ex rel. Turner v. Younker Bros., 210 N.W.2d 550 (Iowa 1973); State of Iowa, Acts and Joint Resolutions Passed at the 1974 Regular Session of the Sixty-Fifth General Assembly of the State of Iowa, ch. 1250, 879–956.

20. M. L. Jablonski, Answers to Interrogatories—Second Series, July 11, 1974; First of Omaha Service Corporation and Coralville Bank and Trust, Agent Bank Agreement, January 10, 1969, plaintiff's exhibit 4; Order on Pretrial Conference, Fred Fisher v. First National Bank of Omaha, Nebraska (No. CV 72-0-156); sales draft signed by Mrs. Fred J. Fisher, Harmony Hall, July 3, 1969; sales draft signed by Fred J. Fisher, Hawkeye Chrysler Plymouth, n.d.; Analysis of Account No. 418–731–194–969 (Fred Fisher), plaintiff's exhibit 52, Fisher Case File.

21. M. L. Jablonski, Answers to Interrogatories, February 12, 1973; brief of Appellee, March 10, 1976, 39, Fisher Case File; John C. Coffee Jr. Entrepreneurial Litigation: Its Rise, Fall and Future (Harvard University Press, 2015). Meeker's strategy was increasingly common. Bankers complained that bankrupt debtors would file Truth-in-Lending claims, hoping that banks would forgive the debt rather than incur the cost of defending themselves. Oversight on Consumer Protection Activities of Federal Banking Agencies, 94 Cong. 121 (statement of Jonathan Landers, Visiting Scholar, American Bar Foundation).

22. Plaintiff's brief, January 14, 1972, Fisher Case File.

23. Deposition of James Doody, January 3, 1975, Fisher Case File.

24. Plaintiff Memorandum of Authorities and Argument, November 1, 1971; plaintiff's brief, January 14, 1972, Fisher Case File; Felix Cohen, "Transcendental Nonsense and the Functionalist Approach," Columbia Law Review 35, no. 6 (June 1935): 809–849.

25. Memorandum Opinion and Ruling and Order on Defendant's Motion to Dismiss, February 22, 1972, *Fisher* Case File.

26. Fisher v. First Nat'l Bank of Omaha, 338 F. Supp. 525 (S.D. Iowa 1972); Fisher v. First National Bank of Omaha, 548 F.2d 255 (8th Cir. 1977); Fisher v. First National Bank of Chicago, 538 F.2d 1284 (7th Cir. 1976), cert. denied, 97 S. Ct. 786 (1977).

27. State of Iowa, *Acts and Joint Resolutions* (1970), ch. 1250; news release, Iowa Department of Justice, November 1, 1974, box 1, Consumer Protection Press Releases and Reports, Attorney General, Iowa State Archives; Iowa ex rel. Turner v. First of Omaha Serv. Corp. of Omaha, Neb., 401 F. Supp. 439 (S.D. Iowa 1975); State ex rel. Turner v. First of Omaha Serv. Corp. of Omaha, 269 N.W.2d 409 (Iowa 1978).

28. "The Bank Credit Card with a $10 Annual Fee"; "Banks Edging toward Card Service Charges," *Banking* (August 1976), 58; First Nat. Bank of Omaha v. Marquette Nat. Bank of Minneapolis, 482 F. Supp. 514, 516 (D. Minn. 1979); United States, Comptroller of the Currency, *Annual Report of the Comptroller of the Currency* (1975), 138–139.

29. Jim Doody quoted in Szmrecsanyi, *First National Bank Story*, 126–127.

30. State of Minnesota, *Session Laws of the State of Minnesota, Enacted by the Sixty-Ninth Legislature at the 1976 Regular Session Commencing January 26, 1976 and Adjourning April 5, 1976*, ch. 196, 664; *First Nat. Bank of Omaha*, 482 F. Supp. at 516; Minutes, Minnesota Senate Labor and Commerce Committee, February 3, 1976, Senate Labor and Commerce vol. 58, box 129.C.7.4F, Senate Committee Books, Minnesota Historical Society.

31. Brief of the Minnesota AFL-CIO, as Amicus Curiae Supporting Petitioner Minnesota, at 5, Marquette Nat'l Bank of Minneapolis v. First of Omaha Serv. Corp., 439 U.S. 299 (1978) (Nos. 77–1265, 77–1258), 1978 WL 223582; Minn. Stat. § 48.185 (1976); *Marquette*, 439 U.S. at 304; Marquette Nat'l Bank of Minneapolis v. First Omaha Serv. Corp., 262 N.W.2d 358 (1977) at 366n.2.

32. Brief for Petitioner the Marquette National Bank of Minneapolis, at 8, *Marquette*, 439 U.S., 1978 WL 223581 (U.S.); *Marquette*, 262 N.W.2d at 365.

33. Julian B. Garrett to Clerk of the Supreme Court, June 26, 1978; Order, Justice Harry A. Blackmun, No. A-500 (78–846), First of Omaha Service Corporation, dba Bankamericard, et al. vs. Iowa, et al., November 28, 1978; State v. 1st of Omaha, 61053, box 84, Supreme Court of Iowa, Iowa State Archives; State ex rel. Turner, 269 N.W.2d at 415; William E. Morrow Jr. to Robert H. Bork, November 10, 1978; Morrow to Bork, November 21, 1978, box I:27, Bork Papers.

34. Daniel T. Rodgers, *Age of Fracture* (Harvard University Press, 2011), 56–63; George J. Stigler, "The Law and Economics of Public Policy: A Plea to the Scholars," *Journal of Legal Studies* 1.1 (1972): 1–12; State ex rel. Turner, 269 N.W.2d at 416; Lawrence M. Ausubel, "The Failure of Competition in the Credit Card Market," *American Economic Review* 81, no. 1 (March 1991): 50–81. In chapter 11 I argue that banks charging higher rates can afford to heavily market cards and can market cards to riskier borrowers, crowding out low-margin, low-priced rivals.

35. State ex rel. Turner, 269 N.W.2d; Harry Blackmun to William Brennan, November 28, 1978, 77–1265 folder, box I:479, Brennan Papers. Blackmun (or his clerk) borrowed the sword metaphor from Marquette's brief (brief for Marquette National Bank, at 11, 1978 WL 223581).

36. Brief of the Minnesota AFL-CIO, at iii, 1978 WL 223582; brief of Petitioner State of Minnesota, at 13, 1978 WL 206921. For a regulatory arbitrage, see Bruce G. Carruthers and Naomi R. Lamoreaux, "Regulatory Races: The Effects of Jurisdictional Competition on Regulatory Standards," *Journal of Economic Literature* 54, no. 1 (2016): 52–97.

37. Justice Blackmun, dissent draft memorandum, May 10, 1978 (emphasis original); Blackmun conference notes, November 1, 1978, 77–1265 folder, box 284, Blackmun Papers; Robert H. Bork oral argument, "Marquette National Bank of Minneapolis v. First of Omaha Service Corporation," *Oyez*, October 31, 1978, www.oyez.org/cases/1978/77–1265; Robert H. Bork to William E. Morrow Jr., September 12, 1978, box I:27, Bork Papers.

38. *Marquette,* 439 U.S. at 312; William H. Rehnquist to William Brennan, December 11, 1978, 77–1265 folder, box I:479, Brennan Papers.

39. *First Nat. Bank of Omaha,* 482 F. Supp.; First Nat. Bank of Omaha v. Marquette Nat. Bank of Minneapolis, 636 F.2d 195, 198 (8th Cir. 1980).

40. Bork oral argument, "*Marquette*"; Bork worried about the lack of industry attention and urged William Morrow to drum up support (Robert Bork to William E. Morrow Jr., November 6, 1978, box I:27, Bork Papers).

41. Memo, Hugh McPheeters to Paul M. Ross, April 1, 1977, S317 folder, box 6, Legislative Files, Teasdale Papers.

42. Hugh McPheeters to Paul M. Ross, August 3, 1977, S317 folder, box 6, Legislative Files, Teasdale Papers.

Chapter 9. Profits Anywhere

1. "Citibank Trying to Acquire Idaho Visa Card Business," *NYT,* August 17, 1977; Leonard Wiener, "Citibank Recruiting for Visa Here," *CT,* August 18, 1977; "Competitor Criticizes Credit Card Letters," *Detroit Free Press,* August 19, 1977; Robert Lenzner, "Competition Is Keen for Bank Card Credit," *BG,* August 1, 1978; "Citibank Offering Visa Cards to Pittsburghers," *Pittsburgh Post-Gazette,* August 27, 1977; Roger Smith, "Citibank Blitz," *LAT,* March 9, 1978; Alex W. Hart, quoted in "A Visa-Card Offensive Angers the Opposition," *Business Week,* September 5, 1977, 31.

2. Jens Beckert, "Imagined Futures: Fictional Expectations in the Economy," *Theory and Society* 42, no. 3 (2013): 219–240.

3. Citicorp, "Operating Earnings after Tax," in *Citicorp Annual Report and Form 10K* (1978), 42 (ProQuest ID: 88205180); Brett Christophers, *Banking across Boundaries: Placing Finance in Capitalism* (John Wiley & Sons, 2013), 187–188; Arturo C. Porzecanski, "The International Financial Role of U.S. Commercial Banks: Past and Future," *Journal of Banking and Finance* 5, no. 1 (March 1981): 10; Ranald C. Michie, *Banks, Exchanges, and Regulators: Global Financial Markets from the 1970s* (Oxford University Press, 2020), 37–43.

4. Harold van B. Cleveland and Thomas F. Huertas, *Citibank, 1812–1970* (Harvard University Press, 1985), 5, 24, 32–34, 83–84, 156–157. See also Peter James Hud-

son, *Bankers and Empire: How Wall Street Colonized the Caribbean* (Chicago University Press, 2017).

5. Cleveland and Huertas, *Citibank,* 217–224; Phillip L. Zweig, *Wriston: Walter Wriston, Citibank and the Rise and Fall of American Financial Supremacy* (Crown Publishers, 1995), 46; National City Bank of New York, *Report to the Shareholders of the National City Bank of New York and the City Bank Farmers Trust Company, December 31, 1946* (ProQuest ID: 88184365).

6. Zweig, *Wriston,* 8, 14, 24–27, 63–67; Walter B. Wriston, "Tanker Financing for Independent Operators," *Oil Forum* (Mid-November 1955): 465–466; Christophers, *Banking across Boundaries,* 146–184; Cleveland and Huertas, *Citibank,* 261–263; Wriston, quoted in Zweig, *Wriston,* 87.

7. Monroe Kimbrel and Arnold A. Dill, "Other Sources of Funds," in *The Changing World of Banking,* ed. Herbert V. Prochnow and Herbert V. Prochnow, Jr. (Harper & Row, 1974), 75–97; Cleveland and Huertas, *Citibank,* 243–257; First National City Bank of New York, *Report to the Shareholders of the First National City Bank of New York and the First National City Trust Company, December 31, 1959* (ProQuest ID: 88192475), 6; Zweig, *Wriston,* 113, 142–143, 193; First National City Bank of New York, *The 1967 Annual Report of the First National City Bank* (ProQuest ID: 88199682), 3. On the origins of the eurodollar markets, see Catherine R. Schenk, "The Origins of the Eurodollar Market in London: 1955–1963," *Explorations in Economic History* 35, no. 2 (April 1, 1998): 221–238.

8. Zweig, *Wriston,* 196–199; Cleveland and Huertas, *Citibank,* 259–260

9. Cleveland and Huertas, *Citibank,* 264–268; Porzecanski, "International Financial Role of U.S. Commercial Banks," 10; Zweig, *Writson,* 199–202; 263–265; 398–409; *SEC and Citicorp,* 97 Cong. (serial no. 97-193) (1982); Richard Dale, *The Regulation of International Banking* (Woodhead-Faulkner, 1984), 195–204; Robert A. Hutchison, *Off the Books* (William Morrow, 1986).

10. Cleveland and Huertas, *Citibank,* 291; Thomas O. Paine, quoted in Zweig, *Wriston,* 197–198; Lee Silberman, "Presidency Contest at First National City," *WSJ,* May 5, 1967.

11. Cleveland and Huertas, *Citibank,* 247–252, 272–275.

12. "Hilton Credit Cites Overseas Expansion," *NYT,* August 25, 1965; "New York Bank, Hilton Hotels Unit Set Merge Plan," *WSJ,* September 22, 1965; H. Erich Heinemann, "Diners' Club Stock Would Cost Chase $56.5 Million Cash," *NYT,* November 18, 1965; "Hilton Seeks to Sell 50% of Carte Blanche to New York City Bank," *WSJ,* August 25, 1965; "Carte Blanche Sale to Bank Hit by U.S. Suit," *LAT,* December 31, 1965; "Chase Bank, Diners' Club End Merger Plan after Justice Unit Threatens Trust Suit," *WSJ,* April 13, 1966; "Court Bars Sale of Carte Blanche," *NYT,* December 31, 1965.

13. Christine Zumello, "The 'Everything Card' and Consumer Credit in the United States in the 1960s," *Business History Review* 85, no. 3 (Autumn 2011): 551–575; H. Erich Heinemann, "Credit Cards," *NYT,* August 1, 1967; Wriston, quoted in Zweig, *Wriston,* 230; Andrew F. Brimmer, "Statement to Congress," *Federal Reserve Bulletin* (June 1970), 479–505.

14. "One-Bank Holding Companies: The Case against a Legislative Roadblock," *University of Chicago Law Review* 36, no. 4 (1969): 803–829; Cleveland and Huertas, *Citibank*, 296–297.

15. Zweig, *Wriston*, 255–261; "Implementation of the Bank Holding Company Act Amendments of 1970: The Scope of Banking Activities," *Michigan Law Review* 71, no. 6 (1973): 1170–1211; Treasury Department, "Summary of the Background of Development of the One-Bank Holding Company Problem and a General Outline of the Principle Points to be Included in a Legislative Resolution of this Problem," February 18, 1969, FG 267 (executive), box 1, WHCF, Nixon Library; First National City Corporation, *First National City Corporation Annual Report—1971* (ProQuest ID: 88201283), 5.

16. Milton Friedman, "A Friedman Doctrine," *NYT*, September 13, 197; Zweig, *Wriston*, 182, 194, 215; Robert Metz, "Market Place: A Big Bank Tells What Its Goal Is," *NYT*, October 28, 1971; memo, Sam B. Chase and Ed Wess to Chairman Burns and Governor Mitchell, October 10, 1972, "First National City Bank" folder, box B48, Burns Papers. On the shareholder value revolution, see William Lazonick and Mary O'Sullivan, "Maximizing Shareholder Value: A New Ideology for Corporate Governance," *Economy and Society* 29, no. 1 (2000): 13–35.

17. Richard Sylla, "United States Banks in Europe: Strategies and Attitudes," in *European Banks and the American Challenge: Competition and Cooperation in International Banking under Bretton Woods*, ed. Stefano Battilossi and Youssef Cassis (Oxford University Press, 2002), 53–73; Brett Christophers, *Banking across Boundaries: Placing Finance in Capitalism* (John Wiley & Sons, 2013), 146–184; Citicorp, *Citicorp 1972*, 40–41 (Proquest ID: 88201321); Citicorp, *Citicorp Reports/1976* (1976), 20 (ProQuest ID: 88204130); "Yankee Doodle Comes Home," *The Economist*, March 4, 1978, 35; "Harder Times," *The Economist*, January 22, 1977, 21; Wriston in Carol Loomis, "Citi's Rocky Affair with the Consumer," *Fortune*, March 24, 1980.

18. Andrew L. Russell and Lee Vinsel, "After Innovation, Turn to Maintenance," *Technology and Culture* 59, no. 1 (January 2018): 1–25; Lewis Mandell, *The Credit Card Industry: A History* (Twayne Publishers, 1990), 35. In this sense, bank adoption of cards, their utilization of unsolicited mailing, and their construction of parallel networks offers a case study in DiMaggio and Powell's theory of institutional isomorphism (Paul J. DiMaggio and Walter W. Powell, "The Iron Cage Revisited: Institutional Isomorphism and Collective Rationality in Organizational Fields," *American Sociological Review* 48, no. 2 (1983): 147–160).

19. Dee W. Hock, *One from Many: VISA and the Rise of the Chaordic Organization* (Berrett-Koehler, 2005), 77; Joseph Nocera, *A Piece of the Action: How the Middle Class Joined the Money Class* (Simon & Schuster, 1994), 66–69; David L. Stearns, *Electronic Value Exchange: Origins of the VISA Electronic Payment System* (Springer, 2011), 30–32. The crisis in credit card processing paralleled the back-office crisis among securities firms (Wyatt Wells, "Certificates and Computers: The Remaking of Wall Street, 1967 to 1971," *Business History Review* 74, no. 2 [2000]: 193–235).

20. Stearns, *Electronic Value Exchange*, 32–39; Hock, *One from Many*, 83–85. Hock's National Bank of Commerce was ultimately acquired by Bank of America in 1992.

21. Nocera, *Piece of the Action*, 62–66; Hock *One from Many*, 89–91, 108–113, 115–124; Stearns, *Electronic Value Exchange*, 39–49.
22. Hock *One from Many*, 91–99, 246.
23. Stearns, *Electronic Value Exchange*, 53–90; "Interbank Card Association Report to the Membership, 1973," box 471, CRR; John Getze, "Bankamericard Profit Eludes Many Banks," *LAT*, December 29, 1971; Richard W. Plumb, "The Story of Mellon Bank's Charge Card Success and Plans for Future," *Banking* (December 1971), 21, 36, 43; David T. Cook, "Banks Trim Credit Cards but Purchases Rise," *CSM*, June 12, 1972; "Bank Credit Card Picture Brightens," *Banking* (December 1971), 19. The networks recruited the Federal Reserve to process charge slips, but the Fed declined (Federal Reserve, Subcommittee on the Payments Mechanism, Report No. 2, 5 July 1973, 33, FRBNY Archives).
24. David M. Kennedy, "Required Reading: Credit Cards Provide Meaningful Approach to Banking Procedures," *AB* (n.d., ca. January 1967), folder 4, box 5, Kennedy Papers; Josh Lauer, "Plastic Surveillance: Payment Cards and the History of Transactional Data, 1888 to Present," *Big Data & Society* 7, no. 1 (January 2020): 5–6; memo, Robert M. Fisher and James F. Smith to Board of Governors, February 23, 1976, box 20, Burns Papers.
25. Richard Phalon, "Credit Suits May Result in Refunds for Millions," *NYT*, September 19, 1970; "$3 Billion Antitrust Suit Charges 5 Chicago Banks," *CT*, August 5, 1970; Robert A. Wright, "Consumers Suing Bank of America," *NYT*, December 8, 1971; "178 Banks Accused on Excess Interest," *NYT*, April 10, 1972; "$26 Billion Sought in Bank Credit Card Suit," *LAT*, July 16, 1972; Plumb, "Story of Mellon Bank's Charge Card Success," 21, 36, 43; Frances Cerra, "Dispute Over Truth-in-Lending Act Grows," *NYT*, July 4, 1977.
26. "Bank Credit Card Picture Brightens," 19–20, 46; "Charge It, but . . .," *CSM*, March 12, 1971.
27. M. L. Jablonski, Answers to Interrogatories, February 12, 1973, *Fisher* Case File; Beverly K. Jakub to Lyn Dean, August 14, 1973, box 44, NOW Records.
28. Master Charge press kit, box 471, CRR; John H. Allan, "As Prices Soar, Bank-Card Use Jumps," *NYT*, April 22, 1974; John J. Reynolds, "Expanding Financial Services through Credit Cards," *Credit World* 62, no. 10 (July 1974): 12; "Outstanding Balances, Credit Cards and Related Plans of National Banks," in United States, Office of the Comptroller of the Currency, *Annual Report of the Comptroller of the Currency*, 1970–1973, FRASER.
29. World Bank, "Inflation, Consumer Prices for the United States (FPCPITOTLZGUSA)," FRED; Board of Governors of the Federal Reserve System, "Discount Rate Changes: Historical Dates of Changes and Rates (DISCONTINUED) (DISCOUNT)," FRED; Edwin Dale Jr., "Federal Reserve Pledges Measures to Halt Inflation," *NYT*, February 27, 1969; William Proxmire to Richard Nixon, December 24, 1969, FI5 (executive), box 41, WHCF, Nixon Library; "Credit Controls Are Essential," *BG*, January 12, 1970; Rowland Evans and Robert Novak, "Selective Credit Controls Weighed By Administration as Last Resort," *WP*, March 12, 1970.
30. U.S., President and Council of Economic Advisers, *Economic Report of the President* (Government Printing Office, 1970), 9; memo, David M. Kennedy, Robert P. Mayo,

and Paul W. McCracken to Richard M. Nixon, January 8, 1970, FG 267 (executive), box 1, WHCF, Nixon Library.

31. Edward J. Balleisen and David A. Moss, "Introduction," *Government and Markets: Toward a New Theory of Regulation*, ed. Balleisen and Moss (Cambridge University Press, 2010), 1–9; President's Commission on Financial Structure and Regulation, *The Report* (Government Printing Office, 1972), 9; H. Erich Heinemann, "Structural Unity Favored for Financial Businesses," *NYT*, November 9, 1971; memo, Richard Erb to Peter Flannigan, December 21, 1971, FG 267 (executive), box 1, WHCF, Nixon Library; *Financial Structure and Regulation*, 93 Cong. 20–38 (1973) (statement of William E. Simon, Deputy Secretary of the Treasury).

32. President's Commission on Financial Structure and Regulation, *The Report*, 46; *Financial Structure and Regulation*, 93 Cong. 17–18 (statement of Reed O. Hunt, Chairman, President's Commission on Financial Structure and Regulation).

33. Charles A. Elfrank, "New 'Jobs' Ahead for Bank Cards," *Banking* (September 1973), 115; Reynolds, "Expanding Financial Services through Credit Cards," *Credit World*, 12; John J. Reynolds, "The Future of the Bank Card," *Credit World* 62, no. 3 (December 1973): 21; Stearns, *Electronic Value Exchange*, 159–163, 171–175.

34. Stearns, *Electronic Value Exchange*, 159–163; "Contrasting Viewpoints on How to Attain Electronic Funds Transfer," *Banking* (May 1974), 30; Bernardo Bátiz-Lazo, *Cash and Dash: How ATMs and Computers Changed Banking* (Oxford University Press, 2018).

35. Thomas McIntyre and John Tower to Colleague, December 9, 1975, box 41, series [1]D, Thomas J. McIntyre Papers, University of New Hampshire; Sen. Thomas McIntyre, "S. 3266, A Bill to Establish a Commission on Electronic Funds Transfer," 120 *Cong. Rec.* 8674 (1974); United States, Public Law 93–495, Title II: National Commission on Electronic Funds Transfer (1974).

36. "Customer-Bank Communication Terminals," FR Doc. 74–29950, Filed December 23, 1974, *Federal Register*, vol. 39, no. 248, 44416–44422; *Electronic Funds Transfer Moratorium Act of 1975*, 94 Cong. 14–20 (1975) (statement of James E. Smith, Comptroller of the Currency).

37. "Customer-Bank Communication Terminals"; *Electronic Funds Transfer Moratorium Act of 1975*, 94 Cong., 36, 46–51 (statement of Smith).

38. Robert Lindsey, "Consumers Test Electronic Banking," *NYT*, April 6, 1975; advertisement, Continental Illinois Bank, *CT*, July 23, 1975; Rudolph Unger and Leonard Wiener, "Continental Bank Stations Challenged," *CT*, June 24, 1975.

39. "Citibank Mails Out Bank Cards Encoded through New Process," *WSJ*, October 25, 1973; Reginald Stuart, "Personal Finance: Cashing of Checks," *NYT*, May 9, 1974; Avery Hunt, "A Little Bank without Bankers," *Newsday*, April 28, 1975.

40. Zweig, *Wriston*, 541–549; "'Invasion' by Banks Is Feared," *NYT*, June 1, 1975; "Measure to Restrict Electronic Banking Shelved in Senate," *WSJ*, July 10, 1975; "Curb on Electronic Banks Expected to Be Contested," *NYT*, July 18, 1975.

41. Leonard Wiener, "Judge Ponders: What Is Bank?," *CT*, November 13, 1975; Richard Phillips and Leonard Wiener, "Appeals Court Says 'No' to Money Machines," *CT*, May 29, 1976.

42. Indep. Bankers Ass'n of Am. v. Smith, 402 F. Supp. 207, 209 (D.D.C. 1975), aff'd, 534 F.2d 921 (D.C. Cir. 1976); Indep. Bankers Ass'n of Am. v. Smith, 534 F.2d 921,

933 (D.C. Cir. 1976); "Curb on Electronic Banks Expected to Be Contested," *NYT*, July 18, 1975; Bloom v. Indep. Bankers Ass'n of Am., 429 U.S. 862, 97 S. Ct. 166, 50 L. Ed. 2d 141 (1976); State of Ill. ex rel. Lignoul v. Cont'l Illinois Nat. Bank & Tr. Co. of Chicago, 409 F. Supp. 1167 (N.D. Ill. 1975), aff'd in part, rev'd in part sub nom. State of Ill. ex rel. Lignoul v. Cont'l Nat. Bank & Tr. Co. of Chicago, 536 F.2d 176 (7th Cir. 1976).

43. Fisher v. First National Bank of Omaha, 548 F.2d 255 (8th Cir. 1977); Fisher v. First National Bank of Chicago, 538 F.2d 1284 (7th Cir. 1976), cert. denied, 97 S. Ct. 786 (1977); William Gruber, "Citibank Chief Urges Change in Local Branch Banking Laws," *CT*, April 19, 1978.

44. Allan, "As Prices Soar, Bank-Card Use Jumps."

45. Louis Hyman, *Debtor Nation: A History of America in Red Ink* (Princeton University Press, 2011), 173–219; Lizabeth Cohen, *A Consumers' Republic: The Politics of Mass Consumption in Postwar America* (Alfred A. Knopf, 2003), 370–386; Felicia Ann Kornbluh, *The Battle for Welfare Rights: Politics and Poverty in Modern America* (University of Pennsylvania Press, 2007), 114–131; Josh Lauer, *Creditworthy: A History of Consumer Surveillance and Financial Identity in America* (Columbia University Press, 2017), 233–241; Helaine Blythe to National Organization for Women, January 23, 1973; Susan M. Burkhalter to National BankAmericard, July 13, 1973; Alice Omohundro to Instalment Loan Department, United Virginia Bank of Fairfax, March 12, 1973, box 44; Erma Bursne to Carole de Saram, December 5, [1972], box 45; NOW Records.

46. Memo, Richard L. Peterson to Board of Governors, "Additional Information on Consumer Credit," August 7, 1974; memo, Robert M. Fisher and James F. Smith to Board of Governors, "Growth of Credit Card Credit Outstanding, 1970–1975," February 23, 1976, box 20, Burns Papers; Allan, "As Prices Soar, Bank-Card Use Jumps."

47. Plumb, "Story of Mellon Bank's Charge Card Success," 21, 36, 43.

48. "Bank Credit Card Picture Brightens," 19–20, 46.

49. Will Lissner, "Citibank Imposes Credit Card Fee," *NYT*, April 13, 1976; Stanley Strachan, "Rising Cost of Plastic Money," *NYT*, May 9, 1976; Zumello, "The 'Everything Card,'" 551–575; James A. White, "Consumers Are Charging through a Credit-Card Blizzard," *CT*, January 22, 1978; "Service Fee Is Absurd," *Newsday*, April 27, 1976; Zweig, *Wriston*, 550–551. Citi's John Reed argued that in an average year, convenience users earned the bank $14 in merchant discounts and cost the bank $20 in processing costs; the $6 fee enabled Citi to break even.

50. Frank Claus, quoted in Jane Shoemaker, "Bank Credit Cards," *Philadelphia Inquirer*, April 25, 1976; John Getze, "'Free Ride' Ending for Credit Card Holders," *LAT*, April 19, 1976; Strachan, "Rising Cost of Plastic Money," *NYT*, May 9, 1976; William D. Harrington, "Use of the Proceeds of Commercial Paper Issued by Bank Holding Companies," *Business Lawyer (ABA)* 29, no. 1 (1973): 207–26.

51. "Bank Cards," *Newsday*, April 20, 1976; "Consumers Play Fly to Bank Spider," *CT*, April 26, 1976; Zweig, *Wriston*, 550–551; Roy R. Silver, "Citibank's Card Fee Ruled Illegal," *NYT*, June 14, 1978; Sternberg v. Citicorp Credit Servs., Inc., 69 A.D.2d 352, 419 N.Y.S.2d 142 (1979), aff'd, 50 N.Y.2d 856, 407 N.E.2d 1350 (1980); "Banks

Edging toward Card Service Charges," *Banking* (August 1976), 58; White, "Consumers Are Charging through a Credit-Card Blizzard"; "Citicorp Unit Ordered to Refund Service Fees to Credit Card Users," *WSJ*, June 14, 1978; "Court Orders Citibank to Refund 50¢ to Customer," *LAT*, August 9, 1979.

52. Sam Chase to Chairman Burns, October 7, 1974, "First National City Bank" folder, box B48, Burns Papers; Loomis, "Citi's Rocky Affair with the Consumer"; Cleveland and Huertas, *Citibank*, 276, 294–295; Zweig, *Wriston*, 205–206, 362–636, 534; Reed quoted in Smith, "Citibank Blitz."

53. Brad Knickerbocker, "Credit Card Decides on a New Name," *CSM*, January 25, 1977; Hock, *One from Many*, 213–231; Nocera, *Piece of the Action*, 144–145.

54. Hock, *One from Many*, 181–182; David S. Evans and Richard Schmalensee, *Paying with Plastic: The Digital Revolution in Buying and Borrowing*, 2nd ed. (MIT Press, 2005), 275–279.

55. Smith, "Citibank Blitz"; John F. Lawrence, "Bank's Credit Card Blitz May Backfire," *LAT*, March 12, 1978; Robert A. Bennett, "Citibank's Credit Card Blitz," *NYT*, July 23, 1978; Zweig, 552–553.

56. "Citibank Trying to Acquire Idaho Visa Card Business"; Smith, "Citibank Blitz"; "Citibank's Credit Card Blitz"; Zweig, *Wriston*, 553; Walter Wriston, "Looking Backward at the Nineteen Eighties," March 31, 1980, "Citibank 1980–1982" folder, box 35, accession 94–4, Janklow Papers.

57. *The Consumer Credit Protection Act Amendments of 1977, Part 1*, 95 Cong. 365 (1977) (statement of David Phillips, Senior Vice President, Card Product Division, Citibank).

58. Wiener, "Citibank Recruiting for Visa Here"; "Perils of Plastic," *WSJ*, July 3, 1979; Lenzner, "Competition Is Keen for Bank Card Credit"; White, "Consumers Are Charging through a Credit-Card Blizzard"; David J. Ginzl, *Barnett: The Story of "Florida's Bank"* (University of Tampa Press, 2001).

59. Priscilla Meyer, "Citicorp Is Apparently Trying to Become a Major Force in the Credit Card Industry," *WSJ*, August 19, 1977; Smith, "Citibank Blitz."

60. Lauer, *Creditworthy*, 245–248; Zweig, *Wriston*, 552–553, 615–616; Citicorp, *Citicorp Annual Report and Form 10-K 1978*, 5, 28 (ProQuest ID: 88205180); Dan Dorfman, "Grim Citibank View of Interest Rates," *WP*, October 25, 1978; Citicorp, *Citicorp Annual Report and Form 10-K 1979*, 32, 40 (ProQuest ID: 88205999).

61. Memo, Lyle Gramley to Robert Carswell, October 18, 1979, Staff Files: Gramley, Lyle [3], Staff Office—CEA, box 153, Carter Library; Lawrence, "Bank's Credit Card Blitz May Backfire"; Rebecca K. Marchiel, *After Redlining: The Urban Reinvestment Movement in the Era of Financial Reregulation* (University of Chicago Press, 2020), 135–146.

Chapter 10. Credit Control

1. Jerry L. Hunter, "Letters," *Newsweek*, April 14, 1980.

2. Lyle Gramley, quoted in W. Carl Biven, *Jimmy Carter's Economy: Policy in an Age of Limits* (University of North Carolina Press, 2002), 249. Scholars chronicling the

Carter presidency ignore the CCA's place in Carter's March 1980 inflation-fighting measures, often glossing over this crucial policy action en route to discussions of Edward Kennedy's challenge for the Democratic nomination (Kaufman and Kaufman, *The Presidency of James Earl Carter* [University of Kansas Press, 1993], 204–208; Erwin Hargrove, *Jimmy Carter as President: Leadership and the Politics of the Public Good* [Louisiana State University Press, 1988], 104). Scholars concerned with Carter's economic policies have similarly downplayed the CCA (Anthony S. Campagna, *Economic Policy in the Carter Administration* [Greenwood Press, 1995], 96; Biven, *Jimmy Carter's Economy*, 246–249; Bruce J. Schulman, "Slouching toward the Supply Side: Jimmy Carter and the New American Political Economy," *The Carter Presidency: Policy Choices in the Post-New Deal Era*, ed. Gary M. Fink and Hugh Davis Graham [University Press of Kansas, 1998], 57–62). For the Volcker Shock, see Iwan Morgan, "Monetary Metamorphosis: The Volcker Fed and Inflation," *Journal of Policy History* 24, no. 4 (2012): 545–71.

3. Hargrove, *Jimmy Carter as President*, 6–7, 87; Kaufman, *James Earl Carter*, 8–12; Campagna, *Economic Policy in the Carter Administration*, 6–9, 22–23.

4. Jimmy Carter, *Keeping Faith: Memoirs of a President* (University of Arkansas Press, 1995), 79; Schulman, "Slouching toward the Supply Side," 54–55; Hargrove, *Jimmy Carter as President*, 69–70, 92; Angus Burgin, *The Great Persuasion: Reinventing Free Markets since the Great Depression* (Harvard University Press, 2015); Elizabeth Popp Berman, *Thinking Like an Economist: How Efficiency Replaced Equality in U.S. Public Policy* (Princeton University Press, 2022); Thomas K. McCraw, *Prophets of Regulation* (Harvard University Press, 1984), 222–310; Allen V. Kneese and Charles L. Schultze, *Pollution, Prices, and Public Policy* (Brookings Institution, 1974); Biven, *Jimmy Carter's Economy*, 44; Bruce J. Schulman, *The Seventies: The Great Shift in American Culture, Society, and Politics* (Simon & Schuster, 2001), 129–131.

5. Kaufman, *James Earl Carter*, 52, 80–81, 113–114; Jimmy Carter, "Anti-Inflation Program Address to the Nation," October 24, 1978, APP.

6. Kaufman, *James Earl Carter*, 139; Federal Reserve Bank of Minneapolis, "The Consumer Price Index (Estimate), 1800–," https://www.minneapolisfed.org/about-us/monetary-policy/inflation-calculator/consumer-price-index-1800-; Organization for Economic Co-operation and Development, "Consumer Price Index: Total All Items for the United States (CPALTT01USM661S)," FRED; memo, Charles B. Holstein to Ester Peterson, March 12, 1979, box 13, Special Advisor—Inflation, Kahn; document, "Selective Control of Consumer Credit," March 13, 1979, box 108, Staff Office—CEA; memo, Department of the Treasury to President Carter, March 30, 1979; memo, Department of the Treasury to President Carter, March 12, 1979; memo, Burke Dillon to Charlie Shultze, April 10, 1979, box 13, Special Advisor—Inflation, Kahn; memo, Department of Justice to Charlie Schultze, April 12, 1979, box 14; memo, Charlie Schultze to President Carter, May 25, 1979, box 54, Staff Office—CEA, Carter Library.

7. Memo, Lyle Gramley to Charlie Schultze, January 25, 1979; memo, "Selective Controls of Consumer Credit," March 13, 1979; memo, "A Proposal to Limit the Terms of Consumer Credit" (n.d., ca. April 1970), box 14; memo, Charlie Schultze to President Carter, May 25, 1979, box 54, Staff Office—CEA, Carter Library.

8. Memo, "Selective Controls of Consumer Credit," March 13, 1979; memo, Burke Dillon to Charlie Schultze, April 10, 1979, box 14, Staff Office—CEA, Carter Library. The Fed was also worried about household debt burdens during this period (memo, "Burden of Consumer Debt," Division of Research and Statistics [Charles A. Luckett] to Board of Governors, June 20, 1977; memo, "Consumer Credit Developments," Division of Research and Statistics [Charles A. Luckett] to Chairman Burns, June 29, 1977, box 20, Burns Papers).

9. Meg Jacobs, *Panic at the Pump: The Energy Crisis and the Transformation of American Politics in the 1970s* (Hill and Wang, 2017); Daniel Horowitz, *The Anxieties of Affluence: Critiques of American Consumer Culture, 1939–1979* (University of Massachusetts Press, 2004), 205–206; Daniel Bell, *The Cultural Contradictions of Capitalism* (Basic Books, 1976); Robert N. Bellah, *The New Religious Consciousness* (University of California Press, 1976); Christopher Lasch, *The Culture of Narcissism: American Life in an Age of Diminishing Expectations* (W. W. Norton, 1978).

10. Carter, "The Energy Problem: Address to the Nation," April 18, 1977, APP; Carter, *Keeping the Faith*, 120–121; memo, Pat Caddell to President Carter, April 23, 1979, box 40, Staff Offices: Press, Jody Powell, Carter Library; Horowitz, *Anxieties of Affluence*, 229; cf. Jimmy Carter, *White House Diaries* (Farrar, Straus and Giroux, 2010), 323.

11. Carter, *Keeping the Faith*, 121–125; Daniel Horowitz, *Jimmy Carter and the Energy Crisis of the 1970s: The "Crisis of Confidence Speech," A Brief History with Documents* (Bedford/St. Martins, 2005), 126, 152; Carter, "Address to the Nation on Energy and National Goals: 'The Malaise Speech,'" July 15, 1979, APP.

12. J. David Woodard, *The America That Reagan Built* (Praeger, 2006), 4–7; Biven, *Jimmy Carter's Economy*, 273; Kevin Mattson, *"What the Heck Are You Up to Mr. President:" Jimmy Carter, America's "Malaise," and the Speech That Should Have Changed the Country* (Bloomsbury, 2009), 159–161.

13. Thomas Karier, *Great Experiments in American Economic Policy: From Kennedy to Reagan* (Praeger, 1997), 40; "Straight and Narrow with Mr. Volcker," *NYT*, July 26, 1979.

14. Biven, *Jimmy Carter's Economy*, 240; Karier, *Great Experiments*, 41, 43; Paul A. Volcker, "Monetary Policy Transmission: Past and Future Challenges," *Federal Reserve Bank of New York Economic Policy Review* (May 2002): 8–9; Allan H. Meltzer, *A History of the Federal Reserve*, vol. 2, book 2 (1970–1986), 1008–1018.

15. Biven, *Jimmy Carter's Economy*, 240; Paul Volcker and Nancy Teeters quoted in, Board of Governors of the Federal Reserve System, Open Market Investment Committee for the Federal Reserve System, "Meeting of Federal Open Market Committee: October 6, 1979," Federal Open Market Committee Meeting Minutes, Transcripts, and Other Documents, 1933–2018, FRASER; "Support Mr. Volcker," *WSJ*, October 8, 1979; Meltzer, *Federal Reserve*, vol. 2, book 2, 1019–1043.

16. Steven Rattner, "Inflation Rise Seen," *NYT*, February 16, 1980; interview with Charles Schultze, July 25, 2013, notes in author's possession; memo, Anne Wexler to President Carter, February 23, 1980, box 172, Presidential Handwriting File; memo, Ester Peterson to Stuart Eizenstat, February 19, 1980, box FI-25, WHCF, Carter Library.

17. Herbert J. G. Bab, "The Fed's Latest Folly," *CSM*, November 23, 1979; "Pro & Con: Would U.S. Credit Controls Whip Inflation?," *CT*, February 24, 1980; Paul Volcker, quoted in "Volcker Says That Any Political Pressure on Fed to Ease Its Policy Will Be Resisted," *WSJ*, October 29, 1979; Volcker, quoted in Stacey L. Schreft, "Credit Controls: 1980," Federal Reserve Bank of Richmond, *Economic Review* 76 (November/December 1990), 33.

18. Memo, CEA and Treasury Staff to Economic Planning Group, February 26, 1980, box 95, Staff Office—CEA; memo, William Miller to President Carter, February 28, 1980, box 172, Presidential Handwriting File; memo, Burke Dillon to Charlie Schultze, February 27, 1980, box 147, Staff Office—CEA, Carter Library; Shreft, "Credit Controls: 1980," 33; Schultze interview.

19. Memo, William Miller to President Carter, February 28, 1980, box 172, Presidential Handwriting File; letter, Alfred Kahn to Betsy Hamilton, February 2, 1980, box 13, Special Advisor—Inflation, Kahn, Carter Library; "Withdrawal Pain for Credit-Card Holders," *Newsweek*, March 31, 1980, 29; memo, Burke Dillon to Charlie Schultze, February 27, 1980, box 147, Staff Office—CEA, Carter Library; Stephen H. Axilrod, *Inside the Fed: Monetary Policy and Its Management, Martin through Greenspan to Bernanke* (MIT Press, 2011), 94.

20. Memo, Burke Dillon to Charlie Schultze, April 10, 1979, box 14, Staff Office—CEA, Carter Library; Biven, *Jimmy Carter's Economy*, 246–247.

21. Memo, Al McDonald to President Carter, March 7, 1980; memo, Department of the Treasury to President Carter, March 12, 1980, box 173, Presidential Handwriting File, Carter Library; ad, Citibank, "Credit Controls—Pushing a String," *NYT*, March 3, 1980 (the ad also appeared in *WP*, March 3, 1980, and *WSJ*, March 3, 1980); Shreft, "Credit Controls: 1980," 33.

22. Carter, "Anti-Inflation Program Remarks Announcing the Administration's Program," March 14, 1980, APP.

23. Roger S. White, "Federal Reserve System Special Anti-Inflation Programs Announced March 14, 1980: A Brief Description," Congressional Research Service Rep. No. 80-73 E, April 2, 1980, 5.

24. "Federal Reserve Clamps Controls on Credit Cards," *Atlanta Constitution*, March 15, 1980; Robert A. Rosenblatt, "Credit Card Interest to Rise," *LAT*, March 15, 1980; John M. Berry, "Restraints Imposed on Credit," *WP*, March 15, 1980; Stephen E. Nordlinger and James A. Rousmaniere Jr., "Federal Reserve Seeking to Discourage People from Living beyond Their Means," *BS*, March 15, 1980; Robert J. Samuelson, "Credit-Card Debt Isn't the Problem," *WP*, April 8, 1980.

25. Hewitt Crosby, "'Now' Syndrome," *WP*, March 19, 1980; letter, Lloyd C. Yager to Alfred Kahn, April 19, 1980, box 13, Special Advisor—Inflation, Kahn, Carter Library; "Alfred E. Kahn Oral History, Chairman of the Council on Wage and Price Stability; Advisor to the President on Inflation," December 10–11, 1981, University of Virginia, Miller Center for Public Affairs, Presidential Oral Histories, https://millercenter.org/the-presidency/presidential-oral-histories/alfred-e-kahn-oral-history-chairman-council-wage-and.

26. Steve Lohr, "Buying Habits Found Unexpectedly Curbed by Controls on Credit," *NYT*, May 9, 1980; ad, "How Washington's New Credit Guidelines Affect the

American Express Card," *Newsweek,* April 14, 1980, 7; "Americans View Inflation, The Public Policy Response, and the Retail Industry (Cambridge Reports, Inc., April 1980), box 25, Special Advisor—Inflation, Kahn, Carter Library.

27. Lohr, "Buying Habits Found Unexpectedly Curbed"; "Consumer Debt Down Sharply," *NYT,* June 7, 1980; Schreft, "Credit Controls: 1980." The decline in 1980 remained the largest, as a percentage of total revolving debt outstanding, until the 2008 recession. Board of Governors of the Federal Reserve System, "G.19, Consumer Credit, Historical Data," https://www.federalreserve.gov/releases/g19/HIST/default.htm.

28. Memo, Charlie Schultze to President Carter, May 5, 1980, box 54, Staff Office—CEA, Carter Library; *Federal Reserve's Second Monetary Policy Report for 1980,* 96 Cong. 110 (statement of Paul Volcker, Chairman, Federal Reserve Board); Volcker, "Monetary Policy Transmission," 8.

29. Schreft, "Credit Controls: 1980," 42; Jerry Knight, "Confusion Cited on Credit Curbs," *WP,* May 20, 1980; Memo, Charlie Schultze to President Carter, May 5, 1980, box 54, Staff Office—CEA, Carter Library; Jimmy Carter, "White House Briefing for Community Leaders," May 27, 1980, APP.

30. Frederick H. Schultz quoted in Federal Reserve, "Meeting of Federal Open Market Committee: February 4–5, 1980," FRASER; Molly Sinclair, "Credit Card Users Face Higher Charges," *WP,* February 22, 1980; Thomas Timlen quoted in Federal Reserve, "Meeting of Federal Open Market Committee: March 7, 1980," FRASER.

31. Memo, Al McDonald and Anne Wexler to EPG Steering Group, March 5, 1980, box 25, Special Advisor—Kahn, Carter Library.

32. Isadore Barmash, "Debtor Beware," *NYT,* March 30, 1980; "Bank of America Reins in Its Lending, Calls on U.S. to Push Monetary Restraint," *WSJ,* March 27, 1980; Jerry Knight, "Sears, Ward's Move to Restrain Credit," *WP,* March 18, 1980; Jerry Knight, "Fed Tightens Crackdown on Credit Cards," *WP,* April 3, 1980.

33. Walter Wriston, "Outsmarting Inflation," *WP,* March 13, 1980; *Credit Controls: An Evaluation,* Comm. Print 96–20, at 5 (1980) (staff rep.), emphasis original.

34. Marquette Nat. Bank of Minneapolis v. First of Omaha Service Corp., 439 U.S. 299 (1978); *Credit Controls: An Evaluation,* 4, 11–12; Robert D. Manning, *Credit Card Nation: The Consequences of America's Addiction to Credit* (Basic Books, 2000), 5, 294; Phillip Zweig, *Wriston: Walter Wriston, Citibank and the Rise and Fall of American Financial Supremacy* (Crown Publishers, 1995), 550–551; Lucia Mouat, "To Charge or Not to Charge," *CSM,* June 30, 1980.

35. Clyde H. Farnsworth, "Consumer Debt Down for May," *NYT,* July 10, 1980, quoted in Schreft, "Credit Controls: 1980," 43–46. The literature on the 1980 recession is surprisingly thin, but for evidence that controls caused the sharpness and timing, see Victor Zarnowitz and Geoffrey H. Moore, "The Timing and Severity of the 1980 Recession," in *Business Cycles, Inflation, and Forecasting,* 2nd ed., ed. Geoffrey H. Moore (Ballinger, 1983), 14; Raymond E. Owens and Stacey L. Schreft, "Identifying Credit Crunches," *Contemporary Economic Policy* 13, no. 2 (April 1995): 63–76.

36. Ronald Reagan, "Address Accepting the Presidential Nomination at the Republican National Convention in Detroit," July 17, 1980, APP; Dick Wirthlin, with Wynton C. Hall, *The Greatest Communicator: What Ronald Reagan Taught Me about*

Politics, Leadership, and Life (John Wiley & Sons, 2004), 35–36; Woodard, *America That Reagan Built*, 27. John Anderson, a moderate Republican from Illinois ran as an independent but was never a serious contender.

37. Martin Schram, "Carter Goes into Debate with Lead in New Poll," October 28, 1980, *WP;* Jimmy Carter and Ronald Reagan, "Presidential Debate in Cleveland," October 28, 1980, APP; Kaufman, *James Earl Carter,* 205.

38. Ronald Reagan, "Presidential Debate in Cleveland," October 28, 1980, APP; Hedrick Smith, "President Concedes: Republican Gains Victory in All Areas and Vows to Act on Economy," *NYT,* November 5, 1980. There is an extensive political science literature on the phenomenon of economic voting in presidential elections; for a comprehensive overview, see Richard Nadeau and Michael S. Lewis-Beck, "National Economic Voting in U.S. Presidential Elections," *Journal of Politics* 63, no.1 (February 2001): 159–181; Masoud Moghaddam and Hallie Elich, "Predicting the Incumbent Party Vote Share in U.S. Presidential Elections," *CATO Journal* 29 (Fall 2009): 455–468. Sides and Vavreck attribute 40 percent of the popular vote outcome to GDP growth (John Sides and Lynn Vavreck, *The Gamble: Choice and Chance in the 2012 Presidential Election* [Princeton University Press, 2013], 12n2).

39. Daniel T. Rodgers, *Age of Fracture* (Harvard University Press, 2011), 15–40; "New Credit-Card Spending Boom Ahead," *Nilson Report* 257 (April 1981), 1–2; Board of Governors of the Federal Reserve System, "G.19, Consumer Credit, Historical Data," https://www.federalreserve.gov/releases/g19/HIST/default.htm.

40. Schultze interview; "Alfred E. Kahn Oral History"; Yankelovich, Skelly, and White, Inc., *A Study of the American Family and Money* (General Mills Consumer Center, 1975).

41. Cf. CEA Staff Files, Reagan Library. For the relationship between credit, wages, and the promise of prosperity, see: Dirk Krueger and Fabrizio Perri, "Does Income Inequality Lead to Consumption Inequality? Evidence and Theory," *Review of Economic Studies* 73, no. 1 (2006): 163–193; Colin Crouch, "Privatized Keynesianism: An Unacknowledged Policy Regime," *British Journal of Politics & International Relations* 11, no. 3 (2009): 382–99; Dan Herman, "The Missing Movement: A Polanyian Analysis of Pre-Crisis America," *International Journal of Social Economics* 39, no. 8 (2012): 624–641.

Chapter 11. Breakdown

1. This chapter significantly revises portions of my article, "Citibank, Credit Cards, and the Local Politics of National Consumer Finance, 1968–1991," *Business History Review* 90, no. 1 (Spring 2016): 57–80.

2. On the wanning influence of the consumer movement, see Lizabeth Cohen, *A Consumers' Republic: The Politics of Mass Consumption in Postwar America* (Alfred A. Knopf, 2003), 288–397; Benjamin C. Waterhouse, Lobbying America: The Politics of Business from Nixon to NAFTA, Politics and Society in Twentieth-Century America (Princeton University Press, 2014), 140–173.

3. Visa USA Inc., "Credit Controls and Bank Credit Cards: Analysis and Proposals," 794.01 (L) Voluntary Credit Restraint March 1980, FRBNY Archives; Dan Dorfman,

"Grim Citibank View of Interest Rates," *WP*, October 25, 1978; Citicorp, *Citicorp Annual Report and Form 10-K 1979*, 32, 40 (ProQuest ID: 88205999).

4. Jon Walker, "Citibank Could Bring 300–2,000 Jobs to S.D.," *SFAL*, March 5, 1980.

5. For an alternate account, cf. Robert Wright "Wall Street on the Prairie: Citibank, South Dakota and the Origins of Financial Deregulation," *Financial History* 106 (Spring 2012): 24–26.

6. Phillip L. Zweig, *Wriston: Walter Wriston, Citibank, and the Rise and Fall of American Financial Supremacy* (Crown Publishers, 1995), 553, 678–681; "Memorandum on National Bank Issues in Missouri" (n.d.), "Citibank—Visa '80" folder, box 40, Issue Files, Teasdale Papers.

7. "Still Last in Salary Scale," *Pierre Daily Capital Journal*, January 24, 1980; William Janklow, interview, "Secret History of the Credit Card," *Frontline*, PBS, April 24, 2004, http://www.pbs.org/wgbh/pages/frontline/shows/credit/interviews/janklow.html.

8. Douglas Hajek, "South Dakota Takes Center Stage: Remembering the Father of the 'Citibank Bill,'" *North Western Financial Review* 189 (September 2004): 13–14, 16; Thomas Reardon, "T. M. Reardon's First-Hand Account of Citibank's Move to South Dakota," *North Western Financial Review* 189 (September 2004): 15; cf. Paul H. Nordstrom to William Janklow, October 26, 1979, "Banking, 1979–1984" folder, box 34, accession 94–4, Janklow Papers.

9. William Janklow to Charles E. Long, March 12, 1980, "Citibank 1980–1982" folder, box 35, accession 94–4, Janklow Papers; "Executive Council Minutes," March 3, 1980, South Dakota Bankers Association, Pierre, SD; Walker, "Citibank Could Bring 300–2,000 Jobs."

10. Charles E. Long to William Janklow, February 19, 1980; Houston Haugo to William Janklow, March 5, 1980; William Janklow to Charles Long, March 12, 1980; mhb [Janklow's secretary] to Bill [William Janklow], March 27, 1980; C. F. Muckenfuss III, "Opinion of the Comptroller of the Currency on the Application to Charter Citibank (South Dakota), N.A." November 19, 1980, "Citibank 1980–1982" folder, box 35, accession 94–4, Janklow Papers; "Executive Council Minutes"; State of South Dakota, *1980 Session Laws of South Dakota*, ch. 331, 536–537; Hajek, "South Dakota Takes Center Stage."

11. Robert Bennett, "Citibank to Bypass State Usury Laws," *NYT*, February 27, 1980; Morgan and Gianotti, "Citibank Warns of Loan Curb," *Newsday*, February 28, 1980; Robert Bennett, "Carey Said to Study Usury Limit," *NYT*, February 28, 1980; "Citibank Intensifies Usury-Limit Fight of Credit Card Unit," *WSJ*, February 28, 1980.

12. Richard K. LeBlond to Hugh L. Carey, March 3, 1980; Robert M. Stevens to Robert J. Morgado, April 8, 1980; Richard K. LeBlond to Hugh L. Carey, March 25, 1980; Walter Wriston to Hugh L. Carey, March 25, 1980; Morton Rechler to Hugh L. Carey, April 2, 1980; Muriel Siebert to [X Banker, n.p.], July 23, 1980, reel 11, second term, Carey Subject Files; Peter M. Gianotti, "Carey Seeks to Ease Usury Law," *Newsday*, March 23, 1980; Niell S. Rosenfeld, "Banking Bills Unresolved in Albany," *Newsday*, June 10, 1980; Stanley Fink quoted in Selwyn Raab, "Legislators Fail to Agree on a Plan to Raise Some Bank Loan Rates," *NYT*, June, 15 1980.

13. Walter Wriston to Hugh L. Carey, June 30, 1980, reel 11, second term, Carey Subject Files; Siebert, quoted in Peter Gianotti, "Del. Makes Bid to NY Banks," *Newsday*, July 24, 1980.

14. Peter M. Gianotti, "Divisions Linger on Bank Law," *Newsday*, July 3, 1980; James L. Emery to Hugh L. Carey, August 28, 1980; Walter J. Floss Jr. to Hugh L. Carey, August 30, 1980; Hugh L. Carey to News Director, November 14, 1980, reel 11, second term, Carey Subject Files; letter of the AFL-CIO, n.d. (ca. November 1980) at 37, bill jacket L. 1980, ch. 883, New York State Archives.

15. Leon E. de Kalb to Hugh L. Carey, December 8, 1980; Arthur Berman to Hugh L. Carey, December 23, 1980; Richard K. LeBlond to Hugh J. Carey (emphasis added), December 1, 1980; James P. Murphy to Hugh J. Carey, December 2, 1980; Edward W. Duffy to Hugh L. Carey (emphasis added), December 5, 1980, reel 11, second term, Carey Subject Files; Zweig, *Wriston*, 733.

16. Isadore Barmash, "Credit Cards at Crossroads," *NYT*, August 3, 1980; "Citibank, Chase Raise Interest Rates, Charge Fees on Their Credit Cards," *WSJ*, December 19, 1980; David C. McBride, "Birth of a Banking Bonanza," *Delaware Lawyer* 1, no. 2 (Fall 1982): 32, 36–37, 54–55; Zweig, *Wriston*, 692; Robert A. Bennett, "Banks May Shift Units out of State," *NYT*, June 11 1980; Joan FitzGerald, "Making It in . . . Delaware," *BG*, March 24, 1981; William W. Boyer and Edward C. Ratledge, *Pivotal Policies in Delaware: From Desegregation to Deregulation* (University of Delaware Press, 2014), 142–144. For the ways policymakers reimagined urban economies in light of deindustrialization, see Tracy Neumann, *Remaking the Rust Belt: The Postindustrial Transformation of North America* (University of Pennsylvania Press, 2016).

17. Citicorp, *Citicorp Annual Report and Form 10-K 1980*, 11 (ProQuest ID: 88207562); Zweig, *Wriston*, 692; Celia Cohen and Bill Boyle, "Consumer Advocates Wary of Bank Enticement Bills," *Wilmington Evening Journal*, January 22, 1981; McBride, "Birth of a Banking Bonanza," 32; "New York Bankers Invited to Delaware," *NYT*, July 23, 1980.

18. Larry Nagengast, *Pierre S. du Pont IV: Governor of Delaware, 1977–1985* (Delaware Heritage Press, 1985), 106–112; Boyer and Ratledge, *Pivotal Policies in Delaware*, 153; E. J. Dionne Jr., "Further Liberalization of Banking Laws Is Not Planned," *NYT*, March 18, 1981.

19. Eric R. Chabrow, "Bank Bill Debate Heated, Lengthy, but Bankers Win," *Delaware State News*, February 4, 1981. For the development of offshore finance, see Vanessa Ogle, "Archipelago Capitalism: Tax Havens, Offshore Money, and the State, 1950s–1970s," *American Historical Review* 122, no. 5 (December 2017): 1431–58.

20. Pierre du Pont, IV, quoted in Bill Boyle, "Delaware: Banking Mecca?," *Wilmington Evening Journal*, January 15, 1981; Eric R. Chabrow, "Two Large New York Banks Eye State Units," *Delaware State News*, January 15, 1981; Celia Cohen and Bill Boyle, "Consumer Advocates Wary of Bank Enticement Bills," *Wilmington Evening Journal*, January 22, 1981; Celia Cohen, "'Bank Mecca' Bills Go to Senate," *Wilmington Evening Journal*, January 23, 1981.

21. Bill Boyle, "Bank Bills Await Governor's Signature," *Wilmington Evening Journal*, February 4, 1981; Ralph S. Mayed, "Del. and the Banks: Shotgun Wedding?" *Wilmington Evening Journal*, January 23, 1981.

22. Chabrow, "Two Large New York Banks Eye State Units"; Broderick Perkins, "Delaware May Draw New Industries but Job Outlook for Blacks Is Bleak," *Wilmington Evening Journal,* January 29, 1981; Celia Cohen, "Delaware House Narrowly Rejects King Holiday Bill," *Wilmington Evening Journal,* February 4, 1981; Eric R. Chabrow, "Maryland Bank Opts for Delaware," *Delaware State News,* February 5, 1981.

23. Siebert quoted in Robert A. Bennett, "State's Banks Warned on Moving Out," *NYT,* January 30, 1981.

24. Curtis Kuehn to Theodore Allison, "Citicorp Application for a National Bank Charter in Sioux Falls, South Dakota," March 19, 1980, Citibank Correspondence Binder, Sioux Falls Chamber of Commerce.

25. Citicorp, "Application to Organize a National Bank," March 12, 1980, "Citibank 1979" folder; Muckenfuss, "Opinion of the Comptroller of the Currency on the Application to Charter Citibank (South Dakota), N.A.," November 19, 1980, 4, "Citibank 1980–1982" folder, box 35, accession 94–4, Janklow Papers. In its 1980 annual report, the bank wrote: "At Citicorp, we believe the most effective way to raise billions of dollars of funds daily in the money markets of the world is to have highly-trained market-tested treasurers in every market" (Citicorp, *Citicorp Annual Report and Form 10-K 1980,* 29 [ProQuest ID: 88207562]).

26. *SEC and Citicorp,* 97 Cong. (serial no. 97-193) (1982); Richard Dale, *The Regulation of International Banking* (Woodhead-Faulkner, 1984), 195–204; Robert A. Hutchison, *Off the Books* (William Morrow, 1986).

27. Eugene Carlson, "Delaware Grabs Early Lead in Luring Out-of-State Banks," *WSJ,* December 15, 1981; David R. Francis, "State after State Is Lifting the Ceilings on Interest Rates," *CSM,* August 11, 1981; State of Delaware, *Laws of the State of Delaware* 63 (1981) ch. 2, 2–19; "Why Is Plastic So Costly," *Time,* April 4, 1983; Terry Branstad to C. W. Strong Jr., June 29, 1984, box 2, Office of Program Research, Financial Institutions and Insurance Committee, House of Representatives, Washington State Archives.

28. Lawrence M. Ausubel, "The Failure of Competition in the Credit Card Market," *American Economic Review* 81, no. 1 (1991): 70, 72. On U.S. wage stagnation, see Jon D. Wisman, "Wage Stagnation, Rising Inequality and the Financial Crisis of 2008," *Cambridge Journal of Economics* 37, no. 4 (July 1, 2013): 921–45.

29. Robert A. Bennett, "Citibank Sets $15 Fee on Its 2 Credit Cards; Loans to Cost 19.8%," *NYT,* December 18, 1980; "Citibank, Chase Raise Interest, Charge Fees on Their Credit Cards," *WSJ,* December 19, 1980; Robert A. Bennett, "Citibank Will Raise Fee on Charge Cards to $20," *NYT,* January 11, 1982; Daniel F. Cuff, "Waiting for Consumer Rates to Fall," *NYT,* September 5, 1982; Daniel Kahn, "Falling Rates Bypass Credit Cards," *Newsday,* October 17, 1982; "Cash-Rich Banks Seek Credit-Card Customers," *CT,* September 27, 1983; Julie Salamon, "Citicorp Again Touts Credit Cards Despite Lofty Rates, Other Risks," *WSJ,* August 28, 1981; Daniel Hertzberg, "Consumer Credit Rates Will Fall Little," *WSJ,* December 10, 1984; John M. Broder, "Huge Marketing Push for Credit Cards," *LAT,* June 2, 1985; Irvin Molotsky, "The High Cost of Credit Card Credit," *NYT,* October 13, 1985.

30. "Statement of Robert L. Clarke, Comptroller of the Currency, before the Senate Committee on Banking, Housing, and Urban Affairs, May 21, 1987," in Comptrol-

ler of the Currency, *Quarterly Journal* 6, no. 3 (1986–1987), 18, 24; John Henderson and Jonathan P. Scott, *Securitization* (New York Institute of Finance, 1988), 88; James A. Rosenthal and Juan M. Ocampo, *Securitization of Credit: Inside the New Technology of Finance* (John Wiley & Sons, 1988), 119–155; Ausubel, "Failure of Competition," 65–68.

31. Charles E. Schumer and Julius Ganachowski, "The Credit Card Puzzle: Why the Rates Never Fall," *WP*, January 12, 1986; "Credit Card Rate List Released," *NYT*, November 19, 1985; Barbara Bradley, "At Last, Some Banks Cut Credit Card Rates," June 17, 1986; William Gruber, "Banks Resolute about Cards' Interest," August 31, 1986.

32. Jan Wong, "Out-of-State Credit Cards Flooding In: Citibank Most Aggressive," *BG*, November 15, 1983; Jan Wong, "3 Banks May Move Credit Card Operations," *BG*, October 22, 1984; Paul R. Watro, "The Bank Credit-Card Boom: Some Explanations and Consequences," *Federal Reserve Bank of Cleveland Economic Commentary* (March 1988).

33. United States, Office of the Comptroller of the Currency, *Annual Report of the Comptroller of the Currency*, 1980, FRASER; *Quarterly Report of the Comptroller of the Currency*, 1986; Board of Governors of the Federal Reserve System, "G.19, Consumer Credit, Historical Data," https://www.federalreserve.gov/releases/g19/HIST/default.htm; Janklow, *Frontline* interview; U.S. Decennial Census, Industry by Occupation for Employed Civilian Population 16 Years and Over, 1970–2000, accessed through Social Explorer database, http://www.socialexplorer.org. It is possible that financial services jobs were also categorized under retail employment in the case of department store credit processing centers or "other" services, which also increased significantly in South Dakota from 1980 to 2000.

34. *South Dakota Codified Laws* (Michie, 1996), 1996 Revision, V.4A, 474–475; V.15A, 26–27; document, "Tax or User Fee: Bank Franchise Tax," "BOF & M, 1990–1994" folder, box 5727, Exec. Mgmt/ Gubernatorial Div/Gov. George Mickelson/General Files/Bureau of Finance & Mgmt, 1987–1993, South Dakota State Historical Society, Pierre, SD.

35. State of Delaware, Office of the State Bank Commissioner, "Consolidated Statement of All Banks and Trust Companies in Delaware," August 20, 1982, RG1325 (microfiche); Delaware, *Sixty-Third Annual Report of the State Bank Commissioner of Delaware for the Fiscal Year Ended June 30, 1982*, 57; Delaware, *Sixty-Sixth Annual Report of the State Bank Commissioner of Delaware for the Fiscal Year Ended June 30, 1985*, 8, 71; Delaware, *Sixty-Ninth Annual Report of the State Bank Commissioner of Delaware for the Fiscal Year Ended June 30, 1988*, 6, 89, Delaware State Archives.

36. Vincent E. Rossiter, quoted in Gary Bingner, *South Dakota Banking: The Lowdown on High Finance in Middle America, A History of the Citibank Revolution, 1980–1983* (1983), draft copy, South Dakota State Library, Pierre, 68; Nathan Hayward III quoted in Eric R. Chabrow, "Bank Bill Debate Heated, Lengthy, but Bankers Win"; Tim Schreiner, "Citibank May Bring Bitter Aftereffects," *SFAL*, December 29, 1980.

37. Memo, Office of the Governor, Bureau of Industrial and Agricultural Development, "South Dakota: The Frontier of Modern Banking," October 28, 1985, "Banking Laws" folder, Sioux Falls Chamber of Commerce; Michael L. Millenson, "How

South Dakota Beckons the Banking Giants: Fast Governor and Liberal Laws," *CT*, November 20, 1983; "Janklow Defends Legislation That Attracts Banks to State," *SFAL*, September 20, 1983; "Fed Dims the Luster of South Dakota Inc.," *SFAL*, August 4, 1985; Zweig, *Wriston*, 810–811; Rudolph A. Pyatt Jr., "Bitter Harvest in Maryland for Bankers," *WP*, January 18, 1984.

38. Terry Woster, "Bill Puts Citibank on Sliding Tax Scale," *SFAL*, February 1, 1991; Terry Woster, "Governor Defends Tax-Hike Plans," *SFAL*, January 17, 1991; Dale Gullickson, "Citibank Tax Break Doesn't Make Sense," *SFAL*, February 7, 1991; Saskia Sassen, *The Global City: New York, London, Tokyo*, 2nd ed. (Princeton University Press, 2001); Randall Smith, "Handling Money: Some Unlikely Places Benefit from the Boom in Financial Services," *WSJ*, March 31, 1983; DRI/McGraw-Hill and MasterCard International, "A Study of Employment, Regulations and the Credit Card Industry," January 1993, California State Library; Anne Saker, "South Dakota Is Friendly to Credit Card Industry," *SFAL*, March 5, 1993; Jim Hass, "Credit Industry Is Cheap, not Friendly," *SFAL*, March 12, 1993. On worker relocation in industrial strategy, see Jefferson Cowie, *Capital Moves: RCA's Seventy-Year Quest for Cheap Labor* (Cornell University Press, 1999).

39. Citigroup, Citibank South Dakota N.A., *A State of Dreams: A World of Difference* (2006), author's possession; Citigroup, *Citigroup Annual Report 2006*, sec. 1, 3, https://www.citigroup.com/citi/investor/quarterly/2007/ar06c_en.pdf; Board of Governors of the Federal Reserve System, "G.19, Consumer Credit, Historical Data," https://www.federalreserve.gov/releases/g19/HIST/default.htm.

40. Brief of the Minnesota AFL-CIO, as Amicus Curiae Supporting Petitioner Minnesota, at iii, Marquette Nat'l Bank of Minneapolis v. First of Omaha Serv. Corp., 439 U.S. 299 (1978) (Nos. 77–1265, 77–1258), 1978 WL 223582.

41. Walter Wriston to Charles Percy, April 23, 1976, box 33, Walter B. Wriston Papers, Tufts University Library.

42. Smiley v. Citibank (South Dakota), N.A., 517 U.S. 735; Randall S. Kroszner and Philip E. Strahan, "What Drives Deregulation? Economics and Politics of the Relaxation of Bank Branching Restrictions," *Quarterly Journal of Economics* 114, no. 4 (November 1999): 1460–1462.

Epilogue

1. Federal Reserve Bank of San Francisco, "2022 Findings from the Diary of Consumer Payment Choice," May 2, 2022, https://www.frbsf.org/cash/publications/fed-notes/2022/may/2022-findings-from-the-diary-of-consumer-payment-choice/; Federal Reserve Board, "Federal Reserve Payments Study: 2022 Triennial Initial Data Release," April 21, 2023, https://www.federalreserve.gov/paymentsystems/fr-payments-study.htm; David S. Evans and Richard Schmalensee, *Paying with Plastic: The Digital Revolution in Buying and Borrowing*, 2nd ed. (MIT Press, 2005), 240–244. Banks began experimenting with debit cards in the mid-1970s, but the cards did not become a significant factor in payments until the 1990s.

2. In the 1990s and early 2000s, there were two major fights about network "honor all cards" rules and interchange fees. One focused on debit fees (Paul Beckett, "Visa, MasterCard Battle with Retailers," *WSJ*, November 24, 1998). The other focused on issuer fees tied to reward cards (Adam J. Levitin, "The Antitrust Super Bowl: America's Payment Systems, No-Surcharge Rules, and the Hidden Costs of Credit," *Berkely Business Law Journal* 3, no. 1 [2005]: 265–336; Steven Semeraro, "Settlement without Consent: Assessing the Credit Card Merchant Fee Class Action," *Columbia Business Law Review* 2015, no. 1 [2015]: 186–272).

3. Vladimir Mukharlyamov and Natasha Sarin, "Price Regulation in Two-Sided Markets: Empirical Evidence from Debit Cards," (November 2022), https://papers.ssrn.com/sol3/papers.cfm?abstract_id=3328579; Kate Fitzgerald, "Credit Card Fees in the Crosshairs as Sen. Durbin Revisits Interchange," *AB*, May 6, 2022.

4. Andrew Leyshon and Nigel Thrift, "Geographies of Financial Exclusion: Financial Abandonment in Britain and the United States," *Transaction of the Institute of British Geographers* 20, no. 3 (1995): 312–341; Oren Bar-Gill, "Seduction by Plastic," *Northwestern University Law Review* 98, no. 4 (2004): 1373–1434; Rachel E. Dwyer, "Credit, Debt, and Inequality," *Annual Review of Sociology* 44 (2018): 237–261; Paola Boel and Peter Zimmerman, "Unbanked in America: A Review of the Literature," *Economic Commentary*, no. 2022–07 (May 2022); Ed Shanahan and Jeffery C. Mays, "New York City Stores Must Accept Cash, Council Says," *NYT*, January 24, 2020; Raphael Auer, Giulio Cornelli, and Jon Frost, "The Pandemic, Cash and Retail Payment Behaviour: Insights from the Future of Payments Database," December 6, 2022, https://www.bis.org/publ/work1055.htm; Susanne Soederberg, "The U.S. Debtfare State and the Credit Card Industry: Forging Spaces of Dispossession," *Antipode* 45, no. 2 (2013): 493–512; Mehrsa Baradaran, *How the Other Half Banks: Exclusion, Exploitation, and the Threat to Democracy* (Harvard University Press, 2018); Lisa J. Servon, *The Unbanking of America: How the New Middle Class Survives* (Houghton Mifflin Harcourt, 2017).

5. Board of Governors of the Federal Reserve System, "G.19, Consumer Credit, Historical Data," https://www.federalreserve.gov/releases/g19/HIST/cc_hist_sa_levels.html; World Bank, "Population, Total for United States (POPTOTUSA6 47NWDB)," FRED; United States Census Bureau, "HH-4, Households by Size: 1960 to Present," https://www.census.gov/data/tables/time-series/demo/families/households.html; Andrea Freeman, "Payback: A Structural Analysis of the Credit Card Problem Financial Reform during the Great Recession: Dodd-Frank, Executive Compensation, and the Card Act," *Arizona Law Review* 55, no. 1 (2013): 151–200; Randy Hodson, Rachel E. Dwyer, and Lisa A. Neilson, "Credit Card Blues: The Middle Class and the Hidden Costs of Easy Credit," *Sociological Quarterly* 55, no. 2 (May 1, 2014): 315–340; Devin Fergus, *The Land of Fee: Hidden Costs and the Decline of the American Middle Class* (Oxford University Press, 2018). Inflation adjustments made using Bureau of Labor Statistics CPI Inflation Calculator, https://www.bls.gov/data/inflation_calculator.htm.

6. Lawrence M. Ausubel, "The Failure of Competition in the Credit Card Market," *American Economic Review* 81, no. 1 (1991): 64; Board of Governors for the Federal Reserve System, *Report to the Congress on the Profitability of Credit Card Operations*

of Depository Institutions (July 2021), https://www.federalreserve.gov/publications/files/ccprofit2021.pdf, p. 6.

7. For overviews of the financialization literature, see Natascha van der Zwan, "Making Sense of Financialization," *Socio-Economic Review* 12, no. 1 (2014): 99–129; Gerald F. Davis and Suntae Kim, "Financialization of the Economy," *Annual Review of Sociology* 41 (2015): 203–221.

8. An important factor for the further diminution of state authority over finance was the rise of federal preemption of state rules, a process implicit in Citibank's relocation (with the approval of federal authorities) and use of *Marquette* and made explicit by later rulings from federal regulators like the Comptroller of the Currency that nationally chartered banks had no obligation to abide by state consumer protection rules. Robert A. Burgess and Monica A. Ciolfi, "Exportation or Exploitation—A State Regulator's View of Interstate Credit Card Transactions Survey: Consumer Financial Services," *Business Lawyer (ABA)* 42, no. 3 (1987): 929–942. For arguments in favor of preemption on economic efficiency grounds, see Julie L. Williams and Michael S. Bylsma, "Federal Preemption and Federal Banking Agency Responses to Predatory Lending," *Business Lawyer* 59, no. 3 (2004): 1193–1205; Joseph R. Mason, Robert Kulick, and Hal J. Singer, "The Economic Impact of Eliminating Preemption of State Consumer Protection Laws," *University of Pennsylvania Journal of Business Law* 12, no. 3 (2010): 781–806.

ACKNOWLEDGMENTS

I BEGAN THIS BOOK WITH A STORY of some money I once owed a bank. I end it here tallying the personal and professional debts I have accrued since that experience, which have enabled this project to come fully, finally, to fruition. It is an immense privilege to owe so much to so many and to have the chance, however briefly, to say thank you.

This book is the culmination of a long academic journey. As an undergraduate at the University of Georgia, I was fortunate to learn from several historians who managed to steer me away from a career in marketing, including John Inscoe, Ari Levine, Kevin McCarthy, and John Morrow. One reason I applied to graduate school was Levine's claim that he did not work on Fridays, an appealing prospect to an aimless twenty-something. The appeal of that misinterpreted remark, likewise, reflected my preparation for serious graduate study (Levine meant that he did not come to campus on Fridays). In my first attempt, I was rejected by every PhD program I applied to. I reentered UGA as a master's student, thrilled at the prospect of two more college football seasons. I stumbled unwittingly into a seedbed for the new history of capitalism, a then-nascent movement to revive historical analysis of economic topics. My teachers there, especially Steve Berry, Kathleen Clark, Jim Cobb, Shane Hamilton, Allan Kulikoff, Stephen Mihm, Bethany Moreton, and Pamela Voekel dramatically reoriented my perspective. They taught me, especially, that capitalism could be carved open, dissected, and scrutinized—and that doing so would reveal that its inner workings were not what they appeared on the surface. My Bcv Com colleagues Levi Collins,

Ashton Ellett, Franklin Sammons, and Kurt Windisch provided camaraderie and an appropriate amount of mayhem. I emerged from UGA with a research project and some idea of what it would mean to be a professional historian.

After Georgia, I was immensely lucky and privileged to make my way to Princeton University. When I arrived, William Chester Jordan promised our cohort one thousand free lunches, a reflection both of Princeton's largess and the deep commitment to continuous scholarly engagement (over lunch—often, but not always). The department was more than good for it. I had the opportunity to learn from many inspiring teachers, scholars, mentors, and now friends, especially Jeremy Adelman, Margot Canaday, Angela Creager, Alison Isenberg, Harold James, Matthew Karp, Kevin Kruse, Alan Krueger, Beth Lew-Williams, Rosina Lozano, Susan Naquin, Philip Nord, Daniel Rodgers, Emily Thompson, Keith Wailoo, Sean Wilentz, and Viviana Zelizer. If I had space, I would write a paragraph for each of them. At Princeton, I learned how to ask the next question and to recognize that American history is impoverished without an appreciation of its global context. Though good for instilling a global perspective, Princeton, New Jersey, is, otherwise, a very small town—the upside of which was many close, enduring friendships. Rich Anderson, Dan Barish, Olivier Burtin, Katlyn Carter, Matt Chan, Peter Conti-Brown, Henry Cowles, Patrick De Oliveira, Andrew Edwards, Christian Flow, Josh Garrett-Davis, Mike Glass, Dylan Gottleib, Jane Manners, Nikhil Menon, Brian Pietras, Randall Pippenger, Em Prifogle, Morgan Robinson, Joel Suarez, Fidel Tavarez, Veronica Valentin, David Walsh, Jess Winderweedle—many on this list read prodigious amounts of research and writing that evolved into this book, some read none of it, but all made it— and the odd experience of graduate school—infinitely better. In all, Princeton provided what every aspiring writer needs: Time, Strength, Cash, and Patience!

I want to especially thank my dissertation committee: Meg Jacobs, Dirk Hartog, Jon Levy, and Julian Zelizer. If, as the wise scholars say, you can understand a book best by reading the acknowledgments first, then that list is a pretty easy cipher for what appears on the forerunning pages. This is emphatically a book about pocketbook politics, about the things law does and doesn't do, about the career of many forms of risk, and about political institutions and democratic governance. These scholars were and remain enormously supportive. They motivated me to do my best work and still do. I live daily with Julian's admonition: keep writing.

This book examines the ways governments—especially state governments—construct, maintain, and reformulate markets. As such, it has relied heavily on government archives and the hard work of often overextended and under-re-sourced librarians and archivists. I want to especially thank the staffs at the California State Archives, the Chicago Historical Museum, the Delaware Public Archives, the Gerald R. Ford Presidential Library, the Hagley Museum and Library, Harvard Law School Historical and Special Collections, the Illinois State Archives, the State Archives of Iowa, the John F. Kennedy Presidential Library, the Lyndon B. Johnson Presidential Library, the Library of Congress Manuscript Division, the Massachusetts Archives, the Archives of Michigan, the Minnesota Historical Society, the Missouri State Archives, the National Archives (in Washington, D.C., College Park, and Kansas City), New Hampshire University Special Collections, the New Jersey State Archives, the Richard M. Nixon Presidential Library, the Federal Reserve Bank of New York, the New York State Archives, the New York City Municipal Archives, the Princeton University Mudd Manuscript Library, the Schlesinger Library, the Ronald W. Reagan Presidential Library, Rutgers University Special Collections, the South Dakota State Historical Society, SUNY Albany Special Collections and Archives, Tennessee State Archives, Tufts University Archives, University of Georgia Special Collections, University of Pennsylvania Law School Archives and Special Collections, the Washington State Archives, and the Wisconsin Historical Society. In addition to these public and educational institutions, I also want to thank: the staff at the Sioux Falls Chamber of Commerce, who let me rummage around in their basement long before I knew what I was doing; the archival staff at HSBC and Barclays, the two banks whose records I accessed directly; and the archivist at Citigroup, who offered to let me search for records among 2 million boxes held in an abandoned iron mine (I declined, a decision I now regret). Special thanks to staff at the National Archives who helped me track down the *Fisher* case file and shipped it to Kansas City for me to view, and to the librarians at the Kalamazoo, Michigan, Public Library who kept marketing pamphlets from the First National Bank of Kalamazoo's Charge Account Service from the early 1950s.

So much travel was expensive, combining long road trips, cheap hotels, and more than a few craft breweries. I was fortunate to receive research

funding from the University of Georgia and Princeton University, as well as
the Business History Conference, the Center for the Study of Social Organization, the Harvard Business School, the Institute for New Economic Thinking, the Lyndon Baines Johnson Foundation, the National Endowment for
the Humanities, and the University of Illinois Foundation. I also benefited
from archivists who made material available remotely, whether by request
(Brigham Young University, South Dakota State University, and the Western
Reserve Historical Society) or through dedicated online collections (Federal
Reserve Archival System for Economic Research).

My friends at FRASER, particularly Genevieve Podleski, made a few last-
minute scans of images that appear in this book, which I deeply appreciate.
I would also like to thank Sally Christensen at First National Bank of Omaha,
Jim Griffin at PNC Bank, Patricia Gonzalez at Unisys, Nils Huehnergarth,
and Helen Koshy at the Federal Reserve Bank of Chicago for their kind assistance securing permissions for the other images and copyrighted material
that appear herein. Also, thanks to Cambridge University Press for their permission to republish two articles initially published in their journals *Business
History Review* and *Enterprise & Society*.

A number of scholarly communities offered me opportunities to refine my
arguments, present my work, and receive valuable and supportive feedback.
I'd like to thank the American Bar Foundation, the American Society for Legal History, the Columbia University Seminar in Economic History, the
Hagley Museum and Library, the Law and Society Association, the Policy History Conference, Seminar in American Capitalism at Johns Hopkins University, the Social Science History Association, and the Triangle Legal History
Seminar. All provided important forums for working out my ideas, but my
true scholarly home has been and will remain the Business History Conference. The BHC has been an enormously welcoming, encouraging, and gen-
erative group of scholars. It is a great pleasure to thank so many of them for
nurturing me as a young scholar (and to occasionally—if quietly—curse
them for the many "service opportunities" they will no doubt offer me in the
future): Marcelo Bucheli, Bernardo Bátiz-Lazo, Manuel Bautista-González,
Brent Cebul, Christy Chapin, Nathan Delaney, Walter Friedman, Bart El-
more, Eric Hilt, Lou Galambos, Shane Hamilton, Roger Horowitz, Vicki
Howard, Louis Hyman, Pam Laird, Naomi Lamoreaux, Marc Levinson, Carol
Lockman, Jan Logemann, Ashton Merck, Stephen Mihm, Sharon Murphy,

Dael Norwood, Julia Ott, Atiba Pertilla, Andrew Popp, Mark Rose, David Sicilia, Jesse Tarbert, David Thompson, Dan Wadhwani, Ben Waterhouse, and Mark Wilson. Five members of that community—Ed Balleisen, Dan Bouk, Richard John, Josh Lauer, and Susie Pak—read this manuscript cover to cover. They improved it immeasurably through their incisive comments and thoughtful feedback, even if I failed to follow their more radical advice to consolidate or cut various chapters (readers may have appreciated it if I had).

Like many early career academics, I revised this book while spending many nail-biting years watching the job boards, Hail Marying applications, and bouncing across temporary appointments. Still, I was fortunate. I had some lucky breaks. At the Princeton Writing Program, under the inspired— if often silly—leadership of Amanda Irwin Wilkins, I learned the mechanics of scholarly writing by trying to teach them. An NEH fellowship at the Hagley gave me the space to write the proposal for this book. Colleagues at New York University's Gallatin School, especially Millery Polyne, Ngina Chiteji, and Kim Phillips-Fein, encouraged me to develop courses which shaped many of my ideas about American capitalism and American democracy. I finished my last semester at NYU over Zoom from a gardening shed in our backyard and then relocated to the University of Glasgow under Covid's dark shadow. Colleagues at the University of Glasgow, especially Hannah Clark, Rose Elliot, Jeff Fear, Ewan Gibbs, Chris Miller, Niall MacKenzie, Jim Phillips, Neil Rollings, Duncan Ross, and Ray Stokes, have been incredibly welcoming and supportive. They have helped shield me as best they could from my other duties as I worked to complete this book.

The last of my professional acknowledgments goes to my editor Adina Popescu and to the staff at Yale University Press. I secured a contract early because I thought it would help me on the job market. Delivery of the manuscript was delayed, delayed, and delayed again. Adina was more patient than I had a right to expect. Eliza Childs provided thorough and thoughtful copy editing. Enid Zafran contributed expert indexing. Margaret Otzel and Eva Skewes provided additional—essential—support to move the manuscript through to publication.

This book owes its greatest debt to the love and support of my family, whom I appreciate all the more being an ocean away from home. My mom, Kathy Lamb, has been unstintingly supportive, insisting on weekly phone calls to keep the communication channels open. She has always listened closely and carefully, eager to understand this arcane business, to better celebrate the small triumphs, and to offer genuine encouragement when it is needed. My parents-in-law, Kevin and Nancy Vogelsang, have been unrelentingly helpful as we have done our best to build a family on the uncertain foundation of academic life. They embody love and kindness; they open their door wide to our family's mobile chaos machine. Greg, Alison, Justin, Penelope, Junior, Oliver, Amy, Gerry, and Sandy: their love has meant the world to me.

More than anyone else, Sara Vanatta, my partner and faultless navigator, has lived with this book through its long development, its many revisions, interruptions, and frantic pushes. It has been the background music to the life we have built together, under Japanese magnolias and steely Scottish skies. When this book quietly gathers dust, that life will continue flourishing through the boundless unpredictability of our children—Elliot, Sawyer, Finlay, our dear, sweet, adventurous girls; Cole, our spirited baby boy. Scotland may be a cold, dark country, but we have made a warm home, full of light.

Lastly, I want to thank my dad, Lee Lyon Vanatta. My dad was a history buff, the kind who would fall asleep reading the latest Churchill biography. He was a Southerner, who inherited from his Texan parents an admiration for the bravery and heroism of the losing side. Becoming a historian has meant wrestling with that legacy, often by needling him about the many points—social, cultural, political—on which we disagreed. My dad was the best man he knew how to be. He was unfailingly proud of me. This book is dedicated to his memory.

INDEX

Italicized page numbers refer to figures and tables.

ABA. *See* American Bankers Association

Adams, Felix, 177

affiliate system, illustration of, *90*

affinity organizations partnering with banks, 295

AFL-CIO, 109, 124, 127, 129, 204, 289

African Americans. *See* Black consumers; race

agent bank structure: Bank of America and, 185, 188; Citi and, 215, 238; First of Omaha and, *187*, 188, 237, 240; Midwest Bank Card and, 95; Minnesota banks and, 191–192, 194–195; Omaha Service and, 190; role of agent banks, xiii, 9, 50–51, 88–90, 185–186

Agriculture, U.S. Department of, 48

airline ticket fraud, 162

Alm, Raymond, 54–55

American Banker (newspaper): on charge account growth and revenues, 43–44, 52, 58, 60, 69; on Charge-O-Matic, 50; discontinuing charge account coverage, 77; on discounting of charge accounts, 48; on service charges, 319n23

American Bankers Association (ABA): on bank cards as entry to multiple finan-

cial services, 226; Bank Card Standardization Task Force, 221; on commercial banks, 25, 64; on competition pressures and unsolicited mailing of cards (1967), 103–104; National Installment Credit Conference (1954), 44

American Express (Amex), xi; Carter's policies and, 256; bank credit cards competing with, 80, 106; fraud investigators employed by, 166–167; funded through merchant discounts and cardholder fees, 142; growth in 1950s, 77; lobbying for sanctions to deter card criminals, 139; model card fraud legislation developed by, 160, 164, 167–173, 177, 180; origin of, 57; Uni-Serv acquisition by, 86

American Law Institute, 169

American Retail Federation, 256

American State Bank of Rapid City, 287

annual fees and service fees: after Carter's policy changes, 259–260, 265; Amex, 142; Chase and, 281; Citi and, 233–235, 259–260, 267, 281, 349n49; convenience users and, 233–235, 263, 265; debit cards and transaction fees, 293; Delaware legislation to allow,

369

107, 185, 209, 218–223, 238, 240;
New Deal preserving structure of, 15,
17–19; tension with national, centralized credit management, 26, 237. *See
also* agent bank structure; financial
federalism; place-based social
contract
Long, Russell, 155, 174
Lorenz, Otto C.: death of, 77; on networking of bank card plans, 87; on
retail charge accounts, 34, 43–46, 52,
54, 58, 68, 76–77; Rockefeller and,
60; on unsolicited mailing of cards,
73
Los Angeles, credit card fraud in, 167
Los Angeles Times: on Carter credit measure resulting in higher borrowing
costs (1979), 254–255; on Citi's nationwide Visa campaign (1977), 237;
on State Credit Card Crime Act
(1967), 169
lost or stolen cards: consumers' liability
for, 139, 143, 144, 153, 159–160; criminal use of, 152–153, 160–166; Proxmire proposing to shift risk to card
issuers, 141

Mafia. *See* organized crime
mail fraud statute and jurisprudence,
176–178, 180–182
mailings of unsolicited credit cards. *See*
unsolicited card mailings
Malcolm, Walter, 121, 123, 125
Manhattan Company, merger with
Chase Manhattan, 66, 69
Manning, Robert: *Credit Card Nation*, ix
Manufacturers Hanover, 258
Manufacturers Trust Company (New
York), 39, 311n9
Margolius, Sidney, 124
Marine Midland Bank (New York): Bank
of America's proprietary software
and, 87; card industry role of, 59;
charge card (Marine Midland
Charge Plan), 49, 52–55, 107, 222; on

effectiveness of unsolicited card mailings, 144; Master Charge issued by,
215; nationwide network development, 96–98. *See also* Midland Trust
(Buffalo)
marketing and promotion: charge accounts, 43, 51–52, 52, 73; Chase Manhattan Charge Plan, 70. *See also*
unsolicited card mailings
Marquette case (*Marquette National Bank
of Minneapolis v. First of Omaha Service
Corp.*, 1978), 13, 183–184; Citi move to
South Dakota predicated on, 13, 265,
269, 271, 280; continued application
of, 289–290; financial federalism
and, 204; First of Omaha's actions in
Minnesota, 186, 190–195; *Fisher* as
deciding precedent for appellate
court, 202; Iowa Supreme Court dis-
tinguishing *Fisher*, 203; Minnesota
law and, 200–207; Minnesota's Bank
Credit Card Act and, 201; negating
financial federalism, 9, 184, 297; subsequent suit by First of Omaha for
malicious prosecution and equal protection violations, 206; transfer to
federal court and suing solely Omaha
Service, 201–202; U.S. Supreme
Court's grant of cert. as stay on Iowa
Supreme Court, 203; where is credit
plan "located" as determinative,
183–184, 204–205, 230
Marquette National Bank of Minneapolis: annual fee charged for
BankAmericard, 200, 233; joining
BankAmericard, 191–192; as only
card-issuing bank in Minnesota, 200;
state installment loan rate used for
BankAmericard balances, 192. *See
also Marquette* case
Marshall, Thurgood, 180
Martin, William McChensey, 223
Maryland National Bank, xi
Maryland's ban on annual fees, xi,
277

New Deal regulatory order (continued)
66–67; constraints on bank growth
and profits, x, 4, 34–35, 60–62, 106;
consumer credit and economic planning, 13, 16, 21–26, 253; encouraging
borrowing and lending, x, xiv, 38;
Hunt Commission proposed modifi-
cations, 224; legacy of, 31; lenders
circumventing and eroding, xii, 1, 17,
28, 78, 81, 160, 216, 296–297; low-
cost credit as priority, xi, xvi, 24, 26–
32, 123, 157; *Marquette* and, 9, 204;
pillars of, 21, 32, 33, 61, 134–135; political economy of, 302n5; purpose of,
7, 15–17, 146; regulatory capture of,
224; roots of postwar financial system
in, x, 17–21. *See also* financial federalism; geographic restrictions; industry
siloing; place-based social contract;
price controls; usury limits
New England Bankcard Association,
95–96
New Jersey: POS terminals as branch
banks in, 229–231; State Credit Card
Crime Act and, 169–170
Newman, Sarah, 118
Newsday: on NY fraud bill (1969), 172;
"The Hot Credit Card Racket" (series),
167, 168
New York (state): Amex's model bill on
credit card fraud in, 168–169; Banking
Board regulating CBCTs, 228; branching restrictions in, 96; consumer
credit regulation in, 267; National
Credit Card Fraud Legislation Project
and, 168–169; Temporary Commission on the Revision of the Penal Law
and Criminal Code (Penal Law Commission), 168–169, 172; usury limits
in, 265–269, 272–274, 281
New York Bankers Association, 272
New York City: consumer affairs office,
122; credit card fraud in, 167
New York Times: on Bank of America's
acquisition of MBNA (2005), xiv; on

"New Banking Era" (1955), 66; Proxmire on front page cutting up credit
card (1970), 152; on Volcker's appointment as Fed chair (1979), 250
Nixon, Richard M.: Bank Holding Company Act and, 216; challenged by
credit card issues, 151–153, 210; de-
coupling dollar from gold, 249; financial reform measures and, 223–226;
FTC action and consumerism supported by, 147–148; low-cost credit
and, 145–146; Saturday Night Massacre, 249; Watergate scandal, 210, 226
no-cash policies. *See* cashless/checkless
society
Nocera, Joseph, 75
non-recourse basis, 47
Northwest Bank Group ("Banco"), 191
Northwestern Banks NWCP Charge
Plan, 319n23
Nugent, Rolf, 27, 32

Office of Price Administration (OPA),
27–28, 32
Olmstead County Bank and Trust Company (Minnesota): in arrangement
with Omaha National Bank (Nebraska) to offer Master Charge, 192–
194; in Minnesota-based suit over its
agent bank role, 194–195
Omaha Service. *See* First of Omaha Service Corporation
Onassis, Aristotle, 211
O'Neil, Paul: "A Little Gift from Your
Friendly Banker," 104–105, *105*
Oregon, interest rates in, 186, 193
organized crime's entry into credit card
fraud, 167, 171, 172, 180
Oster, Richard, 235
out-of-state card-issuing banks, litigation
over. *See Fisher* cases; *Marquette* case
out-of-state card mailings. *See* unsolicited card mailings
overextension of credit. *See* unsustainable credit card debt